THE PHYSICIAN AND THE SLAVE TRADE

THE PHYSICIAN and the SLAVE TRADE

JOHN KIRK, the Livingstone Expeditions, and the Crusade Against Slavery in East Africa

DANIEL LIEBOWITZ, M.D.

W. H. FREEMAN AND COMPANY NEW YORK

Cover and Text Designer: Victoria Tomaselli
Map illustrations: Joe Le Monnier

Library of Congress Cataloging-in-Publication Data

Liebowitz, Daniel, 1921–
The physician and the slave trade: John Kirk, the Livingstone expeditions and the crusade against slavery in East Africa/Daniel Liebowitz.
p. cm.
Includes bibliographical references and index.
ISBN 0-7167-3098-7
1. Kirk, John, Sir, 1832–1922—Journeys—Africa, East.
2. Livingstone, David, 1813–1873—Journeys—Africa, East. 3. Slave trade—Africa, East. 4. Arabs—Africa, East. 5. Africa, East—Race relations.
6. Great Britain—Moral conditions. I. Title.
DT365.655.K57L54 1998 98–47687
916.7604'1—dc21 CIP

Printed in the United States of America

First printing, December 1998

W. H. Freeman and Company
41 Madison Avenue, New York, NY 10010
Houndmills, Basingstoke RG21 6XS, England

This book is dedicated to my wife, Florence Noel, who retraced the Second Zambezi Expedition with me.

CONTENTS

FOREWORD

Sir John Kirk was a British naturalist, explorer, and administrator who played a key role in ending the slave trade in Africa, accompanying the great missionary-explorer David Livingstone on his second expedition. Born on December 19, 1832, at Barry, Scotland, to the Reverend John Kirk, he studied medicine at Edinburgh and served on the civil medical staff in the Crimean War before being selected in February 1858 as the naturalist and physician to Livingstone's expedition. For the next five years, Kirk accompanied Livingstone on most of his African journeys and was one of the first white men to look upon Lake Nyassa. Later, Kirk was appointed British agent, then consul, during a critical period of European expansion into East and Central Africa.

David Livingstone was a real hero to Victorian England. He worked tirelessly to open up "the dark continent" and his arduous trips—with Kirk as his assistant—were meant to explore and open up Africa for Christ, commerce, and colonists, but, above all, to put a stop to the trading of slaves.

During Livingstone's second expedition, letters home to missionary societies, to the Anti-Slavery Society, and to newspapers shocked the moral conscience of Britain. This trip ignited the movement to end the slave trade and led in the 1880s to the partitioning of Africa and to its colonization by European nations.

On May 9, 1863, Kirk was sent home. But his reputation as an explorer with Livingstone and their efforts to end the slave trade led in January 1866 to Kirk's appointment as acting surgeon to the political agency in Zanzibar, and two years later as assistant political agent and vice-consul of Zanzibar. In 1873 he was chosen acting consul-general. In that year, Kirk's most important work was accomplished—he negotiated a treaty with Sultan Bargash that made the slave trade illegal throughout the sultan's dominions, which included not only the island of Zanzibar but also stretched deep into East Africa, for Kirk was grimly determined to stop the traffic in human beings. During these years Kirk remained a champion of Livingstone's mission and fought all those who opposed or impeded this great explorer's efforts to end the slave trade.

Livingstone died in 1873 and was enshrined in Westminster Abbey and in the hearts of the British people as a saintly missionary-explorer and antislaver. But it was left to Kirk, his close companion, to actually bring about the end of the trade in East and Central Africa and to lay the groundwork for the opening up of Africa to partition and colonization.

Kirk was knighted in 1881 and retired in 1887 to Seven Oaks, Kent, where he died on January 15, 1922. During his twenty-one years in Zanzibar, Kirk tried earnestly to uphold the legitimate interests of Sultan Majid and his successor, Seyyid Bargash. Kirk endeavored to protect the sultan's enormous interests against the threats of competing European powers, but their strength and interest in the region was too great to withstand.

Dr. Daniel Liebowitz describes all of this in his excellent account of this doctor-naturalist and explorer-diplomat. It is a moving story, well told, of great men—Livingstone, Kirk, and Stanley—and of great events—the ending of the slave trade in East Africa and the opening up of the area to German, British, French, and Belgian colonization.

Peter Duignan,
Senior Fellow, Hoover Institution
Fellow, Royal Historical Society

ACKNOWLEDGMENTS

Sir John Kirk, physician, explorer, and diplomat, has been virtually forgotten in the United States except by a few historians specializing in African subjects. In England he is remembered by the Royal Geographic Society, where he was secretary, and is spoken of by those stalwarts at the Foreign Office whose roots in the nineteenth century have not been totally severed. But there are no plaques to honor him, not even at the University of Edinburgh where he went to college and medical school. His name is only found today in the village of Seven Oaks near London, in a cul-de-sac called "Kirk's Court," next to the site where his home once stood.

In East and southern Africa, Kirk's name is inextricably linked with the famous missionary-explorer David Livingstone, because of their close association during the Second Zambezi Expedition. Of course, most of all, he is remembered by a few historians in East and southern Africa as the man who singlehandedly persuaded the sultan of Zanzibar to abolish the East African slave trade.

I came across Dr. Kirk quite by accident when I was walking around the Beit al Amani Museum in Zanzibar in 1993. A framed letter, signed by him as acting British consul, hung on one wall. It requested help from the British in Bombay, India, to cope with a hurricane that had just devastated the island. The fact that a physician like myself had become acting British consul intrigued me, but it was tucked away in my memory until one day in 1994, when my flight from Entebbe, Uganda, to Nairobi, Kenya, was delayed. During the three-hour wait, I talked to another American, Mr. Howard Hoffman of Atlanta, Georgia, and told him about my trip to Zanzibar and chance encounter with John Kirk. Mr. Hoffman gave me an address at the Hoover Institution on Stanford University's campus, where I met the senior curator for African affairs, Professor Peter Duignan. With his inspiration and guidance, I began the research on Dr. Kirk that led to this biography.

Many people have given me help and encouragement along the way. First and foremost, I owe a debt of gratitude to my wife, Noel, for her forbearance during the time it took to write this biography. She was a fellow explorer during our 1995 safari to Scotland,

England, Mozambique, Tanzania, Zimbabwe, and Zambia, where we traced Kirk's life.

I also wish to thank my agent, Dr. Paul Insel, for obtaining a fine publisher, providing constant encouragement, and shepherding me through the manuscript revisions.

Mr. Jonathan Cobb, formerly Senior Editor at W. H. Freeman and Company, has done far more than I would have expected from an editor. His wise and patient counsel and painstaking care were vital in preparing this book for publication.

Dr. Don Heyneman, Professor Emeritus at the University of California School of Medicine, contributed his knowledge of parasitology and epidemiology to the manuscript, for which I am most grateful.

Mrs. Sally Hoffman, British archivist, was extremely helpful in obtaining information about Dr. Kirk's residence, Wavertree, in Seven Oaks, Kent, and tracing his descendants.

The Royal Geographic Society, the National Library of Scotland, and the Royal Botanic Gardens at Kew, London, contributed information, materials, and photographs used in this book.

I am also grateful for the comments made by the two reviewers, Professor Harry A. Gailey of San Jose State University and Professor Thomas H. Henriksen of the Hoover Institution.

As I began to delve into the records of Kirk's life and accounts of his times, what captured my interest above all was Kirk's commitment to the cause both he and David Livingstone served, the eradication of the slave trade.

As a physician writing about a physician, I am convinced the voice of this talented man should be heard again by all those interested in his unique contribution to human freedom.

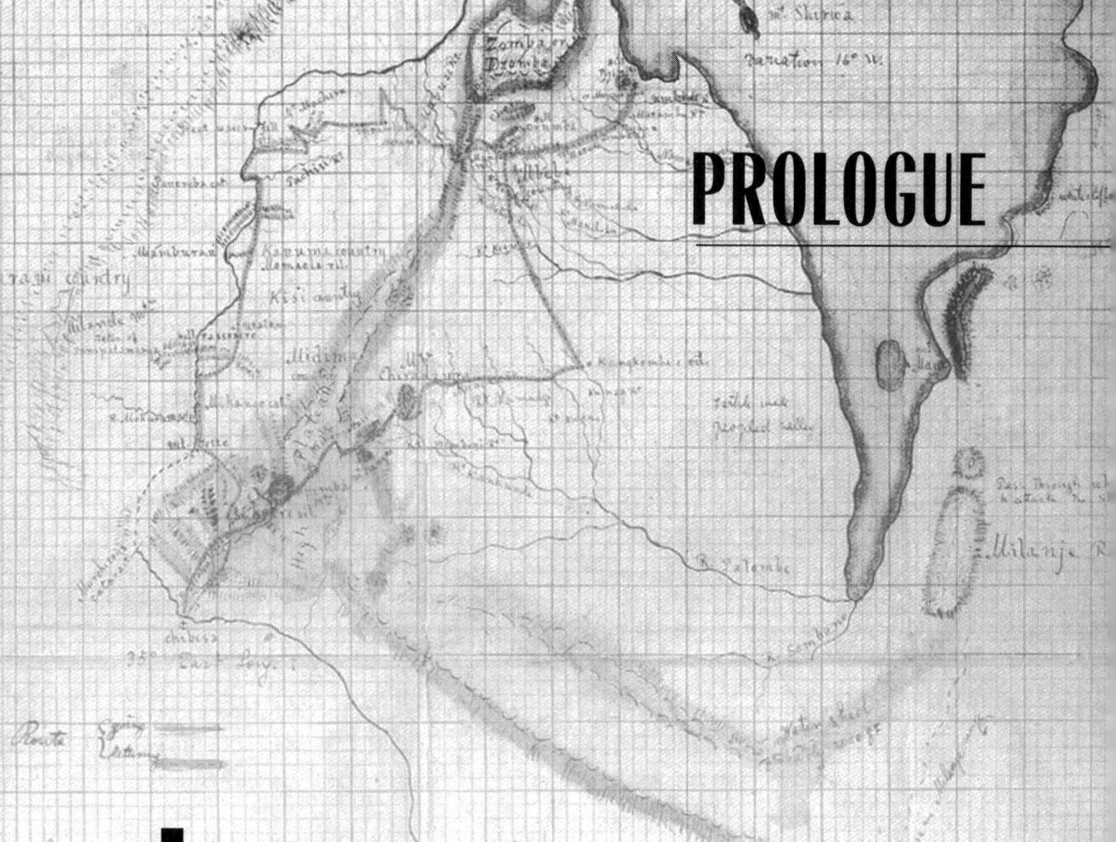

PROLOGUE

John Kirk steamed up rivers and roamed the jungles of East Africa for more than five years in the late 1850s and early 1860s with the famous Victorian missionary-explorer David Livingstone. Together, they endured blistering heat, hordes of insects, tropical diseases, attacks by wild animals, quarrels among themselves, and occasional clashes with local inhabitants. Kirk killed two men in self-defense, and he himself nearly died several times while trekking with the quixotic Livingstone and his party.

Once Kirk nearly drowned when a storm capsized his boat. He managed to right the craft and climb back in, only to have a hippopotamus upend it, again with near-fatal results. Later, the expedition's steam launch was mired for a month in a swamp full of decomposing corpses while vultures circled above. Living with rampant tropical diseases and dangerous animals, such as snakes that crawled over the explorers' faces as they slept, and risking attack from potentially hostile Africans, Arabs, or rival Europeans, Kirk more than once despaired of ever seeing the coast of his native land again.

Kirk was one of a surprising number of nineteenth-century Victorian explorers who were Scottish by birth. Among them were Mungo Park, a medical practitioner who died exploring the Niger River in 1805; George Maclean, an explorer who became governor of the area that is now Ghana; Joseph Thomson, who explored present-day Kenya and West Africa; and Livingstone himself.

Together, they expanded European geographical knowledge of sub-Saharan Africa, sometimes unwittingly preparing those areas for colonization.

Kirk, however, was much more than an explorer. Though he spent five years with Livingstone exploring the Zambezi River and the surrounding territories, that was just the beginning of his encounter with Africa. A specialist trained in botany and medicine, Kirk was one of the first Europeans to investigate a number of important indigenous plants. He went on to serve for twenty years in East Africa, first as a physician and then as the region's most powerful statesman and diplomat, playing a key role in ending the trade in slaves.

Returning to England after the Zambezi Expedition, Kirk found himself again invited to live amongst Africa's haunting amalgam of extraordinary natural beauty and the immense cruelty wrought by the trade in slaves. He returned to Africa in 1866, not as an explorer this time, but as an agent of the British Crown.

Kirk, at heart a humanitarian, would soon find his character, his intelligence, and his patience tested again by his posting to Zanzibar. Twenty miles off the coast of present-day Tanzania, the emerald green, low-lying, spice-rich island was an important center for trade between Africa, the Middle East, and India. Arabs from Oman had ousted the Portuguese from the island in the eighteenth century, and the Arab Sultanate of Zanzibar, whose territory included vast portions of the adjacent mainland, had become the most important slave center in eastern Africa as well as a major exporter of ivory and cloves.

Not long after his arrival in Zanzibar, Kirk was promoted to the position of consul general. As such, he was the highest-ranking British official in that part of the world, and by force of personality, he would become, in effect, the de facto ruler of East Africa. A diplomat by nature, but not by training, Kirk would soon not only be subject to home-country political pressures but also be the focal point of endless political intrigues among the area's Arab chieftains and slave traders. Ultimately, he would himself be a victim of shifting European geopolitics.

The central issue in Kirk's prime years in Zanzibar was the flourishing trade in slaves. For more than a half-century British abolitionists had been campaigning for an end to slavery and to the slave trade, which, at its peak, placed more than 100,000 Africans into bondage each year. Partly in response to these campaigns, the British Parliament had passed laws in 1807 and 1834 outlawing the slave trade at home and abroad. Other imperial powers also officially frowned on slavery, though the trade was so lucrative they often looked the other way while their nationals engaged in it. When he became a British diplomat, Kirk quickly set himself the goal of persuading the local sultan to ban the slave trade in Zanzibar and its possessions. This would be an important step in both stopping the whole East African slave trade and realizing David Livingstone's lifelong dream of ending slavery on the African continent.

The odds against Kirk's success were heavy. A ban on the slave trade would deprive the sultan, now Kirk's friend and Zanzibar's volatile ruler, of his major source of income. Worse, the sultan realized he would face enormous hostility, perhaps death, at the hands of other powerful Arabs. Thus, Kirk found himself caught between a temperamental Arab sultan and the British Empire's moral indignation, between his own deep sense of injustice and the belief of many others that slavery was a highly lucrative boat that should not be rocked. Diplomacy, Kirk was beginning to learn, was a calling with its own set of dangers every bit as real as those along the Zambezi.

Slavery's Toll

Africans, like many other peoples, had conquered, enslaved, and sold one another for centuries, but the size of this trade had been relatively small until Muslim traders and the Portuguese began preying on African lands in the 1500s. About a century later England, France, and Holland entered the African slave trade in earnest. The French West Indies Company was founded in 1664 to control the West African slave trade to France's "sugar" colonies in the Caribbean. The Royal African Company was formed in 1672, and colonial America became increasingly involved in the slave trade during the same period. It is estimated that as many as seven million people were taken from West Africa alone to the Western Hemisphere between the seventeenth and mid-nineteenth centuries.[1]

Though the slave trade was not as extensive on the east coast, and not as well known, it was still substantial. According to the most reliable estimates, two million Africans were transported out of East Africa between 1750 and 1867, mainly to Arab lands, but also to Brazil and the Caribbean. During just the five-year period between 1862 and 1867, soon after Kirk and Livingstone had finished exploring the Zambezi River region, 97,000 slaves were estimated to have been exported from Kilwa, one of the sultanate's main ports on the Indian Ocean, and 100,000 from Zanzibar.[2]

The Arab slave owners of East Africa were considered particularly cruel and inhuman by most Europeans, who easily overlooked the great cruelty Americans and they themselves sometimes visited on their own slaves. David Livingstone, referring to the Arab slave owners in East Africa, wrote that

> for every slave sold on the auction block in Zanzibar or nearby ports, five others died during the journey getting there. If food was scarce their captives were treated as a European might treat a pig or a horse. He would naturally regret to see them die of starvation, but would feel the loss to his pocket more. And so it was with these Arabs. They regretted to see their slaves perish of hunger; but as food proved to be so dear, they could not afford to buy them any, as it would have absorbed more than their money value. Hence they were left to starve, without the slightest idea that an inhuman action was being committed.[3]

Often herded in caravans of a thousand or more, slaves lived on roots and grasses, or whatever refuse and garbage they could pick up, while being marched hundreds of miles to markets in the coastal ports. After months on the trail, the captives looked, an observer noted, "like skeletons covered with parchment, through which every bone in the body might be traced."[4] Often they were forced to carry ivory or other treasures to be sold along with the bearers themselves at journey's end.

Published accounts of this trail of death had shocked the British public and had spurred demands that more be done to stop slavery. Kirk himself needed no spurring. In his journeys with Livingstone he had seen firsthand the appalling conditions of those in slave caravans, and in his early days in Zanzibar he had watched Arab sailing vessels, or *dhows*, sail into the harbor with human cargoes wasted by disease, brutality, and malnutrition.

The Physician, the Sultan, and the Treaty

A master of persuasion, John Kirk was outwardly affable, slow to anger, and incredibly hardworking. He was direct in manner and meticulous in everything he undertook. He demonstrated time and again in the jungle with Livingstone that he was a highly resilient optimist who could adapt to changes in conditions that would easily overwhelm others. It was just such qualities that would be critical to Kirk's success in dealing a mortal blow to the slave trade.

During the years of their association, sultan-to-be Bargash frequently expressed his admiration for Kirk and began to depend more and more on his consultation and advice, particularly after he succeeded his brother as sultan in 1870.

When, in January 1873, the British government decided that the Zanzibari sultanate must finally cease its slave trade activities, Kirk joined Sir Bartle Frere, the British governor of Bombay and a gifted negotiator, to draft and propose a comprehensive treaty to the sultan.

However, Bargash immediately challenged the terms presented to him. He claimed they were destructive to Zanzibar's well-being and refused to sign.

Members of the powerful, anti-European, Mlawa sect of Omani Arabs, who were Bargash's advisors in Zanzibar, helped to further stiffen the sultan's resolve not to sign the treaty. His own family applied pressure as well, fearing they would lose substantial income and power if slavery were outlawed. The treaty would cause far too much hardship for plantation owners, Bargash insisted, and could lead to rebellion. Personally, Bargash was afraid that he would be assassinated by the Mlawas or wealthy plantation owners if he signed it.

Kirk was pitted against not only the sultan and his Arab advisors, but the Americans and the French as well. The U.S. consul, perhaps jealous, labeled Kirk an "empire builder." And France, which had territorial ambitions of its own in Africa, backed the sultan.

Despite Kirk's reassurance that if he signed the treaty the British would protect him and his sultanate, Bargash remained stubborn. Kirk knew that if he raised the ante and threatened the sultan with a blockade, it could become a two-edged sword. If the blockade were enforced, Bargash might still hold out. Cloves and other produce would be left rotting on the docks, and unsold slaves, even if they could be freed, would need to be fed and maintained at great expense. At the same time, if Bargash did relent, the influential Arab population might revolt—a prospect that London would not greet with enthusiasm either. The British definitely did not want the strategically important island, whose deep-water harbor could accommodate the largest British warships, in financial or political chaos.

Bargash, recognizing the British ambivalence, was not easily intimidated. Yet he realized that he, too, faced a dilemma. If he signed the treaty, he would suffer a major loss of income and a likely rebellion. If he didn't sign, he could no longer count on British protection from powerful enemies on Zanzibar itself or from other foreign governments increasingly interested in his lands.

Finally, Kirk decided that he had to raise the stakes. So he took the risk and threatened Bargash with a naval blockade. Bargash stalled and again consulted his advisors. At subsequent meetings with Kirk, he insisted that the terms of the treaty be loosened to allow at least some trade in slaves or to require only a gradual reduction in the trade. When Kirk said it was not in his power to grant such major concessions, Bargash flew into a rage and demanded an audience with Queen Victoria herself.

Such a visit would do no good, Kirk replied. The queen, if she would see him at all, was sure to deny his requests. In truth, he said, the slave trade must be shut down now. Why should it be kept open for even a single day more?

Meanwhile, the city of Zanzibar was in an uproar. Rumors were flying that a French warship was waiting to spirit Bargash away, and the French consul was still urging Bargash to refuse to sign.

Bargash finally asked if Kirk would consent to a clause that would limit the sultan's responsibility to enforce the treaty. This qualification might save his throne and his life, he pleaded.

Kirk considered for a moment and then agreed. Unfortunately, this only emboldened Bargash to begin bargaining anew. Abolishing all trade in slaves would cause terrible financial hardship, he argued again. Even if as few as 10,000 slaves a year could be shipped to Zanzibar, it would ease the burden. Kirk, however, refused this latest entreaty point blank.[5]

The palaver continued day after day, and anyone but Kirk might have given up. But he remained polite and firm as Bargash kept coming back with ever new modifications for the treaty. Kirk granted a few and withheld others, all the while acutely conscious that his friend's life was, indeed, in danger; but the lives of untold thousands of others also hung in the balance. During those long, difficult negotiations, Kirk had been careful never to promise more than he could deliver and had managed, despite their disagreements, to maintain Bargash's friendship.

If Kirk could actually pull it off, if he could persuade the sultan to abolish the slave trade in East Africa, it would be a remarkable feat. He would have accomplished more in practical terms than the famous Livingstone or Sir Bartle Frere or any other servant of the Crown, something that England had vainly sought but that other world powers and Arab leaders, working behind the scenes, were eager to block.

In the final analysis, Kirk really had only a couple of cards to play. Both he and the sultan knew that military force wasn't a practical option and that a commitment to defend the Zanzibari lands with Britain's military might would be vital to the sultanate's ultimate survival. Just as important was Kirk's relationship with Bargash, cemented by Kirk's ability to convey a sense of dependability and integrity. Bargash, therefore, had to weigh Kirk's personal commitment to delivering British support against his own fear and the forces arrayed against him. In retrospect, it appeared as if Kirk's career in Africa had been an apprenticeship in preparation for this very moment.

In his years in Africa and beyond, Kirk accomplished much of importance, probably to more lasting effect than Livingstone himself. However, he has never been given the same prominence by history. Kirk lacked the flamboyance of Livingstone, his charismatic public style, and his sense of personal sacrifice that is the stuff of melodrama. Perhaps even more significant, Kirk became the scapegoat of one of the nineteenth century's great self-promoters, the American journalist Henry Morton Stanley.

While Kirk was establishing himself in Zanzibar, Livingstone embarked on a new series of explorations, this time veering farther and farther north and west into the Congo in search of mythical sources of the river Nile. Not heard of for months, Livingstone was presumed dead or lost by the American and British public. But in 1871 he was found starving and malaria-ridden by the American newspaperman. Stanley used his "discovery" of Livingstone to glorify himself and to promote Livingstone as a living saint while attacking Kirk for not having provided his hero with the necessary medicines and material to keep him alive. Kirk was subsequently exonerated. Though he had ordered supplies to be sent to the interior just as Livingstone had requested, the damage had been done. This may explain why Kirk has been overshadowed in the public eye by both Livingstone's martyrdom and Stanley's unscrupulous search for fame.

Yet John Kirk was among those amazing polymaths of the Victorian era. He was not only an accomplished physician and African explorer but also a pioneer in African photography. He made important botanial discoveries, and he played a major role in African politics. Kirk was not only a remarkable man but was in the thick of a momentous change in European-African relations from the time of the great explorations of Africa's interior to the outright colonization of the continent by the major European powers.

1

First Encounters: Kirk and Livingstone

Rain and winds batter the rugged east coast of Scotland where John Kirk was born in the little village of Barry, ten miles east of Dundee, on December 19, 1832. His mother's maiden name was Christian Carnegie; his father, also named John, was Barry's Church of Scotland minister. When Kirk was only a few years old, his father was promoted to the more lucrative parish of Arbilot eight miles away. The family's fortunes began to fall in 1843, however, when young Kirk was eleven. His father, like many other churchmen at the time, had grown sick of government interference in religious affairs and defected from the official Church. Not only did he lose his salary, but he was forced to move his family to a more modest house in the coastal town of Arbroath, three miles away. The family took their economic downturn with good grace, though, and in a way it turned out to be a boon for young Kirk. Since his father could no longer afford a tutor, he now spent much of his free time with his children.

Kirk was the second of four children. His younger sister, Elizabeth, was later to die in her twenties of an unknown cause. John's younger brother, James, was sickly and emigrated to South Africa, where he also died relatively young. Alexander, however, who was three years older than John, became a successful engineer, inventing a method of separating lighter oils from paraffin, an ice-making machine, and the triple-expansion marine engine, patented in

1874. Alexander eventually became very wealthy as director of Scotland's largest ship-building firm. More importantly, in terms of John's future, Alexander developed a close friendship with David Livingstone.

A man of strong will and stubborn devotion to principles, Kirk's father was no ordinary preacher, being, in addition, both a scholar and amateur botanist. Under his father's tutelage, young John became an expert at identifying and classifying various plants and trees. Though little is known of young Kirk's early life, we do know that he loved to scale nearby seaside cliffs for fossils and that he showed an aptitude for chemistry as well as biology. He also hunted and was a good shot but only a moderately good horseman, according to a fellow classmate, John Beddoe.[1] His parents must have noted his keen intellect, for he passed his college entrance examinations at fifteen and entered Edinburgh University, Scotland's most prestigious teaching institution.

In those days classics, history, and geography were taught during the first two years at the university. A student with a particular penchant and talent could then apply to one of the specialty schools. With Kirk's interests in the sciences, he had no trouble getting into the university's School of Medicine, where he proved a brilliant student. In his senior year he wrote his thesis on the structure of the kidney, demonstrating great knowledge of anatomy and physiology.

When time allowed, Kirk continued his study of botany. Though an amateur, his reputation in that field was sufficient to earn him election as a Fellow of the Royal Botanical Society, most unusual for a student, particularly one specializing in a quite different discipline. Kirk also showed an interest in the budding science of photography, and he was making high-quality prints by the late 1850s. Some of these still survive as the only visual records of his life in Africa.

An early photograph, taken by another while Kirk was on the resident staff of Edinburgh's Royal Infirmary, shows a good-looking, thin, athletic young man. His wide-spaced eyes have a slightly mischievous look suggesting a quiet sense of humor. Once he teamed up with other medical students to steal a quack doctor's wooden advertisement and solemnly burn it. The ability to poke fun at himself, too, helped him bear the adversities he was to experience later in life. Though he would occasionally retreat into a shell to avoid confrontation, he learned to control that tendency.

His fellow classmate, John Beddoe, called him a master of logic. He did not boast or try to dominate in class discussions but when called upon voiced his ideas in a polite and precise manner. When he was twenty-two, he attended a lecture by a pathology professor on carboniferous flora in coal deposits. The topic was fossilized plants, which Kirk had studied since he was a boy, and it was evident to him that the professor did not know his subject. According to Beddoe, Kirk stood up at the back of the room and demolished the professor's thesis.[2]

After receiving his M.D. degree in 1854, Kirk became one of only seven applicants accepted for a year's residency at Edinburgh's prestigious Royal Infirmary. It was to become an accomplished group, with four of his fellow residents attaining fame. John Beddoe became a distinguished ethnologist, Patrick Watson one of Scotland's finest surgeons; David Christison studied archeology and gained notoriety for his work on Scottish ruins, while Joseph Lister became the founder of antiseptic surgery.

In the Crimea

The disastrous Crimean War, which pitted Great Britain, France, and Turkey against Russia, began in 1854, the winter Kirk spent his residency at the Royal Infirmary. Toward the end of his term a call was issued for physicians to supplement the inadequate British Medical Corps in Turkey. Of the 700 who volunteered, 50 were chosen, including Beddoe, Christison, and Kirk.

When they arrived at Istanbul the three doctors found that most of the casualties did not result from military action but from infectious diseases—especially cholera, an intestinal infection causing massive diarrhea, dehydration, and often death. There is no record of their meeting Florence Nightingale, however, though she and her corps of nurses were there revolutionizing care for the wounded and reducing the terrible loss from sickness by enforcing cleanliness and separating disease-ridden soldiers from healthy ones.

It was apparent to Kirk that many of the often inadequately trained military doctors were jealous of the new physicians fresh from their residencies. Kirk and his friends were at first told there was no work for them and assigned miserable quarters at Scutari across the Bosporus from Constantinople. During their enforced idleness, they decided to visit the city of Bursa, a site of antiquities, and to climb Mount Olympus in Greece. Kirk, who had already shown an inordinate capacity for work, collected plants that had not yet been seen or classified. One was a new species of muscari, a fungus he found on Mount Ida in Greece, which William Hooker, curator of the Royal Botanical Gardens at Kew, London, subsequently named *Muscari latifolium.*

In the spring of 1855 the young doctors were finally, after repeated complaints, assigned decent quarters and put to work at the British-built Erenkevi Hospital in the Dardanelles. In the remaining six months of the war, Kirk, while assigned to a full caseload, still found time to take lessons in Turkish and to learn something of the Muslim religion and customs. After the successful siege of Sebastopol, the war was brought to an end in early 1856 by the Treaty of Paris. Though Russia had been defeated, England was left bone weary, having suffered tremendous casualties, mainly from disease, and having accomplished little, if anything, in the costly conflict.

Kirk returned to England, but his wanderlust, whetted by his Turkish experience, led him to leave again as physician for a tourist group visiting Spain, Egypt, and Syria. During this period he took up Arabic, continued to collect plants, and learned more about Muslim culture, a knowledge that would serve him well later.

Returning to Scotland in 1857, Kirk's friend and advisor at the university, Professor D. H. Balfour, urged him to teach natural science because he was so accomplished in botany as well as medicine. A professorship was open at Queens University in Ontario; but, after careful consideration, Kirk turned it down in favor of something much more exciting. He had learned that his brother Alexander's friend, David Livingstone, was planning a second expedition to explore the Zambezi River's far reaches. Livingstone needed a combination physician and botanist who could both treat anticipated illnesses and accidents and collect and classify plants unknown to Europeans. Kirk felt he perfectly fit the qualifications and applied for the job.

It was to be a fateful decision for the twenty-six-year-old. For the next sixteen years Kirk's life would be entwined with the erratic Livingstone's, a man who would become his tormentor as well as his mentor. These two men, so dissimilar in so many ways, would share ideals and hardships, fame and calumny. And even after that period and after both men were dead, Livingstone's place in history would affect how Kirk would be viewed, if he was remembered at all.

Commerce, Christianity, and David Livingstone

With fifteen years of missionary work and some extraordinary travels through the Dark Continent, David Livingstone was already world-famous. He was the first Englishman to have traversed Africa on foot, to have explored extensive portions of the Zambezi River, and to have laid eyes on Victoria Falls. He had returned to England in the late 1850s to organize the Second Zambezi Expedition and to write what became a best-selling book recounting his adventures, *Missionary Travels and Researches in South Africa*. It sold 12,000 copies before publication and received international recognition. Talk of Livingstone—and by him—still permeated the air when Kirk met him.

In 1857, the same year that Kirk returned from the Middle East, the British Parliament had awarded Livingstone £5,000, a considerable sum of money at the time, to explore more thoroughly the Zambezi and its tributaries in central, southern, and eastern Africa (see Map 1 on page 14). In addition, £3,000 was raised at his former medical school in Glasgow and by public subscription. Entrepreneurs as well as missionaries, other explorers, and the British government were eager to find out if the Zambezi, as Livingstone claimed from his earlier trip, was navigable for most of its length. If so, it could double as an important new avenue of commerce and an easy way to reach Africans in need of conversion to Christianity.

In his speeches to the British missionary societies and scientific circles, such as the Royal Geographic Society, Livingstone galvanized his audiences with his sincerity and impressed them with his spirit of self-sacrifice. He told his listeners that he had decided to dedicate his life to converting Africans to Christianity and to abolishing the slave trade. In his grand vision, British ships would soon be sailing up the Zambezi filled with missionaries who would settle along its banks to show Africans how to improve their benighted lives. Among other benefits, the missionaries would give the tribes[3] they encountered instruction in more efficient farming methods, such as growing and selling a superior strain of cotton for processing in British mills. With this legitimately earned money, Livingstone predicted, African chiefs would no longer need to sell their people to the Arab and Portuguese slave traders who crisscrossed the eastern side of the continent.

After the debacle of the Crimean War, the nation wanted a hero, and Livingstone fit that need. As a physician, missionary, and explorer, he stood for everything Queen Victoria's Britain considered noble. Talented and self-reliant, passionate and altruistic, fearless and even at times fanatical, he was obsessed with the conviction that God had chosen him to stop slavery in Africa and open up that continent to Christianity and commerce.

Surviving photographs show Livingstone as a sparse figure of medium height, without an ounce of fat on his wiry frame. His face was gaunt with a slightly receding, dimpled chin, but attention is

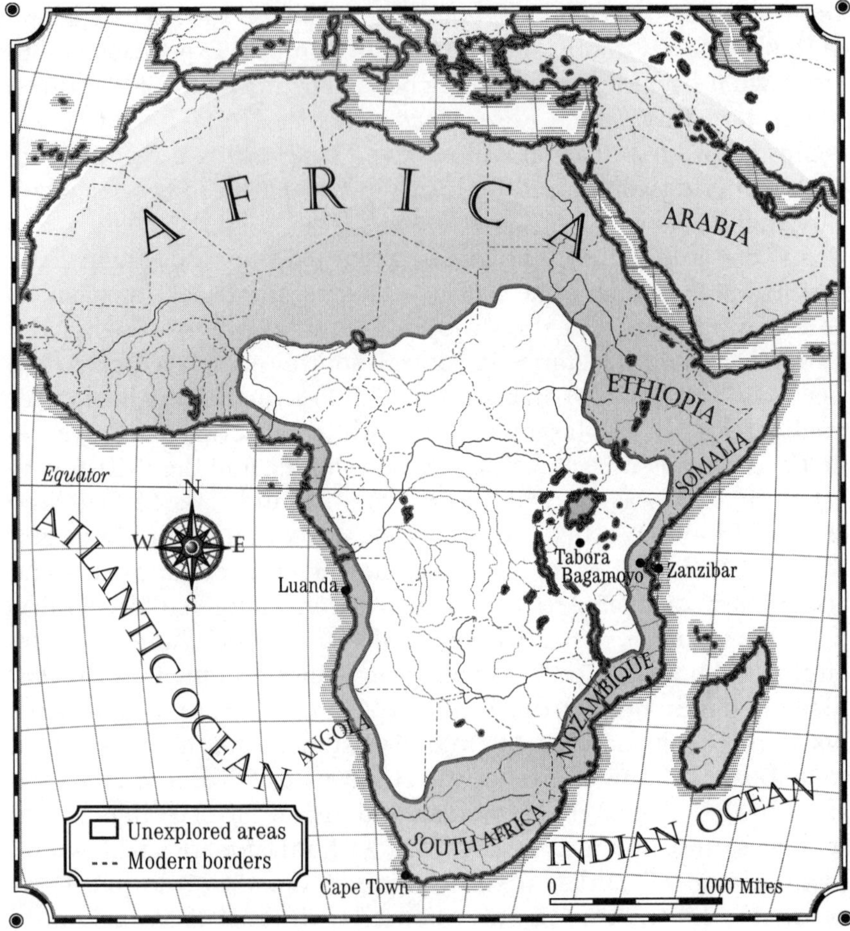

MAP 1 *Unexplored Territory, prior to 1850.*

immediately drawn to his eyes, which appear to gaze at some far distance, not with an unfocused look, but with evangelistic fervor.

The then forty-four-year-old David Livingstone had come up the hard way. Born in Blantyre, Scotland, of poor parents in 1813, he had begun working at age fourteen as a mill hand. After returning from a fourteen-hour workday, he would study until the early morning hours. He was burning with the desire to become a medical missionary, and he managed to pass the entrance exams for Glasgow Medical School. In the early 1800s this was not as prestigious an institution as the University of Edinburgh, Kirk's alma mater, and this would irritate Livingstone later. After graduating, he joined the officially nondenominational, but mostly Congregational, London Missionary Society. He was ordained as a minister and then sent on a mission to South Africa[4] that ultimately led to his first great journey through the continent.

Kirk, as far as we know, initially did not think himself better than Livingstone for having graduated from a more prestigious school. He viewed Livingstone with some awe, given his stirring accomplishments and reputation and his friendship with Kirk's older brother. Yet Kirk would soon find that this man he was hitching his star to was much more complex and sometimes less admirable than he had been led to believe.

Those who met Livingstone in Britain were immediately struck by his passion and conviction and later, in Africa, by his almost foolhardy fearlessness. They were equally impressed by the manner in which his extreme self-confidence, coupled with his earnestness and apparent altruism, disarmed native suspicions. Some of the more friendly African chiefs, it appears, considered him their spiritual father, a kind of super shaman with a pipeline to the Great Spirit. If the great doctor said God had a son and that son was called Jesus and He died for our sins, perhaps, they thought, that was not so different from the human sacrifice which some African religions decreed. Livingstone also gained a reputation as a great healer, for he was able to accomplish some cures with strange and powerful European medicines.

If some groups stubbornly refused to let him pass through their territories, Livingstone would show amazing patience, waiting for weeks until his request for safe passage was met by the local chief. Great tenacity was another aspect of his character which, more often than not, permitted him to succeed where other Europeans failed.

But Kirk would soon find that Livingstone had a darker side to his personality. In contrast to his reputation in dealing with Africans, Livingstone had little patience with his compatriots, including fellow missionaries, even when they were beset with serious illness. He made many enemies, and most of his fellow missionaries agreed that he could not tolerate criticism of any kind. Often moody, he would at times become so completely immersed in his own thoughts that he cut himself off almost completely from his companions.

Dr. Oliver Ransford, a physician and one of his biographers, insists that Livingstone suffered from manic-depressive illness. Kirk would have agreed, for he found it hard to adjust to Livingstone's swinging moods. There were periods when his mentor was bitter, short-tempered, morose, secretive, and even paranoid—the depressive phase of his illness. Yet during his manic phase, he could be quite foolhardy and unrealistically optimistic, causing him to lead others into life-threatening situations on more than one occasion.[5]

Kirk's amazing patience would wear thin, but he never confronted Livingstone openly. He kept his thoughts to himself and, luckily for us, to his journal and letters.

Dark side or not, Kirk, like many others, had become fascinated by Livingstone's extraordinary exploits after reading his *Missionary Travels and Researches in South Africa*. It was a tale of love, good works, heroic sacrifice, and high adventure in an exotic and little-known land that stirred Kirk's imagination.

When Livingstone was sent by the London Missionary Society to Kuruman in South Africa in 1841, he met there the dynamic missionary Robert Moffat, who had gained fame by translating the Bible into the language of the populous Bechuana tribe. Livingstone was even more entranced by Moffat's daughter, Mary, whom he married in 1845 when she was twenty-three.

The couple spent the next eight years in southern Africa, first founding a mission at Mabotsa, 200 miles north of Kuruman, and then again at Kolobeng, another 70 miles farther north. In 1849 Livingstone said farewell to his wife and their three children and traveled another 870 miles north, where he discovered Lake Nagami on the border of the Kalahari Desert (see Map 2 on page 17). The following year Livingstone repeated this journey, this time with his family.

After seeing many Africans sick with malaria, Livingstone decided that the Lake Nagami region was not healthy enough for a permanent mission. Then, driven more by a thirst for exploration than his desire to proselytize, he continued north again with his family, ignoring the possibility that they might be killed by hostile inhabitants or succumb to malaria, amebic dysentery, or one of the other tropical diseases prevalent along the route.

In 1851, the Livingstones became friendly with Sebutane, chief of the important Makololo tribe. It was then that they first came face to face with the dreaded slave trade. Sebutane, who had been waging a desperate war against the Matabele, a branch of the Zulus (now called N'Debele), asked for firearms to give him a winning edge, but Livingstone claimed he was a man of peace and refused. The Makololo chief, who had previously denied that he participated in the slave trade, in his haste to acquire guns now sold eight fourteen-year-old slave boys for eight muskets, powder, and ball. Then, after capturing two hundred Matabele, he sold thirty of them to Arab traders for three more muskets.[6]

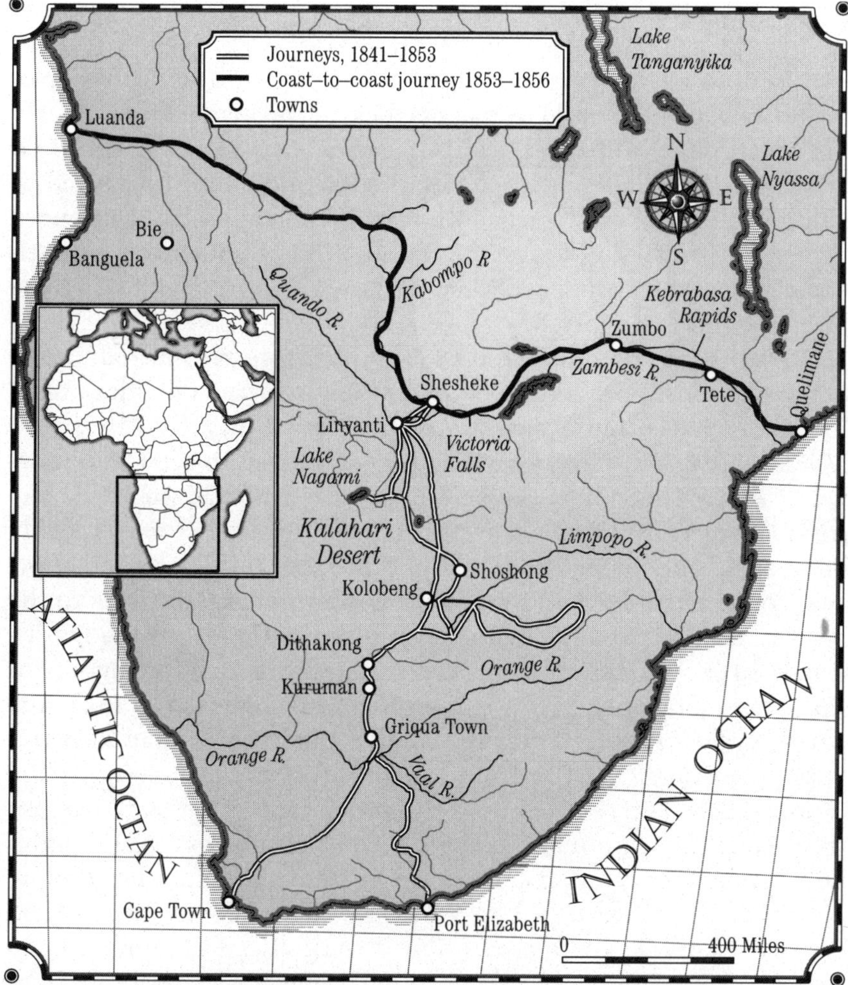

MAP 2 *Livingstone's Journeys in South and Southern Africa, 1841–1856.* From O. Ransford, *David Livingstone, The Dark Interior* (London: John Murray, 1978).

When Sebutane died of pneumonia, his daughter Mamochisane became chieftess and provided guides to accompany the Livingstones to the northern limits of her kingdom. It was at the Makololo's town of Sheshеke, in what is now Zambia, that Livingstone first cast eyes on the great Zambezi River, which flows 1,400 miles from the mountains of northern Zambia westward to Angola before looping, snake-like, back on itself to flow along the boundary between Zambia and Zimbabwe and thence southeast through Mozambique to empty into a mangrove-lined delta.

A Pioneering Trek

The Moffats had criticized Livingstone's astonishing effort at exploration as being foolhardy; it had needlessly endangered their daughter and grandchildren. But Livingstone had laughed off their criticism, and, indeed, the Moffats's second-guessing turned to admiration when they learned that the Livingstones had befriended the powerful Makololo chief Sebutane. But Livingstone himself decided it was time to send Mary and the children back to England to live with his parents.

Returning to the Makololo 1853, Livingstone was introduced to Sebutane's son, Sekeletu, who had taken over the chiefdom from his sister. He called Livingstone "my new father." While at the Makololo capitol, Linyanti, Livingstone refused to see Lazlo Magyar, a young Hungarian explorer and trader who had made the trip from Benguela in Angola expressly to meet him. This was probably because he did not want England and the rest of the world to know that someone had already made the trip from central Africa to the west coast that he was then contemplating. He also played down the voyage of Caetano Jose Ferreira, who had left Angola for Linyanti, by labeling him a half-caste and slave dealer in his book. Another Portuguese living in Angola, Silva Porto, had also traversed southern Africa from the west coast to Linyanti and described the trail he had used to Livingstone. This fact was also omitted from *Missionary Travels* so that Livngstone could claim he was the first European to make the crossing. In a later book, *Narrative of an Expedition to the Zambesi and Its Tributaries and of the Discovery of the Lakes Shirwa and Nyassa,* he mentioned that two Portuguese black slaves might have crossed together from Angola to Tete, the main Portuguese outpost on the Zambezi, in 1809, but then dismissed this as mere Portuguese pretention.[7]

Accompanied by fresh Makololo porters lent by Sekeletu, Livingstone now began his own trek across central Africa to the west coast. His journey was marred by an attack of probable cerebral malaria compounded by dysentery which laid him up for weeks at a time. In the course of his travels he was also forced to give all of his trade goods in bribes to various hostile chiefs. He finally arrived at Luanda, the capital of Angola, starving and destitute, six months after leaving Linyanti, on May 31, 1854.

The bishop of Angola, alarmed by his skeletal appearance and persistent dysentery, sent his own physician to treat Livingstone. When the British missionary-explorer was eventually restored to health, he refused an offer of free passage back to England. He felt responsible for returning his Makololo porters to their homeland.

It took Livingstone another sixteen months after leaving Luanda to reach Linyanti. There, in September 1855, he met Syde bin Habib, who had anticipated Livingstone's journey by completing the same trip thirteen years earlier and who was leaving again for Angola. The Arab trader also told him that between 1808 and 1811 three *pombeiros,* Portuguese traders of mixed blood, had made the same journey.[8]

It would have been true to Livingstone's character to have been jealous of men who had been there before him, and he accordingly emphasized in *Missionary Travels* that Syde bin Habib had sold as slaves in Zanzibar ninety-five Makololo porters lent to him by Sekeletu. Livingstone used his own contacts in Parliament to have the slaves freed and returned to Sekeletu.

From Linyanti, Livingstone went in search of the gigantic waterfall named Mosi-O-Tunya (The Smoke That Thunders) that Sekeletu had told him about. Six weeks later, on November 16, 1855, he landed his canoe just above the site he described as "so lovely [it] must have been gazed on by angels in their flight."[9] As Livingstone cautiously leaned over the edge, all he could see was the dense mist rising from the thunderous 600-foot drop into the rocky gorge below.

Livingstone was both surprised and upset to see the river suddenly divide into five separate falls from a height that dashed his hopes of bringing boats to the upper Zambezi. Nevertheless he continued to assume at first that the roughly 800 miles it took to reach the Indian Ocean below this point would still provide a means of bringing commerce and Christianity to the virtually unexplored hinterland he had traversed. And he comforted himself with the realization that he was the first white man to have seen these falls, proudly naming them after Queen Victoria.

Livingstone then veered east of the Zambezi and walked across the Batoka Plateau to the Kafue River, which led back to the Zambezi. In letters home, he described the region as ideal for British settlement, ignoring the fact that it was infested with malaria mosquitoes and occupied by the warlike Matabele.

Two months later he arrived at Tete. He was now only 250 miles from the Indian Ocean, but he had chosen a trail that bypassed the treacherous Kebrabasa Rapids (spelled Cabora Bassa by the Portuguese) and was under the delusion that the river would provide a means of bringing missionaries and trade goods to the hinterland.

The Portuguese commander at Tete, Colonel Sicard, graciously offered to keep Livingstone's Makololo porters for him should he wish to return to England. Livingstone accepted his offer as he wanted to be reunited with his family and speak and write of the wonders he had seen. Continuing down the Zambezi to the Indian Ocean, he arrived in England on December 12, 1856, almost four years after being separated from his family.

Livingstone was given a hero's welcome. He was awarded the Royal Geographic Society's gold medal for his discoveries, enterprise, dedication, and bravery, and he was granted an audience with Queen Victoria's husband, Albert, the Prince Consort. He also received the keys to the city of London and several honorary fellowships, and he was elected to England's most prestigious scientific institution, the Royal Society.

By August 1857, Livingstone had begun a round of lectures in England, Scotland, and Ireland in preparation for his next expedition. He explained to his audiences the potential for growing cotton along the Zambezi, extolled the fertility of the lands bordering the river, and described them as a potentially huge cotton field that would bring untold wealth to its planters, though, actually, he had seen only sporadic attempts to grow the crop. His glowing report appealed to the British cloth manufacturers and the Scottish cotton spinners and weavers, especially since they were fearful that, should civil war erupt in the United States, they would be cut off from their major supply of cotton in the American South.

While young Dr. John Kirk was preparing to follow Britain's hero to Africa, Livingstone was winding up his impassioned speeches against slavery and for further African settlement, which had inspired Sir Robert Murchison, the Royal Geographic Society's president, to predict that the Zambezi River would become God's highway for bringing Christianity to the heathen. It was a metaphor Livingstone could easily embrace.

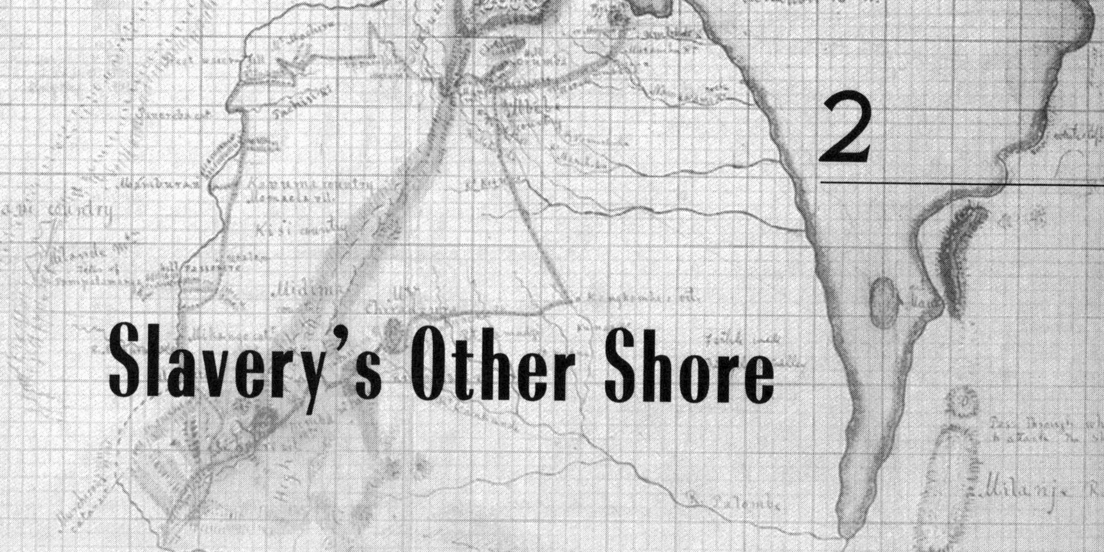

2

Slavery's Other Shore

When John Kirk and David Livingstone were making plans in 1858 for the Second Zambezi Expedition, the enormous West African slave trade, which had supplied most of the labor for the cotton, tobacco, and other plantations of the American South, was winding down. But the much less familiar East African slave trade, which Livingstone was particularly passionate about and whose abolition would figure so prominently in Kirk's later efforts, was just reaching its peak. More than 100,000 human beings were being shipped each year from Africa's eastern shores, primarily to the Arabian and Persian Gulf states but also around the Cape of Good Hope to Brazil and to the sugar plantations of the Caribbean islands.

In eastern Africa, the slave trade was conducted primarily by Arabs and by Swahili-speaking progeny of Arab men and Bantu women in the more northern areas, and by African-Portuguese to the south. The expeditions of these traders were frequently financed by Muslim Indians, known as Banyans, who had settled in the coastal ports and on the islands of Zanzibar and Pemba.

In what is now called southern Africa, the main slave thoroughfare at the time of the Kirk and Livingstone explorations was the Zambezi itself. The 1,400-mile-long river flowed for 400 navigable miles through Portuguese-controlled territory and, compared to overland routes, provided an ideal way of lowering the cost of transporting slaves and ivory to Portuguese seaports on the Indian Ocean.

In the regions to the north of the Zambezi that Kirk would later be most concerned with, Arab slave dealers had for centuries rarely ventured into the interior, being content to receive African-led slave caravans at their trading towns on the coast. But by the 1850s they had begun to travel many miles inland to deal directly with village chiefs who kept a supply of slaves penned and ready for sale. This shift resulted in a dramatic increase in the numbers of slaves exported to the Persian Gulf states.

Arab caravans would leave Zanzibar, cross the 20-mile stretch of Indian Ocean to Bagamoyo on the mainland, and wind their way inland until they reached Tabora and then Ujiji on Lake Tanganyika. From there they would fan out to the west, north, and east, raiding villages or trading guns for slaves and ivory with local chieftains. Such excursions along the foot trails to the interior could often last a year or more.

Trade in animal products, though less profitable by itself than traffic in slaves, provided a substantial additional source of revenue to the slavers, especially after the widespread introduction of firearms made big-game hunting far easier and more successful than it had been. Among various products, most important was ivory. In the eighteenth and nineteenth centuries the European demand for ivory was particularly great, for use in buttons, piano keys, billiard balls, and inlay work on furniture, boxes, carvings, combs, mirrors, and hairbrush handles. There was also a subsidiary market in rhinoceros horns, from which the powder was used as an aphrodisiac by aging Arab men with the misbegotten hope of satisfying the demands of multiple wives.

The great advantage of this secondary trade from the slaver's point of view was that transportation from Africa's interior was virtually free. Newly introduced four-legged beasts of burden succumbed to the tsetse fly, source of the often deadly "sleeping sickness" in much of the region (see Map 3 on page 23), and the existence of only foot paths ruled out wheeled vehicles, so the slaves being sent to market themselves were used to carry the tusks. If an elephant tusk was heavy—one could weigh as much as 200 pounds—it had to be carried by two slaves or more. If a female slave couldn't carry a tusk because she was nursing a baby, the baby might be killed or abandoned. Despite sizable losses from sickness, disease, and "disciplinary" killing, profits from slave trading and ivory could be huge.

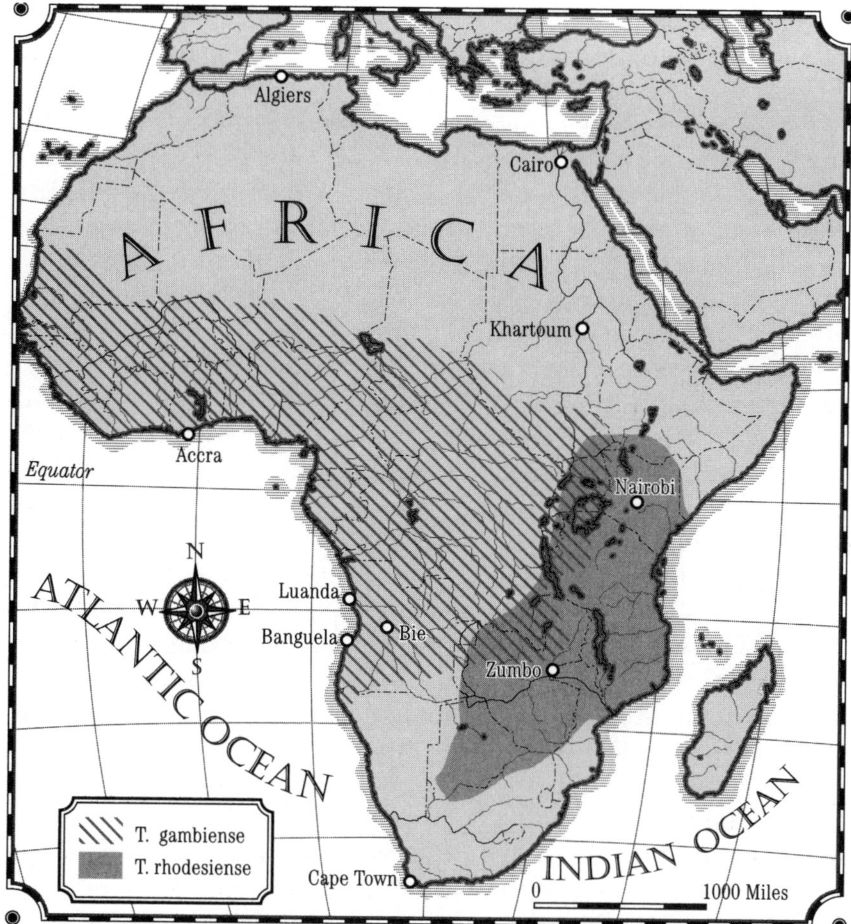

MAP 3 *Tsetse fly belt in Africa, showing approximate distribution of the two types of trypanosomiasis (African sleeping sickness),* Trypanosoma gambiense *(G) and* Trypanosoma rhodesiense *(R).* From J. H. Steel, ed.,CRC Handbook Series in *Zoonoses* (Boca Raton, Fla.:CRC Press, 1982, p.123).

First Slavers, the Torch of Islam, the Portuguese Arrival

As far back as the Sixth Dynasty (2280 BCE), an Egyptian trader, Harkhuf, penetrated south of Sudan into the northeastern Congo. The inscription on his tomb, in a cliff across the Nile from Aswan, says that he returned with a dancing Pygmy for the young pharaoh, Pepi II.[1] Greek classics were part of Kirk's curriculum and he must have known that Euripedes, in the fifth century BCE, had called slavery "that thing of evil." He also read the Koran when in Turkey and came across the passage, "Ye are also forbidden to take to wife free women who are married except those women your right hand should possess as slaves. . . ."[2]

The slave-trading systems—Arab and Portuguese—that Kirk and Livingstone would encounter had a long history, starting with the Arabs. By the end of the seventh century CE, Muslim traders had already entered the sub-Saharan region to capitalize on what became a seemingly insatiable demand for slaves for Egypt, Arabia, Turkey, Persia, and India. Syrian traders were said to have settled in East Africa during the Umayyad Califate (685–705 CE), and, according to the ninth-century Arab writer Al Baladhuri, Lamu in present-day Kenya and Kismayu in Somalia were also settled by Arab slavers at that time.[3] By the tenth century, Arabs had established new slave depots all along the eastern coast from Somalia to Mozambique, spreading the Muslim faith by force when necessary.

In 922 an Omani captain lured an African king accompanied by 200 slave children on board his dhow near Sofala, Mozambique, and sailed north to sell them in Arabia. An observant sailor wrote of the kidnapping that "the visitors to this country steal their children, enticing them away by offering them fruits. They carry the children from place to place and finally take possession of them and carry them off to their own country."[4]

In the sixteenth century, Arab control of the East African coast was subverted by the rising European power of Portugal. When Vasco de Gama sailed around the Cape of Good Hope in 1497, he anchored for several weeks at the mouth of the Quelimane River in modern-day Mozambique, and before crossing the ocean to India he stopped at Arab-controlled ports on Africa's east coast. His remarkable voyage of discovery spurred Portuguese colonization of Africa by soldiers, traders, farmers, and government officials, most of whom sooner or later participated in the lucrative slave trade. Portuguese trading facilities were established at the Arab ports of Sofala and Kilwa in 1505, and two years later on the island of Mozambique, across a narrow channel from the large Portuguese mainland colony of the same name.

Hostilities soon broke out between the two powers, with the Portuguese besting the Arabs at the Battle of Diu in 1509 and soon thereafter capturing Zeila in Somalia and Muscat and Hormuz in Oman. After only twenty years in East Africa, the Portuguese had become rulers of these former Arab ports, and they had built a powerful stockade in Mombassa, Fort Jesus, a structure which still stands. Not content with just these territorial acquisitions, the

Portuguese sent their caravels into the Indian Ocean along Arab sea routes to trade with the Persian Gulf states themselves and to Goa, a Portuguese enclave on India's western shore. They also began a thriving slave trade to the New World and extended their sphere of influence into present-day Malawi and Zambia.[5]

A hundred years after the Portuguese settled in the coastal trading cities of East Africa, the Arabs recovered much of what had been taken from them. Backed by the British, Dutch, and French, who were now determined to limit Portuguese expansion, the Omanis reconquered Hormuz in 1622, and Muscat, the capital of Oman, in 1650. By 1698 the Omani Arabs had taken Mombassa's Fort Jesus.

The contending powers finally reached an agreement to end overt hostilities, dividing the area into spheres of influence that would last down to the days of Kirk and Livingstone. The coast north of the Rovuma River was ceded to the Arabs, while the Portuguese successfully retained control of the area to the south that corresponds roughly to present-day Mozambique (see Map 4 on page 26).

Paths to Enslavement

Because neither the Portuguese nor Arab traders wanted their paths into Africa's interior known, it was only when British explorers like Livingstone and Kirk ran into the slavers and followed them that they were able to record the brutalities of the trade. A slave caravan was typically led by two or three Arab or Portuguese merchants, the former carrying the sultan of Zanzibar's scarlet flag. The leaders of an expedition could command a small army of as many as a thousand slaves and porters.

Kidnapping of Africans was commonplace. "The victims were sometimes caught while walking in the bush quite close to their villages," a Livingstone biographer wrote.[6] Occasionally a chief would be tempted to punish a crime by selling the culprit to the traders, and Livingstone reports the case of an old chief selling his "young and good-looking wife for unfaithfulness," as he alleged.[7]

The Arabs might conduct a raid themselves, but more often they incited a chief to attack another tribe, lending him their own armed slaves and guns to ensure his victory. The result was an increase in intertribal warfare to the point where "the whole country was in a flame."[8] One group, the Ajwa, now called Yao, who lived at the southern end of Lake Malawi, even became specialists in kidnapping their fellow Africans and selling them to the Arabs.

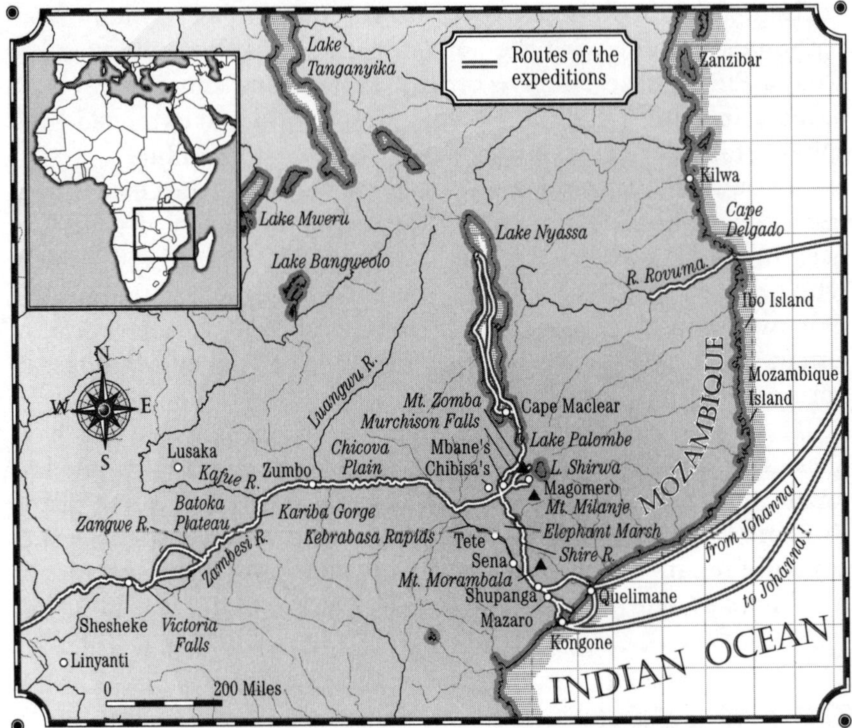

MAP 4 *The Second Zambezi Expedition.* From R. Coupland, *Kirk on the Zambezi* (Oxford: Clarendon Press, 1928, p. 287).

Published reports of slave capture and its aftermath shocked the British public. "A village having been carried by assault, all the inhabitants who had not escaped or been killed in the fighting were rounded up—except those who were too old or decrepit to be salable—and the huts were then set on fire," read one Livingstone account.[9] In addition, livestock might be driven off and standing crops left to rot. To any survivors who might return to this devastating scene of half-burned huts and blackened ground strewn with household goods and bits of furniture was the awful silence and the putrescent stench of the unburied dead.

Such destruction was often widespread. The explorers spoke of "miles of ruined villages." If the slave raids occurred in the sowing season, the havoc they wrought meant insufficient crops and famine, and that, in turn, meant more human losses. Some might starve, others might be sold in exchange for food. "I have known children from the age of 8 to 10 years bought for less corn that would go into one of our hats," wrote Livingstone.[10]

Apart from the personal agony that enslavement caused, it devastated the stability of societies that rested on the extended family. Since polygamy was almost universally practiced, a man's many wives, offspring, cousins, aunts, and uncles formed the extended family, which could consist of several hundred members. Typically, in the nomenclature of the time, a number of extended families formed a clan ruled by a sub-chief, and several clans formed a tribe ruled by a paramount chief or king. This social structure was undermined, sometimes decimated, by the capture of significant family members. Furthermore, slavers consciously intermixed slaves of different tribes to undermine solidarity among captives. Since the tribes spoke different languages or dialects, they were forced to learn Swahili, that mixture of Bantu and Arabic which became the *lingua franca* of East Africa.

Wooden neck-yokes, called gorées, which were secured by chains, fastened recalcitrant slaves in a line while they were marched from the point of capture for hundreds of miles under horrific conditions to the coastal ports. The longest route took as much as three months to traverse, and more than a third of the captives might die on the way. Profits were so great, however, that the traders felt they could afford such high losses.

The explorers often found plenty of grim evidence to indicate that they were on the heels of a slave caravan, so much so that they feared people at home would not believe them. Some of Livingstone's observations were recorded by his biographer, W. G. Blaikie:

> We passed a woman tied by the neck to a tree and dead. Today we came upon a man dead of starvation. . . . We passed a slave woman shot or stabbed through the body. . . . An Arab early that morning had done it in anger at losing the price he had given for her because she was unable to walk any longer. . . . One woman, who was unable to carry both her load and young child, had the child taken from her and saw its brains dashed out on a stone.[7]

In the latter half of the nineteenth century, most Portuguese-controlled slaves were shipped out of Mozambique's port of Quelimane while the Arab slavers took most of their captives by boat to Zanzibar for shipment overseas. Newly arrived slaves were herded into pens or barracoons and fattened. They were then placed in the great weekly slave markets to be sold to the highest bidder. In Zanzibar, captives were held near the auction yard in rooms that can still be visited today on a tourist route. These rooms were constructed under the streets with slit windows just above street level to provide minimal air. Just before the auction, the slaves' hair was inspected for lice and treated if necessary. The slaves were washed and groomed and their skin oiled. Savvy buyers inspected the captives for skin diseases such as yaws and leprosy. They prodded the men's muscles and testicles to see if they could reproduce. They examined the women for pregnancy, and fingered their vaginas to check for an abnormal discharge or to see if any were still virgins. Pregnant women and virgins cost more, as did comely young women who were sold as concubines. Some young men were castrated to become eunuchs in the harems of wealthy Arabs.[12]

After a sale, cruelties could abound, but, many observers claimed that once slaves were purchased, they were usually treated with as much care as any of the owner's other living possessions, such as a horse, a dog, or a cow.[13]

The Arab Slave Trade in East Africa in the Nineteenth Century

With the seventeenth-century agreement with the Portuguese, the Arabs once again controlled the East African littoral from Mozambique's northern boundary at the Rovuma River north to Somalia. During the first decades of the nineteenth century, Kilwa on the coast was superseded by Zanzibar as the center of Arab slave trading. In 1840, the sultan of Oman, Seyyid[14] Said, decided to make Zanzibar his permanent seat of government, and he proclaimed the coastal mainland of East Africa his domain.

When Sultan Said had cloves planted on Zanzibar and its sister island of Pemba a few years later, the need to have the produce hand-picked triggered an upsurge in slave marketing. Ivory and gum copal (the resin from the copal tree used in Europe for varnish) were sources of lesser but nevertheless significant revenue that flowed through Zanzibar's custom house. By 1851, Zanzibar was exporting 8,000–10,000 slaves annually. An additional number was shipped out of Kilwa to the Persian Gulf states, India, and Egypt. This number was to double in Kirk's heyday.

Mozambique in the Eighteenth and Nineteenth Centuries

The mouth of the Zambezi, where Kirk was heading with Livingstone, was a key location in the Portuguese-dominated slave trade. According to custom-house figures, the annual slave trade had grown to 11,000 in Mozambique in 1788. James Prior, a surgeon on the British frigate *Nisus,* reported in 1811 that 10,000 slaves were shipped annually to Brazil and the West Indies.[15] In 1820 the annual shipment of slaves to Brazil had risen to 15,055. By 1858 Ibo also had become a "great warehouse for slaves," according to H. Lyons McLeod, the first British consul to Mozambique.[16]

Yet Portuguese rule over the Mozambique region was relatively weak, and the Portuguese lived in perpetual fear of being overrun by the far more numerous Africans. Annual tributes in cloth and beads were paid to the most warlike groups, such as the Lundeens, a branch of the Zulus, to keep them from attacking Portuguese settlements.

"Quelimane is now the greatest mart for slaves on the east coast," British Captain Owen wrote in 1822. "They are purchased with blue dungarees, coloured cloths, arms, gunpowder, brass and pewter, red coloured beads in imitation of coral, cutlery, and various articles. The free blacks of the country and Banyans carry on the trade inland for the merchants. . . . From eleven to fourteen slave-vessels come annually from Rio de Janeiro to this place, and return with four to five hundred slaves each on an average. . . ."[17]

Though Portugal had signed a treaty in 1842 agreeing to confiscate slave vessels, interest in enforcing it among local administrators was minimal or nonexistent. A year after Portugal signed, another British observer described a caravan of slaves as thin as skeletons brought from the interior. "They had a ring round the neck and a chain through it, thus connecting together 40 or 50 in a line. At night they were shipped off in boats to be taken down the river to barracoons erected near its mouth where they were kept. When the coast was clear of cruisers, they were hurried on board a vessel kept in waiting for them and taken to Rio de Janeiro for sale."[18]

In 1846 the governor of Quelimane was recalled for having dabbled in the slave trade. The governor of Mozambique Island himself departed hastily for Rio de Janeiro with a cargo of five hundred slaves—a fortune—while the governor of Ibo bribed a British translator to keep his slave dealings secret.

In 1852 British Commodore Wyvill wrote, "I regret that the Portuguese authorities, instead of repressing this traffic, afford every facility for its continuance. I learn that the Governor of Inhambane permitted a slaver to lie at anchor off that port for three weeks and capture 1000 slaves in December 1851, and the governor of Ibo connived at the trade."[19]

By the 1850s the slave trade to Brazil had decreased as a consequence of a crackdown on slavers by the Brazilian government, but the French had taken up some of the slack in calls on Ibo and Mozambique for slave laborers. Under what they termed the Free Labor Emigration Act (and the British called a travesty), the French had been shipping slaves under the pretext that they were using them only as indentured servants for seven years. There was great demand for labor from sugar planters on Réunion (formerly called Bourbon) and the Comoro Islands in the Indian Ocean. At one point early in the century, the French demand was so great that two-thirds of Mozambique's yearly export of slaves was shipped on French vessels to their sugarcane islands in the Indian Ocean and the Caribbean.[20]

Antislavery Treaties

The export of slaves from the eastern side of the African continent was occasionally hampered by antislavery sea patrols, but for decades these were generally ineffective. In 1841 Britain, France, Prussia, and Russia agreed to confiscate vessels engaged in the slave trade; a year later Portugal also agreed.[21] Enforcement mostly fell to the British by default, but the home government did not invest heavily in it. The British provided only three navy vessels to patrol the 2,000-mile-long eastern African coast in the wake of the treaty, and two were subsequently taken out of service.[22] Chasing slave-trading dhows was thus a frustrating endeavor for the British patrols until Livingstone and others were later able to arouse the British government sufficiently to reinforce the East African navy. It was only after 1869 and especially after 1873 that more ships were assigned to the task.[23]

To circumvent the right-to-search portion of the treaty, slavers began to use the U.S. flag, as if a prior U.S. search-and-seizure treaty with Britain did not apply.[24] The British patrols were ardent if not always effective in their pursuit of slavers sailing under false colors, and also managed to stop three fast American clipper ships packed with slaves.[25] The Americans had been engaged in the slave trade to supply manpower for the cotton and sugarcane fields and for the rice paddies of the southern states prior to their Civil War.

The Antislavery Movement

The advent of the treaties aimed at eliminating the slave trade that began to spring up in the nineteenth century was due in no small part to pressure from European and American antislavery groups, such as the one to which Livingstone belonged. Though the eastern African trade in human beings was thriving in the middle decades of the century, international opposition to the practice was growing, most notably in Great Britain.

The antislavery movement in England originated from three broad concepts: that of the "rights of man" propounded by Voltaire, Rousseau, and other eighteenth-century philosophers; the mainly Protestant ethos that equated slavery with sin; and the burgeoning theories of capitalism based on the economic value of free labor. Even before the French Revolution, the "rights of man" became a cause célèbre in Great Britain and abolishing the slave trade became the rallying cry for a plethora of activist societies that sprang up.

The first of these societies—the Society for the Abolition of the Slave Trade—was formed in 1783 by William Wilberforce, Granville Sharp, Thomas Clarkson, and a group of other Quakers and clergymen. The organization's seal was designed by Josiah Wedgewood, producer of fine china, and showed an African holding up his chained hands over the stirring motto, "Am I not a Man and a Brother?"[26]

Wilberforce, the Society's most prominent spokesman, advocated the manumission of slaves throughout the world. Elected a member of Parliament in 1780, he described the evils of the slave trade in the House of Commons, arguing that Britain should pass an emancipation act. Finally, responding to public pressure and wishing to free its own slaves, Parliament outlawed slavery in Britain in 1807. In 1834 a second act of Parliament affirmed the British government's determination to end the practice in its own colonies and elsewhere, and it ordered the British navy to set up antislavery patrols along both African coasts. Britain's main and most successful efforts were focused not on Africa's eastern shores, however, but on West Africa, where slaves were being shipped by the thousands to the West Indies and to the southern United States.

The Anti-Slavery Society, which Wilberforce established in 1823, petitioned the government to incorporate antislavery legislation in treaties with other governments. A sizable segment of the upper and middle British classes saw a moral justification in freeing Africa from the terrible scourge of human bondage though the lower classes, beset by the poor wages and unsanitary conditions of the Industrial Revolution, played little role in the campaigns to free African slaves.

It took another ten years of proselytizing before Parliament enacted, in 1833, a new British Emancipation Bill into law. In that same year, a grandiose scheme for worldwide suppression of slavery was fostered by Joseph Sturge, resulting in the British and Foreign Society for the Abolition of Negro Slavery and the Slave Trade. Six years later the furor against slavery and the slave trade reached new heights, culminating in the founding of the British and Foreign Anti-Slavery Society, whose aim extended to stopping the trade overseas. Yet another antislavery society was born that year, the Society for the Extinction of the Slave Trade and the Civilization of Africa, referred to as the African Civilization Society, which Livingstone joined.

The British antislavery activist William Buxton, having been defeated in a run for Parliament in 1837, nevertheless had devised a plan to put teeth into the antislavery legislation by not only urging Parliament to fund more British antislavery patrols around Africa, but by establishing a showpiece society in Africa governed by Christian principles. In 1841 he prevailed on Parliament to send three iron steamships up West Africa's Niger River. After sailing 350 miles upstream, 41 of the 193 Niger Expedition members died of "river fever"—probably malaria. Because most of the other expedition members were very sick, the ships turned back without discovering the Niger's source, without founding any missions or showpiece societies, and without affecting the practice of slavery. Buxton died in 1845, a very disappointed man.[27]

The strides being made in Britain toward the abolition of the slave trade were supported by American abolitionists. Though the United States had passed antislavery legislation in 1807, it was deliberately ignored by the southern states. The most vocal leader of the North American movement was William Lloyd Garrison, who, like Sturge, was a pacifist. He visited his British counterparts three times. In 1840 he attended the first international antislavery convention held in London, but his liberal ideas did not include equality for women, and a delegation of American women failed in their attempt to be included. In 1846 he returned to England with the African-American slave-abolitionist Frederick Douglass. Along with their supporters in Britain, they founded the radical Anti-Slavery League, which accused the British and Foreign Anti-Slavery Society of failing to sufficiently help American abolitionist efforts. Garrison also antagonized the British by insulting the monarchy, deriding the Sabbath, and commenting that the British "were crushed beneath an overgrown monarchy and bloated aristocracy."[28] Frederick Douglass, however, charmed his British audiences and a collection of £150 bought him his freedom.

The antislavery movement in Britain and America reached its apogee on the eve of the American War between the States. Though many of the wealthier British members of the antislavery societies invested large sums of money in the "cause," most of these prominent and well-to-do antislavery activists shared the racial prejudices of their age. Rare was the abolitionist who would do more than shake the hand of a visiting black person.[29] But this prejudice in no way stilled the ardor of many, including Livingstone.

African Social Structure and European Imperialism

David Livingstone was already experienced enough to recognize that black Africa was no undifferentiated mass. Precolonial African cultures were as varied as others elsewhere in the world. Sophisticated merchants in Benin, Songhai, and Mali or accomplished artisans in Meroe and the Great Zimbabwe had little in common with hunter-gatherer Pygmies and bushmen or the pastoralist Nandi, Samburu, and Masai of Kenya and Tanzania. Nevertheless, Livingstone himself was also a child of the imperial ethos of the time and to some extent accepted imperialist views.

Imperialism obviously meant different things to different people. But by the latter half of the nineteenth century, the concept was being used extensively to justify European involvement in African affairs, even including the slave trade and other extremely exploitative practices. Some of the proponents of white involvement in Africa, however, such as Livingstone, saw their work leading potentially to an agrarian paradise that would uplift blacks while it improved the lot of whites. White settlers, in addition to acquiring land for themselves, would aid the indigenous Africans by teaching them farming and instilling in them good work habits. With this tutelage they could become efficient servants who would be paid a low but living wage, comparable to what factory workers received in Britain. It went without saying that conversion to Christianity would be part of the process. This conversion would be key, they believed, to ending slavery, idolatry, intertribal warfare, polygamy, superstitions, and some of the African traditional initiation rites such as circumcision and clitoridectomy.[30]

The Victorian romantic writer James Anthony Froude even proposed ameliorating the evils of industrialization and its associated pollution and sickness by sending poor, homeless British citizens to colonize Africa, where they would be transformed into healthy traders in legitimate goods and hardworking farmers.[31] Others considered imperial acquisition of colonies simply a tangible demonstration of British national greatness. Extension of the Empire, to them, was progress, and progress was social evolution, all for the good of the savage and benighted African who otherwise wouldn't hesitate to enslave his own people or even eat them, given the opportunity.

This ethos of economic and moral imperialism was endorsed by most British explorers and missionaries. Many subscribed to the idea of the "white man's burden." Like the antislavery societies to which many belonged, they believed that it was their God-given duty to care for and educate their black cousins. And if trade with the heathen could help both the natives and the British economy, so much the better.

Many Victorians, then, while they hated to see Africans enslaved and treated like beasts of burden, felt that they were, for the most part, like children, "laughing easily, carrying heavy loads without undue complaints, grateful for the white man's handouts, fearful at following their white masters into territory occupied by strange tribes, avaricious and cruel at times towards their fellow Africans."[32] On the other hand, British social activists equated African tribes with the European proletariat of the slums. Both were to be uplifted and saved. Given a proper education, some Victorian explorers thought Africans could rival any white person's accomplishments.[33]

And what of Kirk? He, too, was a man of his time. But he was never as much the enthusiast for "civilizing" the Africans in the European mold or for Christian evangelism as were Livingstone and others. He was one of a new breed of physician-explorers who were scientifically trained to carefully observe and record the flora and fauna, and the peoples, cultures, and diseases they encountered. In his journals and letters, Kirk attempted to describe objectively his experiences with Livingstone and the hardships they endured. While he shared some of the prejudices of his fellows and belief in the imperial venture, in his later dealings in Africa he earned time and again a reputation for fairness.

Further British Efforts to Stem the East African Slave Trade

Best estimates suggest that after 1850 as many as 20,000–25,000 slaves were shipped annually overseas from holding pens on Zanzibar and Kilwa. Another 10,000 passed through Somalia, and well into the 1870s Egypt absorbed up to 20,000 annually from the Sudan and upper Nile. R. W. Beachey estimates that a total of over two million slaves were shipped out of East Africa in the latter half of the nineteenth century.[34]

In 1858, at the beginning of Kirk's journey with Livingstone's Second Zambezi expedition, two-thirds of the 200,000 inhabitants of Zanzibar Island were slaves. The Englishman George Keppel, who visited the Zanzibar slave market in the 1830s, described it as "being dispersed in a series of small, squalid squares" with "some twenty or thirty fat little negresses from 12 to 14 years of age . . . giggling and chatting with the utmost nonchalance."[35]

When Sultan Said died, his son Majid became the next sultan. Majid made no serious efforts to stop slavery, and the slave trade prospered. A new slave market was built a mile from the port and not far from the palace.

The Arab dhows, which transported freight including slaves, had been in use for over a thousand years. Blown by the trade winds, they would leave the Arabian Peninsula for Zanzibar and other East African ports in November, their single, lanteen sails catching the wind from behind. The voyage would take a month or more. The following April, with the wind blowing in the opposite direction, the dhow flotilla, packed with newly purchased slaves, would return to the Persian Gulf states to sell their human cargo. During the long voyage slaves were piled one above the other in tiers with only three or four feet between, which prevented them from sitting up.

In boarding a suspicious dhow, the first thing British antislavery patrol vessels looked for was the amount of water stored on board. If water casks held more than the crew needed, this was strong evidence that the vessel was hiding slaves in the hold, and a search below decks was made.

There are varied accounts describing the condition of seaborne slaves. Though they were not always fettered, they were forced to lie or sit in their own excrement. They were hosed down once a day, their refuse piling up in the bilges. One can imagine the stench. If the dhow was delayed at a hidden harbor on the coast, waiting to slip past a British naval vessel, or if it was becalmed on the way to the Persian Gulf, slave rations were cut.[36]

The Zambezi River

A word should be said at this point about the riverine route used by Portuguese slavers up to and including the period when Kirk and Livingstone explored the region.

The roar of the Zambezi could be heard for miles as it spilled over Mosi-O-Tunya or Victoria Falls, the name bequeathed by

David Livingstone in honor of the British queen. Pouring through the narrow and treacherous Kariba and Cabora Bassa (Kebrabasa) gorges, the river lost its fearful force when the dangerous rapids were dammed in the twentieth century. The flow has consequently slowed from about seven miles an hour to three miles an hour. Today lakes Kariba and Cabora Bassa (the Portuguese name for the rapids Kirk and Livingstone called Kebrabasa before they were dammed) cover these areas which caused such agony to these early British explorers.

Untamed and treacherous in Livingstone and Kirk's day, the lower Zambezi is now navigable to shallow draft boats past the Portuguese river towns of Tete, Sena, and Shupanga before it empties into the Indian Ocean in a mangrove-lined delta. Some ninety-five miles upstream from the delta, the Zambezi receives water from the Shire River, its main tributary and the outlet for the huge Lake of the Stars, Ninyesi, later known as Lake Nyassa and now as Lake Malawi.

When Kirk and Livingstone arrived on the scene, Portuguese soldier-conscripts and a few slave and ivory traders were living in forts on the lower Zambezi River's malarial floodplain. Livingstone was incensed with the Portuguese colonial government, which had, for several centuries, turned a blind eye to the lucrative slave trade despite an antislavery treaty in 1836 with Britain. However, this two-way trade did bring some benefit to East Africa. The African diet was enriched by crops imported from South America such as manioc (cassava), Indian corn, tomatoes, avocado, guava, tobacco, and the cinchona tree bark which yielded quinine. Quinine was the only remedy for malaria until the twentieth century (with the exception of "guinghaosu," or wormwood, an older remedy used in China).

3

Preparations for the Unknown

Twenty-six-year-old John Kirk signed onto the Second Zambezi Expedition as an enthusiastic, if somewhat naive, young man eager to make botanical discoveries, indulge his new hobby of photography, and learn about unusual tropical diseases. Little did he know that he would be inextricably entwining his life with David Livingstone's. The spirit of adventure and the glamour of going on a trip to an unexplored part of Africa with an already well-known explorer undoubtedly were strong motivating factors.

From the outset, though, Livingstone made it clear to Kirk that this would be no garden party. He wrote prophetically on January 4, 1858, "The contemplated length of the expedition is two years, but there is a possibility of its being prolonged beyond that period by circumstances of which we are not at present aware."[1] It ended up taking over five years.

Kirk had, with due Scottish sagacity, questioned Livingstone about what expenses he might incur while on the expedition. Livingstone wrote back somewhat dryly, though perhaps he thought he was being humorous,

> With regard to "necessary expenses" I am not quite clear as to what you mean. Suppose you shoot a buffalo, there will be no expense in cooking and eating it. There are no inns or hotels in the country. The lodging will be all free. The expedition will have supplies of plain food—coffee, sugar, etc; anything else will be got, I suppose, in the usual mess fashion, each member contributing a share of the expense of the extras. I shall not be answerable for luxuries of any kind whatever. And expeditions of this kind cannot be successful unless all the members are willing to "rough it."[2]

Although officially a government-sponsored expedition under the Foreign Office's Lord Clarendon, Livingstone, a private citizen, was put in command. With public and private donations totaling £5,000, there was money enough to properly equip the new expedition and furnish it with a steamboat with side paddle wheels to cruise up the Zambezi.

A Diverse Crew

Unfortunately, Livingstone, at age forty-four, had no experience and little acumen in choosing or commanding white men. Some members of his new team were friends, others came highly recommended. Captain Norman Bedingfeld of the Royal Navy, whom he had met briefly in Angola in 1854, was chosen to command the steam launch. Richard Thornton, a young graduate of the Royal School of Mines, was hired to investigate possible coal, gold, or other valuable metals or minerals. Livingstone's younger brother, Charles, was to be in charge of evangelizing. Thomas Baines, an artist, was to supervise the stores. George Rae was to be the boat's engineer, and Kirk the physician and botanist. In addition to these principals there were twelve Africans from Sierra Leone called Krumen, as well as a couple of sailors lent by the *Pearl,* the ship that would take them around the Cape of Good Hope to the place where they would begin their riverine journey in Portuguese East Africa.

Each of the men Livingstone had selected had his own idiosyncrasies, which in the cramped quarters of a 75-foot-long paddle wheel steamer intensified and eventually turned to friction with their leader as the group plunged deeper and deeper into Africa's interior. Bedingfeld, for instance, thought himself in virtual command of not just the boat, but of the entire undertaking. This did not augur well with Livingstone,whose sensitive mood and fiery temper almost immediately caused a clash between them.

Baines had been the official military artist for the British expeditionary force in the South African Kaffir War of 1848–51 and again for an exploration in Australia three years later. His paintings and lithographs were admired in England, and Baines presumably volunteered to have a chance to paint the exotic landscapes and other sites that Livingstone had so enthusiastically described. But the main assignment given him by Livingstone was to keep careful records of the expedition's food and supplies. That Baines' artistic temperament might be unsuited for bookkeeping was something Livingstone did not consider.

Livingstone's younger brother, thirty-six-year-old Charles Livingstone, almost immediately became a problem to the others. With no experience in expeditions of this kind, he became a constant complainer. Charles had graduated from New York City's Union Theological Seminary as a Congregational minister. He happened to be in England for treatment of a nervous condition, probably depression, when his older brother persuaded him to join the expedition. This meant leaving his wife and children for a trip into the unknown, disease-ridden African interior for an indeterminate period of time.

George Rae was a competent engineer who came from Blantyre, Scotland, Livingstone's birthplace. But Rae turned out to be an inveterate gossip, usually bad-mouthing people who did not see eye to eye with him.

Twenty-year-old Richard Thornton had been recommended by Sir Robert Murchison of the Royal Geographic Society as a talented young geologist and graduate of the Royal School of Mines. He, like most of the others, was to demonstrate his worst characteristics while suffering from malaria.

Kirk, for his part, was a gentleman by training and background. He had distinguished himself in both medicine and botany, whereas Livingstone was a self-made man who had gotten through medical school without distinction and had focused his life on missionary work. Livingstone may have felt inferior to the handsome, athletic, bearded young physician, almost twenty years his junior. In any case, in the months and years to come he acted at times as a tyrant and at times as a protective father toward Kirk. There is no question that Livingstone went through periods of depression as described by Kirk and also periods of manic behavior in which he took risks no other man would.[3] Kirk felt these moods would come on when things didn't go Livingstone's way, for the expedition leader would lash out at the others unmercifully. A different man might have been driven to despair, but Kirk managed to transcend Livingstone's tantrums.

Livingstone was empowered by Lord Clarendon to run the expedition along quasi-military lines. This meant he could send home anyone who failed to live up to his expectations. But morale wasn't improved by the fact that salaries were low. Captain Bedingfeld was to receive £650, which included his naval pay, per year. Charles Livingstone, Kirk, and Thornton would each receive £350 annually. Rae and Baines complained about the meager £200 allotted to each of them. Although the Foreign Office was sympathetic, nothing could be done about it as Livingstone had already spent the rest of the money on other items for the expedition.[4]

The *Ma Robert*

Captain John W. Washington of the Admiralty took a personal hand in the construction of the shallow-draft steam launch which was designed to be shipped in sections for assembly at the mouth of the Zambezi. The boat, which could burn either coal or wood, would carry provisions, medicines, collections of flora and fauna gathered during the expedition, instruments, guns and ammunition, and trade goods, primarily bolts of cloth which Livingstone had found to be dearly prized by the natives. The boat was named the *Ma Robert* in honor of Mary Livingstone's son Robert, according to the custom of South African natives, who named it after the mother, Ma, and her firstborn son, Robert. Ironically, Robert resented his father, joined the Union army in the American Civil War, and died in a Confederate prisoner-of-war camp.[5]

The side paddle wheeler was powered by a twelve-horsepower steam engine. It had been designed by Macgregor Laird, who had built a similar boat for use on the Niger River in West Africa. It had an eight-foot beam and three watertight compartments. The wooden hull was covered with steel plate, but to help keep the boat light, this armor was only one-sixteenth of an inch thick.

There was a small salon on deck and a couple of tiny cabins. There were fore and aft awnings to protect the crew from the sun as well as two masts, each with a sail in case of engine failure or a fuel shortage. The *Ma Robert* had been tested on the Mersey River by Bedingfeld. It only had a twelve-inch draft, eminently suitable for river cruising, and was reported to raise fifty pounds of steam pressure from wood fuel, enough to average nine knots, which would have made it a fast boat in those days.

The Political Threat

Before the expedition got under way, there were signs of trouble brewing with the Portuguese, who controlled the lower 400 miles of the Zambezi, including the delta where the *Ma Robert* would need to enter (see Map 4 on page 26). Although the Portuguese had been friendly to and supportive of Livingstone during his previous expedition, he knew the Portuguese authorities at Quelimane, Mozambique's international port on the Indian Ocean, were concerned about his plan to steam up the Zambezi. They soon issued a *portaria,* the equivalent of a British white paper, stating that Zumbo, a Portuguese fort far up the river which had been abandoned, would be rebuilt and other forts in the Zambezi river towns of Tete, Shupanga, Sena, and Mazaro would be equipped with fresh troops. A new customs house on the Luabo River, one of the mouths of the Zambezi, would levy tariffs, and all shipping would occur under the Portuguese flag and with a permit.

The Portuguese government in Lisbon knew, only too well, how tenuous a hold it had over its East African colony. Although it recalled governor after governor for corruption and connivance in the officially illegal market in human beings, it had not been able to eliminate the slave trade or find a governor immune to its financial temptations.

Livingstone did go to the trouble to reassure the Portuguese ambassador to England that the express purpose of the expedition was to stamp out the slave trade, not claim territory. The Portuguese also were afraid that with their northern boundary still in dispute with the sultan of Zanzibar, Livingstone would try to claim the area for Britain. A "joint venture" was therefore proposed by the Portuguese with the ultimate objective of bringing the "fruits of civilization" to the natives of the region. They also asked that one of their representatives accompany Livingstone on this joint venture, but the British Foreign Office, possibly prompted by Livingstone, declined.

At Livingstone's own suggestion, however, the Foreign Office gave him some legal standing by appointing him consul to Quelimane. He also wanted them to appoint him consul to the Zambezi river settlements of Shupanga, Sena, and Tete, but the local Portuguese and their African-Portuguese descendants, whose major source of income was the slave trade, were alarmed by Livingstone's antislavery stance. Caught between the threat of British intervention and the Livingstone expedition's avowed purpose of eliminating the slave trade, they refused to allow him more than the Quelimane consulship.

Livingstone wrote to Lord Clarendon indicating how much he despised the Portuguese, who

> are so few and weak that they can scarcely hold the few forts they possess. They have no authority on the south bank of the Zambezi until we come to Sena. . . . The Portuguese inhabitants of Sena, about half-a-dozen in number, have several times paid tribute to the independent tribes adjacent to them. There is a hiatus again in their authority until we come to Tete, another village and fort. There is a stockade on the river below Tete which commands the river, and this is possessed by a chieftain who has at various times waged war with the Portuguese . . . if we ascend the Zambezi . . . we enter an immense extent of country of which the Government of Portugal never had any cognizance. . . . The Makololo people possess the chief power therein.[6]

In order to further counter any British claims in the area, the Portuguese government hurriedly decreed that, "the name, Zambezia, shall be given in all official documents to all territories to which the Crown of Portugal has a right in the valley of the Zambezi from the mouths of that river to beyond the fortress of Zumbo."[7] There was, however, one concession given to Livingstone: he could carry trade goods through Shupanga, Sena, and Tete duty free.

The Medical Threat

Apart from the anticipated political problems, the risk of contracting serious disease was substantial. Livingstone advised Kirk on the kinds of medicine to bring along, but, in truth, medications were few and their actions were understood poorly if at all. Anesthesia was in its infancy. There was no cure or prevention for amebic dysentery or shigellosis, both intestinal infections, or yellow fever, a frequently fatal disease. Schistosomaisis, a disease affecting the liver or urinary bladder depending on the type, leishmaniasis, another debilitating disease involving the glands, spleen, and liver, and malaria, especially the falciparum variety endemic to the lower Zambezi, were the major causes of chronic illness and death. In a world where the germ theory had not yet been accepted and where antibiotics had not yet been discovered, the results of medical care remained abysmal.

Due to a very high infant mortality rate as well as disease, famine, and war, the average life expectancy in Africa in the mid-nineteenth century was thirty-five years and had not changed much over the centuries. Even in Europe and America, where epidemics such as cholera still killed thousands of people, the average life expectancy was not much more than forty. Disease prevention was rudimentary, the importance of sanitation was barely understood, and surgery was associated with a dreadful rate of infection.

With few meaningful therapies available, native healers, with their incantations and a few native drugs of possible value, played an important psychological role among the people, both in Africa and in the so-called civilized countries. Even well-trained physicians were handicapped in achieving success. It was only in the latter half of the nineteenth century, when Kirk's former classmate, Joseph Lister, popularized antiseptic techniques that reduced infection, and the French scientist Louis Pasteur, the German bacteriologist Robert Koch, and others demonstrated that germs caused infections and convinced governments of the need to enforce sanitary measures, that life expectancy began to improve in America and Europe.

The Menace of Malaria

Malaria was, at the time of Kirk and Livingstone's expedition, and still is the most prevalent disease in the tropical Zambezi lowlands; it kills one to two million people a year in Africa, mostly infants.[8] *Mal aria* means bad air in Italian. It was also called "swamp fever" because it was believed to attack persons living near swamps. It was not until 1898 that Ronald Ross, by experimentally infecting canaries, proved that mosquitoes transmit malaria. His Italian rival, Grassi, proved that the female *Anopheles* mosquito transmitted the parasite.

If a mosquito bites a person carrying the malarial parasite, it sucks up that person's malaria-infected blood. The malarial parasite reproduces both sexually and asexually while in the mosquito.

When the next person is bitten, thousands of the parasites ingested by the mosquito are injected into the victim and rapidly invade the liver cells (usually within an hour), where they multiply at regular intervals of forty-eight to seventy-two hours, depending on the species. Bursting out of the liver into the bloodstream, they then enter the victim's red blood cells, causing the red blood cells to rupture and thus to release thousands of additional parasites into the bloodstream in a vicious cycle. The rupture and destruction of parasite-infested red blood cells causes a characteristic anemia.

Malaria was responsible for most deaths among the explorers, traders, soldiers, missionaries, and colonists. The only ones immune were some Africans with hereditary sickle cell disease (sickle cell anemia), because the deformed, sickle-shaped red blood cell is impervious to the malarial parasite.

Of the four types of malaria, the most severe and frequently fatal variety for the Livingstone expedition was falciparum malaria. The liver and spleen became enlarged and tender. Sometimes the spleen would rupture, causing rapid death. Even after recovery from an acute attack, the spleen remained enlarged in many cases.

The falciparum parasite is unique in that it can cause cerebral malaria by distorting and rupturing the human red blood cell. The parasite forms numerous projecting knobs on the red blood cell's otherwise smooth surface. The knobs cause the diseased red blood cell to plug or embolize small blood vessels in the brain. This blockage of the cerebral circulation causes severe headaches, epileptic fits, delusions, and hallucinations and is frequently fatal.

Without prompt treatment with intravenous quinine, not available in Kirk's day, there was a 50 percent or greater mortality rate. Mental changes frequently made the victim unmanageable, violent, or even suicidal.

This same embolization of small blood vessels can occur in the kidney. Urine production becomes scanty or ceases altogether. The concentrated urine is filled with albumen and disintegrating red blood cells, which turn the urine dark. The descriptive term, "blackwater fever" has been used to describe this frequently fatal complication.

The other three species of malaria—malariae-malaria, vivax, and ovale—have generally fewer side effects. Almost all the members of the expedition would become infected with at least one of these species.

Quinine, extracted from the bark of the South American cinchona tree, was eventually shown to prevent most types of malaria.

But at the time of the Livingstone expedition, it was not fully recognized as a preventative medicine. However, Livingstone had read studies of how quinine had been remarkably effective on the Second Niger Expedition. None of the twelve whites on that trip died. This was remarkable since the mortality rate among whites on previous West African expeditions had ranged from 25 percent to 100 percent.

To be effective, quinine had to be given daily in controlled amounts. Too much, and one could get a ringing in the ears, temporary deafness, and blindness called *cinchonism.* Too little, and quinine would cease to be an effective preventative. One problem was that the potency of the preparation varied. In some cases the amount of quinine would be far less than therapeutic. Since the disease was so deadly, Livingstone and Kirk decided to issue quinine as a prophylactic to be taken daily.

Terrible Attacks

According to Livingstone's and Kirk's descriptions of malarial attacks, at first there was a feeling of profound lassitude followed by high fever, shaking chills, and muscle spasms. Drenching sweats are followed frequently by a subnormal temperature and profound, lasting weakness. Malaria can also mimic other diseases. Muscle aches before an attack can suggest acute arthritis or gout, called "ague" in Kirk's day. Severe headaches can presage an attack. Other symptoms include lethargy, prostration, loss of appetite, vomiting, and diarrhea. If only 5 percent of the victim's red blood cells are infected, this is sufficient to cause a severe anemia.

Both Kirk and Livingstone described attacks in four stages. In the first, the patient's face would suddenly turn pale, hands and feet would blanch, and nails would turn blue. The patient would complain of dizziness, nausea, difficulty in breathing, dryness of the mouth, and feeling very cold. This cold feeling would persist up to four hours in spite of being warmed with blankets or the day being hot. Then, quite suddenly, it would be replaced by a pervasive sensation of heat followed by profuse sweating. This third stage would normally last eight to twelve hours and would be accompanied by a rapid pulse rate and urgent thirst. In the fourth stage, severe fatigue would occur. Then, during a brief symptom-free period, the patient might claim that there was nothing wrong, until the cycle repeated itself with another sequence of severe malaise, chills, sweating, and profound lassitude. New cycles would occur over the next ten days or so, but the intervals would begin to lengthen until the patient eventually recovered, or became comatose and died. Other variations were described, especially the cerebral, renal, and hepatic complications of falciparum malaria associated with convulsions, delusions, hallucinations, and violent behavior requiring restraints.[9] Thus, malaria attacks could hamper and in some cases paralyze an expedition, and deaths from malaria could annihilate whole communities.

Livingstone's Advice to Kirk

Kirk was also given advice concerning the native healers by Livingstone. Livingstone, with unusual insight, described them as:

> . . . the most observant people to be met with. It is desirable to be at all times on good terms with them. . . . Slight complaints, except among the very poor, ought to be referred to their care, and severe cases, before being undertaken should be inquired of the doctor himself and no disparaging remark ever made on the previous treatment in the presence of the patient . . . never neglect the opportunity which the bed of sickness presents of saying a few kind words in a natural and respectful manner and imitate as far as you can the conduct of the Great Physician whose followers we profess to be.[10]

He also wrote more humorously:

> The native medical profession is reasonably well represented. In addition to the regular practitioners, who are a really useful class, and know something of their profession, and the nature and power of certain medicines, there are others who devote their talents to some specialty. The elephant doctor prepares a medicine which is considered indispensable to the hunters when attacking that noble and sagacious beast; no hunter is willing to adventure out before investing in this precious nostrum. The crocodile doctor sells a charm which is believed to posses the singular virtue of protecting the owner from crocodiles.[11]

While in an exalted and paternalistic mood, perhaps manic, Livingstone showed unusual compassion for animals in an era that had not yet realized the concepts of ecology and conservation. "In many parts of the country we hope to traverse," he wrote, "the larger animals still exist in large numbers and being relatively tame may be easily secured."[12] He implied that some of them might be headed for extinction. This was amazing foresight at a time when most people had no interest in animals other than as beasts of burden or for fur or hides and anything else that could be worn or eaten.

Knowing about Kirk's botanical experience and interest, Livingstone encouraged him to collect plants. Drying paper was purchased especially for this purpose. Livingstone even offered to let him use his drying iron and suggested glycerine for preserving them.

He also advocated patience, forbearance, and justice in dealing with the natives. Money or trade goods should be given to the man actually performing the job, not to sub-chiefs or contractors, as this could lead to trouble. The paramount chief, on the other hand, was to be given every courtesy because he had the power to annihilate the expedition if he chose. "We come among them as members of a superior race and servants of a Government that desires to elevate the more degraded elements of the human family. . . . Depend upon it a kind word or deed is never lost."[13] This condescending attitude—we would call it racist today—was a prerequisite to justifying the immense effort needed to send missionaries to convert the Africans. Livingstone also urged Kirk to study Sechwane, the language of the Tswana people in Bechuana (Botswana) in southern Africa, since Livingstone's father-in-law had translated the Bible into this native language.

Livingstone ended his advice and admonitions with a last warning: "Finally, you are strictly enjoined to take the greatest care of your own health and that of the Expedition. My own experience teaches the necessity of more than ordinary attention to the state of the alimentary canal. Constipation is always sure to bring on fever."[14]

This is certainly not current medical thinking, but at that time there were theories about toxic products from retained fecal matter poisoning the system. There was, however, another reason for Livingstone's obsession with constipation. His hemorrhoids had become chronic, causing pain and bleeding almost each time he passed a hard stool. (Hemorrhoids, or piles, are enlarged rectal veins which, like varicose veins in the legs, have lost their functioning valves. Blood tends to pool in them, forming clots. The clots stretch the veins, causing pain, and should there be straining from a hard, constipated stool, a vein can tear and bleed.) To make sure he and the others did not get constipated, Livingstone added resin of Jalap and calomel (a laxative, mercuric chloride) to the list of medicines Kirk was to bring along.

On March 3, 1858, just before sailing from Liverpool for Africa aboard the warship *Pearl,* Kirk received a terrible blow: he learned his father had suddenly died. Father and son had been close, and it was Kirk's father who had given him much of his early schooling, who had imbued in him a love of nature in general and knowledge of plants and fossils in particular, and who had inculcated in him a sense of responsibility coupled with a zealous spirit. Kirk didn't even have time to attend the funeral or to grieve with his mother. All he could do was write a quick note to her, swallow his sorrow, and join the others en route to the Zambezi River.

4

En Route

The warship *Pearl*, en route from England to the Zambezi, stopped to take on coal, vegetables, and meat at the British colony of Sierra Leone on Africa's west coast. All went smoothly for the first nine days after leaving Sierra Leone. Then Livingstone, who was accompanied by his wife, Mary, and their youngest son, Oswell, discovered that Mary, who had been constantly nauseous and frequently vomiting, was pregnant. When the ship docked at Cape Town, Livingstone decided Mary and Oswell should remain in South Africa with her missionary family and not travel up the Zambezi with the rest of the group. During the week they stayed at the Cape of Good Hope, Kirk had a pleasant time botanizing and meeting many of the missionaries, traders, and their families.

The *Pearl* took on stores at Cape Town and, accompanied by the British naval vessel *Hermes,* left on May 1, 1858, for Portuguese East Africa. The day after their departure Kirk had to treat Livingstone with opium and rhubarb for an acute intestinal illness. Ten days later, Kirk described Livingstone in his diary as again suffering "slight pain in the bowel with looseness. I gave him 4 Pil. Plumb Opiate." The following day he was no better and "suffered from great pain in the right iliac region. Which he says is relieved slightly by pressure. His bowels have been opened about thirty times since night. . . . I gave him 1/2 gr. Morph: Hydr: in suppository and Tinct. Hematoxylin and with ten pills with 5 gr. special powder compound, ii. to be taken every hour. . . . at night he felt considerably easier, the pain slight and diarrhea less, nothing but mucus, tongue foul. At 11 P.M. another 1/2 gr. of Morphia."[1] Given the pattern of symptoms and their course, Livingstone's illness was not a chronic intestinal disease such as amebic dysentery, but this acute abdominal pain and dysentery could have been due to one of several viruses.

Scouting the Approach

From the available British and Portuguese maps, Bedingfeld, who was to command the steam launch, and Livingstone concluded there were at least four separate entrances to the Zambezi River from its delta. The northernmost was at the Portuguese port of Quelimane and was connected to the Zambezi by a narrow stream which had to be cleared periodically. But Livingstone, wanting to avoid prying Portuguese eyes, decided to find another inlet.

Two weeks after leaving the Cape, the two ships anchored across the bar from what they believed was one of the other mouths of the Zambezi, the West Luabo. But the map of the coast was imperfect, and it turned out to be a separate river, the Luawe, with no connection to the Zambezi. The following day Captain Lister brought the *Pearl,* which had a shallower draft than the *Hermes,* across the bar at slack tide to reconnoiter.

Livingstone asked Kirk and Captain Skead, the naval surveyor from the *Hermes* who had come to survey the lower Zambezi, to take one of the rowboats upriver to survey its course. Equipped with food, camping gear, and rifles, the two men paddled up the river for three days. Not one to waste an opportunity, Kirk studied the plethora of plant and animal life along the hot, steaming banks. He had his first look at hippopotami in the wild as well as buffalo, antelope, and local species of birds and plants. But Kirk soon realized that the *Pearl* would never get through to the Zambezi proper, for the water had become shallow and disappeared in a large marsh, and the two men returned to the ships.

Livingstone, however, did not yet trust Kirk's judgment and decided to investigate the inlet himself. Kirk immediately went to work helping the engineer, Rae, prepare the *Ma Robert*'s steam engine. Once the launch was assembled and placed in the water, Livingstone had it stacked with supplies for an extensive reconnaissance trip. But the boat soon grounded on a sandbank, and the party, after getting it off, returned to the ships.

Steaming north, they found a second inlet. A preliminary survey showed shoals at the harbor's entrance. It was running high tide to boot, so the ships' captains decided it was too risky to try to get even the relatively shallow-drafted *Pearl* over the bar until the tide became slack. Livingstone, on the other hand, eager to move forward, persuaded Skead, the naval surveyor, to cross the bar in the *Hermes* cutter. The ship's captain, afraid they would capsize, ordered them back. In a dispatch to Cape Town, he made it clear that Livingstone had been not only obstinate but foolhardy, willing to risk not only his life but Skead's: "Dr. Livingstone made a further exploration of the bar of the Luabo, but only ran a useless risk of getting entangled in the breakers towards dark, and so far from the ship, that I was obliged to get under way and enforce the cutter's return on board."[2]

On June 3, a little more than a month after leaving the Cape, the ships dropped anchor outside the bar at Kongone Harbor, the third mouth of the Zambezi. There was a deep, straight bay which they subsequently found to be connected to the main river by a natural channel. There were no signs of the Portuguese there, either, so Livingstone thought that British ships could resupply them every few months unobserved.

Forty miles up the Zambezi they discovered an island, which Livingstone named Expedition Island, and landed there. By June 20 they had assembled a prefabricated house made of sheet iron for termite-proof storage of their provisions. Livingstone heard from local Africans that rebels and Portuguese soldiers were fighting farther north, and soon a detachment of Portuguese soldiers arrived from Mazaro, the nearest fort on the river. Livingstone was handed a polite letter from the commanding officer offering assistance and protection to the Englishmen. Livingstone's attempt to hide from the Portuguese had failed miserably. Livingstone gave the Portuguese a cold reception and the surprised Kirk noted: "The Doctor turns up his nose at protection from the Portuguese as he seems to take the side of the rebels."[3]

Thanks to its relatively shallow draft, the *Pearl* had been able to accompany the *Ma Robert* forty miles upstream after entering the main flow of the Zambezi. Before returning downstream, the officers of the warship treated the explorers to a farewell dinner. The next morning the crew of the *Ma Robert* watched as the *Pearl* steamed out of sight. The small group now would be entirely on its own, cut off from English civilization for months until they would rendezvous with another British ship expected to bring mail, supplies, and new orders from the Foreign Office.

Kirk may have felt a twinge of loneliness as he watched the *Pearl* disappear around the bend. But, along with the others, he probably looked with excitement as well as apprehension at the sight of the huge river stretching ahead of them. No matter that the Portuguese had for 300 years been sailing up and down the river as far as their fort at Zumbo. It was now up to Livingstone and his party, as emissaries of Great Britain and leaders of the spiritual faith that sought to break the shackles of human bondage, to investigate, settle, and commercialize this mighty river and its adjacent lands as well as to convert its inhabitants to what they believed was the one true religion.

Sights of the Delta

In his classic novel *Heart of Darkness,* Joseph Conrad described the eerie silence and sense of estrangement which greeted a little steamer chugging up the uncharted reaches of the Congo River. The ominous atmosphere, heavy with promise and risk, must have been akin to what Kirk and his shipmates felt on the Zambezi. Conrad wrote:

> It was the stillness of an implacable force brooding over an inscrutable intention. . . . I had to keep guessing at the channel; I had to discern, mostly by inspiration, the signs of hidden banks; I watched for sunken stones; I was learning to clap my teeth smartly before my heart flew out, when I shaved by a fluke some infernal sly old snag that would have ripped the life out of the tin-pot steamboat and drowned all the pilgrims. . . . On we went again into the silence, along empty reaches, round the still bends, between the high walls of our winding way, reverberating in hollow claps the ponderous beat of the stern-wheel. Trees, trees, millions of trees, massive, immense, running up high, and at their foot, hugging the bank against the stream, crept the little begrimed steamboat, like a sluggish beetle crawling on the floor of a lofty portico. It made you feel very small, very lost. . . . The reaches opened before us and closed behind, as if the forest had stepped leisurely across the water to bar the way for our return. We penetrated deeper and deeper into the heart of darkness.
>
> It was very quiet there. At night sometimes the roll of drums behind the curtain of trees would run up the river and remain

> sustained faintly, as if hovering in the air over our heads, till the first break of day. Whether it meant war, peace, or prayer, we could not tell. . . . We were wanderers on a prehistoric earth, on an earth that wore the aspect of an unknown planet.[4]

Like Conrad's description of the Congo, the river banks around Kongone Harbor and for some distance upstream were lined with mangroves. Only at higher elevations would they be replaced by other species. Livingstone described this tropical vegetation in his *Narrative:*

> Huge ferns, palm bushes, and occasional wild date palms, peer out in the forest, which consists of different species of mangroves; the bunches of bright yellow, though scarcely edible fruit, contrasting prettily with the graceful green leaves. In some spots the *Milola,* an umbrageous hibiscus, with large yellowish flowers, grows in masses along the bank. Its bark is made into cordage, and is especially valuable for the manufacture of ropes attached to harpoons for killing the hippopotamus.[5]

Kirk, too, was enthralled by the huge trees behind the mangroves festooned with thick creepers, some the thickness of a man's thigh. The buffalo also fascinated him, and he described in his diary a sentinel bull which stood guard, his horns encasing his forehead in a hump thick enough to deflect a bullet, while the rest of the herd grazed quietly like stone statues.

Being Victorians and without long-distance communication, the explorers were proficient and prolific letter writers and diarists, luckily for us. In his an almost-daily diary Kirk recorded the boat's latitude and longitude, made sketches, and painted watercolors, of which several have been preserved. He also made detailed observations of zoological and botanical specimens and lists of native words he learned. He had even brought along the crude camera with which he had been experimenting and managed to develop photographs in a makeshift darkroom on the launch.

The tropical flora was slowly left behind as the expedition gained altitude. Sandy banks began to line the river, which was still several miles wide in places. Towing the *Hermes'* pinnace and two whale boats, the paddle wheels of the *Ma Robert* laboriously cut through the muddy water filled with debris of grass and branches and an occasional floating log. Hundreds of Egyptian geese, ibis, and storks rose in the air at the sound of the steam engine, and occasionally the explorers would see a startled fisherman looking at them from his dugout canoe.

Kirk noted hundreds of wild animals coming to the river's edge to drink. As the boat continued into the interior, its crew saw Africans on the banks staring incredulously at the slow-moving, smoke-belching monster making its way upstream. Soon, the explorers would begin to see pitiful men, women, and children yoked together in slave caravans led by Portuguese drivers.

Based on descriptions of similar wood-burning steamers in those days, the *Ma Robert* was most likely very uncomfortable. Because of the engine's insatiable demand for wood, the decks were piled high with logs, leaving little or no room for the passengers to walk about. Instead, they were stuck in the small, crowded salon or the tiny cabins, drenched in sweat in over 90 percent humidity with an outside temperature of over 100° Fahrenheit. The only alternative was to rest on the roof or the deck when space became available. Of course, that meant being bitten by clouds of mosquitoes, which thrived in the delta's humid lowlands. At night, whenever possible, they camped on the sandy beaches.

The First Attack of Illness

It wasn't long before the explorers aboard the stuffy, crowded little ship were afflicted by a variety of ailments. Livingstone began to suffer from recurrent abdominal cramps, possibly due to constipation. Some of the others had graver difficulties.

While he and the remainder of the crew would take the *Ma Robert* upstream, Livingstone ordered Kirk, Baines, and Charles Livingstone to remain at the storage house on Expedition Island with a few porters until he returned to pick them up. But Baines had developed a respiratory infection followed by fever, headache, chills, vomiting, and diarrhea. Kirk noted in his journal:

> July 11th. On turning out to take guard at 4 A.M., Baines complains of having had no rest and having been troubled with fearful dreams. . . .At 6 A.M. he is worse, vomits everything, opium, quinine, tea etc. 8 A.M. tongue dry, pain in the forehead and constant tendency to vomit . . . his breath is very foul. He vomits any medicine given. At 11 takes a cup of tea and quinine which remains on the stomach. . . . At noon Baines begins to talk to himself and becomes quite delirious, talking incoherently of the Kaffir war. His pupils are contracted.

> At 2 P.M. Baines continues delirious, his pulse is very full, skin dry and hot. In the evening he takes a cup of tea, which he vomits and quinine in pills.
>
> Baines . . . says that he is aware that he has been talking incoherently and says that he could not find words, that he knew what he wished, but the wrong word always came out. He has lost all reckoning of time and cannot distinguish between night and morning.[6]

Kirk's was a classic description of the cerebral complication of falciparum malaria. Fortunately Baines began to recover from this attack, but Kirk was kept very busy, for that same day Charles Livingstone developed diarrhea, fever, and buzzing in his ears, presumably from too much quinine. Kirk thought that he, too, might have malaria. The next day Baines had a relapse, and Kirk prescribed calomel and rhubarb.

The two men improved slowly on a regimen of daily drops of quinine in wine, just as Livingstone had advised. After a couple of weeks they were well enough to shoot fowl from the boat. Amazingly, Kirk remained healthy throughout this period, but trouble of another sort was brewing. When Livingstone returned after his preliminary exploration up the river, it became clear to Kirk that the expedition's leader and Captain Bedingfeld had been quarreling constantly.

Livingstone had accused Bedingfeld of having tested the *Ma Robert*'s boiler in Scotland with coal rather than wood, thus misleading them as to the boat's realistic capacities. Coal yielded a much hotter fire and therefore produced more steam to propel the craft. On the river, all they had was wood, and they could not seem to generate enough steam to make much headway against the current. Livingstone also accused Bedingfeld of trying to replace him as leader of the expedition and of downplaying the importance of quinine in preventing malaria. "I heartily wish all this dispute were settled as it is very disagreeable to all others and makes work far from pleasant," wrote Kirk.[7] More importantly, it *was* frustrating to have to spend a day and a half to cut enough wood for each day of steaming up the river at an infuriatingly slow pace.

Bedingfeld continued to fight Livingstone, continually countermanding his orders. Kirk was appalled at both Livingstone's lack of tact and Bedingfeld's repeated claims that Livingstone never consulted him. This was too much for Bedingfeld, who resigned. But soon he had second thoughts and talked the still-sick Baines into writing a joint letter to Livingstone in which Bedingfeld stated that

Livingstone did not have the necessary experience to command and navigate the launch; therefore, Bedingfeld offered to stay on as captain until a replacement could be found.

Livingstone, piqued by Bedingfeld's criticism of his navigational abilities, refused to accept the letter and ordered him to leave. Bedingfeld was lent a few porters to make it back to Quelimane and thence to England. After his departure, the quiet, unassuming Kirk, who had wisely stayed out of the fight, was named second in command by Livingstone.

On July 21, the *Ma Robert,* averaging only ten miles a day, reached Shupanga, the first sizable Portuguese settlement on the river, and four days later Sena, sixty miles above the confluence of the Shire and Zambezi Rivers. With Livingstone navigating and Kirk taking soundings, the *Ma Robert* had managed to go seventy miles in one stretch without running aground, which delighted the men. On August 2, Kirk said he thought he had seen the distant mountain the Portuguese said was populated by the Manganja people. But, having run out of food and trade goods, the party was now forced to reverse course and steam back downriver to their warehouse on Expedition Island for new supplies.

All this while, Kirk had been recording the nature around him. He noted pandanus trees growing at elevations somewhat higher than the mangrove swamps on the delta. He was impressed by the ferns, creepers, and wild figs, as well as the unusual baobab trees that looked like they grew upside down with roots in the air when they were devoid of fruit and flowers during the dry season. He also identified bamboo, hyphanea, mimosa, and rubber vines. He wrote about countless herds of hippos, elephants, and antelopes, such as water buck, kudu, bush buck, and elands. He mistakenly called crocodiles "alligators" and remarked on a cuttlefish he found. Whenever he could, he shot specimens for their skins so that they could be sent back to England with his botanical samples.

Moving on to Shupanga

By the time the men reached Expedition Island, Baines had suffered another relapse; Kirk wrote in his journal a description of what seemed to be recurrent falciparum malaria with mental changes: "August 8th, Baines is worse again. This is similar to his first attack. He has slight shivering, severe and continued vomiting with prostration of strength, hot skin, contracted pupils and tendency to delirium. Gave him Calomel and Jalap with quinine."[8]

Livingstone ordered the men to dismantle the iron storehouse and ship it with their stored supplies to Shupanga on the *Ma Robert*. This way they wouldn't have to return so far to get new supplies each time. Baines, however, remained too weak and confused to help, and Livingstone was provoked into a fury when his brother Charles and the trip's geologist, Thornton, also claimed they were too weak to assist. Ignoring the likelihood that they were suffering from recurrent bouts of malaria, Livingstone called them shirkers but praised Kirk in front of the others for not getting sick and impeding the expedition's progress. Kirk judiciously maintained a low profile during this period of turmoil.

After stowing the storehouse parts on board, they steamed back to Shupanga, where Livingstone asked Kirk to remain with Baines until the latter recovered. With the storehouse reassembled there, Livingstone continued up the Zambezi to Tete on the *Ma Robert* with the rest of the expedition members.

In Shupanga, Kirk and Baines roomed with a Colonel Nuñez in a house "about 150 years old," Kirk wrote, "built of stone and brick with mortar; the walls are of great thickness; the roof is of the stems of the palmyra, squared outside and covered with tiles; in front is a verandah with seats, a very pleasant place to sit and talk with the Portuguese. . . . Our room is a back one and the only objection I have to it is that the room looks into the court where are all the slaves who keep up singing and shouting their war cries all night and day."[9]

Kirk talked to some of the slavers, one of whom mentioned that he himself had shipped 4,000 slaves from Angola and Mozambique. With adequate food and water, he explained, they lost almost no one. But, in trying to evade patrols, they had to lengthen their journey, which meant they sometimes ran out of drinking water. Then the death rate was tremendous. Kirk may have been horrified by this close proximity to the slave trade, but he often recorded his experiences without much commentary.

While at Shupanga, Kirk collected and pressed many plants and even made a successful photograph of the Nuñez house where he was staying. From the verandah, he could gaze northeast across the river at undulating forests of palm trees ending in the massive bulk of Mount Morambala, and to the north the distant headlands of the Shire River.

While Kirk waited at Shupanga, he met the Landeens, a branch of the Zulus, who marched into the village one day carrying short spears (assegais), battle axes, and shields of painted cowhides. They had come to collect tribute from the Portuguese, who paid them to keep the peace. Kirk later described the Landeens as controlling

". . . the right bank of the Zambezi; and the Portuguese, by paying this fighting tribe a pretty heavy annual tribute, practically admit this. Regularly every year come the Zulus in Sena and Shupanga for their accustomed tribute. The few wealthy merchants of Sena groan under the burden for it falls mainly on them. They submit to pay annually 200 pieces of cloth, of 16 yards each, besides beads and brass wire, knowing that refusal means war."[10]

Because Livingstone wasn't expected to return to Shupanga immediately, Kirk decided to do a little exploring on his own. Accompanied by a few porters, he walked twenty miles to a small lake the villagers had told him about. There, he encountered the Zulu Landeens again; they greeted him politely and even provided him a hut to sleep in.

Caught in a Portuguese-African War

Slowed by the shallowness of the Zambezi and many shoals, Livingstone finally reached Tete on September 8, where he was greeted by the Makololo porters whom he had left there two years earlier after they had accompanied him on his first expedition. Sadly, thirty-five had died of smallpox, and six more had been killed by the renegade chief Bonga for body parts to be used in preparing strong medicine. The others had settled down and married local women, and some no longer wanted to return to Makololo land.

On his first visit to Tete, Livingstone had met Major Tito Sicard, the Portuguese commander of the settlements along the Zambezi. Unaware of Livingstone's anti-Portuguese bias, Major Sicard now did the expedition a big favor by having his slaves cut bundles of *lignum vitae* for the *Ma Robert*. This hard, ebony-like wood burned almost as well as coal and saved the expedition many days of work.

By the time Kirk returned to Shupanga from his local explorations, he found that Livingstone also had returned from Tete and that the Portuguese garrison had attacked Bonga near Mount Morambala. The rebels put up a stiff resistance. Portuguese soldiers and their armed slaves were cut to pieces with axes, and iron stakes were knocked into their heads in the vicious fighting. Soon, casualties were flowing into Shupanga. Of what ensued, Kirk wrote:

> Dr. Livingstone . . . [f]ound himself in the sickening smell and among the mutilated bodies of the slain; he was requested to take the governor, who was very ill with fever, across the river to Shupanga, and just as he gave his assent, the rebels renewed

> the fight, and the balls began to whistle about in all directions. . . . He went into the hut, and dragged along his excellency to the ship. He was a very tall man, and as he swayed hither and thither from weakness, weighing down Dr. Livingstone, it must have appeared like one drunken man helping another.[11]

Kirk worked night and day treating wounded Portuguese, their slave-soldiers, and their Makololo allies. Medical supplies were limited and he did his best to prevent infection, but in the sultry climate it was a common and often fatal complication. Kirk received a letter later from the Portuguese governor of Quelimane thanking him for his medical services. The governor general of Mozambique also sent British navy officials a letter expressing gratitude for Kirk's help.

The war in which Kirk had unwittingly become embroiled expanded rapidly when the rebels began a scorched-earth policy of destroying villages to make it harder for the Portuguese troops to live off the country. The whole region to the north was thick with smoke from burning fields and villages, Kirk noted in his diary. Finally, the flow of wounded dropped to a trickle, and it appeared that the fighting was over for a time, though Bonga had escaped with many of his men.

New Supplies

Livingstone had taken the *Ma Robert* back to Tete while Baines, whose health had improved somewhat, had also left for Tete, taking the pinnace and two canoes loaded with supplies. Kirk was still at Shupanga relaxing on the makeshift hospital verandah one day when he heard shouts. He recognized one of the Portuguese's slaves running toward him and shouting excitedly that a white man's boat was nearing the dock. Kirk ran down to the river and a few minutes later saw a boat containing four white men landing. The boat's two officers, Medlicott and Cook, were from the British gunboat *Lynx* that had arrived at Kongone Harbor with new supplies for the expedition. Would Kirk send a boat downriver to fetch them? He had none, Kirk replied, but he hoped the Portuguese governor would lend him canoes and crews. He left with the two Englishmen and they headed north to the confluence of the Shire and Zambezi Rivers, where Kirk was told the Portuguese troops were now fighting another renegade, Mariano. Kirk and the British officers traveled up the Shire a ways to find the governor celebrating a great victory.

His troops had routed the rebels and entered their main stockaded village, which had been abandoned without a fight.

After the Portuguese victory, Kirk had no trouble borrowing a flotilla of canoes, and, with the help of the naval officers, he took the boats down to Kongone Harbor. On the way down Kirk recorded that he caught a young gazelle that had "played dead" and was able to tame it. He was also badly bitten by what he called hornets, more likely African killer bees, when he inadvertently dislodged their nest while climbing a tree to pick oranges. "My shirt and breast were covered, and a good many had got down my coat. . . . I soon tossed them off and ran into the reeds. . . . I took vengeance on them by firing the long grass. . . . I then got a couple of oranges that were first rate."[12]

They arrived at Expedition Island on September 14, and forty miles downstream crossed the bar to the *Lynx*. An African courier had been sent to find Livingstone, who arrived six days later on the *Ma Robert* with Rae and Thornton. Livingstone's brother, Charles, who claimed he was too ill to travel, had been left at Tete, and a new man from the *Lynx*, Quartermaster Walker, joined the expedition.

Equipped with fresh supplies, medicines, and manpower, the Second Zambezi Expedition headed back to Tete via Shupanga. They stopped briefly upriver at Sena, where Kirk took a picture of the 300-year-old dilapidated Portuguese fort, where cows grazed on grass growing on the broken-down walls. Many of the houses, including a monastery, were in ruins and had been reclaimed by the jungle.

Another nine laborious days were spent getting the *Ma Robert* over the shallows, for the river had dropped several feet because it was now the dry season. They traveled through the seventeen-mile-long Lupata Gorge, forty miles southeast of Tete, where cliffs narrowed the river and navigation became treacherous until the river broadened out again. Another two days and they were in Tete. Kirk commented on what a contrast the condition of this town was compared to the more or less abandoned Sena. A wall surrounded the fort and homes of the Portuguese, while African huts were clustered outside.

Meanwhile Livingstone wrote sardonically of a native African he and Kirk had met who had voluntarily enslaved himself:

> . . . a free black, an intelligent, active young fellow, called Chibanti, who had been our pilot on the river, told us he had sold himself into slavery. On asking why he had done this, he replied that he was alone in the world . . . so he sold himself to Major Sicard, a notoriously kind master, whose slaves had

> little to do and plenty to eat. "And how much did you get for yourself?" we asked. "Thirty three yard pieces of cotton cloth," he replied; "and I forthwith bought a man, woman, and child, who cost me two of the pieces. And I had one piece left." His master subsequently employed him to carry ivory to Quellimane, and gave him cloth to hire mariners for the voyage; he took his own slaves, of course, and thus drove a thriving business . . .[13]

Livingstone remained in Tete only two days and then pushed on upriver in the *Ma Robert*. With him were Kirk, Rae, Walker, and some of the Krumen and Makololo porters. Charles Livingstone, Baines, and Thornton continued to run fevers, perhaps from taking a poor batch of quinine, too little, or skipping it altogether, and were left at Tete.

A Critical Juncture

On November 24, 1858, after having traveled about seventy-five miles up the Zambezi from Tete, Livingstone and the crew saw something that turned their blood cold. During his first trip down the Zambezi Livingstone had bypassed this part of the river by choosing an easier path some distance away. Now they were faced with an unexpected obstacle, the awesome Kebrabasa Rapids. Kirk described giant boulders and waterfalls between high, bluish quartz cliffs, and it seemed obvious to him that there was no way of continuing by boat. Had Livingstone been less obsessed by his conviction that he was God's chosen one to open up Black Africa, he might have cut the expedition short at that point, but blind to the dangers, he insisted they try steaming through.

The Kebrabasa Gorge was the equivalent of the Grand Canyon in Mozambique; giant crags squeezed the river into a narrow, furious torrent dashing over huge basalt boulders, some higher than three-story houses, according to Kirk's description. Today, however, a giant hydroelectric dam looms above the gorge, impounding the wild river into the large Kebrabasa Lake.

One critical study of Livingstone contends that if the explorer had bothered to ask any native African or Portuguese officials, they could have told him the rapids were unnavigable. Other Livingstone scholars state that, in fact, Jose, the group's Afro-Portuguese guide, had told of far greater cataracts ahead, but Livingstone thought this was a case of native African duplicity and kept the news to himself. When it appeared they had no chance of negotiating the rapids, Livingstone, disheartened, ordered the boat turned around and they headed back to Tete.

Livingstone, however, now entered another period of what can be termed, at worst, manic delusion and, at best, wishful thinking. He wrote to the British Foreign Secretary on December 17, 1858, that he saw no reason why a steamer doing fourteen or fifteen knots could not pass the rapids when the water was high after the rains. In his *Narrative,* published later, he implied that even his brother and Baines supported him in this view.

But this phase passed rapidly and Livingstone, again depressed by the existence of this apparently insurmountable obstacle, took out his frustration on Baines and Charles. According to Kirk, who tried as usual to look at things dispassionately, Charles Livingstone was the main instigator of the endless arguments. He wrote, "Things are not going well here between young Livingstone and the others. On the one side they have been sick and are more sensitive on that account, on the other, he is one who has never had any one under him and is awkward and ungracious in his dealings."[14] Kirk considered Charles weak-willed and a complainer, lazy and a hypochondriac who sometimes feigned illnesses, "lounging indoors and never exposing himself to the sun without an umbrella or a felt hat with all the appurtenances of an English gentleman of a well regulated family. I fear most of us are not too particular about appearances when there is work doing. . . . Mr. C.L has become so tired with the walk as to be fit for little more than sleep."[15] Perhaps, though, Kirk suggested diplomatically, Charles acted as he did because he couldn't stand the rigors and demands of travel in the African heat on rivers filled with crocodiles and hippos and in a boat that was totally inadequate for the job.

David Livingstone was also far from healthy. He had developed a chronic skin disease which Kirk diagnosed as herpes. "It is a curious fact that everyone I have met here with the least fever or sickness of any sort becomes very irritable, and thus I can now tell the state of health and guess a coming attack," Kirk remarked in his journal.[16]

Assaulting the Gorge

One calamity followed another as they tried again to steam up the Kebrabasa Gorge. "As matters look now," Kirk wrote, "if it is impossible to get the launch up, which I believe it to be, I think the Doctor will as soon see us all back again and go on alone with his brother."[17]

In a new effort, Livingstone hiked along the cliffs above the rapids to reconnoiter with Baines and Kirk. Baines became so exhausted that Kirk had to carry his gear. Kirk understood Baines's condition and thought that especially as a physician and humanitarian, Livingstone was being too hard on him.

By the time of their return to Tete, all the members of the expedition were feeling the effects of stress. Then the rainy season began and the river started to rise. David Livingstone decided to keep the other principals at Tete and to once more canvass the rapids in the *Ma Robert,* this time alone.

Kirk became upset and expressed dissatisfaction with Livingstone's decision. "On this I suggested that it was an insult given to the members, and there were some who had not been sick nor been behind with any work. . . . Dr. L, reflecting a little, said that, if I chose to volunteer I might go: so of course I was only too glad of the chance of seeing new country but also of avoiding the slur offered to us by the Doctor. In fact all felt their honor rather touched by the insult."[18]

Livingstone not only liked Kirk for his mettle but continued to give him more responsibility and occasionally even followed his advice. After steaming past two more rapids near the opening of the Kebrabasa Gorge, they found themselves in a very difficult situation. The boat could go no further, so they anchored it and Livingstone, Kirk, and some of the Makololo porters who had volunteered to accompany Livingstone began to climb the cliffs on one side of the river. Kirk relates that they rose to 2,600 feet. "Footing is treacherous as the slopes are covered with a loose scree of polished black rock. The heat, however, is like Hell if that place is what I imagine it—you cannot hold on any time to the rocks."[19]

The burning heat of the stones blistered the feet of the porters as they climbed the boulders, some of which were twenty feet high. Ignoring the shouts and moans of the Africans, Livingstone insisted on continuing, but Kirk gently and firmly persuaded him to make camp and resume the hike the next day.

The following morning it took them four hours to go a mile and a half on the burning, slippery rocks. They finally reached a waterfall where the river plunged from a height of thirty feet. This ended all speculation and even Livingstone's fantasies about the feasibility of sailing farther up the Zambezi.

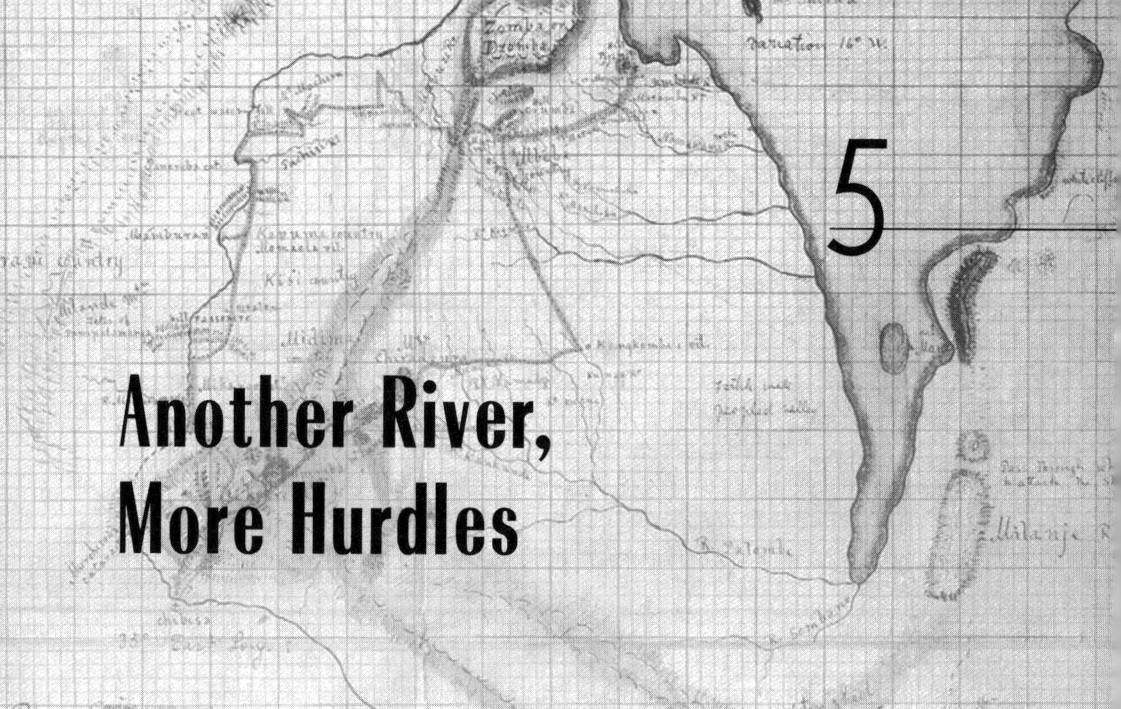

5

Another River, More Hurdles

Blocked by the huge rapids, Livingstone struggled for another route farther up into the country. On Christmas Day, 1858, the expedition steamed into the mouth of the Shire River, located between Shupanga and Sena. The Manganjas, armed with bows and poisoned arrows, stopped the explorers until friendly gestures satisfied them that these particular white men were not seeking slaves.[1]

Livingstone and Kirk, the only healthy Englishmen left, climbed the 4,000-foot Mount Morambala near the confluence of the two rivers. At this point the Shire was almost as wide as the Zambezi, and the explorers were cheered that rains had caused the former to rise high enough to allow the *Ma Robert* access.

Six days up the Shire, however, they found themselves in a foul-smelling marsh full of rotting vegetation and innumerable islands. Elephant Marsh, Kirk called it, because of the great herds of elephants they saw there, perhaps as many as 800, Livingstone estimated, complete with egrets perched on their backs.

Kirk wrote:

> The whole surface of the marsh, as far as we could see, was covered with long grass and sedge about seven feet in height with wet places and branches of the Shire. In the afternoon we saw herds of elephants in all directions. . . . We came up to a small herd of cows, had the engine stopped and fired a volley

> into them. The result was confusion and the herd ran off, leaving two wounded. One remained on the spot while the other moved off some distance and stood to fight us. . . . I gave it the first ball in the head. . . .
>
> It instantly turned to us, spread out its enormous ears, curled its proboscis up like a butterfly and raised its tail in the air like a bull . . . some of our men got near it and certainly would have been killed, so we charged and gave it a running fire in the head. We heard the bullets rattling on her and she instantly gave up the charge and ran off, nor could our fire which was kept up to 300 yards stop her. If we could have followed, there's no doubt that we should have got her as she was severely wounded. We heard her shrieking occasionally with pain.[2]

In spite of Livingstone's reminder to Kirk and the other members of the expedition to avoid needless slaughter, elephants were still considered fair game. Neither Kirk nor anyone else in their group considered it cruel to kill or even wound an animal. Elephants were plentiful, and ivory was the most lucrative trade item next to slaves. Shooting birds and other animals for specimens to bring back to England was also customary, as was hunting them for meat and occasionally for sport.

In fact, despite his relatively advanced conservationist views, Livingstone retained an eye for what would play well back home. For example, he described one incident in which a young elephant was caught alive, and he wrote that to escape its enraged mother,

> . . . we steamed off and dragged him through the water by the proboscis. As the men were holding the trunk over the gunwale, Monga, a brave elephant hunter, rushed aft and drew his knife across it in a frenzy of the sort peculiar to the chase. The wound was skillfully sewed up, and the young animal soon became quite tame, but unfortunately the bleeding prevented the cut from healing, and he died in a few days after the loss of blood. Had he lived, and had we been able to bring him home, he would have been the first African elephant ever seen in England.[3]

Murchison Cataracts

Eventually, the explorers passed through the Elephant Marsh and continued upriver until they spied a village atop a cliff on the river's right bank. The place, now called Chikwawa, was the home of powerful Manganja chief Chibisa, who, fortunately, welcomed the white men. Elated by their warm reception and the cooler weather in the highlands, Livingstone wrote later to Sir John Russell on November 20, 1859, ". . . by affording free passage from England or from the Cape of a few volunteer settlers of good character [who] might render essential service to the cause of African civilization . . . the presence of a small body of colonists, with their religious and mercantile institutions, industrially developing the resources of the country, would materially accelerate the movement."[4]

The Manganjas in some districts smelted iron; they used iron-tipped, poisoned arrows and spears. They also grew two types of cotton. In some regions, Kirk noted, the men were addicted to beer which had a pinkish color and somewhat the consistency of gruel. Some of the women, according to Kirk and Livingstone, were very good-looking, but they considered them disfigured due to the lip-ring, or *pelele,* they wore. Livingstone interrogated an old chief about this custom, who told him: "For beauty, to be sure! Men have beards and whiskers; women have none; and what kind of creature could a woman be without whiskers, and without the pelele? She would have a mouth like a man and no beard; ha! ha! ha!"[5] The practice, and that of creating disfiguring tribal scars, did help make them ugly and seemingly less desirable to the Portuguese and Arab slave traders. Livingstone, obviously fascinated, described the *pelele* in more detail in his *Narrative*:

> The middle of the upper lip of the girls is pierced close to the septum of the nose, and a small pin inserted to prevent the puncture from closing up. After it has healed, the pin is taken out and a larger one is pressed into its place, and so on successively for weeks, and months, and years. The process of increasing the size of the lip goes on till its capacity becomes so great that a ring of two inches diameter can be introduced with ease. All the highland women wear the pelele and it is common in the upper and lower Shire. . . . No woman ever appears in public without the pelele except in times of mourning for the dead.[6]

Warned of rough water ahead but lured by the promise of seeing a great lake to the north, Livingstone and Kirk resumed their journey. On January 10, 1859, they found the width of the Shire narrowed to forty yards between high, rocky banks: a mini-Kebrabasa Rapids.[7] Rushing water tumbled through cataracts for thirty miles before the river widened and calm water resumed. Discouraged but not beaten, Livingstone thought about building a road around the rapids for, unlike the Kebrabasa Rapids, the land was fairly level above the river. Then, in a fit of playfulness (or perhaps mania) he carved the queen's initials, V.R. (Victoria Regina[8]), on a large rock on the northeast bank of the river and named the rapids Murchison Cataracts after the president of the Royal Geographic Society.

Because Livingstone, Kirk, and their party could not get the boat any farther upstream than to Murchison Cataracts, they returned to Tete. On the return trip Kirk wrote in his diary that one of the *Ma Robert*'s paddle wheels smashed on a rock.

Lust for the Lake

Livingstone and Kirk wanted to find the great lake the Manganjas had described, although the trip was expected to be a long and partially overland one, perhaps as much as four months to go there and return. After renewing supplies, Livingstone chose Kirk and the two sailors from the *Lynx*, Rowe and Walker, for this next foray up the Shire, enabling the rest of the party to remain at Tete during their absence.

But Kirk had qualms about going on this latest foray, considering Livingstone's short temper and lack of caution. Everyone seemed to be in a bad humor, and Livingstone seemed to have no patience with himself or the other expedition members.

While preparing for this new venture, Livingstone's attacks on his crew worsened. In a depressed state in February, Livingstone wrote that Thornton "declined to geologize" and sometime later that artist-storekeeper Baines was forgetting to give the Makololo porters their daily ration of food. Kirk was sure Baines was still suffering from the mentally and physically debilitating effects of malaria. Then Livingstone found out that Baines, while at Tete, had given the Portuguese some bottles of wine, a few casks of butter, and sugar, and he accused him of stealing the expedition's stores. Rae and Charles Livingstone also complained about Baines, who would sit for hours in a listless and dazed state. The Baines matter would fester and soon cause Kirk, not to mention Baines, great distress.

Up the Shire Again

It was mid-March before the travelers entered the Shire a second time. This time the Manganjas, seemingly reassured that the English were not slavers, appeared friendlier, and anchoring the launch once more below Chibisa's village, the explorers met the chief again. After numerous palavers with his counselors about the expedition's intent, Chibisa gave them a guide and an interpreter. Rowe and Walker were left with the *Ma Robert* at the base of the cataracts, and Livingstone, Kirk, and twelve Makololo porters left on April 3, 1859, skirting the cataracts on foot as they marched north in search of the great lake they had been told about.

The guide that Chibisa had provided proved worthless and was sent back, so the party resorted to compass headings to navigate the course of the Shire. Soon they saw the 7,000-foot Mount Zomba and the 50-mile-long Zomba plateau to their right, where the villagers cultivated small patches of cotton bushes. Livingstone's wishful eyes imagined fields of prime cotton extending for miles.

On April 16, Kirk and Livingstone climbed a high hill that overlooked Lake Shirwa. While a large lake, it wasn't the enormous one called Lake Ninyesi or "Lake of the Stars" (subsequently renamed Nyassa and then Malawi). The local Africans told them it was still a day's march away.

The cool Shire highlands contrasted pleasantly with the lowland humidity and heat, and the area seemed to Kirk as well as Livingstone suitable for European settlement. Kirk wrote, "We inquired whether any white man had ever been seen in these regions, but all agreed that we were the first ever. . . . This is very singular as the region is so near the Portuguese settlements, but is quite unknown to them; or, if it is, the discovery must have been kept a dead secret from all foreigners."[9] Kirk, swept up by Livingstone's conviction that they were the first Europeans to see Lake Shirwa, was as wrong as his leader about the uniqueness of their discovery. Two hundred and thirty-seven years earlier, Gaspar Boccaro, a Portuguese merchant, had passed by the lake on a new route to Kilwa on the east coast. The lake, then called Lake Maravi, subsequently appeared on a French map by de Lisle in 1722 and one by Jean Baptiste d'Anville in 1727.

The truth of the matter is that Livingstone was well aware that the Portuguese knew all about the lake. Candido Jose de la Costa, who had visited Lake Maravi in 1846 and who now lived at Tete, had drawn a map of the lake for Livingstone when the Scottish explorer first visited his town. When Livingstone returned to Tete with Kirk during the Second Zambezi Expedition, he deliberately avoided de la Costa. He not only failed to give either Boccaro or de la Costa credit for having seen the lake, but claimed that de la Costa had deliberately misled him and had not seen the lake at all. Livingstone's slight was not lost on the Portuguese.

Propelled by a combination of grandiosity and insecurity, the hero of the United Kingdom had deliberately lied to promote himself as the lake's first discoverer. The region was not only well-known to the Portuguese and Arabs, it was a prime slaving area. In fact, Portuguese and Arab slave caravans crisscrossed the lake trading firearms, enamel pots, and brass bangles with the Ajwas who had become middlemen, kidnapping Manganjas and trading them to these slave dealers.[10]

Because Livingstone and Kirk's supplies were running low, the party decided to return to Tete. On their way downriver Kirk took photographs and tried his hand at painting watercolors of Elephant Marsh, Mount Zomba, a native village, and Lake Shirwa. On reaching the *Ma Robert,* the party found Walker bedridden with a high fever. Kirk treated him with quinine for malaria and was relieved to see him recover rapidly. Then, when Kirk and the rest of the party arrived back at Tete, they found Baines complaining of severe lassitude. Kirk thought again that he was suffering from recurrent or chronic malaria.

Livingstone, who now considered himself quite an expert on malaria, wrote in his *Narrative*:

> In general an attack does not continue long, but it pulls one down quickly, though when the fever is checked the strength is as quickly restored. It had long been observed that those who were stationed for any length of time in one spot, and lived sedentary lives, suffered more from fever than others who moved about. . . .
>
> Whatever may be the cause of the fever, we observed that all were often affected at the same time, as if from malaria. . . . For a number of months our men, except two, took quinine regularly every morning. The fever sometimes attacked the believers in Quinine while the unbelievers . . . escaped. Whether we took it daily or omitted it altogether for months, made no difference; the fever was impartial.[11]

Had Walker and Baines taken less than the four grains needed to prevent an attack? We have no way of knowing. Since quinine is very bitter, it was supposed to be mixed with wine to make it more palatable. The men may have disregarded Livingstone and Kirk's orders, dumped their daily dose, taken a partial dose, or just drunk the wine alone, or perhaps their prescribed dose might not have been large enough. In any case, Kirk decided that by taking enough quinine to cause mild cinchonism (ringing in the ears and scintillating flashes of light that were symptoms of quinine overdose) and then backing off to a slightly lower dose, this test would show if enough quinine had been taken.

But he was worried and for the first time wrote in his diary that he and the others were experiencing profound lassitude. He even thought he himself might have hepatitis. Meanwhile, Thornton continued to claim he was too weak to carry on his geological work. Livingstone, however, believing that the best way to prevent and treat fever was to engage in an interesting endeavor, pushed Thornton to investigate what he believed were coal deposits nearby.

In June 1859, Kirk wrote that Thornton's geological work "has been very limited indeed, and he can say very little in respect to the coal fields which it was his especial work to examine minutely." He added in the same paragraph in his diary that Baines was not cut out to be a storekeeper and that he and Livingstone were not getting on at all.[12]

Walker and Rowe, now feeling better, left with Kirk for Kongone Harbor for a prearranged meeting with the supply ship *Lynx*. They arrived July 11, 1859, but the British ship was not there, so they returned to Tete on July 23 without any new provisions. During that trip Kirk became fascinated by the multitude and variety of shore birds: brilliantly colored bee eaters darting in the hot sunshine from their nests in the cliffs on the river's edge, emerald kingfishers swooping down to fish, yellow bill, spoon-bill storks, goliath herons and their smaller counterparts, cranes, pelicans, ibises, pigeons, eagles, flamingoes, guinea hens, francolin, Egyptian geese, and ducks.

Then came another letdown. The voyagers to Kongone noticed that Portuguese soldiers had just built a customs house at the harbor. Livingstone was infuriated at their effrontery when he heard the news, but Kirk thought it only reasonable from the Portuguese point of view.

Crew Discontents

The expedition's crew had been in Africa a year and a half, and their contracts were due to expire in another six months. Walker, Rowe, and Rae wanted out. The sailors from Sierra Leone were disgruntled and rebellious. Kirk's lassitude had turned to fever and painful muscle ache symptoms which he called the "ague." He may have had symptoms of the musculoskeletal form of malaria or, more likely, dengue fever, also called "breakbone fever" because of the severe bone pains accompanying the infection. During this period his diary also reflects a gloomy frame of mind: "£350 per annum minus income tax (especially if there is war going on) won't be much to go ashore with, after one has had one's liver fried for two years and no one knows how much longer."[13]

On July 18, the African crew became mutinous and Livingstone beat one of the Makololo crew members who talked back insolently to him with a cook's wooden ladle. This is the first reference to the previously gentle Livingstone resorting to force against one of "his Africans." But he was becoming increasingly impatient and irascible, in general, with everyone.

Eleven days later, hoping once again to rendezvous with a British vessel, the party returned to Kongone Harbor. This time luck was in their favor, for the following day the British ship *Persian,* carrying fresh provisions, dropped anchor outside the bar. But by this time, the thin steel plates forming the hull of the *Ma Robert* were worn and rusted, causing innumerable leaks and requiring frequent bailing. The launch had to be beached, and Rae and a seaman from the *Persian* tried to make repairs.

During the rendezvous with the *Persian,* Kirk arranged to send more of his pressed plant collection to Professor Hooker at Kew Botanical Gardens in London.[14] On March 30, 1859, Kirk had discovered a poison used by African hunters called Kombé.

Livingstone also sent back letters detailing their discoveries of iron and cotton, and birds, animals, and plants never seen before in England. These created quite a stir when they were published. The captain of the *Persian* also carried news of Richard Burton and James Hanning Speke's spectacular discovery of Lake Tanganyika and of Speke's discovery of the great inland sea to the north, which he had named the Victoria Nyanza (now called Lake Victoria). Livingstone realized the geography of Africa was being filled in with great rapidity, but that there were still places for Europeans to discover, such as the great lake to the north he had heard about but not yet seen and the source of the Nile.

Walker, who had remained chronically ill, and some of the expedition's disgruntled sailors from Sierra Leone were sent off on the *Persian.* The *Ma Robert* had to fight the Zambezi's current, entering the Shire once again, this time in a heavy rain.

Livingstone was anxious to get to Chibisa's so that he could begin a more through study of Lake Nyassa. He decided, in spite of Kirk's warning him not to push on after nightfall in the storm, to steer the launch upstream where it shortly ran aground on a sandbar, and one of the boats it was towing capsized. Tragically, a

Makololo drowned, but others in the boat were rescued. No comment was apparently made to Livingstone by the others about his foolhardiness as the cause of the man's death, and Kirk controlled himself as usual, but perhaps seethed inwardly.

After eleven days of almost constant bailing, they reached Chibisa's. Rae and a seaman, Hutchins, were left with the sidewheeler below the cataracts, and this time Kirk, Livingstone, and the other whites, accompanied by their porters, continued north on foot.

Mopane, or ironwood, trees were in flower; their fruit, appearing later on in the season, was usually a favorite food for elephants. Kirk shot some zebra to be cooked and eaten. The days were not as hot and the nights were decidedly cooler once they reached the Shire highlands. But the villagers there were hostile due to new losses from slave raids; Kirk surmised that "No doubt, many a child or unarmed person has been carried off and never heard of again."[15]

They couldn't buy food because the headman of each village refused to negotiate with them. Kirk wryly related how very superstitious the natives became when it suited them:

> We found ourselves the sudden cause of general panic in the town. . . . For some time no reasonable answer could be got from them. . . . After a long time the old fellow . . . made his appearance. . . . He had cast the dice and found that by receiving us he would not be killed. This dice throwing thing is a most important thing among the Manganja. There is the dice doctor who carries in a bag a number of bits of bone or tortoise back, anything in fact that can be marked and has two sides to rest on. These, he shakes in his hand and throws on the ground. . . . There is no doubt that the Doctor, being commonly a clever fellow, makes up his mind how things had best be done and casts accordingly.[16]

Others they encountered threatened them with bows and arrows as well as the long, machete-like knives called *pangas*. Finally, at a village called Mikena, they met an apparently friendly chief. After drinking the chief's beer, however, they came down with cramps and diarrhea which lasted several days. Some believed they had been poisoned, but Kirk, again drawing on his sense of humor, noted that maybe their own cook had used too much pepper, and wrote, "Now at dinner we had Mulligatawney soup of amazing strength. In fact it blistered the mouth and we had beer, a small quantity, given by the chief. . . . This was a noisy night. I had to turn out towards morning with diarrhea. . . . Heavy artillery had been at work on all sides of me. . . . It was a mistake by the boy. . . . Dr. L. asked me how much, and I suggested a teaspoon full. The boy was careless and mixed the lot up at once."[17]

At the beginning of September 1859, they encountered an Arab caravan with many enslaved children. Kirk was horrified: "The slaves were forced on by a long pole forked at one end in which the slave's neck was fastened while the other was carried on a man's shoulder behind; at night the free end was fastened to a tree." A day or two later, a man offered Kirk a slave in exchange for a piece of red cloth.[18]

Lake of the Stars

On September 14, they passed shallow Lake Palombe or Pamalombe (called Malombe today), and after another two hard weeks of walking, they finally found the great "Lake of the Stars" (Malawi) stretching north as far as the eye could see. This inland sea is also called "the calendar lake" because it is 365 miles long and 52 miles at its widest.

The discovery came as welcome news. After the terrible disappointment of the Kebrabasa Rapids and the realization that the Zambezi was not navigable from the sea beyond Tete, Livingstone needed a new claim to fame. Yet he was still curiously reticent, perhaps because he suspected he was not the first white man to have seen the lake, only the first Englishman, and he was aware of the 1722 map of the lake. More troubling was that a German explorer, Albrecht Roscher, was approaching the lake from the east.[19]

However, in his *Narrative,* Livingstone takes total credit for the lake's discovery. "We discovered Lake Nyassa a little before noon of the 16th of September, 1859. Its southern end is 14 degrees, 25 minutes S. Lat. And 35 degrees 30 minutes E. Long. A long time after our return from Lake Nyassa we received a letter from Captain R.B. Oldfield . . . that Dr. Roscher, an enterprising young German who unfortunately lost his life in his zeal for exploration, had also reached the lake but on the 19th of November following our discovery."[20]

In his next letter to Whitehall, he requested authority to claim the lake in the name of the queen. But the British government, fearful of further antagonizing the Portuguese, refused.

The more populous Manganjas lived along the lakeside, but the Ajwas, at the southern lake, would catch them and sell them to Portuguese slavers and especially to the Arabs who traveled to the lake from the east coast. Many of these dealers were coastal

Swahili, ethnically Arab and Bantu. They came to trade not only in slaves but also in copper, mined nearby, and in malachite, a copper ore used for jewelry. Kirk saw many in the area wearing copper ornaments and dressed in cloth woven from cotton which was grown in small amounts near the lake.

Livingstone was shocked not only by the marketing of the Manganjas by the Ajwas but also by the miserable condition of the Manganjas themselves. He wrote:

> The Manganja chiefs sell their own people, for we met Ajwa and slave dealers in several highland villages who had certainly been encouraged to come among them for slaves. . . . The temptation to sell their people is peculiarly great as there is but little ivory in the hills and often the chief has nothing but human flesh with which to buy foreign goods. The Ajwa offer cloth, brass rings, pottery and sometimes handsome young women, and agree to take the trouble of carrying off by night all those who the chief may point out to them. They give four yards of cotton cloth for a man, three for a woman, and two for a boy or girl to be taken to the Portuguese at Mozambique, Iboe and Quelimane.[21]

As they trekked back to rejoin the *Ma Robert,* Livingstone's mood changed. He talked again of building a road around the Shire's cataracts to open up colonization. Though he wanted to survey Lake Nyassa, he needed more supplies for this great endeavor. On the last leg of an excursion of 250 miles that had taken a month and a half, the group camped, once again, near Chibisa's village.

The Baines Episode

Back at the paddle wheeler, Livingstone's truculent mood reappeared when he heard Thornton and Charles Livingstone claim that they had been too weak and feverish to work on the *Ma Robert* in the time the main party had been away. It worsened when Charles accused Baines of continually stealing ship supplies. It should be borne in mind that most of the explorers by this time were suffering from recurrent dysentery and fevers, and the erratic behavior of Rae, Thornton, and Baines was possibly due to cerebral inflammation from falciparum malaria.

Livingstone, himself weakened by recurrent attacks of dysentery, had become more paranoid than ever and several months earlier had warned Baines that he would be dismissed if he was incapable of fulfilling his responsibilities as crew member, storekeeper, and artist. He now dismissed both Baines and Thornton and ordered Kirk and Rae to take them by canoe to Kongone Harbor, where they were to await a British ship expected by the middle of November.

Kirk was very upset. He hated the idea of being a policeman and wasn't at all convinced that the brothers Livingstone were justified in leveling theft accusations against Baines, who, in his view, was too confused to defend himself in a logical fashion.

Livingstone wrote to Kirk:

> as Mr. Thornton . . . has been honest and failed in his duties as geologist chiefly from ignorance and a want of energy, he is permitted to take the geological specimens with him, but on the understanding that they are government property. . . . The other individual referred to [Mr. Baines], having been guilty of gross breaches of trust in *secretly* making away with large quantities of public property and having been in the habit of secreting Expedition property in his private boxes. . . . It will be necessary for you to examine his boxes. . . . It will be proper for you to ask him in the presence of Mr. Rae, what he did with five jars of butter which he took from a cask and never sent to table or for cooking. . . . If he declines your offer of conveyance he is left to his own resources.[22]

The trip back with the two unwanted men was torture for Kirk. It was the hottest time of the year. Kirk and Rae were forced to get drinking water from muddy ponds contaminated by large numbers of animals. They had brought along dried elephant meat and salt pork, which barely sustained them. Four days after leaving the *Ma Robert* on the Shire, they dragged themselves into Tete exhausted. After resting a day, Kirk dutifully examined Baines, who was feeling a little stronger and vociferously denied Livingstone's accusations. Baines later was to write: "I feel bound to acknowledge that Dr. Kirk performed the duty imposed on him in the most gentlemanly and least offensive manner."[23]

Since Kirk found nothing to substantiate Livingstone's accusations against the sick man, he began to wonder how sane his leader really was and decided that Livingstone was incapable of effectively leading other white men. Although the governor of Tete was friendly, the townspeople, fearful of Livingstone's interference with the slave trade, were overtly hostile and tried to stop Kirk from hiring a crew and canoes for another trip to Kongone Harbor.

After much turmoil and consultation with the governor, someone offered to sell him a canoe. "The Portuguese don't like us as an Expedition," wrote Kirk: "The feeling is mutual . . . they are fools to let us in at all."[24]

As they rowed downstream, Livingstone passed them on the *Ma Robert* and was the first to arrive at Kongone Harbor, November 10, 1859, ostensibly to meet the British gunboat *Lynx* for supplies and mail, and to send news of his discovery to Britain. But what he had were fresh accusations against Baines.

In a pseudo court-martial, Livingstone mercilessly interrogated Baines again. Livingstone now also claimed a cask of sugar and two boxes of sardines had been previously stolen from the stores Baines was supposed to have guarded. But Kirk believed it was never proven that Baines had sold or even used the sugar. One of the Africans could have stolen the cask because not all of the party's provisions could be locked up. Baines did admit, however, giving two boxes of sardines to the Portuguese as a gift for letting him use their canoes.

During Livingstone's inquisition, Baines asked permission to return to Tete for his possessions. Livingstone refused. Baines also asked for a fair trial in any British port. Livingstone again refused. He had acted as judge and jury, much like Captain Bligh of the *Bounty,* and, as in Bligh's case, after Baines returned home and appealed the decision, the British government backed Livingstone. After Livingstone had pronounced him guilty, Baines was forced to live in one of the whaleboats with a sail as an awning, until he could be put on the *Lynx* bound for Cape Town.

Haggard and despondent, Baines landed at Cape Town, where Livingstone's accusations and Baines's denials were eventually published in the *South African Advertiser and Mail.*[25] Livingstone refused to retract his allegations, and the verbal feud continued in the media.

The Portuguese authorities were now very alarmed at the movements of the *Ma Robert* up and down the Zambezi and Shire. The governor of Quelimane met the party on its way back to Shupanga and informed Livingstone that another customs house was to be built there. He also talked of constructing a railroad across Africa, connecting Angola on the Atlantic with Mozambique on the eastern shore, and annexing the territory between them. He further infuriated Livingstone by claiming that the natives would be taught to weave their own cloth from cotton, which would be a blow to the British mills.

Back at Tete once more, Livingstone had another brainstorm. To keep a promise he had made on his earlier expedition, he would return his Makololo porters, who had since settled in Tete, to their chief, Sekeletu, at Sesheke, much farther up on the Zambezi. That was a mere 1,200-mile roundtrip, but it would offer one more opportunity to bring the gospel to more dark, benighted souls in need of redemption.

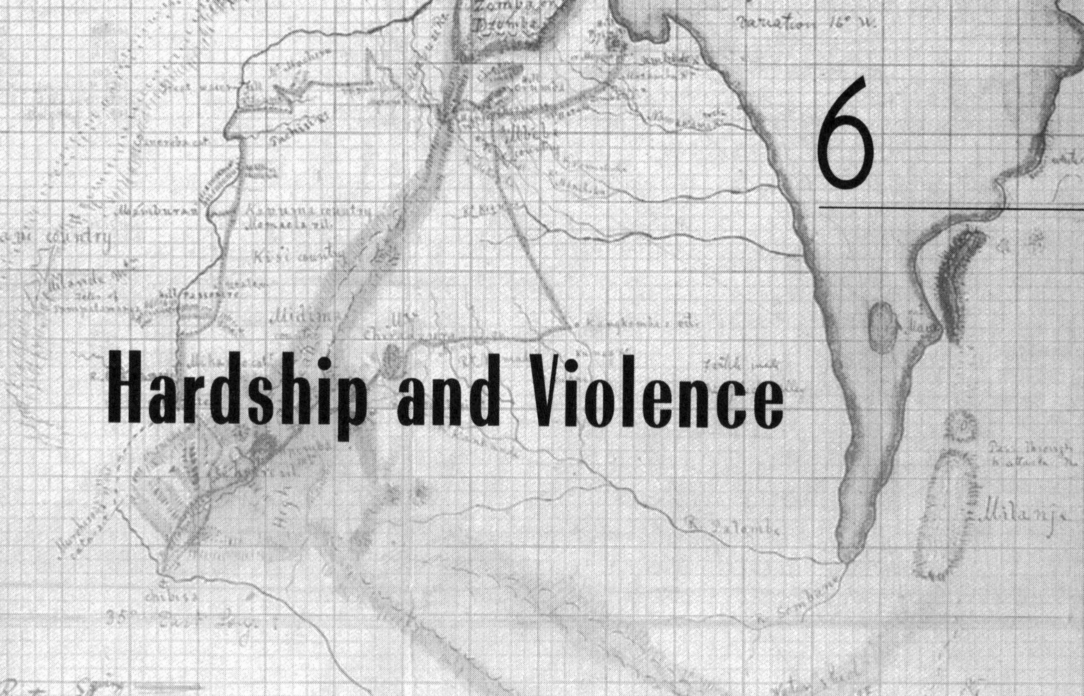

6

Hardship and Violence

Kirk found Livingstone's moodiness to be an increasingly heavy burden. Livingstone's treatment of Baines had seemed petty and vicious and, now, this proposed trip of more than 1,200 miles to Makololo land would be a difficult and dangerous endeavor. Kirk's contract was due to expire two years after the beginning of his employment by Livingstone, and by January 1860 he was having serious misgivings about extending it.

Kirk feared that Livingstone's quick temper and bursts of biting sarcasm would further antagonize the remaining whites on the expedition, including himself. It had been raining steadily for two weeks, and he was fed up with the physical conditions they were forced to endure. He had to write while holding an umbrella over his head. His new plant collection was almost completely ruined by water leaking through the cabin's roof. Complaining, Kirk wrote, "This is an awful place to live in, I mean the ship. My [botanical] specimens . . . are all wet and run the risk of utter destruction. The water floods the floor from the windows while the roof leaks at every joint. . . . Many a pig lives in a better house than we do."[1]

Livingstone recorded in his *Narrative,* "Many of the botanical specimens collected and carefully prepared by Dr. Kirk were destroyed."[2] Then a plague of cockroaches provided the coup de grâce to Kirk's carefully prepared and catalogued botanical collection: "Such a nuisance the cockroaches are. They eat everything. My specimens are going under them," Kirk noted sadly in his journal.[3]

Not only was water constantly dripping into the cramped cabin, but snakes, scorpions, centipedes, and poisonous spiders, which were accidentally brought on board with wood for the boiler, sometimes found their way into the crew's beds. With typical British understatement, Livingstone carped: "To be aroused in the dark by five feet of cold green snake gliding over one's face is rather unpleasant."[4]

But despite the harsh conditions and the mercurial leader, Kirk was impressed by Livingstone's patience and his comparative kindness toward native Africans. Together, they despaired of the terrible suffering and deaths of the people captured and led at gunpoint past them in long slave caravans. It was all still a rousing adventure and a marvelous learning experience, so Kirk stayed on.

Return to Tete

In February 1860, when they returned to Tete from Kongone, Livingstone and his party were given the cold shoulder by the governor, who accused Livingstone of being a "political adventurer." Under the guise of missionary work and stopping the slave trade, he was, the governor claimed, an agent of the British government mapping out areas under Portuguese control for British colonization. Livingstone blamed this sudden change in attitude on a mistranslation of his book, *Missionary Travels,* which had been translated into more than a dozen languages, including Portuguese.

Kirk echoed his leader in condemning the Portuguese, including their sexual practices. They bought nine- and ten-year-old slave girls as concubines, and Kirk commented, "There is not one white man or one who may call himself white in the whole district without venereal disease"; and Livingstone replied with charges of his own, calling the Portuguese "an utterly effete, syphilitic race . . . filthy, diseased settlers who cultivate skin diseases and drunkenness more than horseflesh and are asses themselves."[5]

Perhaps provoked by the stress of this encounter, Livingstone had another attack of dysentery and abdominal cramps early that spring. But by May 16, 1860, he was well enough to leave with Kirk and his brother Charles on the arduous trek to Sekeletu's. With them were eighty-seven of the Makololo porters, the rest having chosen to remain with their new families at Tete.

On their way west, the expedition marched through the Chicova plain with its stretches of parched grassland. In the distance Kirk could see purple, jungle-clad hills. Once again, they passed through the derelict town of Zumbo, where the Loangwa River meets the Zambezi. The region, with its sparsely inhabited forests and hills, appealed to Kirk; but Livingstone, with his distaste for the Portuguese, was more struck by its human dimension:

> There is nothing to remind one that a Christian power ever had traders here; for the natives of today are precisely what their fathers were when the Portuguese first rounded the Cape. Their language, unless buried in the Vatican, is still unwritten. Not a single art, save that of distilling spirits by means of a gun-barrel, has ever been learnt from strangers; and if all the progeny of the whites were at once to leave this country, their only memorial would be the ruins of a few stone and mud built walls and that blighting relic of the Slave Trade, the belief that man may sell his brother man; a belief that is not of native origin, for it is not found except in the track of the Portuguese."[6]

Of course, he was mistaken on his last point. Groups in the area had taken slaves in wars for centuries, albeit in numbers that were small in comparison to those when Arab and Portuguese slavers arrived on the scene.

At Mburuma Pass, fifty miles east of Zumbo, Kirk, who had been experimenting with combinations of quinine and other medicines to find a better treatment for malaria, swallowed the latest concoction himself. Suddenly, complaining of faintness and blindness, Kirk became deathly ill. His sudden prostration and loss of vision was probably due to an overdose of quinine. Livingstone, this time, seemed genuinely concerned. Fortunately, after three days of rest and no quinine, Kirk was well enough to ride the donkey they had with them, and a week later he was marching as well as the others.

Meanwhile, Charles Livingstone complained constantly of what he considered a needless trip and, much to Kirk's embarrassment, began to quarrel openly with his brother. Kirk wrote: "Mr. C.L. is against going up to Sekeletu's; he is for risking nothing in the way of health for these [Makololo] men, although they did bring the Doctor down. They are no worse than most savages . . . and in honor we are forced to undertake a journey which otherwise I should much rather avoid."[7]

After reaching the Kafue River's junction with the Zambezi, they hiked around the Kariba Gorge to follow the Zangwe River north to the undulating Batoka grasslands in present-day Zambia.

Both Livingstone and Kirk thought the region was healthy enough for European settlement and sheep herding. The Batoka tribe, they noted, used ordeal by poison to identify the person who committed a crime. If a suspect promptly vomited the poison, he survived and was pronounced innocent by the chief. If he kept it down and died, he was declared guilty.[8]

All went well until the party became aware of a slave caravan following in their footsteps that was buying ivory and slave girls from the Batokas. The rumor that the African-Portuguese mestizos leading the slave gang claimed to be the Englishmen's children made Livingstone furious on its own account. But it was also dangerous; the expedition leaders might be taken for slavers themselves.

On August 4, 1860, Kirk first saw the great plumes of spray from Victoria Falls and was as impressed as Livingstone had been when he first visited the falls five years earlier. Kirk was especially awed by the incredibly deep chasm cut by the Zambezi below the falls. They visited an island above the falls where Livingstone had planted vegetables and fruit tree seeds. But the island now was a grazing ground for hippos, and signs of Livingstone's earlier visit, save for the initials he had carved on a tree, had vanished.

While admiring the falls, they were surprised to find another Englishman, Baldwin by name, imprisoned in a nearby village. He had broken a tribal taboo by bathing in a sacred spot on the river. To their amazement, he said that he had been so excited by Livingstone's *Missionary Travels* that he had walked over 1,000 miles from Natal, South Africa, guided only by a compass. The chief, who had heard of Livingstone, was subsequently persuaded to release his prisoner.

On August 28, the expedition arrived at Sekeletu's compound at Sesheke. In the five years since Livingstone had seen him, the Makololo chief had developed a serious skin disease. Kirk, remembering Livingstone's advice, conferred with the local African healer, a woman, who said the chief was bewitched and that confinement in his hut was necessary. She did, however, allow Kirk to try his European remedies. Livingstone described the skin condition in his *Narrative*: "His fingers were said to have grown like eagle's claws, and his face so frightfully distorted that no one could recognize him. Some had begun to hint that he might not really be the son of the great Sebutane, the founder of the nation. . . . Having, however, none of the medicines usually employed in skin diseases with us, we [actually Kirk] tried the local application of lunar caustic and hydriotate of potash [potassium chloride] internally."[9] Nitrate of soda was applied externally to each sore and scab daily, and liberal amounts of caustic had to be applied to the hands of Livingstone and Kirk themselves, who feared they had contracted what they thought was a highly contagious disease.

The two physicians thought that Sekeletu was suffering from pemphigus, herpes, or leprosy. Oliver Ransford, a physician and author living in Africa, believed Sekeletu had a form of pemphigus called *Fergo Salvagem* or *Brazilian Wildfire* which, despite its name, is found in Africa's river valleys.[10] Before modern treatment, this blistering skin disease caused blindness and was invariably fatal five years or so after its onset. Yet Sekeletu appeared to improve rapidly in response to treatment, though it was probably only a temporary remission in the cyclical nature of the affliction. In any case, to demonstrate his gratitude, the African chief gave the Englishmen tea, biscuits, and preserved fruits he had obtained from the Portuguese, undoubtedly in exchange for slaves.

Livingstone pleased the chief by showing him a letter from the Foreign Office asking Sekeletu to accredit Livingstone as British consul to Africa's interior tribes. He asked Sekeletu why the Makololo didn't move from the malaria-ridden lowlands along the river to the healthier Batoka plateau. Sekeletu replied he would have liked to, but that the Matabele (or N'Debele) branch of the Zulu tribe occupying the plateau were too powerful. On the other hand, if the English would settle here, the chief added, together they would have enough strength and fire power to force the Matabele out of the area.[11]

Livingstone regretfully refused the offer, explaining that he and the other members of the expedition were there as representatives of the British government. This expression of regret may have been more than politeness. During his stay, in perhaps another manic phase, Livingstone also became uncharacteristically enthusiastic about the attractiveness of the Makololo women:

> The Makololo women are vastly superior to any we have seen. They are of a light, warm-brown complexion, have pleasant countenances and are remarkably quick of apprehension. . . . Sebutane's sister, the head lady of Sesheke, wore eighteen solid brass rings as thick as one's finger on each leg, and three of copper under each knee; nineteen brass rings on her left arm and eight of brass and copper on her right; also a large, ivory ring above each elbow. . . . The men wickedly aver that their two great amusements or modes of killing time are sipping beer, and secretly smoking bang or Indian hemp [cannabis] . . . they do not like their wives to follow their example. . . .

> Nevertheless, some women do smoke it secretly. . . . We had ample opportunities for observing the effects of this . . . smoking on our men. It makes them feel very strong in body, but it produces exactly the opposite effect upon the mind.[12]

The party left Sekeletu's village for a brief excursion to Linyanti, where Livingstone had left a wagon of supplies and medicines on his previous journey. They found it virtually intact, an object of curiosity and veneration by the area's residents. The wagon had indirectly figured in a disaster when the London Missionary Society sent missionaries to Linyanti at Livingstone's suggestion. Four of the missionaries died from fever, most likely malaria. The others then abandoned the site. In Livingstone's view, the victims probably died needlessly. A supply of quinine lay packed in his wagon, which stood only a hundred yards from the defunct mission. If the missionaries had only looked in it, they would have found the cure that could have kept them alive.[13]

When the Livingstone party returned to Sekeletu's village, they found the chief in much better health. He gave them fresh Makololo porters and canoes for their return trip to Tete. Unfortunately, they were never to see him again. After they left, his disease continued its inexorable course, and Sekeletu became blind and died four years later. Following his death, the Lhosi, whom he and his father had subjugated, rose in revolt and hunted down and killed all adult male Makololos. Then, as was the custom, they absorbed the women and children into their own tribe.[14]

After three weeks of traveling back toward Tete, Kirk and the Livingstone brothers again reached the Kebrabasa Rapids on November 11. This time, they did not appear as formidable to Livingstone as they had on the way up, but Kirk wasn't as sanguine as they paddled their canoes into the first series of rapids. Turbulent water coursing around huge boulders appeared to block their further passage. Conditions rapidly got worse. Kirk, who was traveling in a twenty-four-foot-long canoe hollowed out of a tree trunk, commented in his diary:

> For two miles we found the way good, the current very strong. Then the river was divided by a long mass of rock; the sides of the island and of the river were perpendicular and only at a few places could we land. We got up one of these and examined the part in front. On the left the entrance seemed bad; on the right it was very bad, at the farther end so bad that the canoe men desired not to go. The danger on the right was from being

dashed against the opposite bank. We crossed to the north bank to examine. In attempting this the canoe of Ramakukan was taken into the current and almost lost, he however, managed to paddle back and leap on a rock, thus saving his life although the canoe and all its cargo was swept down. In it went my Enfield rifle and 2 sword bayonets.[15]

The current was now too strong to consider turning back. They searched for a break in the high cliffs so that they could portage their canoes around the remaining rapids. Kirk had the best canoeists and went first, the swift current carrying him around boulders into a small pool. When he looked back he saw David Livingstone's canoe caught on a rock and Charles Livingstone's canoe being carried down on it. In the excitement, Kirk's own canoeists failed to keep his canoe headed downstream and they, too, hit a rock and capsized.

The man at the stern got hold of the rock: fortunately there was a slight slope where two could hold on. He held the canoe which was pressed forcibly against the rock, from going down; sometimes it was sucked under. The man at the bow at once jumped into the river, his position was the most dangerous, but he held on to the canoe. I found myself in the water with my body sucked under the canoe. . . . I managed to drag myself up and crawl along the canoe to the rock.[16]

Many years later Kirk further recalled the incident in an interview:

My legs were in the water and the force of the current was so great that I thought at first I had been caught in the jaws of a crocodile. A little further up [down] the stream, about a quarter of a mile off, were some rapids with a drop of fifteen feet. As soon as we had recovered from the effects of our adventure, we let go the canoes to see [out of curiosity] what would happen to them. They were carried by the stream into the rapids where they were hurtled on the rocks below and then they shot up again in the air. The fall had smashed them in half. It was a lucky thing after all that my canoe got into the difficulties I described. Had it not done so, I have not the slightest doubt that the whole party would have been dashed to pieces in the rapids.[17]

Livingstone's canoe was saved and Kirk's also, although obviously not their contents. In Kirk's capsized canoe had been his instruments, rifle, botanical specimens, eight volumes of notes, and one hundred drawings of plants. The group did, however, manage to save most of the expedition's goods.

The strain of the trip was now seriously affecting Charles, who resumed his frequent arguments with his brother. Kirk noted in his journal that he was shocked by the fierceness of their quarrels and the strong language Charles used. In one of his rages, Charles began kicking the Makololo headman. The African raised his spear and was about to stab him, when David Livingstone intervened. It was only out of respect for Dr. Livingstone that the Makololo didn't kill his brother, according to Kirk, but rather than express his gratitude, Charles attacked David, "striking Dr. L. and tearing the coat off his back."[18]

Missionary News

The group returned to Tete weary and in bad humor. Livingstone was upset over the deaths of the missionaries at Linyanti, although he blamed them for their own ignorance and stupidity in not taking quinine. More to the point, he was expecting news from England as to whether the government would renew support for his expedition or recall it. He knew that news of his quarrels and of his firings of Bedingfeld, Baines, and Thornton had reached England, and he was concerned that their critical remarks might tarnish his reputation in the eyes of Whitehall, possibly jeopardizing his new hope of exploring the eastern shore of Lake Nyassa (Malawi) to see if the Rovuma River flowed out of it.

On November 23, 1860, Livingstone read the letter which had been waiting for him at Tete. His dour face broke into a smile. The news was better than good.

The government was not only renewing the expedition's contract, but shipping a new steam launch to them. Lord Russell, head of the Foreign Office, had agreed that the Rovuma River was worth exploring, and, best of all, missionaries from the Universities Mission to Central Africa (UMCA) were due to arrive shortly. Inspired both by Livingstone's book, *Missionary Travels,* and by his speeches, the Universities of Durham, Oxford, Cambridge, and Dublin had collaborated to send missionaries to Africa and build a mission in the Shire highlands. Livingstone's elation was not in the least dampened by Lord Russell's admonition to stop criticizing the Portuguese, since the success of the expedition still depended on their cooperation. Livingstone's dream of founding a

British settlement to fight slavery and "bring Christianity and commerce to the savages" seemed about to come true!

Early in 1861, on the way down the river to Kongone Harbor to meet the British ship, the *Ma Robert* sank despite all hands bailing and the pumps working overtime. Fortunately, no lives were lost, and most of the expedition's possessions were saved. The group arrived at Sena in borrowed canoes. The rainy season had begun for the year, and with it came swarms of mosquitoes, yet Livingstone's mood remained buoyant and the others became more optimistic at the thought of getting a better craft, letters from home, fresh supplies, and the companionship of missionaries.

Livingstone, Kirk, and the others finally reached Kongone Harbor on February 7, 1861. They saw two British naval ships, the *Sidon* and the *Lyra,* anchored outside the bar. Livingstone, wearing his only good suit and cap, rowed out to the *Lyra* to meet the leader of the new mission, Bishop Charles Mackenzie, and his four associates. All were comparatively young, in high spirits, and totally unprepared for what lay ahead. The *Sidon* had brought the new steam launch, the *Pioneer,* in tow.

The *Pioneer,* under the command of Captain May, took on the expedition members. With new apparel brought by the British ship, the explorers discarded their old clothes, mostly rags by now. Dressed in their new clothes, they formed a natty group, according to Kirk. Livingstone wore a jacket and trousers of blue serge with matching cloth cap. His brother was similarly dressed, while Kirk himself received oxford-gray trousers and a shooting jacket along with a broad-brimmed hat to keep out the sun.

The new steam launch was a virtual copy of the seagoing royal yacht, *Elfin.* Although the *Pioneer* was more seaworthy than the *Ma Robert,* its deeper draft meant that the party would have to be even more careful to avoid the frequent sandbars.

But anxious to see how seaworthy the new ship really was, Livingstone had Captain May take them out to sea to the Rovuma River delta on the disputed boundary of Mozambique and the Zanzibari sultanate.

Unfortunately, Livingstone quarreled with Captain May over the chain of command on board, just as he had with Bedingfeld. May resigned, and Livingstone took over as captain and pilot of the *Pioneer* just as he had on the *Ma Robert.* Following an abortive attempt to travel up the Rovuma, for the river was too shallow for the *Pioneer*'s draft, Livingstone next took the *Pioneer* to Johanna in the Comoro Islands, where he bought oxen to provide meat for the crew.

Returning to the Zambezi and traveling up the Shire was a trial for all, but especially for the inexperienced missionaries. Bitten by mosquitoes, they were forced to stay in the hot, crowded cabin much of the time during the rains. They also had to take frequent turns cutting wood for the steam engine, and then there was the strenuous job of rowing small boats to pull the *Pioneer* off the sandbars on which it inevitably got stuck.

Even more sobering, the group got stuck for three weeks in the hot, fetid Elephant Marsh due to low water. For the first time they began to question the judgment of their hero, Livingstone. Then Bishop Mackenzie suddenly came down with malaria, probably due to neglecting to take quinine in large enough doses.

After Mackenzie recovered, the party continued on foot along the left bank of the Shire. As described by Livingstone, their daily trekking routine was this:

> We rise about five, or as soon as dawn approaches, take a cup of tea and a bit of biscuit; the servants fold up the blankets and stow them away in the bags they carry; the others tie their fumbas [woven bags] and pots to each end of their carrying sticks, which are borne on the shoulders; the cook secures the dishes and all are on the path by sunrise. If a convenient spot can be found, we halt for breakfast about nine A.M. To save time this meal is generally cooked the night before, and has only to be warmed.
>
> We continue the march after breakfast, rest a little in the middle of the day, and break off early in the afternoon. We average from two to two and a half miles an hour in a straight line, or as the crow flies, and seldom have more than five or six hours a day of actual travel. . . . After pitching our camp, one or two of us usually go off to hunt. Many of the African women are peculiar about the water they use for drinking and cooking and filter it through the sand . . . the habit may be from observing the unhealthiness of the main stream at certain seasons. . . . It is no wonder that sailors suffered so much from fever after drinking African river water before the present admirable system of condensing it was adopted in our navy.[19]

Interestingly, neither Livingstone nor Kirk mentioned filtering or even boiling their own water. If they had maintained the practice, perhaps they might not have had bouts of diarrhea and fever from parasites such as *Entameba histolytica, Giardia*, or pathogenic bacteria.

Livingstone also described an attack by carnivorous army ants, whose painful bites were known to kill small animals and human babies. "The moist ravines are full of black ants which rushed up our clothes. . . . In a few minutes they cover the whole body and once they fix their mandibles into the flesh, they twist about and cause great pain." (Their mandibles were so strong the natives used them as stitches to close over both edges of a wound and then twisted off the bodies. The pincers remained closed and could be pried off when the wound healed.)[20]

Slave Trade Encounters

After the expedition passed Mount Zomba, its travelers heard of new slave raids on the Manganjas by the Ajwas. Kirk wrote in his journal on July 9, 1861: "When in the village we saw several people. . . . They have fled to tell Chibisa that their village was attacked and their people were carried off as slaves."[21]

A week later Livingstone, who was again feeling sick, halted the expedition near a friendly village. Bishop Mackenzie was bathing in a nearby stream when he heard the sound of horns in the direction of the village. He dressed and ran to the village with the other Englishmen. The sounds came from trumpets (usually made of kudu horns) announcing the arrival of a slave caravan. Kirk counted eighty-four newly captured slaves herded by six Ajwas. The British threatened to shoot the native slavers, and the Ajwas ran off, abandoning their chattel. The slave caravan belonged to the commandant of Tete, Major Sicard, the same man who had befriended Kirk and Livingstone and allowed the Makololo to settle there until Livingstone returned for them. Livingstone's relations with the Portuguese became worse than ever.

Villagers told the explorers that more slave caravans were in the vicinity. Livingstone ordered Kirk to find them and rescue the slaves, but the porters refused to accompany him.[22]

The Ajwas had recently become very active in their attempts at enslavement of the Manganjas. Kirk found out that they had burned two villages, killing all of the inhabitants who resisted. Then they ambushed the Livingstone expedition itself. According to Kirk: "The Ajwa danced about and cut capers, firing their arrows with tolerable aim at 100 yards."[23]

The Englishmen and their Manganja allies chased the Ajwas to their village, where Livingstone tried to speak with the chief. But the Ajwas quickly surrounded the expedition and shot a fusillade of arrows at its members. Outnumbered and realizing this was a life-or-death situation, Livingstone gave the order to shoot back. Bishop Mackenzie wrote, "I had a gun in my hand, but seeing Livingstone without one I asked him to use mine rather than that I should."[24] To make matters worse, the Manganjas accompanying Kirk and Livingstone shouted exultantly at the Ajwas that their great white warrior would avenge them. Livingstone set fire to the Ajwa villages, entangling the mission further in a web of native strife.

After they were liberated, the former slaves the Ajwas had captured ran away, leaving only two children to add to the congregation. (The freed slaves became the nucleus of converts and their descendants remain perfunctory Christians today.) Still, these seemed to be opening shots in an undeclared war between the missionaries and the Ajwas. When news of the fighting reached England, there was an outcry from missionary circles, for they felt the violence would hamper their efforts to evangelize in Africa.

The missionaries traveling with Livingstone appeared eager to join the undeclared war when persuasion failed. They soon chose the village of Magomero for their new home (see Map 5 on page 91). Sixty miles north of Chibisa's and fifteen miles southwest of Lake Shirwa, it would be close to the Shire, allowing supplies to be brought in by boat. Most importantly, it was in the middle of the slave-raiding area and would, it was hoped, help physically separate the Manganjas from the predatory Ajwas. But the stockaded mission was poorly situated from a military standpoint, located, as it was, in the shadow of a hill from which the Ajwas could shoot down at the missionaries.

In October 1861, another fight was to erupt with the Ajwas. The Anglican Church preached conversion through nonviolent means and sent letters to Mackenzie admonishing the mostly Presbyterian missionaries. But the choleric Mackenzie refused to stop his war against the Ajwas. Although he vacillated at first, Livingstone finally agreed that the battles were justified as the only means of protecting the freed slaves from new Ajwa attacks.

At this point, the two Livingstones, Kirk, and a new member of the expedition, Dr. Meller, a naval medical officer recently lent to the expedition by the commander of the *Lyra,* had left Magomero and the missionaries to explore the upper Shire and Lake Nyassa by canoe. By August 16, 1861, the expedition had reached the upper Shire, a wide, serpentine stream filled with hippopotami. One of the animals, wounded by Kirk, attacked his boat a few feet from where Kirk was sitting and nearly killed him.

As they continued up the Shire, people on the western shore could be seen fleeing the Ajwas, while on the eastern side the smoke of vil-

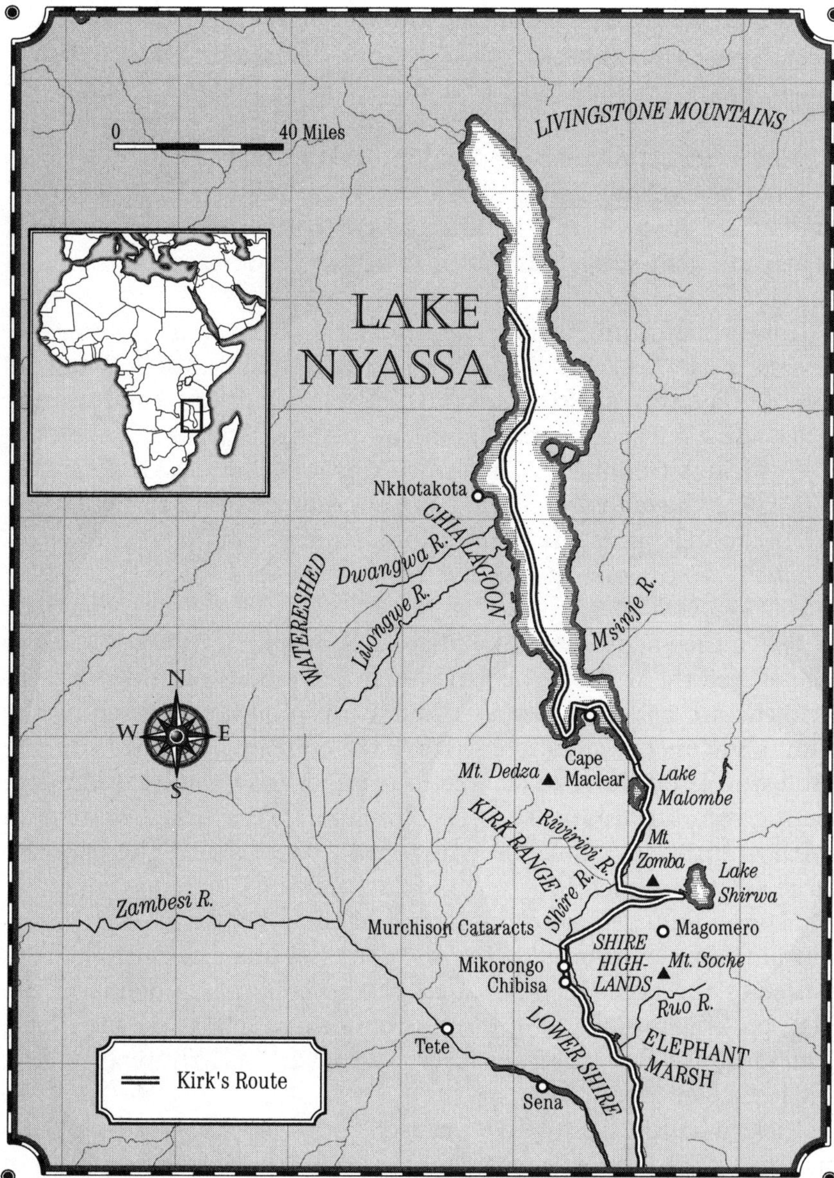

MAP 5 *Lake Nyassa (now Lake Malawi).* From O. Ransford, *David Livingstone, The Dark Interior* (London: John Murray, 1978, p. 156).

lages the Ajwas had set on fire was visible. At the end of August, the group reached Lake Palombe (Malombe). The area around the lake was densely populated, and the people were suspicious of the newcomers. Kirk noticed that many were scarred from smallpox. Some were leprous and others had club feet, eye diseases, and deformities of the limbs that perhaps had been caused by poliomyelitis or spinal tuberculosis. They were armed with spears, bows, and arrows and called the Englishmen "chirombo," or wild animals.

Once the whites had landed and set up their tents, the Africans approached them with a mixture of curiosity and aggressiveness, an attitude that persisted. The next day Kirk commented:

> Towards morning people came down and robbed us of three bags of clothes, one of beads, and several small things. They did it deliberately, seeking out the clothes and leaving such things as boots and specimens. Botanical specimens were smashed by this rough treatment. The birds skins are gone. . . . Dr. D.L and Mr. C.L. have lost their clothing and sundry other things. Fortunately guns and ammunition were not taken, and the cloth, the little we now have, I was using as a pillow.[25]

When they arrived at Lake Nyassa, September 21, 1861, a heavy fog covered the water. When the fog lifted, clouds of midges thickened the air, and Kirk watched the local inhabitants trapping the midges to concoct an edible paste of the millions of insects. Fierce wind storms on the lake cleared the air enough for the explorers to see high mountains to the east, but the lake seemed to stretch north to infinity; and, as they hugged the west shore, the opposite shore was never visible.

Having inquired as to the length of the lake, Kirk wrote in his journal: "One man here gives a very mysterious description of the course of the lake. He says after going far North it bends to the East, passing a place where rocks concealed a passage by which traders could sail in an underground river[26] all the way to the Indian Ocean."[27]

Kirk, who had been having muscle pains, suddenly developed a high fever. This attack was, like his "ague", more likely that of dengue fever than malaria. The disease is caused by a virus which, like malaria, is injected by a mosquito. The incubation period is followed by fever, pain behind the eyes, severe headache, and sometimes agonizing muscle and joint pains. Weakness, prostration, and nausea can be complicated by capillary damage and bleeding under the skin. Though the clinical picture resembles yellow fever, the disease lasts about a week, though with possible relapses, and the death rate is fortunately far lower. Kirk's attack seems to have been short-lived as he recovered quickly.

On October 3, they reached an area where heaps of ashes were all that was left of a group of shoreline huts. The ground was covered with skulls and decomposing bodies. Livingstone learned that a splinter group of Zulus, now called the N'goni, but at that time Mazitu (Mabzwiti by Kirk), was responsible for the massacre. "The only thing the Mabzwiti take is people. They select a few of the strongest young men and women and carry them off. All others they murder that the young may have nowhere to flee to and also to satisfy their desire for blood. As an Englishman loves to kill game, so they kill men for sport. . . . The Mabzwiti are said to kill all over the age of 10. Those under they carry off to increase their tribe."[28]

Livingstone's entries in his diary became terse at this point, and his depression seemed to be deepening. Yet, in one of his more uplifted moods, he generously named the cape at the southern end of the lake Cape Maclear, after his friend, Thomas Maclear, the royal astronomer.

Livingstone then decided to divide his forces. He would lead a party on land which would map the shoreline of Lake Nyassa. Kirk was put in charge of a four-oared gig, which had been towed up the Shire by the *Pioneer,* carried around the Murchison Cataracts, and then rowed to the lake. The mission of those in the gig was to reach the lake's north end and report on the region.

But they had no concept of how long the lake really was. The wind was strong and the waves so big that the two parties soon lost contact with each other. Kirk and others in his group began to run high, nightly fevers, and some became too weak to row. As days turned into weeks, their food supply began to run out, and much of the cloth they had brought to barter for food was stolen. They traveled 220 miles up the lake to about 130 miles from the lake's northern end. But one day in heavy fog, they finally reluctantly decided to turn back.

When they pulled toward shore, to their surprise and relief, they saw Livingstone and two of the Makololo porters emerging from the fog in a native canoe. "What on earth made you run away and leave us?" was Livingstone's comment, Kirk noted in his diary.[29]

Livingstone was now pathologically depressed. Perhaps it was due to encountering dozens of corpses and slave gangs crisscrossing the lake shore. He had concluded that only a British army on land and an armed steamer on the lake could safeguard the Manganjas. His frustration was heightened when he found Arab traders had built a dhow and were transporting newly captured slaves across the lake and then overland for sale at Iboe and Kilwa on the East African coast (see Map 6 on page 94). He was also upset by the estimate from

MAP 6 *The Sultanate of Zanzibar and Equatoria.* From R. W. Beachey, *The Slave Trade of Eastern Africa* (New York: Harper & Row, 1976, p. 308).

the former British consul in Zanzibar, Colonel C.P. Rigby, that "19,000 slaves from this Nyassa country alone pass annually [to the slave ports of Zanzibar, Iboe, and Kilwa]. . . . This is exclusive, of course, of those sent to Portuguese slave-ports."[30]

To make matters worse, the remaining Makololo porters had deserted and returned to Chibisa's. With the firearms Livingstone had given them, they were terrorizing the Manganjas and calling themselves "the children of Doto Livisto." They strutted around like feudal lords mouthing English phrases, such as "Good morning, Sir," "Look here, my man," and "Thank you, Sir" to each other and to the uncomprehending Manganjas, but they carried enough clout to become the region's new chiefs.[31]

Livingstone was also upset by the misty and miasmal climate around the lake, which he thought—inaccurately as it turned out—made the region unfit for white colonization.[32] Furthermore, the group narrowly escaped being massacred one night when their camp was invaded by the Mazitu. By some instinct which caused even his disgruntled crew to admire him, Livingstone, at the last minute, decided to move the sleeping area away from the camp and assigned sentinels to guard them. Thanks to this move, they escaped likely death.

By now they were all sunburned, emaciated, and fever-ridden. When they returned to the Shire River, Kirk, longing for some peace, went off to watch a herd of elephants tearing up trees like matchsticks; he wrote that it felt good to be able to hike on land after sitting in a small boat for days exposed to the sun and wind. But on more than one occasion, when threatened or attacked by Africans, fever-ridden, or upset by his leader's constant vacillations, Kirk would vent his fears, impatience, and irritation in his journal on blacks. "As usual there is a mass of *niggers* ready to stare," he wrote in one place. Yet, underneath this immature ranting, he was genuinely appalled by the deaths and sufferings of the thousands of Africans captured in the slave trade—"this trade in Hell," as Livingstone called it. Later, Kirk was to devote his life to stopping the trade in human flesh.

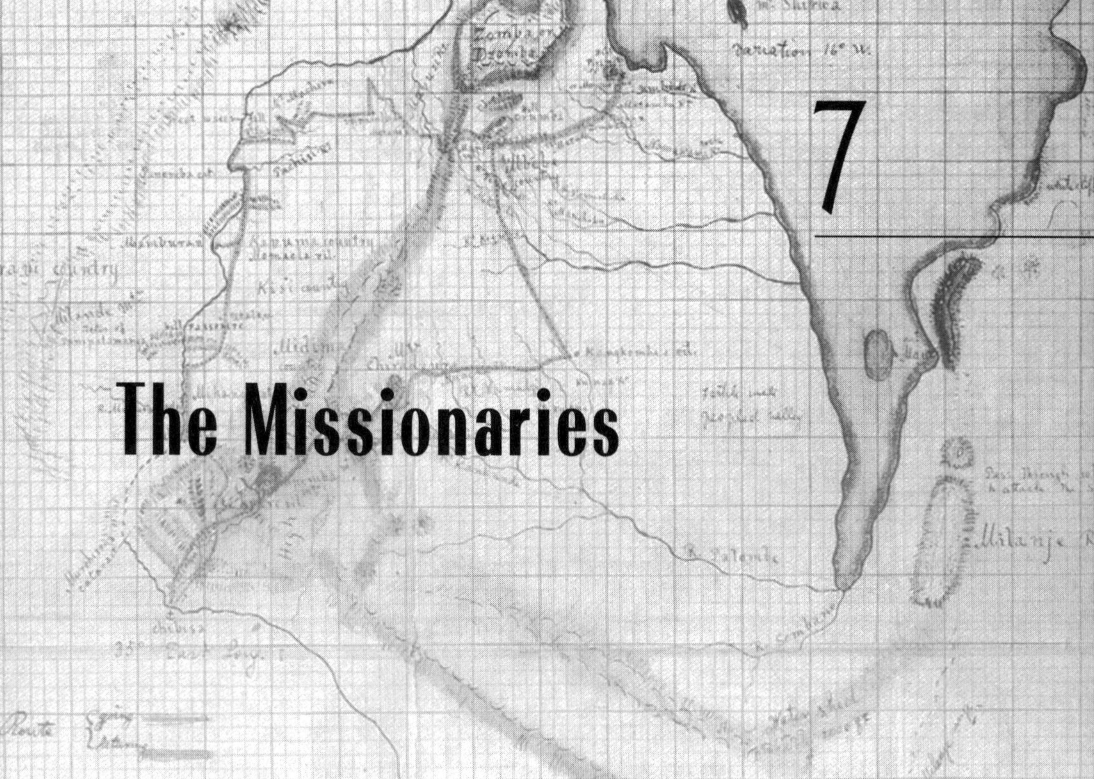

7

The Missionaries

Kirk and Livingstone returned to the *Pioneer* at the end of October 1861, and on November 8, much to their surprise, a young Oxford graduate and missionary, Mr. Burrup, and a Dr. Dickinson arrived by canoe all the way from Quelimane with a few porters. They had been well-treated by the Portuguese and told Livingstone they had come to assist Bishop Mackenzie at the mission. Burrup also brought news that his wife, Helen, along with Bishop Mackenzie's sister, Anne, and Livingstone's wife, Mary, had left England and were expected at the mouth of the Kongone sometime in January.

The news of Mary Livingstone's departure for Africa did not come as a shock to her husband. In fact, he had written to ask her to join him after receiving a disturbing letter from George Rae, the boat's engineer, who had returned to Scotland to supervise the construction of yet a third launch, the *Lady Nyassa.*

According to Ray's letter, he had visited Mary and had been appalled by what he had seen. Mary had begun to drink brandy heavily to assuage her loneliness and help her sleep. She had introduced Rae to James Stewart, a young missionary who, according to Rae, was spending a considerable amount of time with her, including many evenings.

Rae's letter urged Livingstone to act promptly. Rae turned out to be a diligent tattle, and the news of Mary's relationship with

Stewart had spread widely even before Livingstone, deep in the bush, received the letter. Though Livingstone may have felt the calumnies were baseless, he decided it was time to send for her.

The expedition left Chibisa's village on board the *Pioneer* November 14th, 1861, ostensibly in plenty of time to travel downriver to meet the ladies at Kongone Harbor. But the launch was grounded on a shoal for five weeks because the river's level had fallen so much. Then Kirk, Dr. Meller, and one of the crewmen developed the telltale symptoms of malaria: shaking chills, fever, profound sweating, and marked fatigue. In mid-December, Ferger, the young carpenter's mate, died of blackwater fever, the dreaded kidney and liver complication of falciparum malaria.

Though Kirk and Dr. Meller were still weak and feverish, they performed an autopsy, and Kirk noted this description of the effects of falciparum malaria in his journal:

> I was called down and found he had just expired while Dr. Meller was at his side. I had carefully gone over all the abdominal and thoracic organs only two hours before and then he answered quite sensibly. I found nothing out of place . . . the organs were all healthy except the spleen which was enlarged and quite soft and in fact almost fluid. It broke to pieces when lifted up. . . . The duodenum [first part of the small intestine] was congested and contained a quantity of dark fluid like coffee grounds [suggesting internal bleeding]. The blood in the heart was very slightly coagulated and no fibrinous clots existed. It seemed to me that there was no lesion to cause death and the state of the blood must be looked on as the real cause. . . . In many cases we see the kidneys run off fluid like blood. This is a safety valve and a means of clearing out the poison particularly when the liver, which seems to be the natural excretory of it fails.[1]

Illness and hardship continued to surround Kirk. Demands on him, both as a physician and crew member, were unceasing. The danger from malaria was particularly high because Dr. Meller had brought with him unbleached quinine rather than the salt, quinine sulfate. The unbleached variety was quickly shown to be ineffective, for even large doses did not produce a ringing in the ears or the temporary deafness of cinchonism that was expected from the potent preparation.

Making matters worse for Kirk, Livingstone was in a particularly sour mood. Kirk wrote in his journal, referring to his botanical and animal specimens, "My goods at Tete keep me, and they are the only things."[2]

When the *Pioneer* finally arrived at Kongone on January 30, 1862, the explorers saw two British ships already anchored outside the bar, the navy vessel *Gorgon* and the brig *Hetty Ellen,* which carried Mary Livingstone, Anne Mackenzie and her two servants, Helen Burrup, and a fresh crop of missionaries.

The Stewart Affair

It had been three years since Livingstone had left Cape Town and Mary had returned to Scotland with their new baby. She had subsequently quarreled with the Livingstone family and moved with her children into a boarding house. There she had met the missionary James Stewart, a tall, thirty-one-year-old bachelor with a short beard and wavy, auburn hair.

Rumors of their purported affair may have already reached Cape Town because Stewart was given a decidedly cold reception by the church authorities. More likely, however, it was Stewart's Presbyterian, evangelistic fervor that earned him so many enemies among the predominantly Anglican British. The Anglican bishop of Cape Town tried to persuade him to return to Scotland and even offered to pay his fare back, but Mary insisted that if he went back she would go with him.

Clearly, Mary, now forty-one, was deeply attached to Stewart. But there is no objective evidence that their relationship was more than simple friendship. In his own writings, Stewart never admits to anything but being friendly and helpful to her. After reading her husband's *Missionary Travels,* he professed that he had the greatest respect not only for her but for Livingstone himself.

Reunited at Last

At 8 A.M., the *Pioneer,* piloted by Livingstone, crossed the bar separating the Kongone River from the sea and approached the two British ships. Livingstone appeared shocked at first to find Stewart on board the *Hetty Ellen* with Mary, although he had already been warned that the young man was among those on their way to the Magomero mission (see Map 2 on page 17 and Map 5 on page 91).

Stewart described his feelings when he first saw David Livingstone:

> I could not help remarking to Mrs. Livingstone that the Doctor seemed to be a great swell. It must be confessed that in his white trousers, frock coat and naval cap he looked uncommonly smart and really had a commanding air. . . . About 8 o'clock the Pioneer glided in between the Gorgon and the brig. We thought he was going on board the Gorgon and Mrs. Livingstone's countenance fell, but he glided on. . . . Mrs. Livingstone had not seen him and I disturb her or perturb her by saying, "There he is." I allow her emotion to subside and then add he is etc. She gives me a gratified slap for so speaking of the great pioneer and prince of travellers on whom I have just set my admiring eyes.[3]

Was Stewart writing tongue in cheek? We do not know. Nor do we know how Livingstone learned about the slap. Something could have been said by Anne Mackenzie, the bishop's elderly sister, who vied with Rae as the foremost gossip-monger among the new arrivals.

It was certainly unusual for a Victorian woman, a woman whose father and brother were missionaries, to playfully slap a man unless they had been physically intimate. On the other hand, Lady Edna Healey, Mary's biographer, believes Stewart regarded her as a surrogate mother, while Mary leaned on him for help while maintaining platonic comfort in his company.[4] One of Livingstone's biographers claims that as the others got to know Stewart, they agreed that he was innocent, but simply lacked discretion: "His nocturnal visits to Mary's room were to bring comfort to her when she was depressed, laudanum[5] when hysterical and censure when intemperate."[6]

Kirk commented in his journal of the relationship:

> I suspect that all this came out of a scandal caused by the injudicious conduct of both. No doubt, he hoped to gain influence with Dr. L. through her. Certainly he did so and as he knew her character and professes (confidentially to me, so don't speak of it) to have found out early in the day that she drank very freely, so as to be utterly besotted at times, I think any prudent man would have drawn off from such a person, instead of going in late hours into a married woman's bedroom and to prevent the people becoming aware, studiously keeping even the landlady of the house out, lest she should find out the secret. Of course, the truth soon became well known and Mr. Stewart's visits had an interpretation placed upon them and quite naturally too.[7]

In other journal entries, Kirk remarked, "The company, in addition to our former number, is Mrs. L., a coarse, vulgar woman whose behavior with a missionary [Mr. Stewart] seems to have caused some scandal," and "[Stewart] seems to be an active man, but if there is truth in the stories, he will make mischief yet. As to Mrs. L. she seems cut out for rough work, but she is a queer piece of furniture."[8]

From the outset, Livingstone made no effort to be friendly to Stewart, but then again, as far as we know, he did not question either Stewart or Mary about their relationship. On the contrary, at least outwardly, he was elated to have her with him and treated her with great tenderness and love.

Heading for Shupanga

The new steam launch, the *Lady Nyassa,* which Livingstone had paid for with profits from his book, had been built to his specifications under Rae's supervision and brought in sections. Livingstone had the sections put on the *Pioneer*'s deck so that they could be assembled at Shupanga. This diminished available deck space and so overloaded the *Pioneer* that it listed.

Livingstone had arranged with Bishop Mackenzie to reunite him with his sister and Burrup with his wife by the end of 1861, and they were already over a month late. In order to avoid further delay, he asked Kirk to take the women and the new missionaries in the *Gorgon*'s gig and whaler to the prearranged meeting place at the junction of the Ruo and Shire rivers.

They all left Kongone Harbor on February 17, 1862, the *Pioneer* laden with the sections of the *Lady Nyassa* and towing two rowboats. Also on the *Pioneer* were fifty sailors from the *Gorgon* who would be stationed at the Magomero mission to defend it against the Ajwas. In the gig were Dr. Ramsey, the ship's surgeon; Stewart; several other missionaries; the assistant purser of the *Gorgon,* Devereux; four sailors; and five women: Mary Livingstone, Anne Mackenzie, her housekeeper and her maid, and Helen Burrup. Kirk accompanied them in the whaler.

Manned by bluejackets, the four-oared gig with its single sail made its way slowly upstream, and the newcomers quickly learned what it was like to travel on the Zambezi. Lack of mosquito netting caused great discomfort, especially at night, and all aboard suffered from the close confinement and suffocating heat in the open boat during the fifteen-day trip to Chibisa's.

"Our men were growling and moaning incessantly" because of the mosquitoes, Devereux wrote. "They were lying sprawling in every direction, feet bound up with coloured kerchiefs, gaiters, and boots; heads in worsted caps, coats and blankets; bodies in blanket frocks. . . . [they] prefer semi-suffocation to the bites of their tormentors. But it was no joking matter, and want of sleep was telling rapidly on them."[9]

To make matters worse, the bishop's elderly sister, Anne, who occupied the stern, was so badly afflicted by arthritis she couldn't move without help. "She was unable to place one foot in front of the other. If she decided to shift her position, she had to get assistance and to have herself supported with pillows. The daily laundry was a serious job, a bower or shelter had to be constructed and she carried into it. Mrs. Burrup on the contrary was full of life, talked nautical and jumped about," Kirk wrote.[10]

Anne Mackenzie and George Rae continued to fan the rumors of infidelity on the little craft to the point that Stewart, fed up with these two and frustrated by the boredom and difficulty of the trip, felt obliged to write to Livingstone that "to Mrs. Livingstone I always acted with the same ease and freedom as if she had been my mother."[11]

A Rendezvous Gone Awry

Anne Mackenzie and Helen Burrup anxiously awaited the reunion with their loved ones, especially Mrs. Burrup, who had been married only recently. While the gig's crew was securing the boat at Chibisa's, however, a runner came with the terrible news: Both Burrup and Bishop Mackenzie were dead.

The pair had left Magomero for the rendezvous in the rain. Their canoe had capsized and their supplies and medicines were lost. Two days later they reached the rendezvous point, well ahead of Kirk's party, but Mackenzie suddenly began to have abdominal pain and profuse diarrhea, and was soon seriously dehydrated. He managed to write a letter to his sister on January 16, telling her that he and Burrup had passed their time during the torrential rains in an abandoned hut reading Saint Paul's Epistle to the Romans to each other in the original Greek.

Mackenzie's diarrhea soon worsened. In spite of Burrup's efforts, he could not retain fluid or food and became comatose, dying on January 31, 1862. Burrup too was developing the same symptoms and becoming weaker by the day. The Makololo porters had to carry him by canoe and on a stretcher to Magomero, where three weeks later he too died.

Anne Mackenzie handled the dreadful news remarkably well, at least externally, unlike Helen Burrup, a vivacious young woman in her early twenties, barely married three months, who had been eager to finally join her husband in his missionary work. Now she would return home a widow with an uncertain future.

Kirk diagnosed the dead missionaries' symptoms as most likely cholera. Both men had shared close quarters with 200 African converts at the mission, all using the same contaminated drinking water, and others had already died with the same symptoms. Because of the epidemic, Kirk decided to go to the mission to see if he could help the survivors. He left with Wilson, the gig's captain, and a handful of porters. Because it was the height of the rainy season, they were constantly wet and themselves suffered from recurrent fevers. By March 8, they were so weak they stayed in an African hut and sent one of the still-healthy Makololo to the mission for food and medicine. To their surprise, three healthy-looking missionaries returned with him, bringing food, quinine, and morphine. They told Kirk that the epidemic had passed and that most of the other missionaries were now quite well.

In spite of the medications, neither Wilson nor Kirk showed much improvement. Wilson, in fact, got much worse. Kirk thought he would die. "The patient's pulse was weak and irregular and almost stopped. It was a chance which way the case would turn. As I went outside the hut I could not help seeing by the starlight the rocky soil—it seemed all stone and rock—and the idea which came with this was the difficulty in digging a grave. But in the small hours the pulse steadied a little, and later in the day Wilson was fit to be carried in an improvised hammock slung on a bamboo."[12]

Meanwhile David Livingstone and Mary were at Shupanga waiting for the gig to return to the *Pioneer.* When Livingstone heard about the deaths of Bishop Mackenzie and Burrup, he said, "This will hurt us all." He sat with his head in his hands in the boat's dimly lit cabin, but after a moment raised his head defiantly and announced, "I shall not swerve a hairbreadth from my work while life is spared."[13] As always, Livingstone was consumed by the passion and conviction that he must complete what he saw as his life's work, spreading the three C's—Christianity, Civilization, and Commerce—no matter what the cost to himself and others.

Stewart, meanwhile, was beginning to resent Livingstone. This may have been due, in part, to the fact that he was unprepared for the miserable life aboard the boat, the mosquito bites, the rain, and the bouts of fever. He became more and more despondent and withdrawn, and seemed unable to get along with the other missionaries.

Livingstone arranged with Kirk to navigate the *Pioneer* to take Anne Mackenzie, her maid and her housekeeper, and broken-hearted Helen Burrup back to Kongone Harbor, where they could board the *Gorgon* for England. In addition, Dr. Meller, who had also shown signs and symptoms of chronic malaria and who had developed, according to Kirk, an enlarged spleen would travel with them. For so many now, the Zambezi was becoming the river of death.

Mary's Decline

The *Lady Nyassa*'s sections had already been unloaded at Shupanga, but her boilers were still at Kongone Harbor, so before steaming back to Shupanga, Kirk and his crew lashed them to the deck of the *Pioneer.* Amazingly, the heavily laden paddle wheeler grounded only once.

When Kirk saw Mary again at Shupanga, he thought she had been overcome with depression, perhaps because of the continuing talk about her and Stewart. But soon the scandal became irrelevant. On April 14, Kirk observed that she was running a fever. In itself, this was not alarming: most of the expedition members had had fevers from malaria, intestinal infections, or both.

But Mary failed to respond to the new quinine intramuscular injections which had just arrived from England. Her fever rose, and she developed shaking chills, followed by intense sweating. Then her hands and feet swelled, and she became jaundiced. A few days later she developed intractable vomiting and was unable to retain food, fluid, or the medicines Kirk administered, and dehydration set in.

Moved into an empty stone house, she promptly lapsed into a coma. Livingstone asked Stewart to join him in prayer at her makeshift bed, a mattress spread over three empty tea cases. Leaning over his dying wife, Livingstone stammered though his sobs: "My dearie, my dearie, you are going to leave me. Are you resting on Jesus?"[14]

Kirk wrote in his journal: "April 27th Mrs. L. became worse, while medicines proved of no avail. I was sent for at 3 A.M., found her in a half comatose state. It was impossible to get medicine taken. Steadily coma deepened into perfect insensibility and the skin tinged of deep yellow and at 7 P.M. she died."[15]

The rapid sequence of events suggests Mary Livingstone died of inflammation of both kidneys and liver from falciparum malaria.

But it also might have been hepatitis, or cirrhosis of the liver brought on by her heavy drinking, complicated by malaria.

Stewart may have felt at least some relief that Livingstone, in his worst hour, had invited him to pray with him. It seemed that Livingstone no longer harbored suspicions against him since the grieving husband drew on him, of all people, for moral support. He wrote, "I had gone down to the ship to get some tea at 6 o'clock, when a message was brought . . . that the Dr. wished me to come up. . . . When I went into the room Dr. L. said the end was evidently drawing near and he had sent for me. . . . The Dr. was weeping like a child. I could not help feeling for him and felt my own eyes full. He asked me to commit her soul to her maker by prayer. He, Dr. Kirk and I kneeled down and I prayed as best I could. In an hour she was dead."[16]

Livingstone then attempted to hide his grief, and barely spoke to others, but in the privacy of his journal he wrote, "It is the first heavy stroke I have suffered, and quite takes away my strength. I wept over her who well deserved many tears. I loved her when I married her and the longer I lived with her I loved her the more. God pity the poor children who were all tenderly attached to her, and I am left alone in the world by one whom I felt to be a part of myself." Mary's death threw him back into a severe depression. Just a few months later he wrote, "I suppose that I shall die in these uplands, and somebody will carry out the plan I have longed to put into practice. I have been thinking a great deal since the departure of my beloved one about the regions whither she has gone." And even a year later he was writing, "Since the death of my Mary I often feel that I have not long to live, but I will do my duty for all that."[17]

The reconciliation between Stewart and Livingstone at the time of Mary's death proved only temporary. Stewart continued to accuse Livingstone of having distorted the truth when he raved about the salubrious climate for British settlement in his lectures and other writings.

Bitten by fire ants and malaria-bearing mosquitoes, Stewart grew more bitter day by day. He took it out on the Africans he met. To him, they were filthy and indulged in degraded practices worse than the habits of animals. He saw the Manganjas as "great cowards and liars."[18] His view of the town's environment was not much more positive when he visited Tete later that year. In December 1862, Stewart described Tete thusly:

> If one can fancy a bare slope of sandstone ledges, slightly, but very slightly, covered with soil, destitute of grass and almost every

> green thing, and having innumerable water worn ruts, large and small, as if it had been recently the scene of a generous and ruinous inundation, he will have a tolerable notion of the site of Tete. On this site place two parallel rows of detached houses forming two streets. The houses stand apart from each other and are generally raised high above the surrounding level on a sort of small mound. . . . They are built generally of stone and plastered with mud, which the rains wash away. . . . There is a church, a large shapeless building; a public burial ground and a small building used as and called a public hospital. . . . The health of the soldiers is not very good. Fever and dysentery are the prevailing diseases. . . . Conspicuous near the river is that institution peculiar to slave-holding countries, the whipping post.[19]

The *Lady Nyassa*

Preparing the *Lady Nyassa* for launching was a slow, complicated process. Livingstone ordered Kirk to take the *Pioneer* up to Tete and bring back equipment and tools to complete the assembly of the new steam launch. While there, Kirk ran into difficulties with the governor, who upset by Livingstone's anti-Portuguese bias and frequent trips up and down the Portuguese-controlled Zambezi River, denigrated the whole expedition and insisted that the Portuguese had the right to trade in slaves. He refused to acknowledge the discovery of Lake Nyassa by Livingstone, bolstering Kirk's suspicion that the Portuguese had discovered it years earlier. The English should stop meddling in the affairs of others, he said, before announcing that the expedition and the missionaries were no longer welcome. Kirk kept his thoughts to himself, remained courteous, and returned to Shupanga with the necessary equipment. This may have been his first important action in international diplomacy.

When Kirk returned, an embittered but stubborn Livingstone once more took the *Pioneer* down to Kongone Harbor, this time to pick up the remaining supplies unloaded by the British ships. Kirk in the meantime supervised the assembly of the *Lady Nyassa* and photographed its completion.

He also met Richard Thornton, the expedition's original geologist, who had recovered his health and, instead of returning to England, had gone climbing on Mount Kilimanjaro with Baron Von der Decken, a German explorer. Thornton offered to rejoin the expedition on condition that he be given more freedom. Livingstone agreed, and they signed a new contract.

The *Lady Nyassa* was launched at Shupanga, on June 23, 1862, but the stern went into the water too precipitously, almost causing the launch to sink. It was emptied of water, but Rae refused to install the engines until the boat had been towed to just below Murchison Cataracts on the Shire, disassembled, and then reassembled above them. Then it would be able to steam up the rest of the river to Lake Nyassa.

At this point, the missionaries at Magomero were under virtual siege by the Ajwas. After consulting with Livingstone, they decided to move their mission to higher ground at Mikorongo nearer Chibisa's. This change, they hoped, would offer them better protection and reduce the risk of malaria. After the missionaries left Magomero, the Ajwas attacked the Manganjas again, and some of the Makololo converts who had acquired firearms began stealing Manganja cattle, levying tribute and shooting those who resisted. Adding to the turmoil, the Portuguese-African bandit Belchior also raided the Manganjas until he was chased off by the Portuguese.

Stewart showed none of Livingstone's or Kirk's compassion for the victims of these raids. In his journal he described the inhabitants of a Manganja village as:

> saucy, suspicious liars. There was not a soul in this village whose countenance I liked. They were all saucy, insolent and savage. One fatted cow, with an infant at her breast and a load of brass rings on her fat legs and ankles, was particularly loud and noisy. . . . That man must be more or less than human who cannot be disgusted to his very inmost soul at the selfishness, rapacity and vile habits of those savages.[20]

Return to the Rovuma

Above Shupanga, the *Lady Nyassa*'s draft proved too deep for the Zambezi, now shallow again during the dry season. The explorers were forced to wait another six months in the hot, damp lower Zambezi for the water to rise again in the rainy season so that they could take it up the Shire to Lake Nyassa. During the long wait, Kirk thought seriously of returning to England. He had brought his personal effects and scientific collections down from Tete and up the Shire to Chibisa's for storage.

Packing them up and taking them by canoe to Kongone or Quelimane would be no problem. But, he realized, he was the only effective doctor on the expedition, as Livingstone's medicine had become "a little rusty." Kirk was also afraid that if he left so soon after Mary's death, Livingstone might feel he had deserted him in his time of greatest need and would not give him a good recommendation when they returned to England. A cautious and realistic man, Kirk believed his future might well depend on Livingstone's attitude toward him.

Livingstone himself now entered a new manic phase, according to biographer Oliver Ransford. Believing that the *Pioneer* could well manage an ocean voyage, he sailed it at the end of August 1862 to Johanna,[21] the British naval base and coaling station in the Comoro Islands, to pick up more oxen to use hauling the parts of the *Lady Nyassa* in carts around the Murchison Cataracts. But after tying up at Johanna, he suddenly made up his mind to pick up the oxen later and to try once more to explore the Rovuma.

Despite the objections of his party, the *Pioneer* entered the Rovuma on September 9, this time escorted by the British naval ship *Orestes.* Though the river had been shown to be clearly unnavigable, Livingstone hoped it might connect with Lake Nyassa. Very quickly, however, he discovered that the water level was as low as the last time. Then Rae suddenly became acutely ill and had to be evacuated to the *Orestes.*

Kirk himself didn't waste time bemoaning the fact that the *Pioneer* could go no farther upstream. Instead, he concentrated on collecting and observing the local fauna and flora. He found unusual plants growing along the river's banks, such as a *Loranthus* with a spike of scarlet flowers. "The vegetation much resembles that of the Zambezi," he wrote. "Baobabs, Motunda, Sterculius, Borassus [palms], Dates and Hyphanae palms are frequent, the latter having remarkably branched stems."[22]

Livingstone refused to turn back. He ordered Kirk and the other white men into the small boats the *Pioneer* had been towing to continue up the river. Kirk's diary entries over the days that followed show him finally losing patience with the man he wanted to respect. For example:

> September 18. At noon we reach a wide part of the river, very shallow: Still Dr. L. means to drag over it. The infatuation which blinds him I cannot comprehend—getting the boats jammed up a river where they cannot float and where it will soon be impossible to return. . . . It seems madness and to follow a man running such risks for the empty glory of Geographic discovery is more than I would consent to. . . . I can come to no other conclusion than Dr. L is out of his mind.[23]

The next day, a group of armed Makonde tribesmen trailed the canoes Kirk and Livingstone were using for about three miles when a shot fired at a puffadder threw them into panic. The Makonde soon began firing arrows at the boat.[24] "We cannot turn now as they would think we were fleeing and get more insolent," Kirk wrote. After some abortive negotiations, the Makonde drew their arms again, one firing a musket at the whites, who returned the fire. "I at once picked out one of the two men at the bank at one hundred and fifty yards and killed him," Kirk wrote. "Pearce, my coxswain, shot the other standing by him. After this there were no more shots."

But Kirk was conscience-stricken. In attempting to show that his reaction had been justified, he wrote, "We had been driven to this, and have fought in self-defense only. But we must pray God to guide us in the future. We have been doing his work in Africa and trust to his shield. . . . Dr. L's boat's sail has four bullet-holes through it. This shows what was intended . . . we stopped about a mile and a half off and had luncheon. There is no sign of the natives following us, but our sleep tonight will be light."[25]

Two days later they met an Arab who told them that some miles up the Rovuma turned into a little stream too small to navigate and did not connect with Lake Nyassa. He also "advised us not to land among the Makonde as they are robbers, but he did not then know we had just passed them and had a skirmish," Kirk wrote.[26]

On September 25, Kirk wrote: "The river gets worse as we advance. . . . Dr. L. is a most unsafe leader. He never thinks of getting back. All he cares for is accomplishing the object at any risk whatever."[27]

They were still 200 miles east of Lake Nyassa at this point when illness struck again among the party. Kirk's next entry reads, "Sept. 26th. We had not gone half a mile, when we reached the field of rocks, where the water came over with a rush, yet Dr. L. seems intent to take up the boats now. If he does, I can only say that his head is not of ordinary construction but what is termed cracked."[28] On September 30, Kirk remarked that fever in spite of daily doses of quinine—the amount may have been insufficient or it may not have been malaria—had laid three of the crew low.

In spite of hostile encounters and the increasingly unnavigable river, Livingstone only now reluctantly agreed to turn back. It took another twelve days to return to the *Pioneer.*

After deciding he would build a road around the Shire's Murchison Cataracts, Livingstone left the Rovuma on October 18, 1862, for Johanna to purchase additional oxen for the new undertaking.

8

The Expedition Winds Down

Once Kirk and Livingstone had returned to the *Pioneer*, everything that could go wrong almost did. A paddle wheel broke on a rock, and it was hard to repair with the few tools they had. Next, Livingstone sent Kirk and two crewmen upstream to cut wood with nearly disastrous consequences. After much searching, they found the best wood for heating the launch's boiler, ebony, which was also the hardest to cut, only to have a sudden thunderstorm capsize their small boat in the crocodile-infested river; Kirk and his crew were barely able to right the boat. Then Kirk suffered a painful tsetse fly bite, though, fortunately, this particular fly didn't carry sleeping sickness.[1] Finally, a hippopotamus lifted their boat into the air, throwing out the two crewmen while Kirk himself desperately hung on to the craft. The boat miraculously righted itself, and Kirk was then able to rescue the crewmen. The party was thankfully still alive, but once again little progress had been made.

The Expedition's Nadir

The Second Zambezi Expedition seemed stalled in a larger sense, as well. By Christmas 1862, this small, sickly band of Englishmen couldn't point to many signs of success despite almost five years of toil and trouble. True, they had charted a good part of Lake Shirwa and Lake Nyassa and gathered knowledge about the geography and peoples of eastern and central Africa. But, beyond that, legitimate claims had been few and setbacks many.

The explorers had failed in attempts to sail the full length of the Zambezi, the Shire, and now the Rovuma. They hadn't outwitted the Portuguese or been allowed by the Foreign Office to claim Lake Nyassa or any other territory for England. And, of course, they hadn't stopped the slave trade. In fact, they unwittingly aided it by opening up new routes to the interior, which were subsequently used by Portuguese and Arab slavers.

Meanwhile, Livingstone's dream of establishing a string of missions had been thwarted.[2] The few missionaries who were in place—besieged by hostile groups and ravaged by disease—were barely hanging on. Furthermore, despite their peaceful intent, Livingstone's group had again slain Africans, albeit in a pitched battle. In addition, Livingstone had only been able to convert one man to Christianity and that man subsequently relapsed.

When Mary died, something seemed to have snapped in Livingstone's mind. His morbid prediction of his own death worried his friends and his family in the United Kingdom, and the expedition's morale clearly fell as his periods of irrationality increased. It was all too evident to Kirk that Mary's death had changed Livingstone for the worse. Their leader had become increasingly detached from his fellows. He refused to discuss his plans with the others; he gave orders without consulting Kirk; and he would no longer even allow himself to be drawn into arguments with his brother.

Kirk's diary entries during this period indicate not only how upset he was with Livingstone's behavior, but also his own guilt at having killed a man. When he received his medical degree, he had, like other new doctors, taken the Hippocratic oath to heal and do no harm. Yet he had shot a man to death, not in a fusillade where he couldn't be sure if his bullet was actually the one that hit the target, but by deliberately taking aim at a particular person before pressing the trigger.[3]

Though not subject to wide mood swings like Livingstone, Kirk clearly had begun to experience periods of acute anxiety. He appealed to God to protect him and put himself in God's hands for whatever lay in the future. He expressed particular concern over the possibility that the expedition would be attacked again by another tribe.

Kirk thought again about leaving Livingstone and returning to England. Dr. Meller had now rejoined the group after recovering from his acute illness; and E.D. Young, an ex-naval officer, had also been accepted by Livingstone as a member of the expedition. But when Kirk told Livingstone he wanted to leave, Livingstone had a severe attack of dysentery, coincidentally or otherwise, and Kirk loyally decided to stay and treat him.[4]

Trouble at the Mission

Shortly after arrival at Shupanga, Livingstone, Kirk, and their companions met L.J. Proctor, one of the missionaries who was on his way to the coast with porters to get provisions for the new mission at Mikorongo (Mbane). Though the new settlement was on higher ground, the missionaries still suffered from recurrent malaria attacks and one member had died. The mission's physician, Dr. Dickinson, died of blackwater fever, and a tanner employed by the mission, Robert Clarke, began to hallucinate and developed epileptic seizures, though he eventually recovered. This living hell was not improved when Livingstone paid a brief visit and promptly criticized the missionaries for choosing a poor site, drinking too much alcohol, and frittering away their time "collecting butterflies."[5]

Meanwhile, the Ajwas were still raiding Manganjas in the Shire highlands. Charles wrote that the party of a single slaver had captured 450 women to send to the auction block in Zanzibar after killing off their men.[6]

In early January 1863, it rained every day, and the river kept rising. By January 11, the water was deep enough for the *Pioneer* to tow the *Lady Nyassa,* but the party was only able to make two knots an hour against the current.

Unfortunately the *Pioneer* suddenly grounded, and the *Lady Nyassa* immediately crashed into her, bouncing off only to get stuck on a submerged rock. After pulling both boats free, the explorers finally decided to tie them side by side. Four days later they stopped near Mount Morumbala.

Because it was Sunday, Kirk, with Livingstone's permission, went off to stretch his legs and do a little botanizing. After hiking part way up Mount Morumbala, he looked back in horror to see the *Pioneer* and *Lady Nyassa* slowly pulling away from shore. He ran down the mountain as fast as he could and then along the shore, shouting and waving frantically. He could see Livingstone, wearing his pilot's cap, staring steadfastly ahead as he steered the launch upstream. Finally, Livingstone brought the boat into shore and a perspiring, disheveled Kirk hopped aboard.

Livingstone glanced at his pocket watch and said to Kirk without inflection, "This will teach you to be 20 minutes late."

Kirk was furious, but replied only in his diary, where he wrote, "Dr. L's word of honor will not have much value in my mind again.

I have been grossly misused. . . . His subsequent conduct in changing plans which completely tied us to the vessel must have been simply some sort of revenge." Kirk had not only been reprimanded, he had been insulted and treated like a truant by his former idol: "Dr. L told me there were to be no more Sunday excursions, a nice piece of cant piety from him seeing that he had the natives wooding during the very time of Divine Service."[7]

Elephant Marsh Again

When they arrived at Elephant Marsh, they became stuck once more in the fetid swamp. This time the smell was worse as bloated, putrefying Manganja corpses floated around them. How disheartening it must have been for Kirk to stand on the deck amid the stench, listening to the unending croaking of frogs or hearing the flap of vultures' heavy wings as they descended from above while the crocodiles surfaced from below to tear at the rotting Manganja corpses, or else to sit in the small cabin day after day listening to the constant patter of rain on the roof and the water drips inside.

When the weather cleared a bit, Kirk would force himself to return to his scientific pursuits, the best remedy he knew to dispel his gloom. He resumed observing and collecting plants when he could, and once took a small boat to shore to find a hot spring. "The few stones at its source are covered with an encrustation of sulfate of lime and the water smells of sulfurous acid but close to it the grass and trees grow well and show no difference from the increased temperature of the soil or the sulfur and air."[8]

While the boat was stuck in Elephant Marsh, some of the surviving Manganjas paddled over in canoes out of curiosity and to trade. They all looked gaunt, and many were sick and weak. They pointed to their sunken stomachs. The marauders had taken their food, burned their fields and villages, and hundreds of their people were dying of hunger.

After almost a month, the explorers finally freed the launches from the sandbars and reached the new mission, Mikorongo, only to find that Kirk's friend, Reverend H.C. Scudamore, had died on New Year's Day. The weather was hot and sultry, and assuaging his grief, Kirk joined some newly converted ex-slave children playing in the river in an area fenced off from crocodiles. The missionaries had built a rudimentary school for the children, and similar schools were later established at Mombassa on the coast and on Zanzibar Island.

Disease continued to dog the expedition. On February 7, 1863, Kirk made a note in his journal, "Fever plays a great part in making the ship a dull, growling hole."[9] Wilson, one of the stokers, had a severe attack of blackwater fever, and on February 8, the *Lady Nyassa*'s blacksmith also got it.

The missionaries at Mikorongo were short on meat, and Thornton volunteered to try to find some goats. He hiked all the way back to Shupanga before he could buy them, and, after a 330-mile roundtrip, arrived at the mission only to collapse with severe abdominal cramps, chills, and profuse perspiration. Bloody diarrhea and severe dehydration followed. He was unable to sleep; according to Kirk, he would sometimes lie quietly for an hour or two, but then complained of having great mental anguish, with the impression of boiling, thundering noises in his head. His face rapidly became pinched and drawn, and the skin on his neck and fingers shriveled while his pulse became quicker and thinner. After eight days, he began to grow cold. By the tenth day, the pulse and temperature rapidly fell and incoherency set in. He died the next day, April 21, 1863, most likely from cholera.[10]

As if the party hadn't had enough trouble, Rae complained to everyone that he was being persecuted by Livingstone. He wanted to leave, but he was aware that he would have to hike out for miles through rugged and hostile territory. Therefore, he decided to isolate himself on the *Lady Nyassa*. Kirk speculated that cerebral malaria was the source of these personality changes.

Dr. Meller was suffering from recurrent fatigue and despondency in the wake of Thornton's death, and when Meller told Livingstone he wanted to leave again, Kirk reported: "April 28th. Dr. Meller spoke to Dr. L. offering to leave now, believing it would be a saving of rations. . . . There was no longer any need for his services, but he was willing to continue two months longer to complete his time, if that were desired. Dr. L. spoke very harshly accusing him of fear, from seeing so many deaths. . . . Dr. L. said that his time would not be up until 7 months after July and that he should not leave before then without his consent."[11]

The Expedition Recalled

Reports of illnesses and deaths and of continual disagreements among the expedition's members had, by this time, long been reaching England, as had reports of Livingstone's irrational behavior. In spite of Livingstone's grand illusions and tendency to blame others for their setbacks, he was clear-headed enough to realize that he had not fulfilled most of his promises to his supporters. He had failed to find minerals of any worth. The promised rich cotton fields were instead scattered patches. In the long run he had permanently converted no one to Christianity. He thus was not completely surprised when a courier found the *Pioneer* and handed him a letter dated February 2, 1863, from Lord Russell of the Foreign Office:

> Her Majesty's Government fully appreciate the zeal and perseverance with which you have applied yourself to the discharge of duties entrusted to you. They are aware of the difficulties which you must necessarily have met with and they have deeply regretted that your anxieties have been aggravated by severe domestic affliction. Her Majesty's Government cannot, however, conceal from themselves that the results to which they had looked from the expedition under your superintendence have not been realized.[12]

Could anything have been clearer? Lord Russell minced no words. The expedition in his eyes had been a failure. A second letter followed and told Livingstone to expect a British ship at Kongone Harbor sometime in August 1863, to take the remaining expedition members back to England. Livingstone was also ordered to turn the *Pioneer* over to the British navy.

Since Kirk and Charles were still too weak from their bouts of diarrhea to continue overland with him, Livingstone agreed to send them back to England as soon as possible. Kirk, too weary to feel relief at the news that he would finally be going home, and still distressed at the way Livingstone had treated him and the other members of the expedition, added another diary entry describing the leader's attitude: "His manner still very distant, . . . He is savage at being jammed up here. . . . But I believe it is in fact the best thing for him, as he cannot get on with many whites under him."[13]

Kirk became even more upset when Livingstone ordered him to accompany a British sailor and Charles to Quelimane and wait there until they could board a British navy ship. This meant Kirk might have to hang around Quelimane for some time rather than leave on the first available merchant ship. Livingstone also dictated the route he should take back to England, and insisted that if he did not do this, Kirk would have to pay his own passage home. When he saw Kirk's look of dismay, Livingstone, relenting, told Kirk he would pay the fare anyway.

Plate 1

John Kirk at age 28

David Livingstone

Plate 2

Rapids above the Kebrabasa, Zambezi River

Slave caravan carrying ivory tusks

Slave caravan showing wooden slave yokes

Wrought iron slave chains and shackles brought from Africa by Livingstone

Plate 4

Slave woman captured in fishnet

Slave ambush

Zanzibar slave pen

African dwelling with a baobab tree in the background, drawing by John Kirk, c. 1858–1863

Plate 6

KIRKIA ACUMINATA
1. Leaves and fruits. 2. Flowers. 3. Single flower, enlarged.

Kirk botanical specimen, *Kirkia acuminata*

Portrait of Thomas Baines

Mary Moffatt, age 16

The *Ma Robert*, painting by Thomas Baines

Plate 8

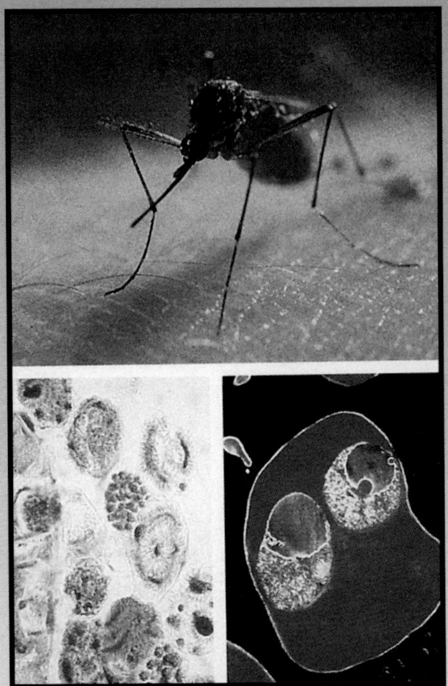

Malaria mosquito

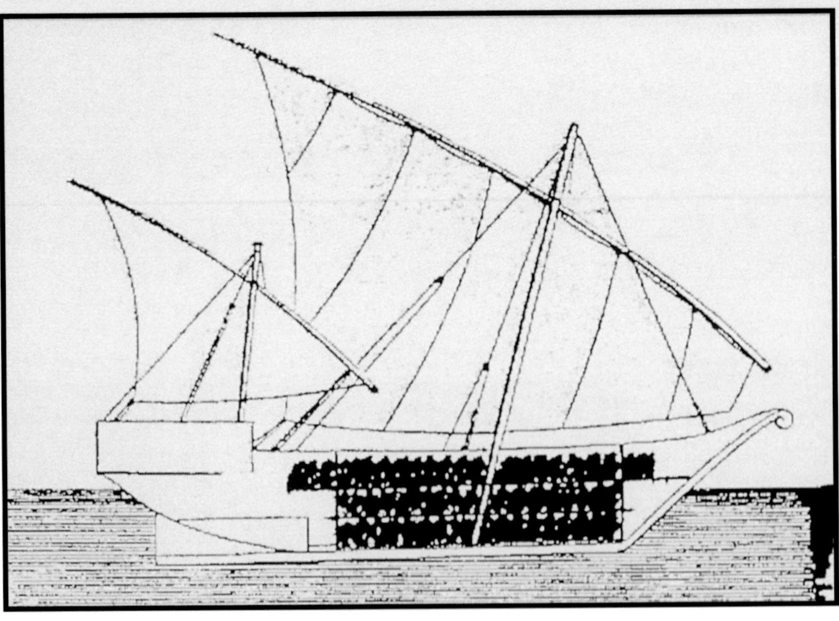

Passenger accommodations on a slave dhow

Livingstone "showed an unkindness that reflects ill on Dr. L's manly character," Kirk commented in his diary. In a later letter to Stewart, he said: "In an underhanded way Dr. Livingstone has given me no cause to thank him . . . , he is about as ungrateful and slippery [illegible] mortal as I ever came in contact with, and although he would be grievously offended to think that anyone doubted his honesty, I am sorry to say that I do."[14]

These were strong words for Kirk. But, trying to be fair, he added: "I believe the explanation to be that he is one of those sanguine enthusiasts wrapped up in their own schemes whose reason and better judgement is blinded by headstrong passion. I don't think he would exactly say what he knew was untrue, but for all practical purposes the result is the same, and in him I believe all kindly feelings to be absolutely extinct."

Stewart was even more direct and plain vindictive. The previous month, when he had been at the mission suffering from fever, he wrote: "Talk at night about Dr. L.: (1) Not fitted for his position (2) His regardless-ness of human suffering (3) Common opinion at Mission that L. in some respects responsible for Bishop's death."[15]

It is remarkable that during the almost six years of dissension and mishaps, Livingstone himself rarely had a bad word to say to others about Kirk. And Kirk, relegating his anger to his diary, would remarkably quickly forgive Livingstone his shortcomings. One could say that Livingstone and Kirk's relationship was ambivalent. Livingstone treated Kirk like a son or a protégé and Kirk did retain enough respect for Livingstone to be a pallbearer at his funeral. After Kirk's departure from the expedition, Livingstone must have realized what a gem Kirk had been on the trip, for he wrote, "our wish to commemorate the name of Dr. Kirk induced us . . . to call the whole chain from the West of the Cataracts up to the north end of the Lake, 'Kirk's Range.'"[16]

Return to the Coast

Kirk, Charles, and the coxswain, Pearce, who was also leaving the expedition early, had a downriver trip beset by more problems. Kirk was suffering from dysentery, Charles was running a fever again, and Pearce had developed a high fever and epileptic fits. Two days after they arrived at Quelimane, one more of the expedition members was added to the list of deaths: Pearce died on June 4.

Kirk's dysentery persisted. After dragging himself to Pearce's funeral, he stayed in bed for a week. Then he and Charles, with whom his relationship had improved, had to wait another month for a ship. Kirk left Quelimane July 4 and landed at Zanzibar on August 20, 1863. He stayed with the British consul, Captain R.L. Playfair, who introduced him to Seyyid Majid, the sultan of Zanzibar. Little did Kirk know at the time that in just a few years he would be returning to this island in a completely different capacity.

Kirk returned to England with the realization that he had helped Livingstone through many difficulties and had saved lives through his medical skills. He had collected plants and animals never before seen by Europeans and, with Livingstone, had laid eyes on places no other white man ever had. He had also faced hostile tribes, observed the awful conditions of slavery, and seen much suffering and death. He had narrowly averted his own death several times. He had been seasoned by discord, war, suffering, and illness and had endured the trial of coping with his famous companion's double-sided nature.

Now, at age thirty-one, Kirk felt it was time to decide where he would practice medicine and consider marriage and raising a family.

Livingstone's Continuation

Freed now from his contentious brother and no longer having to face Kirk as his silent conscience, Livingstone had one more manic spurt on this trip. Hurrying to complete his latest project before the recall deadline in August, he had the Africans in his employ finish the thirty-mile road around Murchison Rapids on the Shire. But, after careful thought, he decided there were neither enough porters nor enough time to dismantle the *Lady Nyassa* and portage her in sections around the cataracts. Therefore, he had Rae, with whom he had become reconciled, install the engines in the *Lady Nyassa* and ready her for return to Kongone Harbor.

Meanwhile, accompanied by E.D. Young, four white sailors from the *Pioneer,* a handful of Makololo who were still loyal to him, and some porters, Livingstone marched 150 miles up the west shore of Lake Nyassa. Instead of completing the trip to the north end of the lake—the long-sought goal—he turned west to follow the Loangwa (Dwangwa) River for another hundred miles, possibly in the vague hope of finding the source of the Nile or the Congo River. He stopped briefly at Nkhotakota, a notorious slave emporium some seventy miles from the southern end of the lake, where he was courteously received by the Arab slave dealers.

Time was running out for Livingstone, but he had to delay his return to Kongone by six months while waiting for the rains to raise the water level so the two steamers could proceed downstream. He finally arrived at Kongone in February 1864, where he dutifully turned the *Pioneer* over to the command of a British man-of-war. By this time more of a geographic explorer than a missionary, David Livingstone had already decided that after visiting England he would again return to Africa and attempt to find the true sources of the Nile and Congo Rivers.

Because Livingstone had paid £6,000 of his own money for the *Lady Nyassa,* he decided to steam on to Zanzibar, where he hoped to sell her; once he arrived there, he found no takers. Then he embarked on a remarkable, 2,500-mile open-sea voyage in the small ship to Bombay, India. Not many days from Zanzibar the supply of wood he had taken on board to feed the steam boilers was exhausted, forcing him to use the sail.

By sheer luck, when less than half the distance to Bombay, he was spotted by the British navy vessel *Ariel,* which offered to tow him the rest of the way. Livingstone accepted gratefully, but no sooner was the *Lady Nyassa* secured by cable to the larger ship than a hurricane swept down on them. Livingstone wrote:

> The captain offered to lower a boat if I would come to the *Ariel,* but it would have endangered all in the boat: the waves dashed so hard against the sides of the vessel it might have been swamped, and by my going away would have taken the heart out of those that remained . . . we then passed a terrible night, but the *Lady Nyassa did* wonderfully well, rising like a little duck over the foaming billows. . . . If we had gone down we would not have been helped in the least—pitch dark, and with wind whistling above.[17]

After reaching Bombay, Livingstone changed his mind about selling the seaworthy little ship. He would use her when he returned to Africa to search for the sources of the Nile and Congo Rivers, he decided. Once back in England, he would see his children and write a book about the Second Zambezi Expedition. If it sold as many copies as *Missionary Travels* had, there would be enough funds for his new exploits.

In the Wake of the Expedition

After leaving for the Seychelles on September 4, 1863, Livingstone arrived in England after a thirty-three-day voyage. The expedition had brought him a sea of disappointments and only a few islands of success; but they were sufficient to prompt him to call for a renewed attempt to bring the three C's to Africa.[18]

Livingstone was welcomed in England warmly, but without the same degree of adulation he had received on the previous occasion. The newspapers had learned from his detractors of his tendency to exaggerate the benefits of the areas he explored and had become a bit more cautious. The recent exploits of Richard Burton and James Hanning Speke in discovering Lakes Tanganyika and Victoria, and Speke's claim that the outlet of Lake Victoria was one of the sources of the Nile,[19] appeared to outweigh Livingstone's accomplishments.

Nonetheless, Livingstone was embraced by the antislavery organizations because he had been the only one among the better-known explorers to point an accusing finger at the Portuguese and Arab slave trade. After seeing his children and his parents in Scotland, Livingstone began a lecture circuit to raise money for a new expedition. He was guest of honor at the Royal Academy and at the Lord Mayor's banquet in London. At Bath he spoke on the evils of slavery to an audience of 1,500, large for that time.

He then spent several months at Newstead Abbey, Mansfield, Nottinghamshire, with his friends, Mr. and Mrs. Frederick William Webb, whom he had met in South Africa while they were on a hunting safari. Livingstone's brother Charles and his daughter Agnes joined him there, and drawing upon his diaries and his brother's, Livingstone spent the next eight months writing *Narrative of an Expedition to the Zambezi and Its Tributaries and Discovery of Lakes Shirwa and Nyassa.* It was agreed that Charles would receive the profits of the American edition.

Kirk, who was frequently called on for consultation and who spent a few weeks with them, provided some of his photographs but was not interested in any kind of authorial collaboration. Nevertheless, Livingstone acknowledged his contribution in the introduction to his *Narrative:*

> The reason Dr. Kirk's name does not appear on the title page of this narrative is because it is hoped that he may give an account of the botany and natural history of the expedition in a separate work from his own pen. He collected about 4000 species of plants, specimens of the most valuable woods, of the different native manufactures, of the articles of food, and of the different kinds of cotton from every spot we visited, and a great variety of birds and insects besides making meteorological observations, and affording, as our instructions required, medical assistance to the natives in every case where he could be of use.[20]

This was magnificent praise from a man who a few months earlier had refused to reveal his plans to Kirk, had verbally abused him, and had forced him to risk his life for reasons that defied all logic. Now Livingstone was brandishing the banner of peace to entice Kirk to write his natural history of eastern and central Africa.

Livingstone wrote once more to Kirk:

> You will excuse me if I urge you to reconsider the subject. I am purposely avoiding anything like a scientific description, having said in the introduction that it is hoped that you will give the botany and natural history of the expedition (in the way that Darwin did of the Beagle's voyage). . . . I would give you the proof sheets, that you might see if I encroached too much on your providence—and give you any information I could on some of the animals—though I dare say you know more on that subject than I do. All the works of natural history would be at your disposal.[21]

Not pushed by the desire to see his name in print, and more interested in securing his future career, Kirk remained only a consultant for the Livingstone book. He never did write a natural history of his own.

Charles Livingstone did not return to his parish in New York state. He entered British politics and, thanks to his brother's contacts, was appointed consul to Fernando Po, a Spanish-owned island off West Africa, in 1864. He died in 1873.

In spite of knowledge of his failures during this last expedition, Livingstone had, in England and most of the Western world, become a mythic figure. His *Narrative* became, as he had hoped, another best-seller, and was read avidly by a British public, which seemed to have an insatiable appetite for vicarious thrills, adventures, and encounters with strange people and their very different customs.

With Livingstone's prestige very high, the Royal Geographic Society asked him to serve as a moderator in a debate between two explorers that had had a falling out. Speke and Burton had discovered Lake Tanganyika, and Speke had gone off on his own to find Lake Victoria and claim it was the source of the Nile. Burton, however, subsequently refused to believe his companion had discovered the Nile's source. Speke had then returned to Africa with another explorer, James A. Grant and, supported by Grant, returned to England convinced he had indeed found the true source of the Nile; but Burton still refused to accept his claim. The public debate between these two protagonists was to be held at Bath in September 1864.

Unfortunately, it never took place. Speke died while hunting, either from a self-inflicted wound or accident, when his loaded gun went off. Though Livingstone was as upset as everyone by Speke's death, he derived some satisfaction from knowing his reputation was still secure enough to have been chosen to moderate the debate.

By the time the *Narrative* was published in 1865, Livingstone had already invited Kirk to join him on his new expedition, but Kirk politely refused. He wanted a stable job, he explained, and he needed a salary sufficient to support the family he hoped to have. Then Livingstone heard of another opening in Africa through the British government and immediately recommended Kirk for the job. It was an intriguing idea to the still-young doctor.

Despite their sufferings, the deaths of loved ones and friends, and their battle with slave raiders and hostile Africans, both Kirk and Livingstone found themselves inexorably drawn back to the land where beauty and cruelty were inseparably intertwined. Memories of their hardships were soon eclipsed by visions of the wide, serpentine rivers bordered with lush vegetation and the greatest variety of wildlife in the world. They were haunted by the majestic sunsets and serene dawns, the horizons framed by lacy acacias, the distant mountain peaks shining roseate in the rising sun, the sounds and sights of the dense jungles, the cliffs and crags, and one of the most spectacular waterfalls on earth.

Both yearned to return to Africa. For Livingstone, it was the dream of becoming even more famous by finding the sources of the Nile and Congo. For Kirk, it was the quieter goal of earning a living in medicine, pursuing his other interests, and settling down with a young woman he had recently met.

9

Making a New Life in Zanzibar

John Kirk had himself been received with enthusiasm back in Britain. Although not considered as great a public figure as Livingstone by his home-country's intellectual community, Kirk was regarded as not only an explorer but also a scientist. After his return from the Zambezi, he worked with Professor Hooker at the Royal Botanical Gardens at Kew, compiling data on many unknown plants and some 350 animal and bird skins he had brought back from Africa. Although tempted to buy a country medical practice he had heard was for sale in the west of England, he decided not to pursue the post. When offered positions as chief botanist at the Botanic Gardens of Bombay and then on the island of Mauritius, he turned them down as well, fearing that promotion was not that certain and that the salaries would remain meager.[1]

In the months following his return, Kirk was invited frequently to races, hunts, balls, and soirées. At one of these gatherings, he met Helen Cook, the charming daughter of a general medical practitioner in Worcestershire. As keen for adventure and exotic places as Kirk was, she listened intently as he told her about the slave-trade horrors he had seen, the ambush by the Ajwas, the fight with the Makondes, the near-drownings, and the many other adventures he had had on the Livingstone expedition.

She soon fell in love with this handsome, soft-spoken man with his sweet, Scots burr, and he with her. With her parents' approval, they became engaged. The man she'd chosen was by now an experienced physician tempered by the almost six years spent in Africa. He not only followed her own father's profession but was a botanist of renown. Best of all, he had a fine, upright character.

Kirk, however, was not one to be rushed. It would be best to delay their marriage until he was sure he could make a decent living, he said, and she reluctantly agreed to leave the date open. They would both be surprised by the place and circumstances of their eventual union.

A Marriage Deferred, an Opportunity Seized

Captain Playfair, the British consul at Zanzibar, whom Kirk had met while passing through on his way home, had become severely ill with malaria and had recently returned to England. When Livingstone heard that the consulship was now vacant, he knew just the man to fill it. He contacted his acquaintance, Sir Bartle Frere, the governor of Bombay, whose jurisdiction included the British consular office at Zanzibar, and recommended Kirk for the position.[2]

On New Year's Day, 1866, Kirk received a letter from Livingstone, who had apparently forgotten the periods of friction between them and thought of Kirk fondly, recalling his steadiness of character and reliability during the Zambezi expedition. He had assured Frere, Livingstone wrote, that Kirk had "no defect of character, or temper. You got on well with people, but were firm in doing your duty etc. And I felt certain, that from your hatred of the slave trade and knowledge of the whole subject, you would be invaluable at Zanzibar." Livingstone went on to suggest that should Kirk get the job, Livingstone might help him set up a slave-free zone near the Rovuma River, which separated Portuguese East Africa from the sultan of Zanzibar's mainland possessions (see Map 6 on page 94).[3]

Frere, however, felt that a more politically experienced individual than Kirk was needed. Since the sultanate controlled most of the mainland of what would become known as East and Southern Africa, the British consular post in Zanzibar was a key one. He appointed instead a man already familiar with Zanzibari politics, Dr. G.E. Seward, the consulate's surgeon.

Livingstone next suggested that Kirk be given the now vacant surgeon's post. To this Frere agreed. Kirk was flattered by the offer, though first he wanted to discuss its ramifications with his fiancée.

Helen Cook had never been out of England. Was it fair to ask her to live so far from her family? He told her what he knew about the tropical island from his brief visit there: the heat, its Indian traders, its masses of black slaves, its veiled women, and wealthy Arab overlords. He described the dangers of malaria and cholera, though he acknowledged that London had just been through its own cholera epidemic. As far as malaria was concerned, he was quite sure that pure quinine in the proper dose would control the disease. There would not be much money, but one could live cheaply on the island. Thrilled at a chance to help Kirk in his new work and excited at the prospect of living with him on an exotic, tropical island, Helen urged him to accept the position.

Kirk, though, felt the salary was really not enough to support a wife and future family. He asked Livingstone to see if it could be augmented. As a result, Kirk was given two other appointments by Frere: assistant to the political officer[4] and vice-consul. Both carried stipends and would give him enough of a salary increase for the couple to live comfortably.

Kirk left England on April 24, 1866, with the idea that Helen would join him after he became established in Zanzibar. Horace Waller, who had met Kirk and Livingstone on the Zambezi, saw him off. In a letter to James Stewart he wrote: "poor fellow, I pity him very much for he of the hard exterior gave way at last. He was engaged shortly before he left to a most delightful girl, a Miss Cook; her friends would not hear of their being married now, so waiting has to be the order of the day, he at the ends of the earth, she longing to be with him for better or worse. . . . She is so nice, refined, hearty, good and very genuine. Kirk, a man of great taste, could not well choose anything else."[5]

After crossing France and the Mediterranean, Kirk spent a sweltering seven hours traveling by train from Alexandria to Cairo. Then he crossed the Sahara to the port of Suez on the Red Sea, where a British ship took him to the Seychelles. There, Kirk boarded the *Highflyer,* a British naval vessel bound for Zanzibar.

At the beginning of June, some six weeks after Kirk had left England, the British man-of-war put in at Zanzibar Harbor. The picturesque town was teaming with Arab dhows, European and American sailing and steam ships, and other vessels from all over the world. The harbor was the scene of constant activity and noise as bundles of cloves, vanilla pods, pepper, cinnamon bark, and other spices, as well as India rubber, gum copal (a resin used to make varnish), wild animal skins, sesame seeds, and ivory were taken to the customs shed to be invoiced and taxed by the sultan's officials before being shipped overseas. And among the cargo were long columns of unfortunates being marched by their guards to the docks for boarding on slave ships bound for Arabia and other lands.

Stonetown

Eighty thousand people—but among them not more than sixty Europeans—lived in Stonetown, the only city and port on the island. Most residents were cramped together in multistoried box-like houses made of stone and plaster. The sultan's palace, the homes of other rich Arabs and Indian merchants, and the European consulates were the only substantial buildings. Even the mosques lacked the grandeur of others in the Muslim world, being only single-story, white-washed structures. Some 220,000 black Africans made up the remainder of the island's estimated 300,000 population. Some were free and lived in a forest of tenements inland, bereft of the cooling sea breezes. But the great majority were slaves, either domestic or plantation workers. Plantation slaves cultivated between the rows of the twenty-foot-high clove trees, dug irrigation ditches, and harvested plantains, oranges, lemons, limes, coconuts, mangoes, vanilla beans, and cinnamon, among other vegetables and fruits. Because so many had been captured or bought from different tribes and often could not understand each other's native languages, they learned to speak Swahili.

Most of the island's commerce was controlled by the 4,000 Arab plantation owners and the 6,000 Indian Muslim merchants then known as Banyans. The energetic Banyan businessmen had gradually preempted the export trade of cloves, spices, India rubber, and ivory from the more indolent Arabs on the island and had gained preeminence in the coastal towns on the mainland that made up the sultanate. Considered British subjects with the same rights as British citizens, the Banyan merchants had also begun to finance the Arab slave trade in great measure by the time Kirk arrived.

The British consulate and those of France, the United States, and Germany lined the waterfront. These were simple two- or three-story affairs, distinguished from each other mainly by the national flag each one flew. A little to the right, as one approached by sea, was the sultan's palace, higher and more ornate, with its blood-red flag flapping in the breeze. Some of the streets nearby were as narrow in places as the width of a Somali donkey, and they remain that way today. The wealthy Arabs, Banyans, and a few European merchants lived in stone houses crowding each other along the waterfront. Their particular architecture had a decidedly Moorish appearance, with balconies framed by ornate iron balustrades. The doors leading to the streets were made of polished hardwoods and were handsomely carved. The cobblestoned, winding lanes teemed with pack animals led by slaves. Kirk could hear the cries of sweating men pulling handcarts and hawkers shouting their wares. He could see slaves trotting along the streets carrying litters in which women dressed in rich Indian gowns or covered from head to foot in black cotton cloth were curtained against prying eyes. And he could observe Zanzibar's men, women, and children, free-born and slaves, who would stop to bargain at the myriad of small shops along the streets or in the market squares, squeezing against the stone-walled houses to let the litter-carrying slaves pass.

The wind from inland brought the smell of spices, but from the sea, all too frequently, there was the stench of the rotting corpses of slaves tossed into the waters and then washed back on shore. Miles of pure, white, sandy beach were also heavily contaminated with piles of refuse and the rotting carcasses of rats, dogs, and cats.

The closeness of the houses to each other, and Zanzibar's general lack of public sanitation, acted as an incubator in the hot and humid climate for malaria, cholera, intestinal parasites, and other such infections. Captain Playfair certainly had not been the first among the British delegation to become a victim, Kirk learned, nor would he be the last. He wrote to Helen shortly after his arrival about the tropical diseases that had killed some of his predecessors at the consulate or forced them to be invalided back to England, and wondered again if he should risk asking her to join him.

While Stonetown may have resembled Elizabethan London in its narrow streets and lack of sanitation, there was one obvious enormous social difference: the presence of hundreds of slaves being auctioned off to Arabs, Persians, and other representatives of the Ottoman Empire at the great outdoor slave market. There, Kirk could hear Arab plantation owners in traditional headdresses and flowing robes vigorously shouting their bids for their fellow humans chained on the auction block.

The captives who had survived the long journey from their mainland villages were kept next to the slave market in an underground holding pen (or barracoon). The pen was divided into male and female sections, each about twenty by thirty feet in size. As a security precaution, the ceiling of the pen was low, less than four feet from the ground, except in a small area in the center where only a few of the captives could stand up at a time. Estimates as to

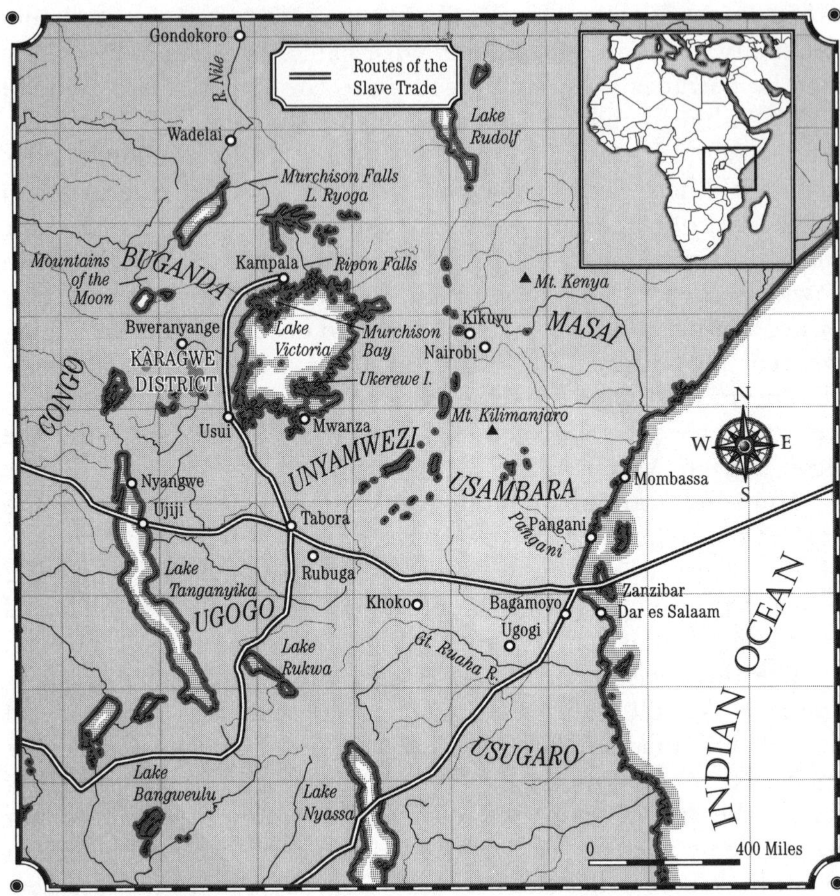

MAP 7 *Arab Slave Routes to Zanzibar Before 1873.*

the number of slaves sold per month ranged from five hundred to two thousand depending on the success of a slave raid and the death rate along the route from the interior (see Map 7 on page 128).

The Economy of the East African Slave Trade

It may have struck Kirk many times as ironic that he, who had been part of Livingstone's attempts to stop the slave trade, found himself now at the very center of its East African market. Colonel A. Hammerton, former British consul to Zanzibar, wrote in 1865: "In no part of the world is the misery and human suffering the wretched slaves undergo while being brought here, and until they are sold . . . ; they are in such a wretched state from starvation and disease that they are sometimes not considered worth landing, and are allowed to expire in boats to save the duty of a dollar a head, and eaten by the dogs."[6]

In 1861, the British consul in Zanzibar, C.P. Rigby, tried to put a complete stop to slavery on Zanzibar and the sultan's other territories. He freed the slaves of 4,000 Indian Banyans only to discover that after he left his post, they were re-enslaved by the Arabs on the island and sold back to the Banyans themselves.[7]

According to a description by British consul Captain R.L. Playfair, "The purchaser walks up to one he liked the looks of and throws a stick at some distance and tells the slave to pick it up. By this he has a chance to see his gait or if there is any lameness. He is then taken apart from the rest of the group and examined from head to foot [every part of their body]." Playfair also made the point that once purchased by an Arab and converted to Islam, the slave's misery seemingly ceased. "Many of the slaves are sent to school [Koranic] and obtain as good an education as some of the head Arabs of the place." This applied only to the men. If a woman was attractive, she could become her Arab master's concubine, and, like the Portuguese mestizos, some African-Arab descendants became slave masters themselves.[8]

Beachey writes, "At Unyanyembe in Unyamwezi, there were unaccountable aspects of the slave trade, at least in the eyes of humanitarians in England. For the Wanyamwezi had entered into the business of slaving with gusto, and were either slavers on their own or acted as agents for the Arabs. They captured slaves in tribal wars and obtained them by purchase. . . . The Wanyamwezi were cruel masters compared to the Arabs, and treated their slaves as if they were on the level of animals. The slaves, however, did not seem to mind this much, and though apparently feeling keenly the separation from friends, rarely attempted to run away. And slaves emulated their masters in the matter of slave holding, and themselves possessed slaves."[9]

The trade flourished in the years following Kirk's arrival. For example, when thousands of slaves died in a cholera epidemic on Zanzibar from 1869–70, Kirk reported to the Foreign Office that to make up for the losses, 17,392 additional slaves were imported in 1871, and 23,392 slaves in 1872, with about half then exported to other lands.

For each slave brought from the coast, the sultan now extracted a customs duty of $1.50 to $2.00.[10] As a consequence of this hike in fees, a much larger number of slaves than before were smuggled directly to the Arabian Peninsula, the Comoro Islands, and Somalia to avoid the sultan's customs duties.

Sultan Majid's wealth came mainly from slaves and ivory, especially slaves, but there were some restraints on his accumulation. He was, for example, afraid to interfere with the twice yearly invasion of the island by what was termed the "Northern Arabs." Arriving with the east-west monsoon in November, agents for these desert tribes of the Arabian Peninsula would leave Zanzibar the following April in dhows filled with black Africans they had kidnapped or bought at auction. In addition, while they were on the island, they demanded a "maintenance fee" of $15,000 to $20,000, which the sultan paid, much as the Portuguese had paid the Lundeen-Zulus, to keep them from making more trouble.

Auctions held during that November to April period provided the greatest profits for the sultan, his Arab subjects, and the Banyans. At the end of each April when the easterlies began to blow, the Northern Arabs took off for their homelands with slaves packed tightly in their ships. The British antislavery patrol was well aware of what was happening, and dhows that could be pursued were followed and forcibly boarded. Nonetheless, with only a few ships for the whole coast, the British patrols could only capture a fraction of the slavers. Of the 39,645 slaves that left Zanzibar for the Persian Gulf between 1867 and 1869, only 2,645 were found on dhows intercepted by the British antislavery patrol.[11]

Should a slave dhow be intercepted by a British antislavery patrol, the slave traders did not hesitate to dump their cargo of slaves overboard.

Consider this firsthand account by an ex-slave:

> The British were the people who had determined to end slavery and the slave trade. Dr. Livingstone and others had seen the cruel deeds done in Africa, the suffering of the people who were bought and sold, and they could not bear it, and they reported the evil in England. The result was that the whole of England felt pity for the Africans, and all the dominions of Her Majesty, Queen Victoria, were moved with compassion. It was for this reason that certain explorers ventured into the interior of Africa.
>
> Having made an agreement with the Sultan of Zanzibar, British cruisers began to patrol the deep sea hunting for dhows, capturing their Arab owners and rescuing the African slaves. . . . It was this way that Mwinyi Upate instructed his slaves on the day that his two dhows sailed. . . . About midday, when the sun

with great heat shone on the center of one's head, the sea became calm and the dhow of Mwinyi Upate stood still, its sails flat down. The captain then saw an object far away on the sea, and he sent for his master, who was asleep, to come and look at it. When Mwinyi Upate came up and saw that object, he knew it for a British man-of-war. . . . He reminded the slaves to say they were all free people. . . . The British cruiser had already sighted the dhow. . . . The Arabs began to curse the British, calling on the names of spirits, even Mohammed. . . . Then old Mwinyi unbound one slave and cut off his head with his sword as a sacrifice to the spirits that held the dhow from sailing, that they might drown the British cruiser instead. When he found he could do nothing else, he told the slaves, "the infidel is coming to steal us. If he asks you whether you are slaves, say NO." And the slaves said, "It is so, Bwana."

Seeing that the cruiser was very close, Mwinyi Upate saluted with all politeness, and so did those who were with him. The British received the salute with their customary good manner. The captain of the man-of-war asked him, "what is your cargo?" Mwinyi Upate answered, "Coconuts" . . . But the captain did not believe him. . . . He came to the dhow holding his sword in one hand and his pistol in the other.

Now Mwinyi Upate objected strongly to this white man stepping on the deck; so he said, "No, no! My dhow will never be entered by a swine-eating infidel!" And saying this he waved his hands high to stop the captain from coming on board. The captain of the man-of-war pointed his pistol at him and said, "Stop this nonsense!" The captain entered the dhow with his native interpreter Serenge. . . . He saw the slaves packed close together, the bonds of those cruel yokes bruising their necks. Serenge was told to ask them whether they were slaves. They all answered with one cry, "Yes! Yes! Ye-e-es!"

The captain of the man-of-war told them, "I feel very sorry for you, and I will do my utmost to give you comfort." Then he signaled to those in his vessel to send the life boats at once.

. . . Now the British hurried to overtake the second dhow of Mwinyi Upate. This was not an easy task, for the tide was up an east wind had risen, the very wind Mwinyi Upate had wanted when the sea was calm. By this time it had pushed the second dhow a long way ahead. But having seen the state of the first lot of slaves, the British gave chase with all their might. . . . When the British cruiser drew alongside, Pwanali (Upate's second in command and captain of the second dhow) knew he faced death.

> The captain of the man-of-war stepped into the dhow with his soldiers, and found every corner of the vessel packed with slaves so close they could not move. Some were sick; four of them were dead; and all still had on their bonds of cruel yokes on their necks. Our parents said that when the Englishmen saw that, the tears came from their eyes.[12]

The truculence of the slave traders increased as antislavery patrols became more active, and some of the Northern Arabs, when they were on Zanzibar, would attack anyone they thought interfered with the slave trade, especially Europeans and Americans, whom they now considered to be antislavery. The Americans had been trading in Zanzibar for cloves, ivory, and other products for over a hundred years, but few slaves were shipped before the American Civil War to the United States from this region, the great part having been obtained from West Africa instead.

Abetted by the French, whose ostensible aim was to snatch dominance of the island away from the British and secure a foothold on the East African mainland, the Northern Arabs, in 1861, had attacked both the British and American consulates, wounding four servants at the American consulate. Fortunately, Sultan Majid had sent soldiers to keep the consulates from being overrun. On another occasion, the slavers had even locked the American consul in his house, and only let him go after he had given them $500.

Majid's father, Said, had been a resourceful ruler who was as much a politician as a businessman. It was he who had worked out a mutual arrangement with the Portuguese for their slave dealings, agreeing to send his caravans only north of the Rovuma River. In an 1822 treaty, he had also promised the British, who had begun to carry the antislavery banner in Africa, that he would abolish the overseas slave trade, but, of course, he never lived up to the agreement. He was not about to relinquish his biggest income producer. To evade British antislavery patrols, he had devised a new land route to Somalia and thence across the Red Sea so he could still sell slaves to his customers on the Persian Gulf. He had also signed trading treaties with the United States (1833), England (1840), and France (1844), cannily giving each one favored trading partner status.

Said had died in 1856 and his son Majid had become Zanzibar's reigning sultan. Majid added to the list of Zanzibar's trading cities in 1859.[13]

The new sultan also claimed dominion over Somalia and all of East Africa north of the poorly delineated boundary with Mozambique and inland about 600 miles. Both the Portuguese slavers and those from the sultanate *harvested* slaves and ivory from the same interior regions, and the sultan was able to tax thousands of slaves brought to the main auction houses at Mombassa, Iboe, Kilwa, and especially Zanzibar.

Palace Infighting

Majid had two half-brothers, Thwain and Bargash, both eager to take his place. After their father's death, Thwain had become sultan of Oman on the northeastern tip of the Arabian Peninsula. Oman's economy was much poorer than Zanzibar's, and Thwain coveted the clove-rich island. The British, who had been active politically and economically in that part of the world for two centuries, had acquired revictualing and coaling stations for their fleet at Aden and the Seychelles. The French had countered by occupying the Comoro Islands, Réunion, and later Madagascar. When Thwain sent a fleet to invade Zanzibar in 1859, the British, fearing loss of control of the island, sent warships to stop him. Thwain backed down and agreed to arbitration. In March 1860, the political agent at Aden, Brigadier W.M. Coughlan, was chosen to look into the dispute. His report recommended that to settle Thwain's demand for the island and the major portion of the slave trade income, Majid pay Thwain in perpetuity 40,000 crowns, or about £8,000, a year.[14] By accepting the settlement, Majid was assured of British naval protection against any future military incursions by his relatives on the Arabian Peninsula. And the annual payment was something he knew he could well afford: his estimated annual income was 206,000 crowns or £43,000.

In 1859 Majid had tried to still, as well, the ambitions of his younger half-brother, Bargash, by giving him $10,000, but the French, who believed Bargash would best serve their interests, urged him to try to usurp his brother's crown. Bargash used the money to send 500 troops into pitched battle with Majid's men. The British intervened on the side of Majid, however, and Bargash was eventually caught and exiled to Bombay. From there, he lavished expensive presents on the influential anti-Majid Zanzibari Arabs, the El Harthi party, hoping they would back his bid for the throne after his brother died.[15]

The Reute Affair

Without Helen, Kirk spent his first Christmas on Zanzibar with four German consulate members whom he had invited to keep him company. One was the merchant Heinrich Reute, who would soon figure prominently in the island's biggest scandal. Reute lived next door to the sultan's half-sister, Seyyida Salme, a sultry beauty with whom he had developed a secret and dangerous liaison.

When Sultan Majid learned of the affair soon thereafter from a slave, he forbade her to see Reute ever again. He became even more incensed when he discovered that she was already pregnant by the handsome German. From the sultan's point of view, two heinous crimes had been committed against his religious faith: a Muslim woman had had sexual intercourse with an infidel, and this had resulted in a pregnancy out of wedlock. Both were punishable by death.

Seyyida Salme's social charm and beauty had brought her acceptance by the island's European society. The captain of the *Highflyer,* which had brought Kirk to Zanzibar, was a friend of both the Arab princess and Reute, and when he learned of their perilous situation, he arranged to send one of the ship's cutters to a secluded cove near the site where devout Muslim women went to purify themselves on a certain religious holiday. Seyyida Salme appeared at the appointed time with two slave girls. For her bathing she had brought along towels and a case for soap. But secretly hidden in its bottom were her most precious jewels and all her money, a fortune in American dollars. When she spotted the cutter and the bluejackets waiting to help her on board, she grabbed her case and ran, beckoning her slaves to follow.

As Kirk wrote some time later to his fiancee, "She'd have been killed, I think, sooner or later, had she remained. . . . I am told she got into the cutter taking down all her boxes of dollars safely and springing into the boat. . . . Her two servants, who knew nothing of the whole affair, screamed, howled and roared . . . but a bluejacket covered the mouth of one with his hands and lifted her in, *nolens volens,* to follow her mistress. The other unluckily got clean away, bellowing up the street."[16]

The slave had run off to inform the sultan, while the British sailors, rowing vigorously, brought the princess and her remaining slave to the *Highflyer.* It steamed off before the sultan could send a boat in pursuit. Heinrich Reute, who had also escaped, joined her at Aden. There, Seyyida Salme converted to Lutheranism and was baptized "Emily." They were married and went to live in Hamburg, where he had his business.

For Majid, his sister was as good as dead. Never would the sultan consider writing to her, answering her letters, or seeing her again. In his letter to Helen about the incident, Kirk added: "Some blame the English consulate—as if the ships of war were under us: and I'm sure no man is more innocent than poor Doctor Seward, acting consul."[17]

Kirk and Seward both realized that the sultan had been dishonored, first by his sister and then by the British sea captain who had connived with her. Sultan Majid was well within his legal rights, according to the Sharia or Muslim law, to demand her return to Zanzibar for trial and almost certain execution. Although Kirk hadn't wanted to alarm Helen, in the wake of the Reute incident the Europeans on the island, especially the British, were in real danger. Consul Seward wrote to Bombay, requesting that a British warship be permanently stationed at Zanzibar. The warship soon arrived in Zanzibar Harbor and, despite mutterings and threats, trouble was averted.

Kirk's New Life

Kirk finally wrote to Helen at the end of 1866, asking her to marry him. In return, he was overjoyed to receive a letter six weeks later in which she consented to his proposal and told him that she was packing and would soon be on her way.

Helen arrived in Zanzibar after a tedious and uncomfortable 8,000-mile voyage. The pair was married in a Church of England ceremony on a British man-of-war in Zanzibar Harbor on March 14, 1867, and settled into a new home.

As the wife of the vice-consul and acting political agent, Helen had to look forward to not only helping her husband in his demanding work, but to entertaining and being entertained by the few Europeans on the 25-mile-long island, including a handful of French Catholic and British Protestant missionaries. The Europeans and Americans were typically engaged in trade, even those who held political agency and consular positions. Kirk was an exception, however, devoting all of his energies to his consulate and political agent responsibilities, his medical practice, and his family.

The couple's first few months together were spent adjusting to the climate and living conditions. Kirk showed Helen how to take simple precautions such as boiling and filtering all drinking water to reduce the likelihood of catching an infectious disease. They also stressed hand-washing and cleanliness to the servants. From the beginning, Helen worked tirelessly with Kirk between her pregnancies and child-rearing. She even functioned as his secretary until he was assigned one by the British government.

During those first years, Kirk wore three hats: vice-consul, political agent, and physician to the British consulate. In addition, he was consulted medically by members of the resident European population and by Indian merchants, but not by most Arabs, who considered their own healers superior. His work was constant, multifaceted, and overwhelming, consuming most of his and Helen's waking hours. Nevertheless, the couple did find time for occasional horseback rides into the country, picnics, and social gatherings in town. Later, they bought a home in the country, where Kirk planted a botanical garden and relaxed in his favorite pastime, cultivating and admiring the rare plants he imported and which grew there in profusion. Harry H. Johnston, an artist and explorer, who subsequently became an administrator, described Kirk's country garden:

> when Zanzibar gets stuffy and the official routine tryingly monotonous, he steals away, often on foot, to a little paradise he has created among the groves of Mbweni, a tiny settlement on the coast of the island. Here he lives a life that is to him ideally happy . . . he wanders . . . amid the groves of cocoa palms and the clumps of panadanus that border the sea; he photographs and above all he gardens. Here among his cycads and his orchids . . . spade in hand . . . a rare flower in his button hole, and rustic contentment irradiating his face—here amid scenery which typifies the botanist's paradise, Sir John Kirk is emphatically at home.[18]

During his years on the Zambezi, Kirk had become proficient in Swahili and Arabic and even spoke and wrote some Spanish, Portuguese, and French. His mastery of these languages enabled him to glean information directly from Zanzibaris in the marketplace and on the docks. Aware of this and of Kirk's cautious and logical approach to problems, the consul began to seek him out for advice.

Through the Banyans Kirk quickly learned about the palace rivalries and the local politics of slavery. The cruelties of the slave trade were, in polite society, sugared over by the profligate use of compliments paid by one Arab slave dealer, merchant, or political figure to another. Such elaborate etiquette wasn't confined to talk only of the slave trade. Court mores also applied to letters on any subject sent to members of the ruling society and foreigners. For this purpose they used scribes, themselves poets of sorts, to weave a string of compliments to the recipient before getting to the meat of the missive. For example, a routine letter from Majid to Lord Stanley, the British Foreign Secretary at the time, asking that a relative be granted an interview, began in the following manner:

> In the name of God the Merciful, the Compassionate. To his excellency Lord Stanley, the honored. A SALUTATION more gentle than the zephyr, sweeter than a shower received by the meadows and the hills, more fragrant than ambergris mixed with musk, and more diffusive than combined civet and aloeswood, and a compliment brighter than the beaming light, and more resplendent than the leafy flowers, are offered to his excellency who possesses perfection and superiority, who unites greatness with virtues; his Excellency the most noble, the most illustrious, the happiness of the age, the rarity of the times, the pillar of the body of Ministers, him in whom the exalted men of counsel glory; the arranger of the jewels of the Kingdoms, to whom the least and the greatest give attention, the Minister of Foreign Affairs, the tongue of the exalted British Government. May God preserve his noble person and his beauteous ascendancy! And may his penetrating views continue to clear up the intricacies of contentions, and the beams of his genius to cast light upon the dark points of opinions! Amen.
>
> And then next the main design and general purpose is to inquire after the health of your noble self—after the equability of your exquisite condition. May you continue in blessings and joy, in honour and happiness! And may your hours never be void of greatness and good fortune; and your days be sheltered from disasters and vicissitudes! Amen.
>
> And if the perfumed mind vouchsafe in kindness to inquire after the friendship of the sincere one and the affection of the devoted one, then thanks be to God the King of Glory, he is in health and well being and in abundant blessings from the Lord, persistent in that friendship and sincere unanimity which he has undertaken, erect for such performance of prayers and requests as are meet, upholding the palms of supplication and entreaty for the eternalization of your exalted Government.[19]

The more practical-minded Kirk sought to limit such poetic preambles. To make things simple and use less space in forwarding Arab letters to the Foreign Office, he usually placed the phrase "Compliments Excluded" to the left and just below the letterhead before beginning with the business at hand.

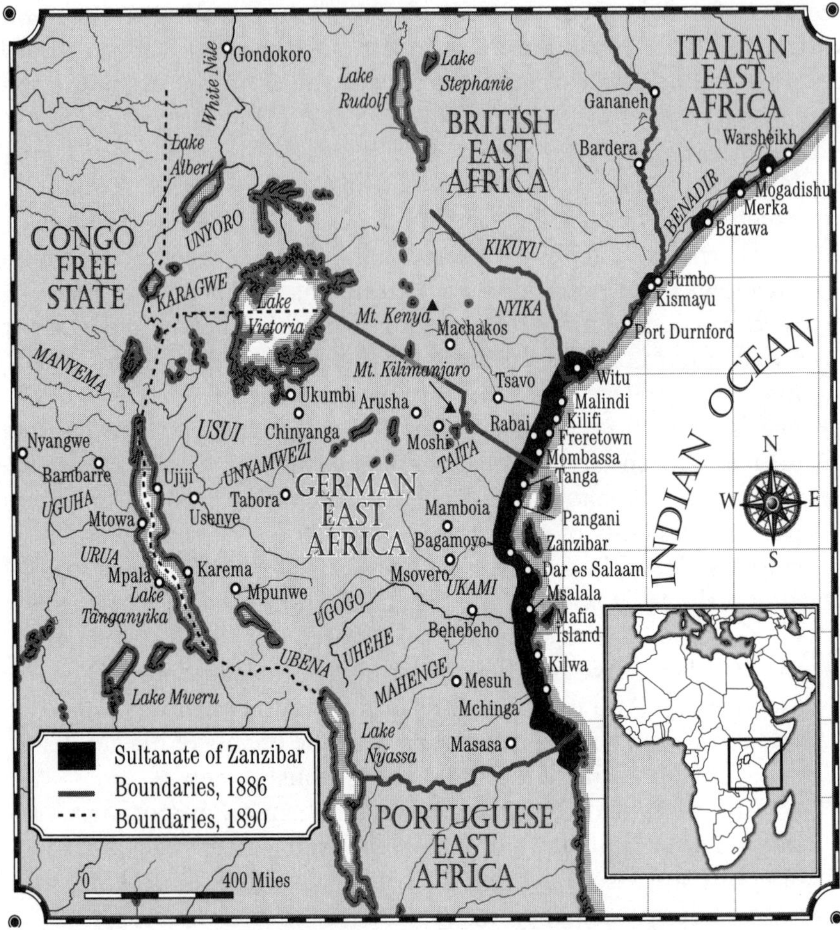

MAP 8 *Partition of the Zanzibar Sultanate, 1886.* From R. Coupland, *The Exploitation of East Africa* (London: Faber and Faber, 1939, p. 508).

The Sultan's Hold Weakens

During the four years Kirk knew Majid before his death in 1870, the sultan had trouble maintaining his hold on the mainland. He exacted customs duties, both legal and illegal. He appointed governors and sent his soldiers to guard the coastal towns of Barawa, Merka, Iboe, Lamu, Mombassa, and Kilwa. But the area between Mogadishu and the Juba River in Somalia was controlled by Sheik Ahmed Yussuf and 40,000 of his warriors (see Map 8, above). Profits were so great from slavery and ivory, however, that Majid found it expedient to pay the sheik off to keep the peace rather than risk having him overrun the coastal towns.

To increase his income, Majid's Arab and Swahili slave caravans began to push farther and farther north and west in search of slaves. But Majid wielded less and less power in the vast territory he claimed. Indigenous chieftains became bolder in their attacks on coastal enclaves, dealing defeats to the sultan's soldiers. One powerful chief successfully raided slave caravans for five years until he was caught and executed by the sultan.

For Kirk the botanist, Zanzibar Island, with its plethora of rare plants, was a delight. For Kirk the explorer, the whole African continent was only twenty miles away, always beckoning with the possibility of another expedition. And for Kirk the budding politician, he knew the battle between those who profited from slavery and those who were repulsed by it was being fought all around him, and he was eager to engage in that battle himself.

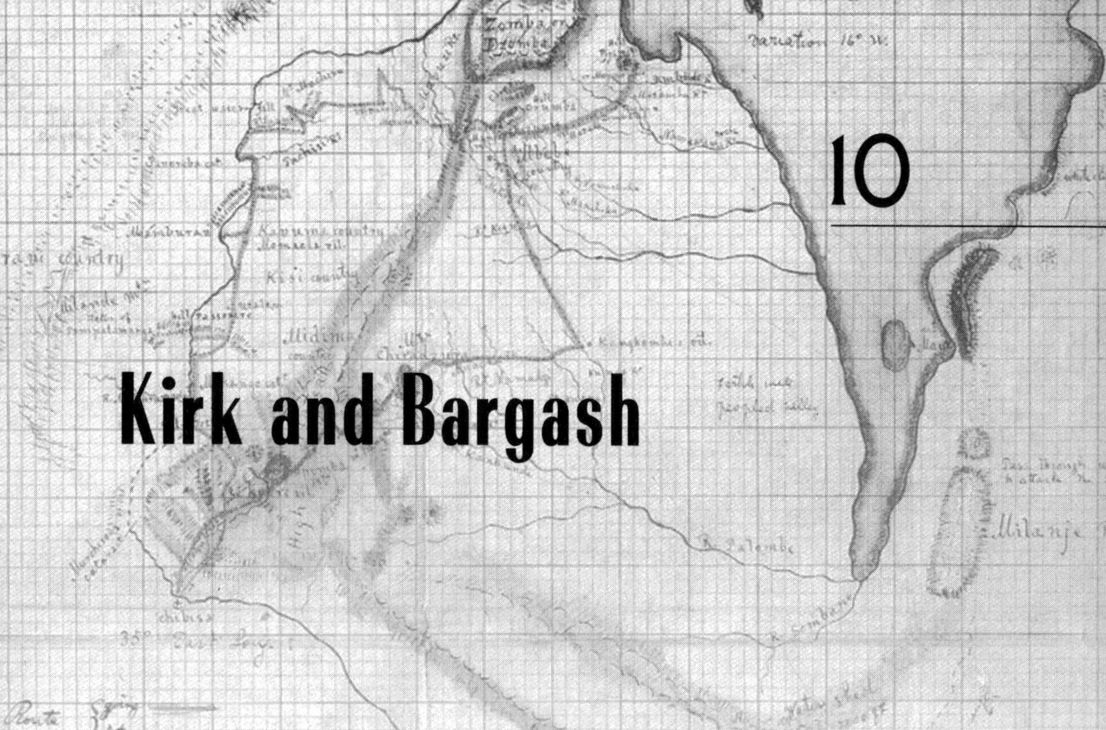

10

Kirk and Bargash

In the summer of 1866, two months after Kirk arrived, Seyyid Bargash was pardoned by Majid. A year of exile in India had broadened Bargash's horizons, and he returned to Zanzibar declaring his loyalty to his older brother. Keeping to his promise, he consorted with neither the anti-Majid faction of Arabs (the El Harthi sheiks) nor the French.

Shortly after his return, as mentioned in the Prologue, Bargash asked Kirk for what would prove to be a pivotal favor: Would the doctor make a house call on a half-sister of his and Majid's of whom he was particularly fond? She was seriously ill in her country house about five miles from town.

Kirk agreed, being willing to undertake almost anything legitimate that would further the British Agency's[1] standing among the Arabs.

The patient's home was located on a hill in the midst of a clove plantation, a stone house with a view of the harbor and a large courtyard in which spices were being dried. Prince Bargash greeted him at the door. It was the first of what would become many meetings. The entrance hall was cool, and Kirk noticed the rich oriental carpets on the marble floor. But he also wrote in his diary of the distressed look on the young prince's round face. Bargash said his sister had complained of severe abdominal pains for several days. Kirk examined the fifty-year-old woman in the presence of her ladies-in-waiting, her face hidden behind a thick veil. He found a hard abdominal mass which he thought was probably advanced cancer of the uterus or an adjacent organ. The patient told him that the trouble had begun five years before. Arab physicians had prescribed the application of hot irons to the abdominal area, and these had left festering scars.

When Kirk explained to Bargash that she had little chance of recovery, the distraught prince thanked him for coming so promptly before ordering him a sumptuous breakfast in gratitude.

Majid then called on Kirk to help resolve a dispute over the export duties that the sultan had been charging French and British merchant ships. The duty had been 15½ percent on all goods coming into Zanzibar from coastal ports. But when the French consul suggested the sultan give his government an exclusive tariff reduction to 5 percent, Kirk suggested that Majid reduce the tariff to 5 percent for all nations trading with the sultanate so as not to show preferential treatment for the French and antagonize the others. Majid acquiesced, and this resulted in a significant victory for Kirk, who was acting for the first time in his capacity as political agent.

Sometime later, when Sultan Majid himself developed a bloody cough and epileptic seizures, Kirk was called and again responded promptly. He believed the sultan to have pulmonary tuberculosis which had spread to his brain and caused an abscess there. As in the case of the sister, Kirk felt he could do nothing. Majid died October 7, 1870, and Bargash, whose gifts to the influential Arabs on the island had paid off, succeeded him as the new sultan.

Not only in his medical dealings, but in other ways, Kirk was showing himself to be a rising star within the consular ranks. Outwardly pleasant, but inwardly careful in everything he undertook, he could, as he had shown while with Livingstone, adapt to difficult conditions and come up with effective strategies to rectify a problem or improve a situation.

For example, one of Kirk's duties as political agent was keeping track of the island's trade figures. Its imports in 1867, he noted, consisted of cotton cloth worth $629,400 from Indian and British mills, $237,000 from the United States, $233,400 from Germany, and $89,000 from France. Beads, mostly from Germany, amounted to $95,600. (Cloth and beads were often used as currency on the mainland.)

That same year, by Kirk's estimates, the value of exports from the sultanate including the mainland were: ivory, $663,500; cloves, $321,000; coconuts, $225,000; gum copal, $100,000; sesamum (sesame) seed, $100,000; and cowry shells (also used as money throughout Africa at the time), $98,000. In 1871, Kirk estimated the slave tax alone brought the sultan over $100,000, or one-fourth of his annual income.[2]

H.A. Churchill had replaced Dr. G.E. Seward as permanent chief consul in 1867, but in 1869 he came down with a persistent high fever, probably from malaria. Considerable friction soon developed between Churchill and Bargash, perhaps because of the consul's irritability induced by his incessant fever, or perhaps because the Mlawa sect of Zanzibari Arabs[3] had pressured Bargash into taking an openly anti-British posture. In any event, Bargash left Churchill's letters unanswered, and spurred on by the jealous Mlawas, Bargash enacted legislation prohibiting the Banyans, who, like all those from India, had been made de facto British citizens, from owning clove plantations or trading outside Zanzibar town. As expected, there was a strong protest from Churchill.

Also at issue was the custom for a new sultan to reaffirm any previous treaties. When Churchill asked Bargash to reaffirm the anti-slavery treaty of 1845 with Britain—in which his father, Said, had agreed to stop Zanzibar's external trade of slaves, but, in fact, had turned a blind eye to the smuggling of slaves to the Red Sea and Persian Gulf—Bargash vehemently refused, claiming Churchill was trying to bankrupt him. Of course, this treaty and the additional ones of 1862 and 1864 had not put a stop to the slave trade, but they did allow British ships to patrol the coast, arrest slave owners and crews, and remand them to the sultan for judgment and sentencing. Churchill threatened retaliation for the sultan's refusal with the might of the British navy, but in a countermove, Bargash asked the German consul, Theodore Schultz, for protection. A crisis developed, with potential international repercussions, when Schultz implied the Germans would back Bargash. At this point, Churchill, now a victim of recurrent malaria, realized he was not up to the task, and asked Kirk to help resolve the controversy. This event was to cast Kirk in a new and increasingly important role in suppressing the slave trade.

The first thing Kirk told Churchill was that he didn't believe the sultan was serious about switching his long allegiance from the British to the Germans. He pointed out that the German government had been too busy consolidating its 1870 victory over the French after the Franco-Prussian War to bother with a little kingdom like Zanzibar. Kirk, to whom the sultan had now begun to listen, managed to quiet the potential controversy, and Churchill subsequently admitted that Kirk had been right in insisting that Zanzibar would not fall to the Germans.

But temporary calm gave way to a new storm, this one created by the sultan's younger brother Khalifa, who, following in Bargash's footsteps, attempted a coup while Bargash was on a pilgrimage to Mecca. To win backers, Khalifa had also given out expensive presents, in his case to the Northern Arabs who had arrived for the yearly slave auctions. But Bargash had left a co-regent, Mohammed-bin-Hamed, who intercepted a note from Khalifa to the Northern Arabs requesting their help in dethroning his brother. The sultan's guard arrested Khalifa, removed his sword and dagger, and placed him in irons to await his brother's return. The Northern Arab co-conspirators on Zanzibar were also rounded up and jailed. In recognition of his own past treatment, when Bargash returned he placed Khalifa under house arrest.[4]

During Kirk's first few years on the island, not only did the pace of political activity pick up, but so did the speed of communications. The average time for the trip from London to Zanzibar was cut in half, to a little over three weeks, by the opening of the Suez Canal in November 1869. British ships could now provide relatively rapid mail and passenger service between British bases in Aden, the Seychelles, and Zanzibar. Also, by 1870, a telegraph line had been built between London and Persia via Constantinople and was connected by cables under the Mediterranean, Red Sea, and Persian Gulf as far as Karachi, India (now in Pakistan).

These two events occurring within a year of each other made consular relations between far-flung outposts and the Foreign Office in London far more efficient. Diplomatic cables which might have taken a month or more could now be delivered virtually overnight. Thus, as Kirk would discover, when Zanzibar's turn to receive the cable came, he would be able to obtain answers and authorizations while an issue was still hot.

Kirk as a Politician

Kirk's political astuteness soon came to be recognized by Bombay, and when Consul Churchill was invalided back to England in 1870, Kirk was appointed acting consul until a replacement could be found. For all intents and purposes, Kirk was now the consul—the most powerful British official in the most important slave center in East Africa.

Kirk immediately called on Bargash in his new capacity. The palace was guarded by smartly uniformed mercenaries from Baluchistan as well as by the sultan's personal bodyguards from Persia. There was an excellent brass band playing "God Save the Queen" and the Zanzibar national hymn when he arrived. Kirk walked up a long staircase and then along a corridor lined with guards and Arab courtiers in brilliant colors wearing ornate gold-hilted swords and knives until he reached the reception room, where the walls were covered with huge mirrors reflecting the sultan's collection of clocks and telescopes.

A contemporary observer noted such a scene:

> The ceiling was loaded with crystal candelabra, and the floor was covered with a rich carpet. Along both sides were gilt chairs with crimson-covered seats on which the Arab courtiers disposed themselves. At the head of the room was the Sultan's arm-chair where he seated himself, inviting us to occupy chairs beside him. There were customary inquiries about our health and voyage spoken in the Swahili language through an interpreter, though after a few sentences his services were dispensed with, and Kirk spoke directly to the Sultan.[5]

Kirk knew that the young sultan was insecure and not above shifting alliances, but he explained to Bargash that it would be in his best interests, financial and otherwise, to reaffirm the treaties curtailing the slave trade that his brother Majid had signed with the British. In return, Kirk promised that the British would continue to safeguard his throne.

Kirk's earlier willingness to do what he could for the sultan's dying sister had left an indelible impression on Bargash. He was by now already coming to consider Kirk a trustworthy friend. When Kirk, in his calm but persuasive tone, suggested that the Mlawas were not giving the sultan the best advice, Bargash began to listen.

Kirk suggested Bargash also reverse his edict to ban Banyans from owning clove plantations and participating in overseas trade. The sultan suddenly relented and gave Kirk full authority to abrogate the earlier edict. This may have been more crafty than impulsive on Bargash's part, however. It spared Bargash the wrath of the Mlawas and other jealous Arabs who blamed the Banyans for reaping huge profits by charging too much interest on their loans to the Arab plantation owners and caravaners.

Bargash also appointed Kirk deputy judge for the sultanate. This empowered Kirk to try illegal slave runners, thus shifting an enormous responsibility to the young physician-cum-statesman, and making it possible for Bargash to appear to be complying with the British, yet at the same time not incurring more wrath from other Arabs.

Toward the end of 1870, the sultan was confronted with another crisis over which he again called on the services of Dr. Kirk. The Mlawa sect in Oman had a great deal of power and their chief religious leader, the Imam, interpreted Muslim law and played a decisive role in determining the policies of Oman's sultan. The Imam threatened Bargash in the following note: "If you bind yourself to follow the Imam, he will continue the kingdom, but if you deny him he will take it from you."[6] Bargash also received a belligerent letter from one of his half-brothers in Oman, Abdul Assiz bin Said, with none of the usual Arab rhetorical fanfare or appeals to God. It warned: "Zanzibar is the fountain of money and we cannot get on without Zanzibar. . . . I have drawn on you for the sum of $5,000.00: pay it at once. . . . You have been my agent of old and are so still, nothing more: so do not make a big man of yourself."[7] This demand was in addition to the annual tribute previously agreed to.

Bargash sent the letters to Kirk, who advised him to stand firm and give nothing to his half-brother or greater demands by the Omanis would be made. "Your Highness will see that I am determined to support your authority and punish those who transgress your orders in slave trade matters," Kirk added by way of emphasis.[8]

Compared to Zanzibar, Oman was a relative wasteland with little irrigated land. Although it grew grapes, dates, pomegranates, and cereals and exported dried fish, the arable area consisted only of a narrow strip along the coast and a few oases inland where camels were bred for export. Shipping the produce overseas took several weeks, by which time most of it would spoil, so exporting much of the fruit grown there was not practical. The Omanis did export metal work, but most of the Omani sultan's income came, as it did for his brother in Zanzibar, from the resale of slaves and from ivory from Zanzibar. Oman's navy wasn't much: a few small steamships, the rest dhows. It more or less matched that of Zanzibar, but the Zanzibaris could now rely on the far more powerful British fleet.

Any attempted attack by the Omanis, however, would put the British in a difficult position. Oman, poised as it was on the corner of the Arabian Peninsula facing the Persian Gulf, was a base from which the British could secure safe passage to India, and Britain wanted to maintain close relations with both sultanates.

In early 1871, Turki, another of Bargash's brothers, overthrew Thwain in Oman, but was no friendlier to Bargash and threatened to annex Zanzibar. Kirk, who now wielded such tremendous influence with Bargash that the sultan consulted him in almost every matter, advised restraint and watchful waiting.

Kirk was by this time so pleased with the close personal and political relationship that had developed between himself and Bargash that in a letter to the Foreign Office he forsook his usual modesty: "So far from keeping at a distance, nothing is done by him without informing me or asking my advice, and justice is obtained for all British claims with a rapidity unknown in the days of Seyyid Majid. . . . With the French, American and German consulates, I find his Highness has greatly lost favor since he has treated the Agency with proper respect, and as taking precedence in everything without question."[9] Kirk's view of the situation was more than imperial myopia. There is no question that Bargash personally liked and began to depend more and more on Kirk in managing his foreign affairs. Kirk's whole personality spelled dependability; and he did try to faithfully protect the sultan's interests to the extent permitted by the British government. Thus, Kirk's statement may not have been bragging so much as expressing confidence based on a realistic assessment of his position.

As judge of the Vice Admiralty Court, which was one of the duties of a political agent, Kirk's judicial powers applied to British subjects as well as to any Zanzibari Arab or Banyan who broke the law. His was the responsibility of deciding which dhow owners were guilty of smuggling slaves, for example. Bargash then passed the actual sentence, usually following Kirk's advice.

In 1872, when Juma bin Salim El Farsi was caught smuggling slaves to Johanna in the Comoro Islands, his ship was seized by a British man-of-war. The defendant insisted the slaves were not his, but Kirk, who sat as judge, determined otherwise. The ship, its tackle, and furnishings were confiscated and the slaves freed.

But Kirk's new position as judge was also frustrating to him at times, if not disheartening, for the capture and prosecution of the tough dhow masters wasn't easy. In an action off the coast of Madagascar, the British warship *Columbine* sent a boat under the command of Sub-Lieutenant Harenc to intercept a dhow that failed to heave to in response to warning shots. Harenc testified before Kirk in Vice Admiralty Court:

> Before going alongside the men's arms were ready in case of any emergency . . . , but the instant the boat touched her side, James Barrett, A.B.[able-bodied seaman] jumped on board, cutlass in hand, and was immediately attacked. Seeing this Mr. Harris boarded her in the waist, and John Harman and himself [Harenc] on the poop. . . . Henry Radley, A.B., was holding the boat on to the dhow. On boarding [Harenc] fired two rounds

> from his pistol. On recovering himself he found the boat dropping astern, the bowman, Henry Radley, having been killed by a spear. Mr. Harris and John Thompson, ordinary [seaman], were in the water. James B. Wheeler, ordinary, in the boat, wounded. . . . James Barrett A.B. was missing. . . . Mr. Harris was severely wounded in the left arm and hand and Thompson in the abdomen.
>
> James Wheeler was wounded a second time in bitter fighting and Harenc pursued the dhow, but the Arab slavers and their captives, assuming they had been hidden in the dhow, had disappeared by the time he was able to locate it.[10]

If the Arab master on the dhow had been captured, he would undoubtedly have been judged guilty by Kirk and remanded to the sultan for sentencing.

Now that Kirk had become the sultan's friend, confidant, and judicial appointee, he felt he was firmly entrenched. Perhaps, just perhaps, he had gotten into a position where he could at last fulfill Livingstone's dream by persuading Bargash to sign a new and far more comprehensive treaty banning the slave trade.

There were incredible odds against his succeeding, even though Churchill had turned over this responsibility to him. Why would the sultan agree to eliminate a major source of income—the slave trade—and risk assassination by the other Arabs who were in the slave business? Although this was just the kind of a challenge Kirk was willing to rise to, he would first have to face a crisis of a different sort. This one would involve David Livingstone and an attack on Kirk's character so severe that it would bring heartache and threaten to end his career in the British Foreign Service.

11

Reverberations from Stanley and Livingstone

Propelled by his own peculiar brand of wanderlust and megalomania, David Livingstone, soon after he finished his book recounting his Second Zambezi Expedition, left again for Africa. He arrived in early 1866, seemingly undeterred by the danger, physical discomfort, and illness inherent in another African expedition, his fourth. At age fifty-two, Livingstone was no longer in the robust health he had once been. A low-grade chronic iron-deficiency anemia caused by repeated malaria attacks, blood loss from bleeding hemorrhoids, or hookworm[1] made him tire far more easily than before.[2]

Livingstone was nevertheless ceaseless in pursuit of his dream to replace paganism with Christianity and to offer Africans the values of European civilization in exchange for commerce with Britain. This evangelical imperialism, with its attendant hope of abolishing slavery, brought him many followers.

Stopping off at Zanzibar, Livingstone bought supplies and firearms with money raised from book royalties, lecture fees, and donations from the public and the British government. The Royal Geographic Society had also contributed again, but this time only the meager amount of £500.

Livingstone was very solicitous of Kirk during his time in Zanzibar, treating him like a preferred son. Kirk, who had often felt terrorized by Livingstone on the Zambezi expedition, now extended every courtesy to his former superior and even arranged for Sultan Majid to lend him a house. Livingstone also left Kirk money to use to re-equip Livingstone during this new expedition. Doubting that he would return for several years, Livingstone wanted the supplies forwarded to the Arab slave town of Ujiji on Lake Tanganyika, 700 miles to the west.

Remembering the problems with his fellow Britons, Livingstone decided to travel only with indigenous carriers. His party consisted of ten porters from Johanna, twenty men from the village of Mikindani at the mouth of the Rovuma, fifteen freed slaves, and thirty Sepoy Indians. He appointed his two faithful servants, Susi and Chuma, both veterans of the Second Zambezi Expedition, as headmen.

Livingstone's Wanderings

As the group pushed into what is now northern Zimbabwe, one of the porters absconded with Livingstone's medicines. Having lost the opium he carried for diarrhea and the quinine he used for malaria, Livingstone was ripe for complications. He collapsed on Lake Tanganyika's south shore and was confined to a hut for over a month. Rumors of his death reached Kirk and the British Foreign Office and preparations were begun for a search, but they were abandoned when it was reported that Livingstone had been seen heading north toward Ujiji.

Kirk had dutifully sent medicines and supplies to Ujiji, where Livingstone could have easily obtained them. But Livingstone continued his wanderings, this time bypassing Ujiji. He was intent on finding the four fountains which had been described by Herodotus as the source of the Nile and suddenly veered west toward the Congo, but had to stop in a village when a new attack of malaria struck. Weak and undernourished, he was found there by a caravan of slave merchants under the command of a Swahili, Muhamad Bogharib, who was kind enough to give him both food and quinine.

Bogharib was a Robin Hood of Arab merchants, so clever at eluding British antislavery patrols that his name became an anathema to the British navy. Having grown rich, he gave money to mosques and other charities and was liked not only by fellow Muslims and local merchants, but even by some Europeans. We do not know how well Livingstone got along with him, but he was in no position to object openly to the slave dealer's activities and was indeed grateful for his help while he regained his strength.

Livingstone spent a month with Bogharib, his retinue, concubines, and slaves at Chief Casembe's village. There, they were apparently forcibly detained, and Livingstone described the chief's cruelties toward his own subjects, whose hands, legs, and ears were lopped off for ostensible offenses. After persuading the chief to release them as well as Mohamed bin Saleh, another Swahili trader, the party began a long journey back to Ujiji. However, instead of returning to the relative safety of Ujiji, Livingstone broke away from Bogharib. Now Livingstone appeared to be entering a manic phase, convinced that he was going to find the headwaters of the Nile. Over the next two years, though his personal porters refused to accompany him, he wandered, accompanied by only a half dozen attendants, in the region between the Democratic Republic of Congo and Zambia. He was sure the Lualaba was one of the headwaters of the Nile, unaware that it flowed into the Congo River. However, he did find two lakes previously unknown to Europeans: Mweru and Bangweolo. Returning then to Lake Tanganyika, he finally crossed it to Ujiji in March 1869. He was short of food again, feverish and emaciated. To his despair, his supplies and medicines, including the quinine that Kirk had sent, had all been stolen.

Of the forty letters Livingstone wrote from Ujiji, only one reached Kirk during that period. In it, Livingstone asked for more medicines, supplies, and porters and complained of chronic foot ulcers which had not only laid him up but killed many of the slaves held captive nearby.

These so-called tropical ulcers were probably due to a fungus with secondary bacterial infection, possibly an anaerobic streptococcus which eats flesh and even bone. Livingstone had to rest for three months before his ulcers healed, in spite of self-treatment with lunar caustic and an Arab salve made of beeswax, copper sulfate, coconut oil, and butter. Slow healing could also have been due to his chronic anemia.[3]

While Livingstone was having trouble with foot ulcers, Kirk was having troubles of his own. A cholera epidemic had spread to Zanzibar, keeping Kirk very busy. Worse, his five-year-old daughter, Marion, had come down with the disease. Her bedroom had become a hospital, its rancid smell from almost continuous diarrhea permeating the rest of the house. Kirk had seen cholera kill thousands in the Crimean War. He knew it was highly contagious and suspected it was passed from one person to another through their secretions; Florence Nightingale had shown that by isolating the sick, casualties were significantly reduced. Now, his own daughter was his patient, and he felt helpless, for at that time there was no such thing as intravenous therapy to combat the vomiting and dehydration which she developed along with the telltale rice-water stools.

With his daughter hovering between life and death, and feeling overwhelmed with fatigue and anxiety, Kirk nevertheless made special arrangements with an agent he had used before, a Banyan by the name of Ludha Damji, to expedite delivery of the medicines and supplies that Livingstone had requested. Ludha entrusted his house slave and tailor, Shereef Basha, with the consignment. But Basha, once on the mainland, exchanged most of the goods for ivory, which he then sold at a good profit for himself. The slave eventually traveled to Ujiji, arriving there in December 1870, with a remnant of the supplies and ten of the fifteen porters requested by Livingstone, the other five having succumbed to cholera on the way.

But Livingstone was no longer there. Before the supplies arrived, like Don Quixote tilting at windmills, he had left Ujiji in his continuing search for the headwaters of the Nile and Congo. He traveled with another slave caravan, this time led by the Swahili slave trader of great renown, Muhammad bin Muhammad bin Juma al Marjebi, also known as Tippu Tib, a nickname given to him because of his frequent blinking. Tippu Tib lectured Livingstone on Muslim teachings and customs, which lauded the faithful for freeing deserving slaves but did not expressly forbid slavery. Later, Tippu Tib explained slavery from the Arab slave traders' perspective:

> My slaves don't want to leave me. They are too content with their lives. If I was cruel to them they might run away, but to what purpose? They would just be recaptured and sold again, or mistreated and even killed. Or perhaps work twice as hard as I make them. There is no lack of dignity among slaves that leave the cruel tyranny of their African master for the enlightened tutelage of the Arab whose religion dictates benevolence and justice.[4]

Livingstone was incensed. Still, by traveling with the Arab slavers he probably survived as a consequence of their hospitality and medical care. He did finally break with Tippu Tib when he witnessed the Swahili slave traders and their men massacre Africans who resisted capture in a marketplace at Nyangwe in July 1871 (see Map 8 on page 138). "Before I had got thirty yards out, the discharge of two guns in the middle of the crowd told me that slaughter had begun: crowds dashed off from the place and threw down their wares in confusion, and ran. . . . Shot after shot continued to be fired on the helpless and perishing. . . . The Arabs themselves estimate the loss of life between 330 and 400 souls," Livingstone wrote.[5]

When Livingstone's description of the massacre by Tippu Tib's men was later published, it inflamed the British public to such an extent that the Foreign Office considered sending a high-ranking diplomat to Zanzibar to force the sultan to abolish the slave trade.[6] Livingstone himself, upset by the horrors he'd seen, and more depressed than ever, barely managed to return to Ujiji, on October 23, 1871.

Enter Henry Morton Stanley

Meanwhile, the adventurer, journalist, and explorer Henry Morton Stanley was approaching Ujiji from the east, having embarked on a mission to "find" Livingstone. By bringing food and medicine, Stanley may have saved Livingstone, but his intent, in the process, was to gain as much publicity as possible for the newspaper he represented and for himself. He would also become the bane of Kirk's existence and a threat to his career.

Stanley had already led a remarkable life. Born John Rowlands in Wales, he was abandoned by his mother as an infant and raised by his grandfather. When the elderly man died, Rowlands, age six, was sent to Saint Asaph's Orphanage until he ran away at fifteen to work on the Liverpool docks. By age eighteen, he was a cabin boy on a British ship bound for Louisiana. Adopted in New Orleans by Henry Stanley, a wealthy southerner who gave him his name and American citizenship, young Stanley enlisted in the Confederate Army at the beginning of the Civil War but was captured at the Battle of Shiloh. As a prisoner of war, he repudiated the southern cause and was allowed to enlist in the Union Army. Invalided out for poor health, he nevertheless enlisted again, this time in the Union Navy, and began to write war dispatches for New York newspapers.

When the war ended, he had no trouble obtaining a job as a journalist for the *New York Herald.* He was sent out west to cover the Indian Wars, to Africa for the British invasion of Abyssinia, and then to Spain to cover a civil war. His reportage was considered so good that William Gordon Bennett, the newspaper's famous editor, took a gamble and sent him back to Africa to find Livingstone. It could be an expensive flop, but if Stanley were to succeed, it would become banner headlines.

Stanley's search for Livingstone had first taken him to Zanzibar to obtain porters for his 820-mile trip from Bagamoyo to Ujiji on Lake

Tanganyika, where Livingstone had last been sighted. He met Kirk at the British consulate, and clearly didn't like him. In *How I Found Livingstone* he portrayed Kirk as crass, unfeeling, and arrogant, and remembered his first introduction to Kirk by the American consul, F. R. Webb, negatively. He described Kirk as "a man of rather slim figure, dressed plainly, slightly round-shouldered, hair black, face thin, cheeks rather sunk and bearded. . . . I fancied at the moment that he lifted his eyelids perceptively, disclosing the full circle of the eyes. If I were to define such a look, I would call it a broad stare." In line with his animus, he described an evening spent with the Kirks thusly:

> The entertainment which the British Consul and his wife provided for the visitors on their reception evening consists of a kind of mild wine and cigars; not because they have nothing else in the house . . . but I suppose because it is the normal and accustomed habit of a free Zanzibarized European to indulge of something of this sort, mixed with a little soda or seltzer water, as a stimulant to the bits of refined gossip, generally promulgated under the vinous influence to sympathizing, interested and eager listeners.
>
> It was all very fine, I dare say, but I thought it was the dreariest evening I ever passed until Dr. Kirk, pitying the wearisomeness under which I was laboring, called me aside to submit to my inspection a magnificent elephant rifle, which he said was a present from a governor of Bombay. Then I heard eulogies upon its deadly powers and its fatal accuracy; I heard anecdotes of jungle life; adventures experienced while hunting, and incidents of his travel with Livingstone.
>
> "Ah, yes, Dr. Kirk," I asked carelessly, about Livingstone— "where is he do you think, now?"
>
> "Well, really," he replied, "you know that is very difficult to answer; he may be dead; there is nothing positive on which we can base sufficient reliance. Of one thing I'm sure, nobody has heard anything definite of him for over two years. I should fancy, though, he must be alive. We are continually sending something up for him. There is a small expedition even now at Bagamoyo about to start shortly. I really think the old man should come home now; he is growing old, you know, and if he died the world would lose the benefit of his discoveries. He keeps neither notes nor journals; it is very seldom he takes observations. He simply makes a note or dot or something on a map, which nobody could understand but himself. Oh, yes, if

he is still alive he should come home and let a younger man take his place."

"What kind of a man is he to get along with?" I said, feeling now quite interested in his conversation.

"Well, I think he is a very difficult man to deal with generally. Personally, I have never had a quarrel with him, but I have seen him in hot water with fellows so often, and that is principally the reason, I think he hates to have anyone with him."

"I am told he is a very modest man; is he?"

"Oh, he knows the value of his own discoveries; no man better. He is not quite an angel," said he with a laugh.

"Well now, supposing I met him in my travels—I might possibly stumble across him if he travels anywhere in the direction I am going—how would he conduct himself towards me?"

"To tell you the truth," said he, "I do not think he would like it very well. I know if Burton, or Grant, or Baker, or any of those fellows were going after him, and he heard of their coming, Livingstone would put a hundred miles of swamp in a very short time between himself and them. I do, upon my word I do."[7]

Many of Kirk's purported comments about Livingstone are inarguably valid criticisms of the famous explorer. Livingstone was irascible, prone to hyperbole and self-promotion, and not known for careful record keeping. Still, it is hard to imagine the cautious Kirk, so admired by many for his tact in general, and his forbearance with Livingstone in particular, saying such things to a foreign journalist he had just met.

In any case, Stanley left Bagamoyo with 192 porters, 23 Baluchi soldiers, and 3 young white men. Their salaries and the costs of the expedition were borne by the newspaper. One of the whites with him, W. L. Farquhar, became acutely ill with dysentery. Stanley, eager to push on, left him in an African village, though he claimed it was actually at Farquhar's request. Stanley's critics later accused him of abandoning the young man, who died shortly afterwards.[8] Later, in his book *How I Found Livingstone,* he implied that Farquhar's death had been brought on by his heavy drinking.

The news of Stanley's search for Livingstone had been carefully leaked to the international press to heighten anticipation, and the world waited expectantly. In his book, Stanley dramatically recounted how his men fired guns into the air as they approached

Ujiji on November 10, 1871, to alert the village. Africans flocked to greet them, then:

> Suddenly I hear a voice on my right say, "Good morning, Sir!" Startled at hearing this greeting in the midst of such a crowd of black people, I turn sharply around in search of the man and see him by my side. . . . "Who the mischief are you?"
>
> "I am Susi, the servant of Dr. Livingstone," and he smiling and showing a gleaming row of teeth.
>
> "What! Is Dr. Livingstone here?"
>
> "Yes, Sir."
>
> "In this village?"
>
> "Yes, Sir."
>
> "Are you sure?"
>
> "Sure, Sir, why I leave him just now."
>
> My heart beats fast, but I must not let my face betray my emotions. . . . I pushed back the crowds and passing from the rear walked down a living avenue of people, until I came in front of a semi-circle of Arabs, in front of which stood the white man with the grey beard. As I advanced slowly towards him I noticed he was pale, looked wearied, had a grey beard, wore a bluish cap with a faded gold band around it, had on a red-sleeved waistcoat and a pair of grey, tweed trousers. I would have run towards him, only I was a coward in the presence of such a mob—would have embraced him, only he being an Englishman, I didn't know how he would receive me; so I did what cowardice and false pride suggested what was the best thing—walked deliberately to him, took off my hat, and said, "Dr. Livingstone, I presume?"
>
> "Yes," said he with a kind smile, lifting his cap slightly.
>
> I replace my hat on my head, and he puts on his cap, and we both grasp hands, and then I say aloud: "I thank God, Doctor, I have been permitted to see you."
>
> He answered, "I feel thankful I am here to welcome you."[9]

Livingstone was restored by the supplies brought by Stanley, and soon was well enough to explore the north end of Lake Tanganyika with him. Two months later they reached Tabora. As it neared the time for Stanley to return to his newspaper, he tried to talk Livingstone into joining him on his trip back to the coast. The great missionary and explorer could recuperate in Zanzibar, or preferably England. But Livingstone refused to leave. Reiterating what he had said when embarking on the Second Zambezi Expedition, he told Stanley that, as God's instrument, he had been chosen to find the sources of the Nile and Congo Rivers so that they could provide a means of bringing Christianity to the interior and thus eliminate the slave trade.

Despite differences in temperament and background, the missionary and the journalist got along quite well. Both were complicated men, but in different ways. Stanley's hard life had made him a survivor; he was an extrovert, a showman, and an opportunist. He had managed to outwit both sides in the American Civil War. More brutal than humane in his treatment of indigenous Africans, he was equally insensitive to the needs of the white men who accompanied him.

Livingstone, by contrast, was a reticent loner. Though usually patient and kind to the Africans who traveled with him, he could be cold and firm when he detected insubordination. With his fellow whites he was impatient and often antagonistic. He seemed sincerely grateful to Stanley and seemed to take a fatherly interest in him.

Basking in the reflected glory of the man he had immortalized, Stanley described Livingstone in glowing terms: "His gentleness never forsakes him; his hopefulness never deserts him." And Livingstone responded with: "He laid all at my service, divided his clothes into two heaps, and pressed one heap upon me; then his medicine chest; then his goods and everything he had, and to coax my appetite, often cooked dainty dishes with his own hand."[10]

The Attack on Kirk

Both men would find for a time a common target: Kirk. In Stanley's now classic account of his meeting with Livingstone, Kirk is the foil for the reporter's good works. Stanley attacked Kirk for shirking his duty to Livingstone and almost causing his death.

Before Stanley left, Livingstone, with Stanley at his elbow prompting him, wrote Horace Waller, a friend of both Kirk and Livingstone: "By some strange hallucination, our friend Kirk placed some £500 of goods in the hands of slaves with a drunken half-caste tailor as leader. . . . It is simply infamous to employ slaves when a number of freemen may be hired! . . . Tell Kirk not to believe every Banyan's tale. It makes him a gape and not a disciple of David Livingstone's."[11]

Then Livingstone wrote a letter to Kirk on October 30, 1871: ". . . I had just reached this place thoroughly jaded in body and mind, and found that your agent, Shereef Basha, had sold off all the goods you sent for slaves and ivory for himself. . . . With due deference to your judgement, I claim all the expenses incurred, as set down against me in Luddha's books. From the Banyans, who by fraud converted a caravan . . . into a gratification of their own greed."[12] Livingstone also wrote a bitter letter to the sultan in which he castigated Kirk as well as the slave who squandered his supplies.

Then, Livingstone seems to have gotten even more upset at Kirk:

> I have just received information and letters that make the matter doubly serious. Mr. Churchill informed me by letter, of September, 1870, that Her Majesty's Government had most kindly sent £1000 for supplies to be forwarded to me. But you had recourse to slaves again, and one of those slaves informs me they remained at Bagamoio four months. . . . A whole year has thus been spent in feasting. . . . I want men, not slaves . . . I may wait twenty years and your slaves feast and fail.[13]

Stanley knew that the more important Livingstone became to his reading public, the more important Stanley himself would become. In revitalizing the Livingstone legend, he had to create a villain. That villain became Kirk.

But why not make Shereef Basha the villain? After all, it was he who had absconded with Livingstone's effects. But Basha was a mere slave while Kirk represented the British Empire and was thus a much larger target. Perhaps jealousy of Livingstone's affection for Kirk may also have been a factor. Or did Stanley sincerely believe Livingstone's pitiful condition was Kirk's fault?

Kirk, piqued and defiant at Stanley's and Livingstone's accusations—which was out of character for him—wrote to the Earl of Granville at the Foreign Office:

> I shall at once open criminal proceedings on the charges of slaveholding and fraud brought forward by Dr. Livingstone against the parties named . . . and report to your Lordship. . . .I refrain from making any observations on the very uncourteous tone of these official letters or the ungenerous personal insinuations affecting myself and Mr. Churchill's conduct in the manner with which we carried out your Lordship's wishes to send aid to Dr. Livingstone, but I shall be ready, when required, to answer any point on which your Lordship may call for an explanation.[14]

When the triumphant Stanley returned to Zanzibar, he ran into Kirk again, this time at the American consul's house. Stanley recorded the conversation,

> "Doctor, I fear I will not be able to dispatch the expedition to Dr. Livingstone as early as I hoped. . . . I shall have to ask you to take charge of it."
> [Kirk replied,] "If you do I shall have to decline it. I am not going to expose myself to needless insult again."
> "Needless insult, did you say, Dr. Kirk?"
> "Yes."
> "May I ask what it consists of?"
> "He [Livingstone] blames me for the failure of the caravans to reach him, and charges me with having employed slaves. If the men did not reach him, how can I help it?"[15]

Stanley's attack on Kirk created a major scandal and the worst crisis to date in Kirk's life. When Stanley reached England several months later, the London crowds cheered him. He received the Royal Geographic Society's Gold Medal and ovations at many other cities in the United Kingdom. When he spoke in Edinburgh, where Kirk had received his medical degree, he spent half his time castigating Kirk. In a melodramatic speech, he suggested Kirk's supposed negligence could have martyred Livingstone:

> I was an utter stranger to both Dr. Kirk and Dr. Livingstone. I cared for the one no more than I cared for the other. . . . If I had seen or known Dr. Kirk to be friendly to Dr. Livingstone it would have been a very happy task for me to convey to you my experience of the kindness which Dr. Kirk had shown Dr. Livingstone. Now, I do not charge Dr. Kirk with any willful neglect, or with any feelings of jealousy. That is far from my mind. . . . The first question I asked myself . . . was . . . if Dr. Kirk, Her Britannic Majesty's consul and political resident, could not start an expedition on 35 men to Central Africa in three and a half months, how long would it take me—an utter stranger, a private individual—to start an expedition of 192 men? Well, if I could start that expedition of 192 men in two months, I certainly have reason to be surprised that this little expedition [of Kirk's] remained there a hundred days. . . . Then also Livingstone adds to this that repeatedly caravans sent from Zanzibar to the central region had failed to reach him and that he wondered what was the matter with his friends in Zanzibar—why Dr. Kirk had sent him slaves—and what should I have said if some man told me afterwards that Livingstone died because the expedition from Zanzibar came too late? (Cheers.)

> When Dr. Livingstone prefers to lodge a formal complaint against Dr. Kirk—not against the doctor, himself, but simply against that dilatoriness; that is all, not against him as a man—he just wished to say, though it was a formal complaint, "My dear Kirk, why did you send those slaves to me?" Was he drawing a parallel with Jesus on the cross where Jesus was reported to have cried out before dying, "My God, why hast thou forsaken me?"

Stanley kept broadcasting the same condemnatory message, painting himself as speaking for the saintly Livingstone, who was inclined to forgive a shameless act of betrayal:

> What had I to do with Dr. Kirk? Was he not alive in Zanzibar, where he could write all he wished to his own government, and explain everything he liked to explain to the people? But Dr. Livingstone was absent; and as he was absent, it was my place, knowing the facts, to explain them to the people. (Applause.) . . . How many a one would have contented himself saying (as Livingstone had), "My dear Kirk, I am sorry to bring this unpleasant subject before you." Would you and I not have expressed ourselves in hot, flaming language, in burning words—with all the force of which the English language is capable? (Applause.) To this man in Africa with the dark midnight of barbarism around him, suffering even on the edge of the grave—a ruckle of bones—as he said himself. . . . I will explain the thing to the people, let them blame whom they may. (Applause.) . . . If God gave me a heart to feel, should I have falsified my own nature and prepared to meet Dr. Livingstone's complaints in connection with his arduous labors for six years with a cool indifference by saying, my dear Dr. Livingstone, you settle this with Dr. Kirk as you like, but do not burden my ears with this tale. (Applause.)

He ended his speech with a vitriolic attack on Kirk.

> But the gentleman who has got his fame and position as the friend of Dr. Livingstone left him in Africa, silent, alone, deserted, and almost at death's door. . . . Dr. Kirk, himself, first wrote to friends at Seychelles that Livingstone was crazy. Rather than blame Livingstone, I prefer that you should blame me as much as you like. (Laughter.) . . . But I have been so led away . . . by the real and

true interest which I knew you felt in Dr. Livingstone, that I could not help speaking as I have done. (Applause.)[16]

Livingstone was still a living saint to the British, and if he had really talked about Kirk the way Stanley said he did, Kirk's career as a government official would have quickly ended. Fortunately, one of Livingstone's letters reached the Foreign Office in time to repudiate Stanley's accusations. "I regret very much to hear incidentally that Dr. Kirk viewed my formal complaint against Banyans as a covert attack upon himself. . . . I never had any difference with him, though we were together for years, and I had no intention to give offense now."[17]

After Stanley began his lecture tour in England, he quickly realized that Kirk was still held in great esteem by the British, and he retracted his accusations in the appendix to the first edition of *How I Found Livingstone.* He even wrote, "Dr. Kirk can rest assured that I have a sincere admiration for himself."[18] In subsequent editions he mentioned Kirk only three times and not at all in the appendix. Sensing Kirk to be a hero in his own right among the British public, and having already successfully used Kirk as a whipping boy for his own self-aggrandizement, he apparently now thought it best to lay his accusations to rest.

Kirk Investigated

Kirk bore his attacks in his typically stoic manner, refusing to become embroiled in a conflict with this flamboyant showman. Perhaps the silent treatment worked best, because Stanley avoided mentioning Kirk in most of his subsequent dispatches. But the press would not let go. How had an American expedition, headed by a New York journalist, been able to upstage the British by arriving in the nick of time to save a "saint," when supplies from a representative of the Crown could not be delivered successfully?

This prompted Granville of the Foreign Office to send a commission of inquiry to Zanzibar in 1874 to investigate Stanley's allegations and to determine if Kirk had been lax in his duties. The commission was headed by Sir Bartle Frere, the distinguished statesman who had appointed Kirk six years earlier to the British consulate at Zanzibar. He was charged with determining if "the complaints of Dr. Livingstone are well founded . . . and whether Dr. Kirk is in any way to blame for the delays that took place in expediting the stores to Dr. Livingstone or for their plunder and failure to reach him."[19]

To Kirk, this was more than an annoyance. It was an insult to think that an adventurer like Stanley could turn the Foreign Office upside down and waste his time and the commission's.

Frere, though, came down solidly on Kirk's side. He replied to the Foreign Office that he'd read all the pertinent material and interviewed Kirk:

> On the first point, as to how far the complaints of Dr. Livingstone were well-founded, there can, I think, be no doubt that they were. The things sent to him did not reach him; those taken by and sent to Mr. Stanley did reach him. Clearly then, there was good ground for complaints of the non-arrival of Dr. Livingstone's packages. On the second point . . . Dr. Kirk availed himself of the agency of the largest and most influential Hindoo house in Zanzibar. They had been, I believe without hardly an exception, always employed by the English Consulate on similar work, and had usually been most successful.
>
> Mr. Stanley, I believe, employed the broker of theAmerican Consul . . . [who] ranks only second to the Hindoo house in general estimation. . . . But judging from all I hear and have read, I have little doubt that Mr. Stanley's own convoy would have failed to reach Ujiji but, for his presence with it, and the extraordinary energy with which he pressed it forward.
>
> On [the] third and last question, whether Dr. Kirk is in anyway to blame for the delays that took place in expediting the stores to Dr. Livingstone, I have no hesitation, whatsoever, that he is not. He seems to have done what any one on the spot, after judging after the event, would have said what was for the best, and his want of success was in no way due to want of care, precaution, local knowledge, or energy or any defect in judgement in the choice of his agents.

Frere adds in this official communication:

> But what appears to be conclusive on this subject is the testimony of the great traveler himself . . . and I cannot find that, even in the first manifestation of natural and pardonable vexation, Dr. Livingstone imputes to his old friend anything more than being taken in by their agent . . . , Dr. Livingstone explains very clearly and distinctly that he imputed to

> Dr. Kirk no more than companionship with himself in the misfortune of putting their trust in men who deceived them, and he disclaims in the most pointed and emphatic manner all intention of accusing his friend of anything more than participation in their common misfortune.

In conclusion, Frere wrote that Kirk:

> is conspicuous for the careful, conscientious, laborious, and most efficient discharge of every duty connected with the important offices he holds here, and is not likely to have failed in what was to him a labor of love and a duty of long and uninterrupted friendship and I cannot conclude this Memorandum without expressing my conviction that Dr. Livingstone never had here, possibly not in any part of the world, a truer and warmer friend than Dr. Kirk.[20]

After Stanley had left, Livingstone had received a letter from his son, W. Oswell Livingstone, who admonished his father for listening to Stanley and attacking Kirk. Livingstone then wrote an apologetic letter to Kirk, "I am sorry to hear by a note from Oswell that you had taken my formal complaint of certain Banyans and Arabs as a covert attack on yourself: this grieves me deeply, for it is a result I never intended to produce. . . . It looked to me as if a band of dishonest persons had conspired to hoodwink you and me."[21]

While the charge of betrayal was never repeated, the idea that Kirk had been guilty of culpable negligence didn't vanish entirely. For example, W. G. Blaikie's *The Personal Life of David Livingstone,* published in 1880 and still the most authoritative biography, praises the "gallant Stanley" and leaves little doubt that the author believed that Kirk failed in his duty.[22] Later biographers have tended to suggest that Kirk was unfairly blemished, giving credence to Sir Bartle Frere's conclusion.

Livingstone "Missing" Again

Once Stanley left, no one saw Livingstone again. His nephew Robert Moffat joined a second relief expedition led by Royal Navy Lieutenant Verney L. Cameron when the Royal Geographic Society selected him in 1872 to find Livingstone. Because of difficulties in hiring porters, they got off to a slow start, not leaving the coast until March 28, 1873. Once in the interior, the members suffered from fever, and two months later Moffat died, probably of falciparum malaria.[23]

We know from Livingstone's journal that on January 3, 1873, he headed west toward Katanga in the present-day Democratic Republic of the Congo in his quest for the sources of the Congo and Nile rivers. By January 9 he reached the village of Chungu in an area flooded by heavy rains. The chief, mistaking him for an Arab slaver, purposely sent him further west into marshlands, where he tramped for days in sometimes knee-deep brackish water. Eventually he grew so weak that his men had to carry him on their shoulders. They were all short of food and lived mainly on dried beans. The beans too ran out, but on February 4 they found a deserted garden where they were able to dig up sweet potatoes and cassava.

Temporarily stronger, Livingstone insisted that they keep going, noting in his journal that he continued to lose blood from his hemorrhoids. On the night of February 17, driver ants, which can jump four feet high and cause painful bites, invaded his tent. Covered with the ants, he ran out into heavy rain. His men picked off the ants and set grass fires to drive them away. Livingstone finally met a friendly chief who lent him canoes to cross Lake Bangweolo and reach drier ground. He set up camp on the left bank of the Chambezi River to recuperate, but after resuming his trek on March 20, he suddenly developed excruciating abdominal pain and became so weak he had to be carried in an improvised litter. With each movement of the litter, his pain became worse.

On April 29, the party reached the village of chief Chitambo, who offered the sick man a hut. He visited Livingstone the next day, but the suffering explorer was too weak to talk, probably from peritonitis from a perforated bowel.[24] At 4 A.M. on May 1, 1873, Livingstone's faithful servant Susi found him kneeling by the side of his bed, his head between his hands in the attitude of prayer. His body had already turned cold.

Chuma and Susi then carefully removed the internal organs and buried Livingstone's heart under a Myonga tree at Chitambo's. His two faithful followers then salted down the abdominal cavity and dried the corpse in the sun for two weeks. Wrapping the body in calico, they fitted it into a cylinder of bark which was then covered with sailcloth. The bundle was suspended from a pole and carried like a litter by two of the men. His followers also gathered up his journals and wrapped them carefully to preserve them.

The little group left Chitambo in the middle of May 1873, led by a drummer boy and followed by natives carrying the Union Jack and the sultan's scarlet flag. The party ran into trouble only once, when it was attacked by drunken villagers who refused to let them into their stockade for the night. The party shot its way into the stockaded village, and chased the assailants off, killing two and wounding several others.

Meanwhile, Lieutenant Cameron's expedition, following the trail left by Livingstone, ran into Chuma at the southern end of Lake Tanganyika. Hearing of Livingstone's death, Cameron tried to talk Chuma out of carrying the corpse all the way to the coast, but Chuma, loyal to the end, refused. Livingstone, he felt, would want to be buried in England.[25]

Cameron went on to explore the lower end of Lake Tanganyika, discover the source of the Zambezi River, and, emulating Livingstone, cross equatorial Africa from the Indian Ocean to the Atlantic, reaching Angola two and a half years later. Chuma and his men, meanwhile, carried Livingstone's body all the way to the Indian Ocean, arriving at Bagamoyo on February 15, 1874. They had walked 700 miles in nine months.

Kirk was on leave in England at the time, so the acting British consul took charge of the remains and Livingstone's journal. Livingstone's body was shrunken and mummified, and when it reached England, it was positively identified by Kirk and some of Livingstone's old friends from the condition of the upper left arm, which had been deformed in an encounter with a lion many years before.

Livingstone had fulfilled the British public's concept of martyrdom. Interred at Westminster Abbey at a huge funeral on April 18, 1874, Livingstone in death was even more popular than in life because he had tried to bring Christian values to Central Africa and, in the popular mind, gave his life in an attempt to suppress the slave trade. His contradictory nature was ignored. His blind pursuit of his goals without regard for the safety of others was forgotten. His inability to get along with his fellow Englishmen was overlooked. Instead, he was eulogized for his compassion, his love of his fellow man, and his understanding of and tolerance for Africans.

In a speech published in the *Journal of the Society of Arts,* Sir Bartle Frere said:

> Livingstone was intellectually and morally as perfect a man as it has ever been my fortune to meet, one who formed vast designs for the good of mankind, and placed his hopes of achieving them in no earthly power, but in Him who created the universe and controls the raging of nations. . . .

In all he did he worked in the same spirit as the great apostles of old, and he has done for civilization and religion a work which has had few parallels since the days of the early martyrs of our faith. Martyr he was and hero, and we may no longer lament him than other heroes who have died in their country's service, or holy men who have entered into their rest.[26]

12

With the Stroke of a Pen

In 1872, while Livingstone was still wandering in Central Africa, Kirk wrote to the Foreign Office, "Never, since coming to Zanzibar, have I seen so many large dhows come in, crowded with slaves, and seldom have the slaves imported been landed in a worse state."[1] Most slaves Kirk would have seen, in fact, would die before the age of thirty-five from diseases, accidents, or malnutrition. His perception of increasing numbers of these unfortunates was most accurate; the slave trade through Zanzibar had increased rather than diminished.

Ten years earlier, Sultan Majid had issued a proclamation forbidding mainland Arabs from buying slaves and shipping them to Zanzibar for sale. But this proclamation was made simply to placate the British, and it merely spurred slave smuggling. The recent cholera epidemic that had swept the island and its neighboring islands of Pemba and Mafia had killed one-quarter of the estimated slaves in 1872. Most had been used in the clove plantations and had to be replaced.

As far back as the mid-1830s, the clove plantations had become widespread on the island. "The easy profits which clove plantations yielded made all the inhabitants of Zanzibar turn their eyes towards the crop . . . almost everybody on the island is clearing away the coconuts to make way for them," wrote Kirk to Granville.[2]

Many of the landowners were of Omani origin, though Shirazi (Persian) and Swahili (Bantu-Arab) also owned a considerable number of plantations. By the 1860s a new landed aristocracy had taken root on the island based on the intense monoculture of cloves. So much land was devoted to the cultivation of cloves that there was no longer enough rice planted to feed the population, necessitating its import along with other cereals and vegetables. Like cotton before the invention of the cotton gin in the United States, the cultivation of cloves was heavily slave dependent. The Swahili slave trader Tippu Tib himself owned seven plantations worked by as many as 10,000 slaves and worth 50,000 Maria Theresa dollars[3] at the end of the nineteenth century.

In 1860, during Sultan Said's reign, the annual income from the slave tax was about $10,000, based on $2 a head for 5,000 slaves imported per annum, most of whom were transshipped to the Arabian Peninsula and Persian Gulf region. By 1871, the sultan's income had risen to $100,000 by Kirk's estimate.[4]

With the increased importation and sale of slaves to make up for the losses following the 1872 hurricane, which had destroyed much of the clove crop, and the cholera epidemic, which had been so devastating to the slave population, the English government, at the urging of British abolitionists, offered a financial subsidy to those slave-owning nations who had the most to lose by stopping the slave trade. This was done in the mistaken belief that if the money was offered, those countries would spontaneously abolish the trade.

The governor of Bombay, Sir Bartle Frere, arrived in Zanzibar on January 12, 1873, hoping to persuade Bargash to sign a new and more comprehensive antislavery treaty. He stayed at the British consulate and held long strategy meetings with Kirk and the Reverend G.P. Badger. An Arabist who knew Bargash from previous visits to Zanzibar, Badger told Kirk they wanted an all-inclusive treaty prohibiting the capture and export of slaves to Zanzibar and their transshipment to the Arabian and Gulf states. This would, for the first time, put teeth into the previous treaties signed by Bargash's predecessors, Sultans Said and Majid.

In the Moresby treaty of 1822 with Great Britain, Sultan Said, the ruler of Oman and Zanzibar, agreed to stop the seaborne trade but not the internal trade in slaves. The seaborne trade was to be eliminated north of Cape Delgado (Mozambique) and to the east of a line drawn from Diu, India, to a point east of the island of Socotra off the Somali coast (see Map 6 on page 94).

In spite of this, slaves continued to be shipped from Zanzibar across the Red Sea to the Persian Gulf nations. In 1845 a second treaty banned all transport of slaves by sea except among the sultan's dominions in Africa, but it was not enforced. Thus, only theoretically was the trade limited to between the coast, Zanzibar, and other dependencies of Sultan Said.

The terms of the 1847 treaty called for the prohibition of the import or export of slaves to and from the sultanate but did not prohibit the traffic between cities within the sultanate. The treaty's full text is in Appendix C on page 268. This treaty, like the other preceding it, was more of a balm to the British antislavery societies than a way of choking out the slave trade, for the sultan did not enforce the provisions, nor did the British have enough ships in the Indian Ocean to stop ships transporting slaves.

Majid, who succeeded his father Sultan Said, then issued a proclamation in 1862 forbidding Northern Arabs to buy slaves and ship them out of Zanzibar. Yet the clandestine trade continued to flourish, forcing Majid to furnish two further proclamations in January 1864:

> I. Know that we have ordained that no owners of boats shall transport slaves in their boats from any part of our dominions during the monsoon (from January 1 to May 1).[The monsoon blew the slave dhows eastward during this time to the Arabian Peninsula.]
>
> II. We have ordered all our subjects not to rent their houses to the people of the north employed in stealing slaves.

Since these proclamations were also ignored, Majid issued a third in March 1868.

> III. Any ship caught carrying slaves anywhere along the coast during the monsoon will be burned. Any subject of the Sultan's convicted of sharing in the slave traffic with Arabia will be fined and exiled from Zanzibar. Any person selling slaves to Northern Arabs will be fined.[5]

Again, the profit was too great, and the enforcement too lax to make a dent in the slave trade. The trade was still openly flourishing when Sir Bartle Frere arrived on the scene. In a letter to a friend he described the conditions he observed firsthand:

> The slave market is a hideous sight—a dirty, uneven space surrounded with filthy huts. The commoner slaves—generally children, seated in lines or batches—were miserably thin and

> ill; hardly any had more than a few rags to cover them; two or three runaways in chains—and all but a few having that look of stolid indifference which a sheep or cow would have. Some of the younger and better fed women were well clad and had a silver ornament on. As we came away we met batches being taken to the market, and in some cases I observed that the guards, when they saw Europeans coming, pushed their charges into the nearest door and stood there till we were past.[6]

Frere's first meeting with Sultan Bargash did not go well. Bargash, on looking over the treaty, which had been translated into Arabic to prevent any misunderstanding, immediately challenged it, claiming the terms were so onerous that they would destroy his sultanate and bankrupt the island's large landowners, including his advisors, the Mlawas. When he met again with Kirk, Frere threw his hands in the air. "I couldn't get anywhere with this fellow," he said, and asked Kirk to have a go at it. Needing to leave the island on other business, he empowered Kirk to act as de facto chief consul and find a way, if he could, to convince the sultan to sign.

A few days later, Kirk entered the palace. Bargash greeted him as effusively as always. But when they were seated, Bargash looked sadly at his friend and said, following the advice of the Mlawas, "When you have heaped a load on your camel that it cannot pass the city gate, do you not lessen the burden and gain your object? Now lessen this heavy burden, be it ever so little, and we are your servants, and you will gain all you desire. Give us some respite and we will accept the treaty."

At his next meeting with Kirk, Bargash was more distant and cold. "We cannot sign the new treaty on account of the hardship it involves to us, on account of dread of insurrection, and on account of the ruin it would cause to the plantations of our subjects. . . . In one word, No!"[7]

Even if he had wanted to, Kirk was powerless to grant significant concessions without Frere's approval. When Frere returned to the island on February 11, he suggested that Kirk should enlist the help of the American, German, and French consuls to pressure Bargash into reconsidering. The American Civil War was over, and Hamilton Fish, the U.S. Secretary of State, promised to lend his enthusiastic support. Captain Wilson of the *Yantic,* an American navy vessel in port at that time, wrote to the sultan, urging him to sign the treaty and to stop "the traffic in human flesh."[8]

But the actual American consul, W.G. Webb, undercut his superior's decision by letting the sultan know he would support him if he would just limit, not necessarily end, slave trading. Since Captain Wilson and Consul Webb had received identical instructions from Secretary Fish, Kirk was perplexed, but he subsequently found out that Webb considered Kirk to be an "empire builder" and someone who discredited Americans generally and threw obstacles in their way. Perhaps Webb resented the fact that Kirk had become the power behind the sultan's throne.

Kirk knew Bargash was responsive to pressure. So he called on Consul Webb and asked him, point blank, if he would assist the British in stamping out the slave trade. Webb replied evasively that his instructions from Secretary Fish were merely to stop the slave trade between Zanzibar and Oman, but not to get involved in the trade elsewhere. Kirk wrote to Fish asking for an explanation, but, as in most foreign office bureaucracies, Fish officially defended his consul's actions.[9]

To compound the situation, the French, who were also envious of Kirk's relationship with Bargash and who had territorial ambitions of their own in East Africa, ordered their consul to back Webb. Thus, emboldened by French and U.S. assurances, Bargash refused again to sign the treaty.

The British Foreign Office put pressure on the French in the name of humanity; three months later the French agreed, at least in principle, to back the British. But Bargash, by now more afraid than ever of being assassinated by the Mlawas and wealthy plantation owners who would "lose a fortune" if the treaty was approved, once more refused to sign it.

Because of these setbacks, Frere decided to terminate his official mission. But before leaving, he left instructions with Kirk to get the sultan to agree, if possible, to a modified treaty:

1. The shipment of slaves from the interior will be considered the equivalent of piracy on the high seas. (Violation would be considered a breach of international law and subject to the death penalty.)
2. The transport of slaves from port to port on the East African coast will be abolished.
3. The slave auctions are to be stopped and the markets closed.
4. If custom houses continued to allow the trans-shipment of slaves, they should also be closed.
5. The anti-slavery patrol will be increased to 14 ships of the line, 10 for the East African coast and four to patrol the coast of the Arabian Peninsula and the Red Sea.

6. All slaves coming into or leaving Zanzibar will be freed by the British Consul unless they are domestic slaves owned by subjects of the sultan on the island or on the mainland so those previously owned could continue to be kept in servitude.[10]

Frere was keenly aware of the tremendous amount of consular and judicial work that had fallen on Kirk's shoulders. He had seen both Kirk and his wife putting in twelve or more hours a day, and he realized that if the health of this talented and hardworking man should fail due to the strain of overwork, the Empire would lose a key player in the fight against the slave trade. He therefore recommended to the Foreign Office that Kirk be appointed permanently as consul general and that the consulate be expanded to include two consular attachés. Captain Frederick Elton, who had been a "frontier agent" pacifying native tribes in India, was accordingly dispatched on Frere's recommendation to Zanzibar as vice-consul and assistant political agent, while Frederick Holmwood became general assistant in the office and in Kirk's judicial court.

For someone of Kirk's background, as mentioned in the Prologue, to be appointed a consul general was highly unusual at that time. Among Foreign Office diplomats and consuls, all but 6 percent had graduated from either Oxford or Cambridge and had military backgrounds. Kirk was in the decided minority, having graduated from the University of Edinburgh.

Furthermore, colonial servants with an aristocratic background —which Kirk did not have—were typically the ones appointed to key positions in the Foreign Office. Physicians, like Kirk, could usually only aspire to consulate positions and almost never to be chief consuls.[11]

Frere's departure and recommendation that Kirk be made consul general suddenly boosted this physician into a position of extraordinary responsibility. As acting chief consul, he had expected to be replaced any day by someone high up in the Foreign Office. Now, should the new position be confirmed, he would be the most important British representative in eastern Africa. His immediate mandate remained, of course, to obtain the sultan's acquiescence to the treaty.

The duties of consuls like Kirk were not only to represent British commercial and political interests and protect British subjects, but also to become standard bearers of British morality and principles. They were also instructed to convey to the Foreign Office the attitudes and mindset of the citizens and government of the country they were assigned to and to request guidance or approval from the Foreign Office before making important decisions.

Frere, after leaving Zanzibar, called on the sultan of Oman and persuaded Turki, Bargash's half brother, to sign a separate, but identical, treaty to the one Bargash had rejected. The $40,000 annual payment that Bargash owed Turki had not been paid for the previous two years, and Frere reassured Turki that the amount would be forthcoming, confident that the sultan would cough up the money, given the pressure that he was being put under.[12]

Kirk, meanwhile, returned once again to the palace, this time with the request that Bargash close the Zanzibar slave market. The sultan agreed, though he knew that the auctioneers would merely move it to another section of town. Sure enough, a new auction building—more modern and with a roof—was promptly constructed.

The Ante Is Raised

When Lord Granville, Frere's superior in London, heard of the treaty impasse, he feared that Kirk might be pushing Bargash into the waiting hands of the French. It was time for a show of force. In a telegram received by Kirk on June 2, 1873, Granville instructed: "You will state to the Sultan that if the treaty . . . is not signed by him before the arrival of Admiral Cumming, who is ordered to proceed at once to Zanzibar, the British naval forces will at once proceed to blockade the island of Zanzibar."[13]

Bargash wanted to avoid a long-term blockade because it would create financial havoc for himself and his subjects. If the blockade were enforced, cloves and other produce would be left rotting on the docks, and unsold slaves would have to be fed and maintained at great expense. A desperate Bargash, if still in power, would need to borrow millions of pounds, if not from Britain, then from France or some other foreign power vying for control of Zanzibar's deep-water port.

Meanwhile, the health of the recalcitrant American consul, W.G. Webb, had been deteriorating, and he was recalled. His replacement, F.R. Webb, no relation, was much more cooperative with the British and urged Bargash to sign the treaty. The German consul, Theodore Schultz, also agreed, in principle, to back the British attempt to convince the sultan to sign.

On June 3, buoyed by the seeming consensus among the Europeans, Kirk returned to the palace, treaty in hand. He spoke Arabic without an interpreter, patiently explaining to the sultan and his four top counselors the ramifications of a blockade.

The sultan fought back. "I thought you were my friend. Of all the foreigners, I only trusted you. How can you do this to me?" When he added that this was negotiating by ultimatum, Kirk reminded him of Bismarck's comment to the defeated Napoleon III at the Treaty of 1870 ending the Franco-Prussian War, "I have come not to discuss, but to dictate."[14] Kirk conveyed the same to the sultan, but then he told him that he wanted to remain his devoted friend and would always do his best to protect him and the sultanate with the backing of British power.

Bargash faced a dilemma. If he signed the treaty, it would mean a major loss of income, though he would hardly be destitute. (Kirk calculated that the sultan's yearly trade in ivory, tobacco, and india rubber alone amounted to $308,000). More frightening was the high probability of an Arab revolt against Bargash, ending, most probably, in his murder. On the other hand, Bargash knew he needed British protection from Turki in Oman and other foreign powers.

At this juncture, Kirk, believing he had to be even more firm, told the sultan, "I am here today as representative of the Queen of England and to tell you that this is an ultimatum. To reject it means British naval power will strangle your island and its possessions and bring the sultanate to ruin."[15]

Bargash countered by saying he had to consult Suliman bin Hamed, an immensely wealthy slave dealer who had been advisor to Said and to Majid. A clever old man, Suliman favored the French, openly disliked Kirk, and vocally opposed the treaty.

That evening Bargash called Kirk back to the palace. When Kirk entered the throne room, he found the sultan surrounded by the Mlawa leaders. They sat on either side of the ruler and listened to Kirk reiterate the demand. Bargash asked Kirk to wait in the hall while he argued with the Mlawas for over an hour. Kirk was then called back in, and Bargash said he and the Mlawas wanted modifications before he could sign the treaty.

He didn't have the power to make major changes, Kirk replied. Bargash, losing his temper, cried out, "I will go to England, myself, and plead my case." Why couldn't the blockade be postponed until he could telegraph Kirk from England after his discussion with Queen Victoria? Kirk perhaps could even act as Zanzibar's regent in his absence.

Kirk replied tactfully, but firmly, that it would be a waste of time to attempt to reverse the decision. The slave trade had to be shut down. The sultan again requested more time to confer with his advisors, and Kirk left with the unsigned treaty under his arm.

In his next correspondence with the Foreign Office, Kirk wrote that Bargash had treated him with great courtesy and respect, and expressed confidence that the sultan was fairly certain to sign. Meanwhile, rumors of all kinds were circulating in the city, including one that had Emily Reute, the sultan's estranged sister, arranging to have a French warship take Bargash away. The French consul was also apparently still trying to undermine Kirk, for Bargash later confided that the French had secretly urged him not to sign.

While this maneuvering was going on, Granville sent Kirk a secret message to grant the sultan some minor concessions. When Kirk was called back to the palace for still another meeting, the sultan was surrounded by his counselors, including all the leading sheiks of the island's Arab community. He asked Kirk if he would agree to inserting the phrase, "to the utmost of his powers?" This modifying clause would acknowledge the sultan's limitations as sovereign to enforce the treaty and, thus, might save his hide with his fellow Arabs.

Kirk considered for a moment, then agreed. But this only led Bargash to begin bargaining in earnest. Abolishing all trade in slaves would cause terrible financial hardship, he repeated. If only as few as 10,000 slaves a year could still be allowed to be shipped to Zanzibar, the sultan pleaded, it would ease the burden considerably. Kirk, however, calmly and firmly refused.[16]

A sample of one of Bargash's letters to Kirk is typical of the verbal maneuvering on Bargash's part. Translated from the Arabic, it reads:

> In the name of God the Merciful the Compassionate:
> To H.E. [His Excellency] our Magnificent and well-beloved friend, Sir John Kirk, may his prosperity be perpetual. "Know, O friend, that we do not doubt the benevolence of the English government and its helpfulness towards us and our subjects. But it may be that the exalted English government is not aware of Zanzibar's need for slaves. The people of Zanzibar can do nothing, not even clip their whiskers, without the servants and slaves they own; if they were deprived of them they would be impoverished and their possessions worth nothing. An Arab would refuse any offer for his servant and would rather perish than manumit his servant. . . .
>
> I see as plainly as I see the sun that the Arabs would revolt. Such being the case, the exalted government—we believe—would not wish this on us or our subjects. This is the time for

the government to help us. We ask of its benevolence that it should delay this clause to Zanzibar. We believe absolutely that it wishes us well; this then is the time for it to do us a favor. . . . As for the governments of *Turks* and of the *Shah of Persia,* they are not in need of servants. Their affairs prosper and provide for them, and it is all the same to them whether slavery is abolished or maintained among them, whereas we the people of Zanzibar would be extremely badly affected. . . . God forbid that the exalted English nation should consent to the ruination of our country and impoverishment of our subjects. . . .

Everything that the Government and its agents have desired we carry out regularly; there is never any defiance on our part. This is what we desire of the Government postponement.[17]

Prescription for Freedom

When Bargash asked Kirk whether existing slaves would still be allowed to travel with their masters by sea, bearing in mind Granville's message, Kirk agreed. Could runaway slaves who made it to the mainland be pursued and returned to their rightful masters? No, Kirk replied, they would no longer be considered legitimate property.

Bargash reiterated that since the greater part of his income would be cut off, he wanted to go to England at once to obtain financial help for his poor country. Kirk gently advised him to postpone the trip until the Zanzibari and Arab merchants on the mainland had time to adjust to the new treaty and had found other means of maintaining their income.

Kirk remained polite and firm while the struggling sultan kept asking him to return to discuss further modifications in the treaty. All were refused. Finally, on the morning of June 5, 1873, five months after the Frere mission began, Bargash grudgingly agreed to sign the treaty while reiterating that his life was in constant danger.

Kirk reviewed the treaty with Bargash line by line:

Treaty between Great Britain and Zanzibar for the Suppression of the Slave Trade

In the Name of the Most High God Her Majesty, the Queen of the United Kingdom of Great Britain and Ireland, and his Highness, the Seyyid Bargash-bin-Said, Sultan of Zanzibar, being desirous to give more complete effect to the engagements entered into by the Sultan and his predecessors for the perpetual abolition of the Slave Trade, they have appointed as their representatives to conclude a new treaty for this purpose, which shall be binding upon themselves, their heirs and successors, that is to say, Her Majesty the Queen of Great Britain and Ireland has appointed to that end John Kirk, the agent of the British Government at Zanzibar, and His Highness the Seyyid Bargash, the Sultan of Zanzibar, has appointed to that end Nazir-bin-Said, and the two aforenamed after having communicated to each other their respective full powers, have agreed upon and concluded the following articles:

Article I
The provision of the existing Treaties having proved ineffectual for preventing the export of slaves from the territories of the Sultan of Zanzibar in Africa, Her Majesty the Queen and His Highness the Sultan above named agree that from this date the export of slaves from the coast to the mainland of Africa, whether destined for transport from one part of the Sultan's dominions to another or for conveyance to foreign parts, shall entirely cease. And His Highness the Sultan binds himself, to the best of his ability, to prevent and abolish the same. And any vessel engaged in the transport or conveyance of slaves after this date shall be liable to seizure and condemnation by all such naval or other officers or agents, and such Courts as may be authorized for that purpose on the part of Her Majesty.

Article II
His Highness the Sultan engages that all public markets in his dominions for the buying and selling of imported slaves shall be entirely closed.

Article III
His Highness, the Sultan above named, engages to protect to the utmost of his ability all liberated slaves, and to punish severely any attempt to molest them or to reduce them again to slavery.

Article IV
Her Britannic Majesty engages that natives of Indian States under British protection shall be prohibited from possessing slaves and from acquiring any fresh slaves in the meantime, from this date. [This meant that the Banyan merchants who made money by lending it to the Arab slave traders to equip their slave-raiding expeditions, and who also owned many slaves, would lose both sources of income.]

Article V
The present treaty shall be ratified and the ratification shall be exchanged, at Zanzibar, as soon as possible, but in any case in the course of the 9th of Rabia el Akhir (5th of June, 1873) of the months of the date thereof.

In witness whereof the respective plenipotentiaries have signed the same, and have affixed their seals to this Treaty, made the 5th of June, 1873, corresponding to the ninth month Rabia el Akhir, 1290.

JOHN KIRK
POLITICAL AGENT,[18] ZANZIBAR
The mean in God's sight,
NASIR-BIN-SAID-BIN ABDALLAH,
With his own hand.
THE HUMBLE, THE POOR,
BARGASH-BIN-SAID,
With his own hand.[19]

A Great Victory

It had been a great victory. After the signing, Kirk received acclamations from all over Europe and America for his role in the negotiations. He had managed to obtain from the sultan, remarkably peacefully, a decree which effectively abolished the slave trade in eastern Africa and parts of southern Africa.

This was a remarkable feat, doubly so given the fact that during these long, arduous negotiations, Kirk had been careful to promise nothing more than to stand by Bargash and do his best to defend his throne for him. What is even more amazing is that Kirk managed to retain the sultan's friendship. Kirk's genius, as he'd shown with Livingstone and now with the sultan, was his ability to convey to others a feeling of dependability and integrity which enabled real progress to be made.

Clearly, the threat of the British blockade was an important factor in Kirk's success. But if Bargash had continued to refuse to sign, the treaty could have been delayed for years. It is also unlikely that the blockade would have been enforced effectively; if it had been enforced, it would likely have been short-lived if for no other reason than that the island and its deep-water harbor were strategically important and, unlike most in the region, could accommodate the largest of British warships. Further, the British did not want a bankrupt and rebellious Zanzibar.

To Bargash's credit, after signing the treaty, he immediately ordered the new slave market torn down and issued another edict: "Know that we have prohibited the transport of slaves by sea in all our harbors and have closed the markets for the sale of slaves through all our dominions. Whosoever, therefore, shall ship a slave after this date will render himself liable to punishment."[20]

There was grumbling among Arab and Indian slave owners on the island but no outright violence because not only the sultan, but leading Mlawas, had agreed to the treaty's terms. As an act of good faith in the British, Bargash also agreed to allow Bishop Steere, one of the missionaries on the island, to build an Anglican cathedral where the slave market had stood as long as the height did not exceed the height of the roof on the sultan's palace.

The Difficulties of Enforcement

Kirk wanted to make sure the provisions of the treaty were also carried out on the sultan's mainland possessions. After all, in light of the treaty and the watchful eyes of the British in Zanzibar, the slavers might simply circumvent the island and organize new centers on the mainland. He visited the coastal towns north of Mombassa in October 1873, while Vice-Consul Elton visited the southern ports. Backed by Bargash and the new treaty, they compelled the Indian merchants on the islands and coastal towns in Bargash's territories to free their slaves, but many men and women thus liberated had nowhere to go and simply became poorly paid employees of their former masters.

Though Bargash had signed the treaty, Kirk was not totally sanguine about the long-term results: "It is not to be imagined that contraband traffic in slaves is at an end. This will doubtless continue as long as slavery is an institution of the coast and of the islands, and on so difficult a coast, ways and means will be found to evade the greatest vigilance on our part or that of the sultan."[21]

His fears were soon justified. A loophole in Article V of the 1873 treaty allowed slave dealers to ship their slaves north along the coast beyond the sultan's jurisdiction. Kirk commissioned a secret agent to report on how many were sold that way. Vice-Consul Elton told him a few weeks later that a caravan of 4,000 slaves had already been shipped north from Kilwa and Dar es Salaam.

Kirk visited Barawa in what is now Somalia in May 1874, and described the countryside as barren and inhospitable to human life. Yet the slavers were willing to take the risk of losing a great many of their victims on death marches to that point on the coast as long as they could make a profit. By the time a slave caravan reached Malindi on the coast of Kenya, at least one out of three slaves had died on the trail. The farther north the caravan went, the greater the numbers of death from disease, starvation, and suicide. Although the death rate was staggering, the price at the end was still worth it to the slave merchants. A male slave, for example, sold for $20 U.S. at the end of the inland slave route to Kilwa. After being marched hundreds of miles north to Somalia, the price increased to $50. A female was $7 less, or $43, except for those judged particularly pretty, who were bought as concubines for the same price as the males.[22]

Following the devastation of the clove crop in the hurricane of 1872, the price of cloves had skyrocketed. Pemba, north of Zanzibar, and part of the sultanate where cloves were also grown, had been spared the devastation. As Pemba's residents grew rich on the high demand for cloves, they wanted more slaves to enlarge their plantations and were willing to pay top price to obtain them. Kirk estimated that the demand so far outweighed the danger of being caught that as many 12,000 slaves were smuggled into Pemba in 1873 and 1874 alone.[23]

With the treaties banning the slave trade concluded and the initial surveys of enforcement accomplished, Kirk left for England on a well-deserved leave with Helen and their children. The Kirks had five daughters. Three survived to adulthood: Marion, Nora, and Helen. Their only son, John William Carnegie Kirk, graduated from Cambridge University, joined the British Army in the Boer War, and became an expert on Somalia, publishing a Somali-English dictionary which is still in use. This 1874–75 period was a happy time for the Kirk family. They visited friends and relatives, including his brother, Alexander, now a tycoon in the Scottish shipbuilding industry, but all was not relaxation for the Kirks.

For some time, Bargash had been clamoring to visit Queen Victoria, and on May 9, 1875, the sultan left on a five-week journey to England while Kirk was still there. He brought with him a large retinue, including five of the leading sheiks of Zanzibar. This was not only a courtesy visit, but one to cement ever-strengthening ties with the British Throne. Bargash was honored by both the royals and Parliament for signing the antislavery treaty and invited to discuss its ramifications with the British government. The sultan and his followers were welcomed by Kirk as well as by Sir Bartle Frere. Queen Victoria invited them to Windsor Castle, and Edward, the Prince of Wales, gave them a tour of several English cities, including the highly industrialized Birmingham, Manchester, and Liverpool. Bargash was also taken to inspect the Woolrich Arsenal, Aldershot Camp, and the General Post Office—the working machinery of the British Empire, which impressed him with its might and modernity.

Bargash's stay in England was a great success. There were dances, dinners, opera performances, and garden parties to attend. Dressed in flowing Arab robes, Bargash cut quite a figure and seems to have impressed the British public as unique in having had the courage to abolish the East African slave trade. His prestige soared in the Arab world as well. Despite his ambivalence toward the British antislavery policy, he had, to all appearances, been received as an equal by the world's most powerful empire.

When Kirk returned to Zanzibar, he was dismayed to find the treaty had been frequently broken. Dhows were still smuggling slaves to the Arabian Peninsula, and slave caravans had begun to operate again around Lakes Nyassa (Malawi) and Tanganyika. He calculated, for example, that 1,500 slaves were marched from Manyema, in the eastern portion of what is now the Democratic Republic of Congo, to the coast in 1875.[24]

Kirk paid an official visit to Bargash to make it clear that he would not tolerate the sultan's lax enforcement of the ban. Suliman bin Hamed had died during Kirk's absence, and Kirk was able to persuade Bargash to sign a stronger antislavery proclamation on April 18, 1876, aimed at the Pemba problem in particular and continued slave-smuggling in general.

> In the name of God, the merciful, the compassionate.
> From Bargash-bin-Said Sultan
>
> To all whom it may concern of our friends on the mainland of Africa, the island of Pemba, and elsewhere.
>
> Whereas in disobedience of our orders and in violation of the terms of our Treaties with Great Britain, slaves are being constantly conveyed by land from Kilwa for the purpose of being taken to the island of Pemba: be it known that we have determined to stop and by this order to prohibit all conveyance of slaves by land under any conditions. And we have instructed our governors on the coast to seize and imprison those found disobeying this order and to confiscate their slaves.[25]

Bargash was now in real danger. His sheiks, the Mlawas, the Imams (Muslim priests), and other slave owners were contemptuous of what they saw as his puppet-like acquiescence to the

British. In fact, the proslavery forces in the coastal port of Kilwa revolted. But after the British navy vessel *Thetis* was dispatched to Kilwa and the sultan sent 200 Baluchi soldiers to restore order, the Kilwa slave merchants gave in.

Bargash was not spared outbreaks in his other dominions either. Salim-al-Yakubi, the governor of Benadir on the coast of present-day Somalia, had done his best to uphold the terms of the treaty but was murdered along with fifty of his men by pro-slavery forces. There was a riot in Mombassa, and a large crowd threatened the Church Missionary Society's headquarters; the governor had to send soldiers to break up the demonstrators.

A third incident occurred when Said bin Abdulla, one of Bargash's relatives and a high-ranking Zanzibari advisor, had his agents smuggle 13 slaves from the mainland to Pemba. The men were caught by the British navy and brought before Kirk. He had them taken in chains to Bargash, who was presiding at a Zanzibar court on other matters. When Kirk presented the evidence, the agents confessed they were in Said's employ. Said was arrested on the spot and imprisoned. The news spread quickly, and for a while the slave trade appeared to have reached a standstill.[26]

Although there was no great resurgence in opposition to the ban on slave trading, by virtue of his new capacity as chief consul, Kirk still thought it prudent to keep a watchful eye on the Arab traders on the mainland. After his return to Zanzibar, he appointed new British consuls to Ujiji on Lake Tanganyika and to the main coastal ports of Kilwa, Mombassa, and Lamu. Kirk also felt it would be prudent for the sultan's troops to be strengthened and disciplined to preserve the sultanate's power and enforce the slave-trade treaties. At his recommendation, Lieutenant Lloyd W. Mathews of the warship *London* was hired.[27] Mathews subsequently trained 300 of the sultan's best Baluchi soldiers into a crack combat-ready force. This helped, along with the British navy, to suppress opposition to the treaty.

Lord Salisbury, who replaced Lord Derby at the Foreign Office in 1878, was sufficiently impressed by Bargash's apparently sincere desire to see that the slave trade was not revived that he sent him a gift of 500 new Snyder rifles for his little army, which grew to 1,300 well-trained men. The sultan then made Mathews a brigadier general in his army; Mathews, in turn, became a friend and confidant of Bargash.

Kirk could now take pride in the fact that he had not only negotiated the final terms of the treaty, but had put in place mechanisms to enforce it. As British consul he had secured a vital antislavery treaty from Sultan Bargash where a far more experienced diplomat, Sir Bartle Frere, had failed. But Kirk was not the kind of a person who sought publicity or glory, and he did not dwell on his achievements. Despite his accomplishments, today Kirk's name is all but forgotten, even by most people in Zanzibar, as is the slave trade he was able to muzzle.

13

Zanzibar's Virtual Sultan

The signing of the antislavery treaty was followed by an enormous improvement in Zanzibar's economy and also brightened prospects for both Kirk and Bargash. Despite losing his cut of the slave trade, Bargash saw his revenues actually increase because the economy boomed and gross exports tripled. The increase in exports—especially of copal, ivory, and cloves—followed the abolition of the slave trade but wasn't necessarily caused by it. Whatever the source, the increase proved a shot-in-the-arm for the local economy and for the sultan's popularity.

It was also fortuitous that the island recovered quickly from the hurricane of 1872, which had caused such severe damage to Zanzibar's plantations. By 1879, the island's clove crop alone brought in $850,000. Ivory brought in another $800,000, and rubber $1 million.[1] Thus, total income approached $3 million, with more than half coming from raw products from the mainland.[2]

As a result of this newfound wealth as well as a likely nudge by Kirk, the sultan began ambitious public works projects. First, he had new pipes laid from a spring outside the city to Stonetown, the old city, to ensure a supply of clean water. Then he had gaslights placed at the corners of the main streets, and he established a permanent police force. His popularity increased further when, in 1882, he purchased four steamships to bring in wheat, which he sold at a price below what the privately owned British East India Company charged. He also abolished a head tax that native Zanzibaris had been paying to the Arabs for generations. No longer the cringing, evasive, impulsive sultan he had been when Kirk first met him, Bargash was becoming recognized as a wise and generous ruler. Distancing himself from the Mlawas and their followers and often ignoring his advisors, he largely entrusted Kirk to run the major relations of the sultanate.

Although he was only a few years older than Bargash, Kirk had become not just a friend, but apparently more or less a father figure to the sultan. Wielding enormous power, Kirk was thus not only chief consul for Great Britain but virtually prime minister of Zanzibar.

In his new capacity Kirk was constantly besieged with demands for trade and shipping concessions by other European powers, especially the Germans and French, whom he treated with impartiality. To cope with the constant intrigues and attempts at rebellion, especially on the mainland, he developed an efficient, behind-the-scenes information network. His "secret service" consisted of Banyan traders who moved up and down the coast and British missionaries who kept up a constant correspondence with Kirk, using native runners from their posts along coastal ports.

Problems to the North

A growing problem for both Kirk and Bargash, though, was that the farther north the sultan's rule nominally extended, the more tenuous was his hold on the mainland societies, especially with the Somalis. Their allegiance was primarily to their respective warlords; and in some towns the Somalis greatly outnumbered the Indian businessmen and Zanzibar traders.

One recurring headache was Mbaruk-bin-Rashid, chief of the Mazrui clan of Arabs that had once ruled Mombassa. He had plotted a revolt against the sultan in 1872; but when he heard that Bargash was sending 400 Baluchi soldiers, he delayed hostilities. The following year, when the chief sent taunting messages to the sultan, Bargash ordered the Baluchis to attack. They forced Mbaruk to retreat into the bush, but peace still did not come. Anti-British protests by the proslavery Arabs culminated in the murder of a British navy officer on antislavery patrol in the mid-1870s. Not long afterward, an English businessman was murdered, but his assassins were never found.[3]

The sultan's hold over former slave ports along the coastal ports below Somalia was also a bit tenuous. At Kilwa, for instance, slave smuggling persisted on a small scale. Local chiefs there and in other towns levied *hongo* (tribute) in the form of customs duties on travelers and merchants and kept the proceeds rather than turn them over to Zanzibar. At Mombassa, Mohammed bin Abdulla defied the governor appointed by Bargash and became, in effect, the real ruler of the town. On January 12, 1875, Mohammed lowered the red Zanzibari flag on the fort and bombarded the governor's house. His men were able to loot the town before the governor's troops finally forced the rebels to withdraw to the fort. Three days later, 200 Baluchis arrived from Zanzibar on the British warship *Rifleman.* The fighting stopped, but Mohammed remained in the fort with 350 followers. Eventually, after bombardment by another British ship, Mohammed surrendered, was taken prisoner, and was sentenced to life imprisonment.[4]

That same year Bargash and Kirk would face another threat to their control of ports to the north. This one, however, was from a quite unexpected quarter.

Consul Kirk and General Gordon

The British had effectively controlled Egypt ever since the French occupation of Egypt had been brought to an end in 1798 with Admiral Horatio Nelson's destruction of Napoleon Bonaparte's fleet at Abukir. Thus, besides Zanzibar, Britain had within its sphere of influence this North African nation which was nominally part of the Ottoman Empire. Britain helped end the hereditary rule of the Mamelukes, and a British official worked closely in Cairo with the Turkish viceroy or "khedive" to ensure that Egyptian policy was favorable to Britain. In 1873, the reigning khedive, Ismail, hired Colonel Charles G. Gordon[5] of the British army, making him a general in the Egyptian army as well as governor of Sudan, which had come under Egyptian control.

Gordon's job was ostensibly to put an end to the still active trans-Sahara slave trade between Tabora and Cairo. This proved to be particularly frustrating as some of the most powerful slave owners held high positions in the Egyptian government. Gordon was a very religious man and, much like Livingstone, a man of passion and conviction. He cared neither for worldly riches nor for increasing his social status. He had achieved recognition for his accomplishments due to a spectacular military career in China. He was convinced of the rightness of his actions and brought extraordinary determination to carrying them through. Like Livingstone, Gordon often persisted in endeavors against great odds and without regard for his safety, sometimes at the expense of his followers.

Gordon and Kirk, two very dissimilar representatives of the British Crown, were about to lock horns. Gordon was considered one of Britain's ablest officers, daring and charismatic, but known to have a fiery temper. Kirk was Gordon's antithesis, calm and highly organized without Gordon's mercurial temperament. Kirk shared none of Gordon's fanatical trust in God, which Gordon used to justify his actions. With the Egyptian government's connivance (under British leadership), Gordon planned to connect Egypt's most southerly province to the Indian Ocean with access at Formosa Bay only 250 miles north of Zanzibar in a region controlled by the sultan (see Map 8 on page 138).

"My idea," Gordon wrote to the famous explorer, Sir Richard Burton, in July 1875, "is that till the core of Africa is pierced from the coast but little progress will take place among the hordes of natives in the interior. The idea is entirely my own, and I would ask you not to mention it; as though you are a consul and I have also been one, you must know that nothing would delight the Zanzibar consul more than to have the thwarting of such a scheme. . . ."[6]

Earlier, the khedive had sent Captain H.F. McKillop and four companies of Egyptian soldiers under Gordon's orders by ship to Formosa Bay to occupy the port of Kismayu (Kisimaio). Four Egyptian warships with 550 more men aboard had threatened Barawa, and the Somali town promptly surrendered. The scarlet flag of the sultan of Zanzibar was lowered, and the Turkish flag (Egypt being nominally part of the Turkish Empire) raised over these two ports which belonged to the Zanzibari sultanate.

Hearing the news of this development and deciding to see for himself what was going on, Kirk arrived at Barawa on the warship *Thetis* on November 30, 1875. Shortly after coming ashore, he and the ship's captain were stopped at gunpoint by Egyptian soldiers. Kirk explained that he was British chief consul and represented the sultan of Zanzibar as well as the government of Great Britain. He asked to meet with the Egyptian commander. When the latter arrived, Kirk told him he wanted to visit Indian traders for whom he had brought letters. In fact, the traders were Kirk's northern listening posts, and he probably wanted to instruct them on how to get messages to him should the Egyptian occupation continue. The commander refused, and Kirk and the officers of the *Thetis* were turned back.

Kirk sent an ultimatum to the Egyptians. The *Thetis* would begin bombarding the town at two o'clock that afternoon if the

Egyptian commander refused to allow Kirk the freedom to go about as he pleased. Half an hour before the deadline, the commander capitulated, and Kirk was able to visit the Banyans.

Ever since he had been officially appointed chief consul, Kirk had happily taken orders directly from the British Foreign Office. But now he was irritated that the Foreign Office had seemingly pitted Englishman against Englishman, and in a way that was symptomatic of the vacillating attitude prevalent in British foreign policy at the time. In a letter to a friend in India he described the Egyptian invasion as a "filibustering expedition organized by the Khedive and commanded by English adventurers worthy of the palmy days of the buccaneers."[7] Bargash issued pleas, supported by Kirk, to the khedive, asking him to withdraw his troops from the "territories of Zanzibar," and to Lord Derby, then head of the Foreign Office, as well as to Badger, the Arabist and erstwhile friend of Bargash who sent a telegram to *The Times* stating it was a wanton outrage for Gordon's troops to invade the Zanzibari sultanate. Though British officials at Aden suggested a warship be sent to rout the Egyptian invaders, Lord Northbrook, then viceroy of India (with control of Aden), ducked the issue by referring it back to the Foreign Office.

The next encounter between the two sides came when an Egyptian freighter entered Zanzibar Harbor and requested a load of the sultan's coal. The sultan filled the ship with fruit as well as coal, and he included a letter to the Egyptian commander: "I send you the coal you desire, also the fruit. The latter may serve to keep you in good health, the former to take you away from my country."[8]

At this point Kirk knew he had no choice but to act forcefully to preserve the integrity of the sultan's lands. He ordered British warships to defend the sultan's other coastal ports and communicated his intent to Lord Derby.[9] Finally, in April 1875, the Foreign Office realized that this comedy of errors must end, and he ordered McKillop to apologize for the intrusions. In order to save Egyptian face, it was decided he should write to General Stanton, the British consul general at Cairo. McKillop tried to defend his actions: "I had no choice as to landing at Kismayu (near Formosa Bay). I had not one ton of coal, a pint of oil or tallow for the engines, and, having drowned two officers and seven men at the mouth of the muddy stream, I was obliged to seek a port."[10]

When McKillop saw that the sultan's troops would fight him there as well, he tried to contact Gordon, but his letter was seized by the sultan's governor of Lamu and sent to Kirk. The last part of the letter indicated that McKillop had had the good sense to decide to remove his troops and return to Suez.

Shortly thereafter, Gordon must have received orders from the Foreign Office, for, uncharacteristically, he, too, backed down; and, in a letter to Lord Derby, he assumed total responsibility for the fiasco. The blame lay in ignorance of the exact frontier, he claimed, and McKillop's actions were not actually intended to annex any territory belonging to the sultan of Zanzibar.

The Egyptian ruler's foreign minister, Nubar Pasha, also apologized to the Foreign Office. He too claimed that the intention had been perfectly innocent and reiterated that Gordon merely wished to provide Indian Ocean access to the inland lakes with a view to stopping the slave trade throughout the vast region.

Bargash's Hold Safeguarded

During this period, Kirk had sent strongly worded communications about the incipient collision between Zanzibar and Egypt to the Foreign Office. His letters clearly influenced the Foreign Office secretary to instruct Gordon to recall the Egyptian troops. So, thanks to Kirk, Bargash's hold on his northern possessions was safeguarded, at least for the moment.

Then the khedive, Ismail, in a new attempt to secure access to the Indian Ocean, asked the British for Egyptian rights over the port of Kismayu, which was within the sultan's jurisdiction. The British government, heeding Kirk, however, only allowed the Egyptians to occupy the port of Ras Asir on Cape Guardafui, which was north of the territory claimed by the sultante. The Egyptian government also announced that it had annexed all the land around Lakes Albert and Victoria, but since this was north and west of the sultan's claims, neither Bargash nor Kirk was in a position to object. This area, encompassing southern Sudan and the region east of Uganda extending to the Congo border, would become the southernmost region of the new Egyptian province of Equatoria (see Map 6 on page 94).

Gordon finally wrote Kirk a conciliatory letter asking Kirk to back his request that "Britain appoint a Governor General of the entire mainland of East Africa to put a stop, once and for all, to slavery, the frequent insurrections against the sultan's authority, and the perils to explorers and missionaries."[11] A more petty man might have blocked Gordon's proposal for fear of having his power diminished; but Kirk, who had earlier requested a British presence to control insurrections, wholeheartedly backed it. Gordon then telegraphed Kirk saying he would like to visit him for further discussions.

Kirk telegraphed back: "Personally would be glad to see you; can say no more."[12] He then wrote to the Earl of Granville:

> In the absence of letters I have no means of knowing what Colonel Gordon's views are in wishing to visit Zanzibar, or in what service he is willing to engage. . . . At the same time I am personally most desirous to learn the views of so experienced an officer. . . . I hope, therefore, that Colonel Gordon will find it possible to visit Zanzibar now, and, if he comes I shall do my best to induce the Sultan to consider favorably any scheme that offers a hope of establishing authority and order in Central Africa.[13]

Kirk seems to have envisioned Great Britain, with its tradition of individual freedom and justice, as still the best hope for peace and for the elimination of slavery in Africa.

Kirk and Gordon never did meet, but through dispatches, Gordon urged that a British governor administer Bargash's interior domain. Kirk enthusiastically approved, and suggested Gordon for the job. But both suggestions were turned down by the Foreign Office, to Kirk's dismay, for the same old reason: fear of taking on responsibility for a vast region of the interior believed to be minimally valuable.

Slavery's Persistence

The Portuguese government, despite its assurances to Britain that it considered the slave trade illegal, made only feeble attempts to stop it in Mozambique. Captain Elton, Kirk's right-hand man, observed the trading and reported to the Foreign Office:

> Slaves are still held in slavery, to all intents and purposes, throughout the whole of the Portuguese possessions on the East African coast. . . . Some masters are liberal, give daily pay in proportion to work done, free and good quarters and ample rations; but from such masters as the Portuguese convicts or half-castes, who are numerously settled on the island, much cannot be expected. They are determined slave holders and live in laziness by what is earned for them by their slaves. . . . Slave punishments are not discontinued such as working with a heavy log attached to the leg by a chain &c. . . . My own servants tell me they can readily buy slaves in town and the mainland at low prices.[14]

Some Portuguese still openly sought to justify the persistence of the Mozambique slave trade. For example, an 1881 letter from a Portuguese official claimed that the slave trade was "an institution that has had centuries of existence, that has firmly rooted itself among the traditions and customs of native races; and lastly it is one to which are attached the greatest profits with very slight fatigues. . . . He will not be far wrong who estimates an average export in these times of between 2000 and 4000 slaves per annum."[15]

The Portuguese claimed it was not them, but Arabs, Swahili, and Banyans who furthered the trade in collusion with their counterparts in Zanzibar. The Portuguese, like the Zanzibaris, used the excuse that they were hobbled in their antislavery efforts by the many hidden bays and inlets which allowed dhows to avoid patrol ships. Although Portugal, per se, did not appear to profit, it was common knowledge at the time Kirk was with Livingstone on the Zambezi that high colonial officials abetted the slave traders in exchange for their share of the profits.

Antislavery patrols had been very effective in drying up the slave trade from Africa's opposite shore by 1858 but were not quite as efficient in East Africa. In 1877, Elton—now promoted to consul, but still under Consul General Kirk's jurisdiction—learned that the enterprising Portuguese in Mozambique had devised a new way of making money: growing opium poppies. The British objected strongly, though they themselves had, of course, introduced opium to China, and British companies were profiting from Chinese drug addiction.

Elton was well aware that the British pot was calling the Portuguese kettle black:

> I cannot refrain from noticing the apparent inconsistency. . . . In most of the officially inspired pamphlets published of late years in Lisbon, it is thrown in our teeth that, whilst on the one hand we suppress the Slave Trade for purely political motives, at the same time . . . we foster a more detestable traffic than even the Slave Trade, namely the opium trade to the prejudice of the Chinese nation, yet now it would appear that Portugal herself has become the willing protector and patron of the free trade in opium on a wholesale scale.[16]

Nor would the Arab world of East Africa let go of the trade in slaves that easily. The main slave-gathering places were still Tabora and Ujiji in Tanzania; but slaves were also being funneled down from Buganda (Uganda) and from as far west as Urua in the present-day Democratic Republic of Congo (see Map 8 on page 138).

Irritated at this flaunting of the sultan's antislavery treaty and proclamations by Arab slavers, Kirk complained again to Bargash:

> I am now anxious to place in your hands all I know in order that steps may be taken and a mutual line of action agreed upon between us for carrying out your Highness's orders and stopping a traffic that has again become a source of danger to your Highness's Government and to the peace and welfare of your dominions. For upwards of six months this traffic was in abeyance after the issue of the Law, and its revival is due to your Governors having themselves again entered the Slave Trade, or participated in its profits by taking money from dealers for permitting them to pass.[17]

This put Bargash's credibility at risk, and one British official in Zanzibar wrote a confidential letter to the Foreign Office in 1881 wondering how much more Bargash knew about the continuing surreptitious trade than he let on:

> Seyed Bargash may become our puppet; [but] he can never be our cordial fellow-worker; for, by force of circumstances, a slender thread of duplicity, more or less visible, runs through all his actions; and the same reasoning will hold good in the case of any Arab prince who may hereafter succeed to the throne of Zanzibar. I think, therefore, that for any real genuine work we must depend upon ourselves alone, and merely look on the sultan as an instrument to be used occasionally when needed.[18]

It wasn't only the Portuguese and Arabs who became involved in the slaver trade, but in one case the English, too. In January 1880, Kirk had to judge the case of a fellow Englishman who had bought a female slave. The deed of purchase read, "In the name of God the Merciful, the Compassionate . . . be it known Mirant bin Ali has declared before me that she has given over her slave to Captain Russel for 50 dollars. . . . Written by the poor Ali bin Nasur with his hand (*professional letter writer*)."

"No one will suspect Captain Russel, formerly an officer in the navy, and at the time director of the Mission and free slaves settlement at the Church Missionary Society at Mombassa," wrote Kirk to the Marquis of Salisbury, "of buying a slave for the purposes of reselling her. . . . That the transaction was illegal is evident, although the open manner in which it was done will show how little Captain Russel thought he was violating English law."[19] The woman was freed and Captain Russel reprimanded and fined.[20] Still, Kirk worried that slave dealers would use this as an excuse for resuming their operations.

The deceptively dormant embers of the slave trade reignited once again in 1881 when Captain Charles Brownrigg from the British naval vessel *London,* cruising in a pinnace along the coast of Pemba Island, sighted a dhow flying the French flag. Thinking the vessel might be carrying slaves under false colors, Brownrigg tried to board the ship. He had guessed right, and the dhow captain, a well-known slaver, Hindi-bin-Khatim, ordered his men to open fire. Brownrigg and three of his sailors were killed. The slavers escaped to Pemba to hide among sympathetic, anti-Bargash plantation owners. The sultan, with Kirk's full approval, ordered General Lloyd Mathews and 350 of the Baluchi soldiers to Pemba, where they killed or captured the slavers.

In another eruption, in February 1882, Mbaruk-bin-Rashid, who had resurfaced from hiding, insolently claimed that his family owned the coast from Vanga, in present-day Kenya, to Pangani in Tanzania, and had every legal right to continue the slave trade. He managed to enlist 2,000 Masai warriors in a raid against the port of Vanga, which was under the rule of the sultanate. Bargash, backed by Kirk, sent Mathews and his men to attack Mbaruk. Most of Mbaruk's army escaped again, and the port was returned to Bargash's control.

Still, Bargash knew his mainland frontiers were not safe from marauders like the Somali and the Masai. Even Tabora, which Bargash's governor had run for several decades, was attacked by neighboring chiefs intent on resuming the slave trade. One of the main perpetrators of these raids was Mirambo, chief of the Nyamwezi, who since 1873 had periodically blocked the trade route to Ujiji from Katanga in the Congo and from Zanzibar to Lake Victoria, grabbing as much copper and ivory as he could and smuggling slaves to the coast himself. He even attacked Tabora while Henry Morton Stanley was there on an expedition but spared his house when Stanley raised the American flag. Now it was said that Mirambo seemed to wield more power in Tabora than the Arabs.

Kirk had received favorable reports from several missionaries in the region, however, that the rebel chief was not only an intelligent man but one who sincerely wanted the best for his people. He treated them kindly, the missionaries noted, and furthermore seemed to show a genuine interest in Christianity. As Mirambo continued his hit-and-run raids, Kirk thought something had to be done to stabilize the region and sent Mirambo a secret, friendly message in which he proposed a political settlement that would benefit all parties.

Mirambo replied that he was willing to listen to the British but not to the sultan. This was the only time Kirk acted independently on an affair of the sultanate without consulting Bargash. He told Mirambo that if he would leave Tabora alone and stop preying on legitimate Arab caravans, the rebel chief could have jurisdiction over all the area north of Tabora, which was sparsely settled. Kirk also promised that the sultan would have no jurisdiction over Mirambo, nor, theoretically, would the British if he promised to confine himself to that region and did not engage in the slave trade. Mirambo agreed. Kirk then told Bargash, who quickly gave his whole-hearted approval to the arrangement. Bargash probably cared little about this remote area between Lake Tanganyika and Lake Albert to the east and Lake Victoria to the north. In any case, the story had a happy ending, for Mirambo indeed troubled Tabora no more. When Bargash received proof of this, it confirmed once again that he could ultimately benefit when he put his trust in Kirk.

Another crisis developed after Kirk learned, in 1880, that at least 40,000 guns had been sent to Tabora and other settlements on the mainland from Iboe on the coast. Stopping the sale of firearms to Africans became a new imperative for Kirk. To safeguard missionaries and explorers, he asked Bargash to prohibit the sale of guns and gunpowder. He also suggested to the sultan that Mathews and 2,000 troops be stationed along the main caravan route to Tabora. After this was done, the illegal sale of firearms was greatly reduced.

However, Kirk remained concerned about future insurrections; in 1881, he suggested to Bargash and the Foreign Office that, in accordance with the agreement he had reached with Mirambo, a commission be set up to draw a definitive boundary between the sultan's dominions and those of the African chief. The proposal, though, was rejected by the Foreign Office with the excuse that it would constitute a formal commitment to protect the sultan's territory as well as Mirambo's.

The British policy in Africa had focused mainly on stopping the slave trade. Following the discoveries of Lakes Tanganyika, Albert, Edward, and Victoria, British explorers and missionaries began to penetrate the region, but the British government refused to officially declare the area a colony or even a protectorate. Thus, attempts by Kirk to establish what might have become a permanent

British presence there never got off the ground; for during twenty years of guidance by Palmerston, Derby, Russell, Disraeli, and Gladstone's first ministry, the British government was reluctant to spend money on acquiring new colonies. It was only after the so-called "Scramble for Africa" began in the last two decades of the nineteenth century that the acquisition of territory became the byword.

Kirk had not only effectively stopped outbreaks of the slave trade within the sultan's realm but had managed to keep emotionally labile Bargash on a more or less even keel in his relations with foreign powers. Finally, in 1880, the British government recognized Kirk's unique accomplishments and rewarded him by appointing him consul general. For seven previous years he had functioned in that capacity, but now it was official.

In January 1883, Kirk and his family went on leave again to England. While living at Strathmore Gardens in London, they bought a large house in Seven Oaks, Kent, where they planned to retire. Seven Oaks was only twenty miles from London and had its own train station. The house, called Wavertree, was on a hill overlooking the green, rolling, Kentish downs.

While in Britain, Kirk renewed old acquaintances. His opinions were solicited by various scientific societies including the Royal Geographic Society and the Royal Botanical Gardens at Kew, where some of his specimens were kept. He was called upon for advice by the Foreign Office. He also kept up a voluminous correspondence with his temporary replacement, Colonel S.B. Miles, who had been transferred from Muscat in Oman to Zanzibar as interim consul general. He also wrote to and received letters from Bargash, who, it appeared, had become very upset with Miles. Bargash claimed that the interim consul did not trust him and treated him contemptuously.

Miles's distrust was evident when he claimed Bargash was secretly involved in the slave trade. Kirk wrote to Granville at the Foreign Office, "It cannot be assumed that the Sultan is actuated in all he does by the disinterested and philanthropic motives which move us; but that is no evidence that he has not loyally and sincerely helped to carry out our policy. It is too well known that between Colonel Miles and the Sultan there exists such a want of confidence and sympathy as must be very detrimental to the influence on which so much of our success depends."[21]

Kirk again had shown loyalty to the man he had befriended and successfully persuaded to abolish the slave trade. This loyalty would last as long as Bargash remained alive and Kirk remained consul in Zanzibar.

With his son now matriculated at Beacon Preparatory School in England and his daughters receiving their education through tutors, as was the custom at the time, Kirk was anxious to return to the tropical island. Kirk would have to end Bargash's stormy relationship with Miles and once again resume his close relationship with the sultan.

14

The Crisis of European Intrusion

Upon Kirk's return to Zanzibar he had to deal with a new problem. Rather than take direct possession of East Africa as protectorates or colonies, Britain began to encourage development by individual businessmen or groups of entrepreneurs as proxies for British presence in the region. These individuals hoped this would lead to a protectorate[1] of the region, but this was not to be the case. The British government, headed at the time by Prime Minister Benjamin Disraeli, refused to commit time and money. There were several reasons, Kirk learned; foremost among them was the conclusion, based on reports from British subjects who had lived in or explored the region, that the land did not contain enough natural resources to warrant the expenditure of stationing troops there or of developing a British military and governmental infrastructure.

William Mackinnon, a Scottish entrepreneur and friend of Kirk's,[2] had been hired by Bargash in 1876, with Kirk's encouragement, to build a toll road to extend 450 miles from the coastline of present-day Tanzania to Lake Nyassa (Malawi). This was meant to open up the area to legitimate commerce and to make it easier for the sultan to transport his troops to areas of incipient rebellion. It proved, however, to be a very expensive and time-consuming enterprise, and only seventy-five miles had been built by 1880, ,when Kirk saw it. When Kirk learned that Mackinnon's company had run out of funds without having added a mile to the already constructed portion of the road, he concluded that this was not the right way of furthering British interest in helping the sultanate. Yet Dar es Salaam, the point on the coast where the road began and which had been only a small village, had, within ten years of the advent of the Mackinnon project, grown to 5,000 people, many of whom had initially been employed in road work.

Commercial Concessions Sought

Kirk was next confronted with a new British company formed and led by Mackinnon and others, including Sir Thomas Buxton, son of the prominent British abolitionist, and Gerald Waller, brother of Kirk and Livingstone's missionary friend, Horace Waller. The new company wanted to develop the trade in such items as rhinoceros horn, gum copal, and india rubber—all valuable export items at the time—and sought a permit from Bargash for mining and agricultural concessions on the mainland.

The Foreign Office gave the petition quasi-official backing, and, on Kirk's advice, Bargash agreed to grant the company the right to pass laws in the region they would be developing and the right to collect taxes to fund such local projects as constructing more roads, drilling wells, and creating a standing army or police force to protect their enterprises. The sultan would benefit financially by receiving 20 percent of the company's profits—after an interest of 8 percent was paid to its shareholders—and an additional 5 percent of mining profits.

Kirk also persuaded Bargash to let the company have a monopoly in the sale of ivory. In exchange, Bargash would be guaranteed an income of $450,000 a year and an interest-free loan of $250,000. But Kirk had to tread a fine line as he went over with Bargash each point in the concession agreement, as the proposal by these English investors was not an official action of the British government. Kirk reminded Mackinnon that he was only involved in this capacity as a representative of the Crown. Bargash favored the enterprise, for it would not only give him a large sum of money, but the private police force, trained by the British, would offer him greater security.

Before giving his final approval to the scheme, however, the Earl of Derby, head of the Foreign Office at the time, wanted Kirk to run the proposal by the viceroy of India, Lord Lytton, and the then Secretary of State for India, Lord Salisbury. In November 1877, Salisbury replied that: "The careful views expressed by Dr. Kirk have our general concurrence."[3]

The concessionaires arrived at Zanzibar in early May 1878 to negotiate the final draft of the treaty. But Bargash had developed qualms about giving up his inland kingdom to the British company and this time, despite Kirk's admonitions, requested several amendments:

1. That he should have the final say in any sale of land.
2. That he alone had the right to approve any new taxes.
3. That he retain the exclusive right to trade in gum copal, india rubber, and rhinoceros horn.
4. That the Arabs be permitted to continue in the ivory trade along with the British.
5. That the sultan be advanced more interest-free loans, if needed.
6. That Kirk was to be the final arbiter of any disputes that should arise pursuant to these amendments or the provisions of the treaty.[4]

One can understand the sultan's reluctance to cede partial control of his mainland domain to the British businessmen, despite the attractive financial rewards. But the Reverend G.P. Badger, a missionary and Arabist who did much of the translating for the businessmen, blew up when he heard Bargash's new demands. In a letter to a friend, Kirk commented:

> If the matter falls through it will be Badger's fault . . . . He has had his usual blow off and threatened, if the Sultan does not agree at once, to go back. . . . I told the Sultan to take it easy and reflect that he has witnessed scenes with old Badger before. . . . Of course the Concessions can easily be spoiled and Badger is a fool to trust to his power and run any risk. He is the most undiplomatic man I ever knew. The way to deal with the Sultan is to approach him on the old draft, point out that some expressions there are dangerous to him. . . . Badger has taken another course. He ignores the old [draft] . . . and rams the [new one] down the Sultan's throat. . . . He has sent the Sultan the most insolent messages.[5]

To Kirk, Badger had behaved like a bully. What Kirk did not know, however, was that Badger had received secret orders from Lord Salisbury to wreck the scheme. Salisbury's motive was not revealed, but some historians have speculated that he suspected that

Mackinnon wanted to turn his concession into a private colony. Were Mackinnon to proceed, Lord Salisbury may have decided, it would not be in long-term British interests, let alone Zanzibar's.[6]

Bargash, whose temper also could be fiery, then further undermined the whole enterprise himself by adding another amendment, one in which he demanded the company take over the collection of custom duties at all ports and inland towns on the mainland by January 1, 1879. This was a huge financial risk, and Mackinnon, among others, also began to have second thoughts. Badger's secret orders were not made public, and the Foreign Office was blamed for the scheme's collapse. But Kirk felt relieved. Better to leave things as they are, he thought, "either a real government or none at all."[7]

By that Kirk meant a British colony or at least a protectorate rather than concessions with quasi-political control over a region. Though a friend of the sultan's, Kirk was, after all, a servant of the British Crown, and he realized that without full official backing by the British government, the project's outcome, like Mackinnon's road, would be highly problematic. A colony or protectorate, on the other hand, would have the political structure in place to facilitate shipment of supplies, provide medical care for the workers, and police the area. Kirk also saw the threat posed by other European countries, which seemed poised to try to slice off pieces of Africa for themselves. Given his belief in the British Empire's tradition of benevolent paternalism, it would be far better, he thought, for Britain to take the Zanzibari sultanate under its protection before other nations tried to. But a British takeover of the Zanzibari sultanate would not happen for another two decades, and by then a huge portion of East Africa would already have been ceded to the Germans. Only with the Allied victory in World War I would a British East Africa be realized, and then for just half a century until the flames of freedom burned the rope binding East Africa to the Commonwealth.

While furthering British territorial interests, Kirk's friend and assistant, Consul Elton, died en route from Lake Nyassa (Malawi) to Zanzibar. Elton's traveling companion was none other than James Stewart; he had returned to Africa with a change of heart about Livingstone and had founded Livingstonia, a mission on Lake Nyassa.

Together, Elton and Stewart had explored the great lake in a mission steamboat, and Elton, a geographer, had taken copious notes of the poorly understood northern end of the lake while identifying streams flowing north into the Rufiji (Ruaha) River. Once back on land, his group spent the night in a small, stockaded village, but they were attacked by the Machinga, a branch of the Ajwa. The Machinga gave up the siege after a few days, when they learned that their own village was being attacked by still another group.

Because the usual land trail back from the lake was blocked by tribal warfare, Elton took an alternative path through the lowlands at the hottest time of the year. There he died, reportedly of sunstroke associated with convulsions, but the real cause was never ascertained.

Kirk wrote, "I consider . . . Captain Elton's manuscripts should be given to the world without delay, and the more since the exploration of Africa now advances so fast that if this is not done at once others will soon follow and reap the credit of what has cost him his life."[8] In fact, Elton's careful exploration of the lake opened up future settlement by the British and led to the formation of the Nyassaland protectorate, now the independent African nation of Malawi.

In 1879 a technological development improved communications significantly in Kirk's part of the world. John Pender wanted to lay a telegraphic cable across the Zanzibar channel to Zanzibar Island from Bagamoyo on the mainland. He had asked £5,000 for the job, but Bargash told him he couldn't afford it. Kirk's renown was so great that he was able to talk Pender into laying it free of charge. The rapid increase in communication from both cable and telegraphy was one of several factors which facilitated European takeover of lands that would become their future African colonies.

The International Plot Thickens

Toward the end of the 1870s, the European nations had begun to look more seriously at East and Central Africa as potential colonies. A marker of this budding interest occurred in June 1877, when King Leopold II of Belgium called an international meeting in Brussels to form the African Exploration Society, the ostensible purpose of which was, besides exploration and scientific observations in East and Central Africa, to eliminate the slave trade wherever it was encountered. Prominent explorers from England, Germany, France, and Italy attended, but the meeting was dominated by the king, who pledged part of his personal fortune to finance further exploration of Central Africa.

The Foreign Office asked Kirk for his opinion of the meeting. Kirk reminded Whitehall that Leopold II's African Exploration

Society might well encroach to the east on Bargash's hegemony and that Britain had a duty to protect the sultan's holdings. Foreign incursions would only be satisfactory to the sultan, he added diplomatically, "[if] philanthropists and merchants were to work with him in ameliorating the conditions of the interior."[9] Kirk did not enumerate these conditions, but they would have included not only enforcing the prohibition on slave trading but also encouraging the development of tropical agriculture and building more roads to enable the export of lumber, rubber, and minerals.

The real purpose of the Belgian king, whom Kirk already suspected was a latter-day Machiavelli, was to gain the Congo and the territory east and north of it (Tanzania and Uganda) as his personal possession. In one move to secure this granddaddy of concessions, an Austrian and three Belgians, led by Lieutenant Cambier and financed by Leopold, began a "scientific" exploration of the Congo in that same year. By June 1877, two of the Belgians had died and the Austrian had turned back, leaving Lieutenant Cambier to continue alone. When three-quarters of his porters deserted him, Cambier, too, gave up the exploration.

The king, in the meantime, had chosen the by now famous Henry Morton Stanley to obtain the territory he coveted. Stanley had learned how to dazzle gullible Africans by offering a gun or two, some whiskey, beads, calico, and other trade items to Congolese chiefs in exchange for their mark on a treaty that they could not read. The treaty did not cede their land to the Belgian government, but to Leopold himself as his personal fief. Cambier, meanwhile, did not remain idle. Two years later, he built the first Belgian military post at Karema, 150 miles south of Ujiji on Lake Tanganyika in territory bordering, if not within, Bargash's domain.[10]

Kirk was concerned about Leopold's attempt to take over the Congo and what this could mean to the political stability of the region. He also believed that if Stanley continued to treat the Africans as he had in the past, he would create more trouble for other Europeans on the continent. This feeling arose from the fact that when Stanley had previously returned to Africa in 1874 to explore Lake Victoria, his men had gunned down the inhabitants of the lake's Bumbire Island, who were armed only with bows, arrows, and spears.[11]

Furthermore, the Reverend J.P. Farler, a missionary on the mainland who interviewed some of Stanley's employees, had written to the Foreign Office claiming that Stanley had himself engaged in the slave trade. The letter was forwarded to Kirk with a request that he investigate the charges involving his old nemesis. Kirk undertook the task in May 1878, with his usual care. After a three-month investigation, he wrote to Derby at the Foreign Office that his inquiry showed that the actions of the Stanley expedition were "a disgrace to humanity" and would hamper future explorers and missionaries in the region.

> The principal charge contained in Mr. Farler's letter is no doubt that of selling as slaves men who had been taken captives; this I have not found denied by any of those with whom I have spoken. . . .While descending the river they say that a village on an island was attacked and plundered, and that a young girl was seized . . . by Mr. Pocock, Mr. Stanley's European companion. The girl was . . . carried off from her country and friends, and used by Mr. Pocock as his mistress. . . . At the time Mr. Pocock kidnapped this girl, Mr. Stanley had twelve captives, taken in the same village, passed on board his boat; nine of these were given up further down the river to his followers to be sold to the tribes, and it is said they were sold and bartered in exchange for food. . . . Mr. Stanley's treatment of his own people would appear on many occasions to have been very cruel, and they speak of one occasion on which a man was kicked and beaten to death by himself. . . . As to Mr. Stanley's doings at Bambire [Bumbire] Island, on the Victoria Lake, reported by himself, which caused so great indignation and led the British Government to disown the use then made of the flag, I find the natives give an account very like that of Mr. Stanley himself. They say, however, that his revenge on that occasion was wholly uncalled-for and impolitic; that taking captives as hostages before the attack on the islanders was an act of foul treachery; they add, however, what Mr. Stanley has not thought wise to tell us—that these captives were taken to Uganda, where the greater part of them were killed in cold blood in Mr. Stanley's presence.[12]

Kirk concluded that he believed these tales to be "substantially true," but Derby refused to meddle with the Belgian king's personal affairs.

A year later Stanley was once again in Zanzibar to enlist porters for an expedition to the Congo. Resentful of Kirk's refusal to see him, he showed surprise, when interviewing Bargash, that he was still on the throne, for he had heard confidentially from top British government officials that there was a secret plan to get rid of Bargash and make Zanzibar a British colony.[13]

When Bargash relayed Stanley's comments and his own concern to Kirk, the British chief consul asked incredulously how Bargash could possibly believe the words of such an unscrupulous person as Stanley? The sultan then apologized for having doubted his good friend.

Developing King Leopold's Congo

Kirk had to direct his attention to the Belgians once more, for King Leopold had conceived the idea that elephants would provide easier and more rapid transportation along the muddy trails crisscrossing the land he coveted, and in 1879, he had four Asian elephants shipped to Zanzibar from India along with their mahouts and an English officer and trainer, Captain Carter.

As a naturalist, Kirk was fascinated by the animals and talked with Carter and the mahouts about their prospects. The expedition started off from Bagamoyo with the elephants at the head of a column of 600 porters and a handful of other whites, including another Englishman, Cadenhead, also employed by the Belgian king. A few weeks later, two elephants died, possibly because of inadequate or unfamiliar forage. The column finally reached Tabora in October of that year. From there, they moved to the new Belgian base at Karema, where the third elephant died.

More trouble for the expedition lay ahead. Before they reached the Congo border, unpredictably Mirambo, despite his agreement with Kirk, ambushed and killed Carter and Cadenhead along with 120 of their porters. Kirk wrote,

> On the arrival of the Belgian party, the camp was fired into and Mr. Cadenhead shot in the head, and several of the expedition were killed. It then became necessary for the party to act in self-defense and several of the enemy were shot down, Mr. Cadenhead, himself, killing six before he fell from loss of blood. After that the Zanzibar men seemed to have broken and fled . . . the bodies of both white men were stripped by Mirambo's men and left where they fell.

This was a setback for Kirk and the sultan, as Mirambo went on to capture thousands of Africans west of Unyanyembe to sell them into slavery and use the proceeds to buy cattle and ivory.[14]

Firearms and the French Interest

Kirk was shortly faced with a new problem with international repercussions. This time it was the French trying to obtain a foothold on the East African coast. When a French ship tried to anchor at the ports of Mogadishu and Barawa in order to sell a load of firearms, it seemed, initially, like an isolated incident. But selling firearms to mainland Africans had been banned by Bargash, and the governors of these towns, following the sultan's orders, refused to let them disembark. The French consul asked Bargash to punish the governors, but Kirk recommended that he reject the request. The French then demanded 180,000 francs in reparations for lost revenue, but in a subsequent communication offered to reduce it to 100,000 francs if paid promptly.[15]

Kirk telegraphed the Foreign Office for advice. The Foreign Office backed the sultan's stand against firearm sales in the sultanate and communicated this to the French government. The French agreed in principle but claimed that the sultan, prior to the time the shipment was made, had not made it clear that the sale was forbidden, and threatened to charge interest at a punitive rate if the payment was not forthcoming. Kirk was indignant, but the Foreign Office refused to intervene further, so Bargash reluctantly paid the fine to avoid further repercussions.

The French subsequently made two desultory attempts to claim parts of the sultan's northern territories in Somalia, but they were only able to obtain a small enclave around the port of Djibouti north of the sultan's holdings. They did conquer the island of Madagascar off the East African coast, but their major colonial effort was directed at Central and West Africa. Imbued with the certainty of its cultural superiority, France even went so far as to reward some of its colonies by making them part of "Metropolitan France."[16]

Leopold, King of the Congo

European attempts to gain territory in East and Central Africa began to gain real momentum. Having acquired the Congo with Stanley's connivance, King Leopold wanted to obtain a port on the Indian Ocean. In 1880 he cast an eye on a place near Malindi in present-day Kenya (see Map 8 on page 138). He had given up an attempt to acclimatize Indian elephants to Africa, and after reading of Hannibal's march across the Alps in the Second Punic War in

210 B.C.E. with thirty-four African elephants, Leopold became convinced that he could train the African species. For a reason not made evident, he wanted the port of Malindi, then part of the Zanzibari sultanate, to become the training center.

When Bargash received King Leopold's request, on Kirk's advice, he promptly refused. Wanting to avoid open conflict with the British, Leopold, using Stanley as his agent, purchased a narrow tongue of land on the Atlantic bordering the Congo River delta. Torrid, plagued by mosquitoes and malaria, it nevertheless gave the landlocked Congo a port, Matadi.

During the 1880s, when the Congo chiefs realized they had been tricked out of their land by Stanley, many rebelled, but their sporadic revolts were savagely suppressed by Belgian guns. Then the slave traders, mostly Arab or Swahili, revolted against the Belgians in the eastern part of the country, where they had formed slave-trading settlements, in one of the bloodiest episodes in Africa's colonial history.

In spite of the fighting and the cruelty of the Belgian administrators and traders toward the Africans, Leopold's personal takeover of this huge territory, a third the size of the United States, was officially "legalized" by the other European powers and by Great Britain in the Treaty of Berlin in 1885. The partition of Africa had begun in earnest. A coalition of the other European nations, shocked by the raping, torturing, and killing of Africans who dared oppose Leopold's brutal colonial regime, at last forced the king in 1908 to turn over his so-called "Congo Free State" to the Belgian government.

The First German Advances

Bargash viewed these developments with the Belgians and the French as direct threats to his kingdom's territorial integrity. Kirk, who, in effect, was serving two masters, Bargash and the British Foreign Office, shared the sultan's pessimism. The best he could hope for was to forestall other nations' hunger for territory while Britain decided if, and to what degree, it should seek greater involvement in the Zanzibari sultanate.

One nation with no such ambivalence was Germany under the aggressive leadership of Chancellor Otto Bismarck. Bismarck felt Germany was being left out in the cold in the European division of Africa and decided it was time to take a large piece for his own country. Both the German African Society of Berlin, founded in 1878, and the German East African Society, started in 1884, provided springboards for this colonization. Germany annexed southwest Africa and the Cameroons and Togoland in West Africa, and began to eye the sultan's domain in East Africa.

During the time the German explorer Hermann Wissmann twice traversed Africa successfully from west to east between 1880 and 1887, the Germans sent agents to secretly make treaties with chiefs in the sultanate's mainland realm (present-day Tanzania) under the very noses of Kirk and Bargash. One of them, G. A. Fischer, in the guise of an explorer, tried to cross the Kenya Highlands in 1883 but was stopped by the Masai. They attacked his men and he shot two of them, but when he asked for a palaver and explained that his intentions were peaceful, they let him pass toward Lake Baringo in present-day northern Kenya. Before he could reach the lake, he was stopped again, this time by an army of 3,000 Masai warriors, and was forced to turn back. Two other Germans, Count Samuel Teleki and Lieutenant L. von Hohnel, using the pretext of big-game hunting, were the first whites to reach northern Kenya, where they discovered Lake Rudolph for the Europeans in 1888, but they also had to battle African tribes along the way.[17]

Although secretly troubled by these developments, Kirk politely hosted a variety of nationals, including the German explorers and businessmen. In fact, his reputation for impartial and upright behavior was so sterling that Kirk was consul general for the Portuguese, consul for Italy, and consul for the free city of Hamburg, part of the Hanseatic League. It was only when the Germans appointed their own consul in 1883 that his consular service to Hamburg was withdrawn.

Still, Kirk had become increasingly concerned with the plethora of European explorers now being sent to East Africa. He believed that most of them had come to gather intelligence in advance of an attempted German expropriation of the sultan's territory, and he wrote to Lord Salisbury of the Foreign Office in 1880 expressing his fears of further intrusion. He also bewailed the fact that England was not making any attempt to stop the Germans or at least make clear to them its own zones of influence, but his pleas largely fell on deaf ears.

Still, his reputation had soared both in Africa and Europe. He was called the great *Belozi,* the Swahili word for consul, and A.J. Mounteney Jephson wrote of Kirk:

> John Kirk—his title was rarely used by the Swahilis—was known as the big man from the coast to the Congo and Uganda, and along the coast from the Zambezi to Mogadishu.

> . . . I do not think it is an exaggeration to assert that even along the coast he had more influence than the sultan, Seyyid Bargash; and he was scarcely less respected and feared than that enlightened potentate. Sir John's knowledge of what was going on, far and wide, was less than downright uncanny. He knew everything of importance and worth knowing.[18]

Now, the great *Belozi* would have to face the infringement on the Zanzibari sultanate by the German government.

15

Europeans Tighten the Noose

Although the British government was slow to respond to the Belgian and German incursions, the Royal Geographic Society, the Royal Society, and the British Association raised £1,500 in 1878 to send an expedition to explore the region between Dar es Salaam and Lake Nyassa (Malawi). The party would map out a path for extending Mackinnon's road in order to increase the sultan's military control of the region and Great Britain's influence. Keith Johnston, a twenty-five-year-old naturalist, was chosen to head the expedition; his second-in-command was Joseph Thomson, age twenty-one.

While they were equipping the expedition, Johnston and Thomson were entertained by the Kirks at the consulate in Zanzibar. Thomson described the Kirk children as being as happy and healthy as if they had been brought up in England. Helen was a warm and wonderful hostess, and Dr. Kirk invited them to visit his Zanzibar country home five kilometers from the city. Kirk emphasized the importance of avoiding hostilities with the indigenous Africans, a suggestion that Johnston and Thomson took to heart and that served their expedition well.

Thomson, a keen observer and ardent diarist, writing two years later in 1880 for the Royal Geographic Society, described the town he had seen as a picturesque place, no longer the filthy and malodorous slave emporium described by earlier Europeans. Clearly,

Bargash's reforms had greatly improved Zanzibar even if, by European standards, it was by no means a beautiful city at that time.

> Dead animals, filth and garbage of all kinds are no longer allowed to be thrown out into the streets to rot and fester in the sun; and dead slaves are at least placed below the soil instead of being thrown upon the beach. . . . No starved or ill-used slaves are to be seen, for on cases of inhumanity being reported to the Sultan, the sufferers are at once set free, and made safe from the brutality of their masters. . . .
>
> Zanzibar . . . possesses all the architectural characteristics of an ordinary Eastern town with this exception, there is a marked absence of minarets and mosque towers. The square, prison-like houses are devoid of ornament and all whitewashed present little variety. They form narrow, crooked lanes whose only recommendation is their shadiness during the greater part of the day. . . .
>
> There is nothing European in the scene with the exception of the ships in the harbor and an occasional white man in the streets. . . . The Arabs are the dominant race, and form the upper and ruling class. They have not, however, the usual conservative character of Arabs, but are rather liberal minded. . . . Each nationality has its separate quarter in the town. Pass along some lanes, and but for the houses you might imagine yourself to be in India. . . . Wander towards the palace, and you leave the business thoroughfares behind and enter Arabia in a twinkling. . . .
>
> We continue our march, and from Arabia we seem suddenly to enter a purely African scene. . . . There is a gabbling crowd of natives in all degrees of undress—the wild-looking Somali from the far north of the Sultan's dominion, Wanyamwesi[1] porters waiting for a return caravan to Unyanyembe, representatives of the coast tribes, and finally Waswahili slaves and freed men from every tribe . . . within the area of the great Lakes.[2]

Kirk suggested Johnston and Thomson hire Livingstone's former guide Chuma as headman because he was familiar with some of the territory they would be exploring. They took Kirk's suggestion, and Chuma proved invaluable in collecting porters for the trip and maintaining discipline among them.

Thomson noted in his journal the respect shown to Kirk not only by the sultan but even by the porters. "The porters were evidently much impressed by the part which Dr. Kirk took in our arrangements. He is looked up to with almost superstitious rever-

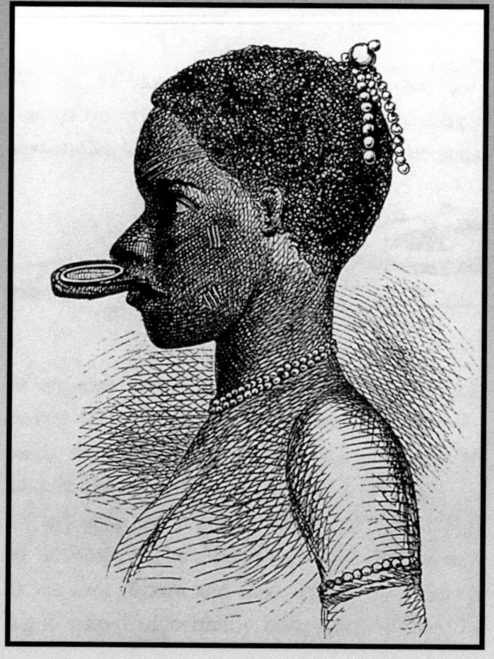

Pelele, or lip-ring of Manganja woman

Mongazi village, drawing by John Kirk, 1859

Plate 10

Mary Livingstone, age 40

Elephant marsh, photograph by John Kirk

James Stewart

Elephant marsh, 1995

Sunset on the Zambezi, 1995

Port Zanzibar, from fort, c.1860s

Zanzibar, from the roof of the British Agency, July 1884, photograph by John Kirk

THE COMMANDANT'S HOUSE AT TETE

Photograph by Kirk

The Commandant's house at Tete, photograph by John Kirk

Plate 14

Lady Helen Kirk

Kirk's daughters

John Kirk in consular uniform

Sir John Kirk, c. 1882, after being knighted

Henry Morton Stanley

Plate 16

Portrait of Tippu-Tib

Bargash (bottom center) and the Mlawas, 1875

John Kirk, age 90

ence. Hence the interest he manifested in the expedition gave it a coherence and a character otherwise unobtainable."[3]

The Johnston-Thomson Expedition

As the Kirk family watched the dhows carry the young men and their porters to the mainland on May 19, 1879, Kirk perhaps thought about his own experiences with Livingstone so many years before. Thomson certainly did. He wrote:

> I shook Dr. Kirk's hand and bid him farewell with a quivering lip, yet with a heart full of great hopes and expectations. . . . We were entering a valley of the shadow of death into which many have passed and few have returned. In that great moment vivid pictures flitted before my excited brain. I thought of Stanley beleaguered by thousands of bloodthirsty natives, and compelled to slay on every side to save himself. Would we have to do likewise? I pictured Livingstone dying in the swamps of Bangweolo. Might such not be our own fate? These and many similar speculations passed with lightning rapidity. But in the proud consciousness of having started a great work, all doubts and fears were stifled in the bud, and waving an answer to the hearty, "Kwaheri, bwana mdogo!" of the Arabs, I turned my back on the Indian Ocean and set my face resolutely for the interior.[4]

Guides and entertainers called Kiringosis traditionally headed caravans to announce their entry into a village. They wore tall feather-headdresses, beat drums, played flutes, and blew kudu horns, and Thomson used them to entertain the porters during rest stops. Describing the preparations made to camp near a native village, he wrote: "The moment we arrived the Kiringosis threw down their loads, and forming a ring around them they executed a breakdown (dance) full of the most grotesque gestures, while the drums were thumped and the horns were blown most lustily."[5] He also gave one of the best descriptions about a rainforest he had entered:

> A forest of the densest nature, formed of colossal trees, with deep, green, shady foliage . . . there are feathery acacias and mimosas, branching hyphene palms, and fan palms with their abnormally bulged trunks . . . fill up the intervening spaces

> between the trees with ivy-green shrubbery, until not a clear bit of ground is seen, and passage through the forest is rendered impossible. From tree to tree hang creepers of every description; slender leafy kinds swaying gracefully in the breeze; giant forms thick as a man's thigh, gnarled and twisted, binding the tree trunks as with bands of iron. The whole forms an impenetrable mass of vegetation through which it is impossible even to see.[6]

Thomson, while sharing Kirk's sense of adventure and enthusiasm for the African people and the environment, also unfortunately encountered many of the same problems his predecessors had. Not long after leaving Zanzibar, Johnston became seriously ill. In a letter to Kirk, Thomson wrote, "My Dear Dr. Kirk, Mr. Johnston being too ill with dysentery to use the pen, he desires me to write to you . . . and informs you of our safe arrival." The weather was poor, and unrelenting rains had added to the difficulty of getting through waist-deep marshes. The rivers, choked by sandbars and snags, made the conditions of their march even more harsh.[7]

Eight days later, Thomson wrote to Kirk, "On the 21st, I wrote to you stating Mr. Johnston's extreme prostration from dysentery. From that date he became gradually worse and weaker, unable even to stand without fainting. On the night of the 27th he suffered dreadful pain and passed into an insensible condition in which he remained all day." Perhaps Johnston had a severe case of amebic colitis with perforation of the intestine ensuing. That could explain the "dreadful pain." He died that afternoon, June 28, 1879.[8]

Although shaken by his partner's death and feeling inadequate by himself, young Thomson courageously chose to continue on to Lake Nyassa. After making valuable meteorological observations there, he explored Lake Tanganyika, keeping in touch with Kirk by mail. This was possible because a new runner service to the coast had been started by missionaries at Ujiji. Kirk, in turn, kept the Royal Geographic Society apprised of Thomson's progress and was instrumental in getting him an additional £500 grant to enable him to continue his explorations.

Thomson seemed to have an uncanny knack for spiritually disarming hostile groups he encountered. He knew most Africans of the interior would be initially suspicious of any light-skinned strangers because, despite Bargash's decree, slave raiders with firearms were still periodically terrorizing the region. Since the older inhabitants remembered Livingstone and Chuma kindly, Thomson usually encountered hostility only from the younger warriors.

In an incident on Lake Tanganyika in 1880, the Masai of the area mistakenly believed Thomson had stolen one of their slaves. They attacked him as well as the missionary E.C. Hore, who had accompanied him from the mission on the lake. Thomson pretended not to understand and moved fearlessly among the warriors while making a show of examining their weapons. His apparent innocence and fearlessness confused the group enough that their intent cooled.

Thomson's letters to Kirk reveal how much real danger he was in almost continually:

> At one village a crowd had got hold of one of my men and I only forced my way in just in time to deflect a descending ax which would have ended his days. And yet we had to show ourselves both firm and yet pacific. The slightest accident or blood drawn and not a soul of us would have escaped. They seemed just to thirst for our blood but still they were afraid to attack us. . . . At last we reached the big chief (Kijombe).
>
> We were informed to our immense disappointment we would not be allowed to pass as they were at war with the country in front, and to make matters worse we were further directed to return exactly the same way we came. And back we had to go, and what a time we had of it! How we escaped with our lives I cannot comprehend. Imagine being wakened in the dead of the night in your tent by your blanket being torn from under you, just in time to catch hold of your azimuth compass and to find your watch gone, such was one of my night adventures.[9]

Kijombe's men stole almost everything Thomson owned and he arrived destitute in Mitova in present-day Kenya. Fortunately, Hore showed up, as did Captain Carter with his last surviving Indian elephant. To his great pleasure and surprise, Thomson was able to ride the elephant rather than hike through an extensive marsh. But this elephant, too, like its three predecessors, shortly succumbed to the different climate and inadequate forage, as noted in Chapter 14.

Return to Zanzibar

Thirteen months after leaving the Kirks, Thomson returned to Zanzibar, having contributed greatly to the geographical knowledge of southern and eastern Africa yet having lost only one porter, a remarkable feat in those days when a large proportion either deserted or died of trauma and disease. He bragged to Kirk that he had "passed in peace through every tribe."[10] This wasn't quite true, but Thomson didn't fire his rifle at any African, and Kirk concluded that his young protégé must have used considerable tact and psychology to keep his expedition intact in the midst of such perilous conditions. He respected the brave young Scot, who, like himself so many years ago, had ventured forth fearlessly in the wilds of unexplored Africa.

Bargash, doubtless at Kirk's urging, hired Thomson as his geologist in 1881 and sent him looking for coal deposits that could be mined. But Thomson returned a few months later with the discouraging news that the deposits he'd discovered were not coal but bituminous shale that was not worth mining.

Thomson soon left on a new expedition to explore the region around Mount Kilimanjaro and the Kenya Highlands to study the possibilities of agricultural development, mining of potentially valuable mineral deposits, and substantial European settlement. To avoid meeting the German explorer G.A. Fischer, who he had heard was traveling ahead of him, he passed around the northeast side of Mount Kilimanjaro.

The Kenya Highlands were heavily defended by thousands of Masai. These brave warriors, with their long spears, colorful cowhide shields, and red toga-like capes, presented a fearsome sight and greatly outnumbered Thomson's little party. They soon surrounded him, entered his tent, handled the strange objects he had brought with him, and, according to his journal, made comments like, "Take off your boots . . . show your toes. Let us see your white skin." It was then that he hit on two ingenious demonstrations that created the impression that he was a great wizard. One was to fire a gun at the same time that he dropped a spoonful of effervescent salts into a heated liquid, which then "blew up." The second was to remove his two false teeth in front of the crowd. The Masai warriors, having never seen anyone who could take his teeth out and put them back again, from then on treated him with the respect a wizard deserved.[11]

Thomson reached Lake Naivasha in present-day Kenya, where he heard of Fischer's retreat, but was himself slowed by an attack of dysentery. After recovering, he climbed a mountain range to the west, naming it "The Aberdares" after Lord Aberdare, then president of the Royal Geographic Society. (Thomson Falls was later named after the young explorer, as was a small gazelle seen in large numbers on the East African plains.) Eight months after leaving

Mombassa, he became the first white man to see Lake Baringo, sixty miles north of Mount Kenya; two months later he reached Lake Victoria.

All along, Thomson had done careful surveys of the soil and mineral outcroppings he encountered in East Africa, and this perceptive young geologist concluded that the land lacked significant minerals. Later, in Katanga (now in the Democratic Republic of Congo), he found rich copper deposits. Thomson's findings were borne out by subsequent geologists, and Mackinnon's fond hopes of finding profitable mining concessions in East Africa were never realized.

Returning to the coast through southwestern Kenya, Thomson passed through country devastated by drought and famine. He ran out of food and barely made it to Mombassa. By the time he landed at Zanzibar on June 11, 1884, he was weak and severely undernourished. Kirk and his wife treated him like a second son, caring for him in their home until he was well enough to leave for England. He eventually recovered sufficiently to return to Africa twice more. He explored the Niger River in West Africa in 1885 and present-day Zimbabwe from 1890 to 1891. He died in England in 1895 at age thirty-eight, probably from cirrhosis of the liver due to schistosomiasis,[12] which he had acquired bathing in freshwater African lakes.[13]

Kirk thought Thomson's Kenya expedition very successful. Heeding Kirk's advice, Thomson was the first white man to pioneer the path between Mombassa and Lake Victoria that was followed sixteen years later by railroad builders who opened up Kenya to colonization and commerce.

Butting Heads with Whitehall

Thomson's successes buoyed Kirk's spirits. But Kirk continued to be concerned about the poorly disguised interest shown by Belgian, French, and German explorers in acquiring portions of East Africa for their governments. At the same time, he was undoubtedly flattered when Bargash, whose health was beginning to fail, asked Kirk to become regent in the event of his death and rule the sultanate until one of his sons became old enough to assume the throne:

> This is my will regarding the succession to the government of Zanzibar and its dependencies.
>
> In the name of God,
>
> From Bargash bin Said, be it known to those who may see this that, finding it for the public good to make an arrangement

for the government of Zanzibar after my death and to remove any doubt or dispute, my wish and intention is that the British Government shall promise the throne of Zanzibar and its dependencies to the eldest of my sons and after him to his son, should he leave one; and the British Government [meaning Kirk] shall be guardian to them until they come of age. . . . The full meaning of this is that the Great Government shall act for us in everything, should God cause anything to come upon us before our sons are of age. And in this we invoke the help of God. And Salaam.

Written by my hand,
30 RAMADAN, 1298 [1881][14]

Thus, Bargash had arranged to place his kingdom, family, and subjects in Kirk's hands. Foreign Office superiors, however, disapproved of this magnanimous gesture. Lord Hartington, then Secretary of State for India, and Lord Ripon, the new Indian viceroy, refused to permit Kirk to assume this added responsibility, explaining their reasons as follows:

It has been our main object in dealing with these States to maintain such relations with the Chiefs as would ensure the safety of trade and the welfare of the numerous Indian subjects of Her Majesty residing at and with the ports on the coast, but at the same time to carefully avoid implicating ourselves in matters over which we could exercise no real influence without an expenditure of money and a display of strength out of all proportion to the advantages to be gained.[15]

The meaning was clear enough. The British didn't think it worth spending a farthing more than they already had on the Zanzibari sultanate.

Bargash was bitterly disappointed but gratified that Kirk was, at last, beginning to win recognition as the man who had stopped the slave trade. In truth, the Foreign Office was more than ever aware of Kirk's crucial role. They had realized that "our man in Zanzibar" was doing his best to prop up Bargash on the swaying dance floor of international geopolitics and had for some time considered giving him the recognition he so truly deserved, a knighthood. In 1879 Queen Victoria finally bestowed the Commander of the Garter, or C.M.G., on Kirk, and in 1881 the Knight Commander of the Garter, K.C.M.G.[16]

Kirk's attention remained focused on the continuing problems besetting the sultanate, however. For example, in 1879, Mirambo's men murdered a British missionary near Tabora. Bargash was so upset that he told Kirk he would pay to have a British officer stationed there to enforce the laws and punish the criminals. Kirk accordingly passed word to the Foreign Office, but the Foreign Office chose to ignore the offer, as it had when both Kirk and Gordon had previously suggested a British governor be appointed for the region.

In 1881, Kirk again recommended to the Foreign Office that a commission be sent to Tabora to define a boundary between the sultanate and Mirambo's territories. The Foreign Office once again refused with the same reasoning—East Africa offered few prospects for obtaining wealth, and the cost of maintaining a protectorate wasn't worth the expense of establishing one.

Slavery's Persistence

In the first years after Bargash signed the antislavery treaty, there were continued attempts to circumvent it. In April 1877, Kirk wrote to the Earl of Derby that he had visited a settlement of former slaves converted by German missionaries at Malindi, but he learned subsequently that Arabs, forcing themselves into the mission, had enslaved them again.[17]

Aside from the Malindi enslavement, there were more sporadic attempts to circumvent the antislavery treaty. In 1884, a dhow displaying the French flag with ninety-four slaves aboard was seized by the sultan's forces. The French consul objected to the seizure, but Bargash followed Kirk's advice and sentenced the culprit to life imprisonment.

In another incident, this one in 1885, Kirk learned that King Sayyid Ali of Johanna in the Comoro Islands had smuggled slaves from the mainland. He sent Consul Holmwood to investigate. Holmwood discovered that schoolchildren had been seized by mercenaries of Sayyid Ali while attending classes in their village. The youngsters were forced on a dhow despite the pleas of their parents, who had followed the abductors to the beach. On Kirk's recommendation, Bargash threatened Sayyid Ali with attack if he did not stop slaving, and slave smuggling to the Comoro Islands subsequently ceased.[18]

Even as late as 1887, the British were threatened by various chiefs on the mainland who were still dealing in slaves. Chief Manje wrote, "If the English Consul wishes to come here, let him come alone, for as soon as he reaches the bank of the river which flows past my village my men will shoot him down. Therefore all Yaos, Machinga, Ajwa and Makololo who are with him should lay down their loads and return home. They are my friends and I wish them no harm. The English are my enemies. If the Consul attempts to march through the pass we will attack him."[19]

There were also instances of British barbarity that did not endear the British to the Africans or Arabs. In 1881, for example, there was trouble at the mission at Freretown, named in honor of Sir Bartle Frere. Established by the Church Missionary Society near Mombassa, the mission educated, trained, and sheltered freed slaves. J.R. Streeter, the lay superintendent at the mission, was accused of unmercifully beating African converts for stealing and imprisoning some of the free citizens of Mombassa for no apparent reason. "There is no concealing the fact that recent events at Mombassa have seriously affected the position in which we stand with the Arabs even here. They cannot disassociate the Mission from being a government agency," wrote Kirk that same year. Bargash was incensed when he heard about the floggings and asked Kirk to act immediately to stop them and punish the man. Holmwood investigated. When he showed Streeter the charges, the lay superintendent insisted he had done no wrong, but grudgingly apologized.

Holmwood wrote to Kirk, "I recommended him to tender an apology to the Arab he had wronged and compensation to the slaves he had beaten. . . . On our way to the boat . . . Mr. Streeter again referred to the charges against him . . . but he added, I regret to say, that if such were the law the Mission might as well be given up for he had found the stick was the only thing that would make the native speak."[20]

Holmwood added on July 7 that the slaves who had been beaten were still suffering. "The strokes they had received had apparently cut into the flesh and left scars which were still raised and inflamed although the floggings had taken place more than a month previously." The Arab community was outraged and claimed that Streeter was far crueler to their former slaves than they had ever been.

Petition after petition was received by Holmwood from Streeter's victims. Esther Smith, a young married woman and a convert to Christianity,

> who dressed as a European and appeared to be well educated, stated she had received lashes from the "bakora" from Mr.

> Streeter himself. Mr. Streeter admitted that he had given her two strokes; he said he had been greatly irritated at the time by her constant appeals to him to release her husband. She would not leave his house, and her crying made a disturbance. He desired me to ask the girl again if he had given her more than two strokes of the "bakora." She at once replied firmly that she was ready to declare on oath that he had struck her five times.[21]

Other newly converted Christian women who had been slaves were among those who complained. One man had been confined for six weeks in prison, and Streeter expected him to remain another six weeks despite festering ulcers which had developed on his legs and buttocks. But Streeter was not the only culprit.

The mission's chaplain, who felt that Streeter had been far too lenient, was found to be an accomplice by Captain Byles of the British man-of-war *Seagull* during his investigation of Streeter on criminal charges.

Holmwood had considered the situation so dangerous he had requested of Kirk that a British man-of-war be stationed at Mombassa to keep the peace. Captain Byles wrote to Kirk on July 12, 1881:

> I consider the treatment of the natives living at the Church Mission station, Mombassa, a disgrace to the honour of Englishmen, and if the facts were fully known in England they would very much militate against the prosperity of that great and useful Society, The Church Missionary Society.[22]

> In the interest of the Church Missionary Society I consider it desirable that, as soon as possible, all the present white officials be removed, and be replaced by those who can carry the Gospel into all parts of the world without bringing disgrace on the name of England. My reason for classifying all white officials together are the following: It was, I imagine, the duty of the Chaplain to report these occurrences as he was fully aware of them, and he stated he considered the Lay superintendent to be very lenient. The medical officer was also of the same opinion, and this officer had not even visited the cells since he had been at the Mission. . . . I furthermore consider that for the welfare of the Christian mission it is desirable that all flogging of both men and women, and above all women, should be abolished immediately.[23]

Consequently Streeter was called back to England.

By 1889, there was no longer any significant seaborne slave trade, but there were a few exceptions. Heavily forested creeks and narrow inlets from the sea provided hiding places for Arab slave dhows that would leave their sanctuaries at night to still attempt the voyage across the Indian Ocean to the Arabian Peninsula.

Although the 1873 agreement had prohibited trafficking in slaves, it did not emancipate existing slaves. In 1875 Bargash closed some loopholes in the treaty with another proclamation and freed his personal slaves. Kirk, as judge, had also ruled that escaped slaves automatically became free men. Swahili, Arabs, and Banyan merchants on Zanzibar and in other parts of the sultanate still retained their domestic slaves, and some slave trafficking continued in the Congo, Somalia, and the Lake Victoria region.[24]

Seven years after Kirk had left Zanzibar, Freretown was shaken again when local Arabs complained that the mission was sheltering their runaway slaves and began to make similar accusations against other missions. Some of these missions were in areas where the Imperial British East Africa Company was involved in road building, agricultural, and commercial activities. George S. Mackenzie, the director of the company, wrote to the new British consul in Zanzibar, Euan-Smith, that the Church Missionary Society, the United Methodist Free Church Society of Sheffield, and the German Evangelical Lutheran Mission of Hersbruk, Bavaria, should end their bickering and reimburse the Arab owners for any runaway slaves who sought refuge in the missions.

Though Bargash had outlawed traffic in slaves, he still had not emancipated those already owned within his domain, where domestic slavery was still promoted as an economic necessity, even by some of the British. "Slavery under existing circumstances here is an absolute necessity," wrote Mackenzie. "If suddenly abolished, the country would be utterly ruined." But he did make one gesture toward emancipation: "I am now seeking to induce the owners to grant all the slaves at present in the hands of the missions their papers of freedom at 25 dollars per head."[25]

After determining that there were 1,421 escaped slaves at Freretown, Mackenzie wrote a sarcastic letter to the director of the Church Missionary Society, Reverend Price: "I regret to find the Missionary Societies at Mombassa are exceptional in harbouring runaways. . . . This may be accounted for by the fact that your Society is a large holder of land and shambas [farms], the cultivation of which improves their value, but I scarcely think it is the purpose with which the generous public at home subscribe to the Society's fund." He believed the mission was evidently using runaway slaves to provide cheap labor for its farms.[26]

New Attempts to Acquire African Territory

As was true of Joseph Thomson, much of the push for British control over the lands of the sultanate was made by private citizens, sometimes even Africans themselves. Twenty-five-year-old naturalist Henry H. Johnston,[27] who was to become a British administrator, was commissioned by the Royal Geographic Society in 1884 to make a detailed investigation of the flora and fauna around Mount Kilimanjaro. He carried with him a letter of introduction from Kirk, who had helped him plan his expedition. When he arrived at Moshi in present-day Tanzania in early 1884, he met Chief Mandara, who had been a friend of Livingstone's. The naturalist persuaded the chief to sell him a few acres of land at Taveta as a settlement for British colonists in exchange for a quantity of cloth and beads. The transaction was completed with the total sum of "4 gora merikani, 5 gora sahari, 1 gora handkerchiefs and 1 frasilah of beads." (A gora was thirty yards of cloth. Merikani was colorfully dyed cloth from New England mills, sahari cloth was for turbans, and a frasilah was the equivalent of £35).[28]

Johnston wrote enthusiastically to the Foreign Office that land could be cleared and houses built there economically. "What I feel impelled to say to you is this. . . . Here is a land currently suited for European colonization, situated near midway between the Equatorial Lakes and the coast. Within a few years it must be English, French or German."[29] The other European explorers had already proposed colonization schemes to their governments and the British would be left out if they didn't act promptly.

Kirk received a telegram from the Foreign Office, "Johnston reports Mandara asks for British flag and protectorate. What is your opinion?"[30] Although Kirk had toyed with the idea of Britain consolidating its sphere of influence in order to keep France and Germany out of East Africa, he had not yet come out unequivocally for the establishment of a British colony. In fact, he hesitated to recommend such a course, because a British colony in the interior would need access to the sea or it would be at the mercy of whatever power controlled the coast. And, if the British annexed a coastal town like Mombassa to gain such access to the potential colony, that would clearly infringe on Bargash's rights, which Kirk had vowed to defend, so, again, with no backing by the Foreign Office, nothing came of the proposal.

Changing Geopolitics

In other regions of Africa, the British were facing renewed difficulties. In February 1884, Charles G. Gordon returned to Khartoum for a second time as governor for the Egyptians. He had very few troops with him and was quickly besieged by a huge force of Sudanese led by the now powerful Mahdi. The Mahdi, backed by the slave-owning chieftains, proposed to rally all of Islam in a jihad, or holy war, to rid the country of the perfidies and intrusions of the heretics (Christians) and to protect the slave trade. His troops, called "Whirling Dervishes" by the Westerners because of their gyrating motions while praying, believed themselves immune to gunfire. They managed to surround the city. While sending a call for reinforcements which never arrived, Gordon held out for over six months in one of the epic sieges of the nineteenth century. Toward the end of the siege a military force under British General Wolesley was sent to Khartoum to rescue him and the other Europeans and Egyptians besieged there. As the British general approached the outskirts of the Sudanese capital, he saw the Mahdi's flag raised over the city. Khartoum had fallen three days earlier, on January 26, 1885, and Gordon, along with many of the Europeans and all the Egyptian soldiers, had been killed.

Much has been written about Gordon's heroism at the siege of Khartoum, but few if any Western writers have examined the outcome from the point of view of the Sudanese, who were implacably opposed to the Anglo-Egyptian occupation of their country. The Mahdi wrote the following letter to Bargash after Khartoum had fallen to him:

> Know, O friend, that in accordance with the promise of the unfailing God and His inscrutable grace the city of Kartum [fell] with the help of the Living and Self-existing One. This was on Monday . . . after the break of dawn with the instrumentality of the Ansar [soldiers]. With trust in the Lord of the World they prepared themselves and rushed the trench. In barely a quarter of an hour or even less the enemies of God had undergone their fate in that they were exterminated or surrounded—this in spite of their great preparations.
>
> At the first shock, they turned tail retreating before the soldiers of God . . . thinking they would be safe if they entered the yards and closed the gates. But the Ansar pursued them, cutting them down with their swords and piercing them with their spears until there was much shouting and groaning. In a

> trice they laid them low. Then they laid hold of the remainder, those who had locked the gates for fear that punishment should overtake them; they seized them and made great slaughter until only a few subordinates and riff-raff were left. As for God's enemy, Gordon, despite all our admonishing and cajoling him to turn back and repent to God, he failed to do so because of his previous misdeeds and his excessive folly until he came to the end of his appointed time. . . . So have the unjust been exterminated. . . . Ten of our companions were crowned with martyrdom in this victory. We have prostrated ourselves in thankfulness to God for having supported the Faith; do you likewise.[31]

After the debacle of his troops at Khartoum, the Egyptian viceroy or khedive, Twefik,[32] sought to modernize his army by hiring more foreign military men. Unemployed American officers were readily available, even more than a decade after the U.S. Civil War, and one, Brigadier General C.P. Stone of Massachusetts, was made chief of staff. Eduard Schnitler, a German physician who had served as medical officer with Gordon at Khartoum, but who was away at the time of the disaster, was appointed to replace Gordon. He served as governor of Equatoria, the southernmost province under Egyptian control, although much of it was now in the hands of the Mhadists. Part scientist, part military man, and part adventurer, Schnitler had converted to Islam and had taken the Turkish name Emin Mehemet Pasha.

The geopolitics of the region was changing dramatically, and the Africans were justifiably concerned. The French, otherwise intent on colonizing much of West and Central Africa, took Madagascar in 1885. In West Africa, the Cameroons and Togo became German protectorates by 1885. More German explorers meanwhile had traveled through East Africa trying to get native chiefs to sign treaties accepting German protection. Lord Granville, who was aware of the intent of the other European powers to divide and conquer sub-Saharan Africa, wrote to Kirk in 1884, "It is essential that a district situated like that of Kilimanjaro . . . should not be placed under the protection of another flag to the possible detriment of British interests."[33]

Kirk wrote that maintaining the intactness of the sultantate's mainland territory was doubtful: "We cannot expect it to go on. . . . There are mysterious Germans traveling inland and a German man-of-war is reported on the coast." These movements, under the guise of scientific expeditions, had not fooled Kirk. To protect both British interests and the sultan's, he convinced Bargash to issue a proclamation on December 6, 1884:

> ***By the Grace of God***
>
> I, Bargash-bin-Said, Sultan of Zanzibar and of the Interior of Africa, will not accept the protectorate of any nation whatever nor cede my sovereign rights or any part of my dominions which are in the islands or on the mainland of Africa from Tungi in the south to Warsheik in the north to any Power or Association without consulting the English, and this I do for myself and my successors.
>
> Be it known by all who shall see this.
>
> WRITTEN BY MY HAND: 17 SAFAR 1302. [6 DECEMBER 1884][34]

Kirk, with the British government's approval, then asked the sultan to send Mathews, with reinforcements from the British army, to Chief Mandara to obtain a treaty recognizing the sultan's authority over him. Similar treaties would be made with other chiefs, and Britain would continue as the sultan's protector with free access to his territories.

When William Gladstone became British prime minister for his third term in 1886, he was against making East Africa either a protectorate or colony. The territory was reported to have few resources other than a little gold and copper, mining of which had just started. Britain, in Gladstone's view, had already sunk enough money into this part of the world, having spent an estimated £5,000,000 to eliminate the slave trade.[35]

But there was another reason—and an important one—for not acting to protect British interests in all of East Africa. Gladstone believed he needed Germany as an ally, and when he received word that Bismarck was interested in making a German protectorate of the vast area claimed by Bargash from Lake Tanganyika to the coast, Gladstone told Kirk to follow a hands-off policy.

Bismarck wasted no time in pursuing his African schemes, and in December 1884, one of Bismarck's agents, Dr. Carl Peters, obtained signatures from various chiefs pledging their allegiance and accepting a German protectorate for the large territory the Germans called Tanganyika after the lake, now known as Tanzania.

16

Germany Makes Its Move

By the 1880s, the continent of Africa was coming to resemble the board of a frantic game of chess, with nations and peoples being acquired and discarded like pawns. Germany, though a newcomer to the game, was playing particularly aggressively.

Not even a unified country until 1870, when Bismarck joined together many quasi-independent states, the new German Federal Republic nonetheless was driven by a fiercely nationalistic spirit. Its government wanted to acquire colonies as England and France had done, and Africa was a prime target.

Initially, East Africa did not appear as good a choice as the western regions of the continent, where Germany was already colonizing southwest Africa, Togo, and the Cameroons. There were few exploitable natural resources in much of East Africa, and even the harvest of ivory was dwindling as the great elephant herds of the past were decimated by modern guns. More importantly, from the point of view of maintaining a self-sufficient population, drought was a recurring problem, as it is today, and periodic torrential rains leached out the thin topsoil in many areas. There was also a possibility of famine as in the winter of 1884–85, when parents even began to sell their children to slavers in exchange for food.

Along the coast and in the foothills, however, there was forest for timbering and good soil for crops, but it was limited. Indigenous peoples still continued to prey on one another in the inland portion of the sultanate from time to time, while human diseases, especially malaria, as well as locusts and an epidemic of rinderpest (a cattle disease) further reduced the potential profitability of other investments in the region, such as rubber and palm oil.

East Africa was not the ideal land for colonization, surely. Still, the desire for imperial domination gave impetus to German explorers and entrepreneurs. Dr. Carl Peters arrived in Zanzibar with three companions in November 1884, by a devious route. He, Count Joachim Pfeil, Dr. Carl Juhlke, and August Otto had left Trieste for Aden disguised as mechanics and then hired on as deckhands for a British East India Company ship bound for Zanzibar.[1]

Although Bismarck telegraphed them not to expect the protection of the German government—a state's standard denial of responsibility made to spies—they left Bagamoyo with a well-equipped expedition using funds the German government had indirectly provided. And, like Stanley in the Congo, they carried with them absurdly simple treaties for African tribal leaders to affix their thumbprints to, such as the following Treaty of Eternal Friendship: "Mangungo offers all his territory with all its civil and public appurtenances to Dr. Carl Peters as the representative of the Society of German Colonization for exclusive and universal utilization for German Colonization."[2]

By the time they reached Usambara 130 miles north of Bagamoyo (see Map 8 on page 138), the Germans had collected twelve such treaties. Soon Peters was back in Zanzibar with the signed agreements in hand. Meanwhile, the brothers Clarence and Gustave Denhardt, who had conducted scientific studies in 1878 on the river Tana in present-day Kenya, had come to Zanzibar in 1885 to organize a new "geographical" expedition to benefit Germany.

Aware that they were up to more "back-door" acquisition of territory, Kirk's informers told him that when the German brothers had landed at Lamu, an island off Kenya that had been a slave-trading center, they had contacted Ahmed Fumo Luti, otherwise known as Simba ("lion" in Swahili). Simba was a bandit who, even so many years after the abolition of the slave trade, maintained himself by raiding, looting, and selling slaves in Somalia, where Bargash's rule was less and less effective.[3]

August Haggard—brother of the novelist H. Rider Haggard, who became famous with his adventure stories of East Africa—was now British vice-consul at Lamu, and he expressed his misgivings to Kirk about this unholy alliance between the Denhardts and Simba. In order to confront the African leader directly about his connection with the Germans, August Haggard decided to enter the lion's den himself. He took a small guard with him to Simba's heavily fortified village of 3,000 followers and as many slaves.

The bandit-chief greeted him pleasantly enough, but that night Simba sent his brother-in-law and chief advisor to Haggard's hut with a request that he smuggle guns and ammunition from Lamu for the African chief. If he refused, Haggard would be killed. "The man's manner towards me was so sinister and ferocious that I could not but feel uneasy at my helpless position in a town full of savages and so securely walled that a cat could not escape," Haggard later wrote to Kirk. He had managed to talk his way out of the situation by threatening British naval bombardment if he were not released.[4]

While Peters was enlisting or forcing local chiefs to relinquish their land, Kirk heard that Bismarck and Lord Granville had quarreled over Germany's annexation of New Guinea and neighboring New Britain. But if Great Britain and Germany were at odds over this issue, the split was short-lived: events were soon to push them into an embrace. On January 26, 1885, the Mahdi of Sudan declared his country independent of Egypt and its overlord, Great Britain. Simultaneously, the imperial Russian army was advancing on Afghanistan and France had thrown its support to the czar. The Foreign Office was deeply concerned that if the Russians took Afghanistan, they could pose a serious threat to India, the "Jewel of the Crown" itself.

Britain then sought Germany's backing, turning a figuratively blind eye to Bismarck's plan to acquire Bargash's mainland holdings. At the same time, the Foreign Office began to look at the possibility of establishing its own protectorates in East and Central Africa. The loss of the Sudan, although hardly thought by Gladstone and his party to be a catastrophe, prevented, at least temporarily, a new breed of English entrepreneurs like Cecil Rhodes[5] from executing their dream of British hegemony from the Cape to Cairo, which included control of the Nile.

Birth of a Protectorate

Peters had returned triumphantly to Berlin with the treaties from the African chieftains. Now Germany, in the face of Britain's insecurity, could declare much of East Africa a German protectorate without fear of repercussions from other European nations. On February 26, 1885, Kaiser Wilhelm did just that. He issued a *schutzbrief*—the equivalent of a British white paper— announcing the official appropriation of the sultan's mainland territories (which the Germans denied belonged to the sultan). The German parliament gave Peters's German Colonial Society the exclusive right to administer the region, which they named Tanganyika after the lake within its borders. On March 3, Gerhard Rohlfs, the German consul in Zanzibar who like Richard Burton and Kirk had been an explorer before becoming an administrator, notified Kirk that Germany had formed a protectorate from the area east of Mount Kilimanjaro to the Indian Ocean (see map 8 on page 138).

Bargash, when he heard the German announcement, was so upset that he immediately sent a telegram of protest to Kaiser Wilhelm. "These territories are ours," he wrote, "and we hold military stations there, and those chiefs who profess to cede sovereign rights have no authority to do so."[6]

Under Kirk's nose, a good part of Bargash's territory was swallowed by Germany. These various events seriously eroded Kirk's influence and the relationship with Bargash that he had striven to build up over the previous fifteen years. Torn by his divided loyalties to his home country to do nothing to interfere with the German government's policy in East Africa and to Bargash to preserve the integrity of his lands, Kirk still urged the sultan to keep a tight grip on the Mount Kilimanjaro area. Mathews was quickly dispatched with 180 troops to reaffirm the sultan's hegemony. After landing at Mombassa, Mathews marched inland to Taita, where Chief Mandara, who had signed a treaty with Peters, obligingly switched sides again and formally acknowledged the sultan's rule.

Mathews then continued west to Moshi and convinced the chiefs of the Kilimanjaro and Chaggas to sign a declaration no less absurdly simple than the model German treaty affirming their allegiance: "We are subjects of . . . his Highness, the Sultan of Zanzibar." Kirk then telegraphed Granville, "Mathews says it is a nice country and a pity if we lose it, but the fertile part is thickly peopled already and land is not to be had in any amount without fighting."[7]

Rohlfs had told Bismarck that Bargash listened only to Kirk. Consequently, Bismarck complained to Granville that Kirk was responsible for Bargash's initial insulting telegram of protest. He was especially irritated by the fact that it had been addressed not to him, but to Kaiser Wilhelm.[8]

Granville telegraphed Kirk immediately: Had he encouraged Bargash to send the telegram? Kirk insisted the sultan had independently written his own message. Then an agitated and depressed Bargash impulsively decided to go to England to plead his case with Queen Victoria, and then to Germany to meet the kaiser on a king-to-king basis and reassert his claim to his East African lands, just as he had during his negotiations with Kirk over the antislavery treaty of 1873. Kirk, pessimistic about the outcome of Bargash's latest impulse, was able to dissuade him from going. The old adage that when Zanzibar plays the flute, all of East Africa dances was no longer the case, Kirk reminded him.

The Sultan Cannot Stand Alone

A less principled man might have withdrawn to the sidelines, content merely to follow the Foreign Office's directions. But Kirk could not passively watch the dismemberment of the sultanate and all he had worked to foster. On May 9, 1885, he wrote to Granville, "If neither England nor France considers their interests and historical associations worth defending or if they are for the time so preoccupied elsewhere as to be unable to attend events here, the Sultan cannot stand alone, and he will soon see that the longer he opposes German aspirations, the more he will lose." Kirk was deploring the fact that while both England and France had had similar interests in Zanzibar, France was backing Russia's adventurism in Afghanistan and England was being thrown into Germany's treacherous arms.[9]

Kirk followed up his letter with a telegram to Granville: "Collision in the district [between English and German agents] . . . German agents elsewhere active. Sultan helpless. Unofficial influence used to place himself under Germany. . . . Her Majesty's Government must be prepared for possible consequences."[10]

When Salisbury became British prime minister in June 1885, he took control of the Foreign Office as well. More conservative than Granville, he had been quite content to sit by while Germany acquired the sultan's mainland territory of Tanganyika. He was also irritated by his Zanzibar consul's persistent defense of the tiny island's sultan.

The consequences followed shortly when the German battleship *Giesenau* arrived at Lamu, where the Denhardt brothers had just persuaded Simba to accept the German protectorate. Bargash was scared and angry. He threatened to send troops and ships to Lamu—but what troops and what ships? Mathews with 2,000 men and a few coastal vessels could not stand against the mighty German navy.

Kirk and Bargash both knew that only the British could stop the German expansion. Desperate, Kirk telegraphed the Foreign Office: "It would assist me much if I did know whether under any circumstances the British Government in case of any opportunity offering, could now consider acquisition or a protectorate of a district with a naval port. I mention this believing that Zanzibar must soon break up or pass bodily to Germany."[11] Lord Salisbury replied: "You should not permit any communications of a hostile tone to be addressed to German agents or representatives by Zanzibar authorities."[12]

News of the discord between Kirk and the Foreign Office spread fast, and the former Arab slave dealers took advantage of it. Aware of the sultan's political impotence, they sent five dhows crammed with slaves from the mainland, but Mathews's soldiers caught them.

Kirk then received word that Juhlke, one of Carl Peters's cohorts, had obtained ten more treaties, this time from the groups around Mt. Kilimanjaro who had so recently sworn allegiance to the sultan. Juhlke made eight treaties public in which Mandara and other chiefs ceded sovereignty to the German East Africa Company. He also made public a statement he attributed to Mandara, "I love the Germans above all other people, and in particular above Englishmen and Arabs."[13]

Mandara, asked by the German visitors why he flew the sultan's flag, answered that Mathews and his soldiers had been there and had given him 600 rupees to hoist the flag of Zanzibar. "Let there be no misunderstanding," Mandara said, speaking of himself in the third person. "This did not mean he was subject to the Sultan of Zanzibar, on the contrary he was free as a bird and perhaps of equal power to the Sultan. He would hoist the German flag instead if Julhke would bring him a better flagstaff."[14]

Because England believed it needed Germany to stop Russia's foray into Afghanistan, Lord Edmond Fitzmaurice could say to general approval in a Foreign Office discussion, "On the part of Her Majesty's government there is nothing except an anxious desire to meet the views of the German Government." And Gladstone, who returned to the prime ministership for his third term in February 1886, could openly say, "If Germany becomes a colonizing power, all I can say to her is God speed her."[15]

A Bold Plan

Kirk had spent the better part of his mature years cultivating the sultan's trust. Because of that trust, he'd been able to persuade the sultan to outlaw the slave trade in his dominions. Consequently, Kirk had risen in esteem in the eyes of the British public and politicians alike. Now in an ironic twist of fate, his relationship with Bargash was being undermined by British appeasement of Bismarck.

Bismarck's vendetta against Kirk and the sultan came to a head when the "Iron Chancellor" asked Salisbury, now serving his second term as prime minister, to recall Mathews. On this point Salisbury refused, giving the excuse that Mathews was in the sultan's, not British, service.

Reacting to this, Frederick Holmwood, Kirk's former assistant who was now consul under Kirk at Mombassa, suggested that since the sultan had lost control over most of the mainland, the British should occupy the port of Tanga, 100 miles north of Bagamoyo and Zanzibar. A railroad could be built from there to Lake Victoria and on to Lake Albert. Thus, Khartoum, the capital of the Sudan, would be only a fortnight's travel from Zanzibar. If the British reconquered the Sudan and Equatoria from the Mahdists, they would then be linked from the Cape of Good Hope in South Africa via the Nile all the way to Alexandria, Egypt. In one bold stroke they would control the eastern half of the African continent, with the exception of the Congo, and the dream of British hegemony from the Cape to Cairo would be fulfilled.

This bold plan envisioned British settlers raising all kinds of crops on the fertile plateau that would become Kenya Colony less than twenty years later. Holmwood, obviously an ardent imperialist, assured the Foreign Office that, with the exception of the Masai, who would have to be "tamed," the other African societies were agriculturists and would hire out to English owners. He described the area, 120 miles as the crow flies from the border of the new German protectorate of Tanganyika, as lush, basing many of his recommendations on Thomson's reports of the healthy, high, and fertile plateau now known as the Kenya Highlands. "A more charming region," Thomson had written, "could not be found in all Africa . . . undulating uplands at a general elevation of 6000 feet, varied and lovely scenery, forest-crowned mountains, downs land clothed with heather and flowering shrubs, park-like country with cattle knee deep in the luxuriant grass, a network of babbling brooks and streams, a land, in fact, where there was little to suggest the popular idea of the tropics."[16] Holmwood was backed by J.F. Hutton, president of the Manchester Chamber of Commerce and a business associate of William Mackinnon's. These two British businessmen and others would form an East Africa Association, which would operate, they envisioned, independently of the British government, just as the East India Company once had.

Many influential imperialists in Great Britain seriously considered Holmwood's plan. Mackinnon met with Lord Aberdare in 1885, who by then had retired as president of the Royal Geographic Society. Lord Aberdare, along with two other notables, signed a secret letter urging Lord Granville, who was still influential though no longer head of the Foreign Office, to pressure the British government into putting Holmwood's plan into effect.

An Ultimatum

While these British machinations were going on, Bargash's distress would worsen. On August 11, 1885, a German naval squadron, already anchored at Zanzibar, presented him with an ultimatum. Bismarck demanded the sultan withdraw his letter of protest and immediately accept the treaties made by Carl Peters, Julke, and the Denhardt brothers. If he refused, the squadron commander would bombard the city.

Kirk advised Bargash to stall, hoping that the British would intervene. When Bargash failed to respond to the ultimatum, the ships were lined up in firing position, their guns ready. Telegrams flew between Kirk and Salisbury, and back and forth to Bismarck. Salisbury ordered Kirk to convince the sultan to accept the German terms.

Deeply troubled by the British acquiescence to Bismarck's brutal methods, Kirk telegraphed Salisbury, "My position throughout has been delicate and difficult, and at one time I hardly expected to induce the Sultan to yield without losing further influence over him. There was and is still a real danger that at any time he might think it his interest to make terms with Germany alone in a manner perhaps prejudicial to the interests and influence of other nations, especially of Great Britain, in these parts."[17]

There was no room for negotiations, Salisbury replied; Bargash must agree to Bismarck's terms. On August 13, Kirk, much against his will, managed to get the depressed and fearful sultan to withdraw the letter of protest. "His Highness objected strongly at first to complete submission, saying that he would agree to withdraw his troops and cease to interfere in those countries, but maintained his protest," wrote Kirk to Salisbury.[18] Continuing to act on Salisbury's orders, Kirk finally persuaded Bargash to accept the German takeover of the kingdoms of Witu, Usagara (where the sultan kept troops), Nguru, Useguha, and Ukami (see Map 8 on page 138).

The Return of Emily Reute

Ever since his sister had become pregnant by the German attaché, Heinrich Reute, nineteen years before, Bargash had maintained an unrelenting distrust of the Germans. Now that the Germans had taken the greater part of his realm, the unceasing stress under which he had suffered had resulted in his rapid physical deterioration. Bismarck then delivered a final psychological blow to the bewildered and melancholy sultan. A German warship, the *Adler,* pulled into Zanzibar Harbor. Aboard were Bargash's sister, Emily Reute, and her children. Before her arrival, she had written to her brother telling him that the German kaiser had been kind to her and that it would be in his best interests to side with Germany. "Should you wish me to act for you with the German Emperor, I can go personally to him and speak with him for you. . . . My brother, I want you to understand that the British only wish to destroy your power and your name; they only await a fitting time to seize Zanzibar and everything in it, just as lately they seized Egypt and its dependencies by stratagem. . . .It is the only government that wishes to seize your realm as it does the whole world."[19]

Kirk knew why Bismarck had sent Emily Reute back to Zanzibar. Bismarck figured that Bargash would imprison and execute her for the dishonor she had brought to the royal house of Zanzibar. Because she was now a German subject, this would provide a perfect excuse for the German annexation of Zanzibar. The British ambassador to Berlin, however, reported that all Bismarck hoped for was a reconciliation, and that as a German citizen, Emily Reute had financial claims against the sultanate that Germany was required to support.

Bargash did not attempt to contact, arrest, or imprison his sister. After several weeks, the Germans gave up and shipped her home. Probably at Kirk's urging, Bargash agreed to avoid further trouble by providing Emily with the sum of money the Germans thought she was entitled to. But as a way of lodging his protest, he sent it directly to the German government rather than to Bismarck himself.[20]

At this point Salisbury had shown himself to be flagrantly pro-German,[21] and Kirk had no choice but to follow the prime minister's orders. The treaty ceding most of the sultan's mainland holdings to Germany was finally signed between the sultan and German Rear Admiral Knorr in November 1885. It included ceding control over Dar es Salaam, which would become the main German port for the new protectorate. The only concession Kirk was able to obtain was the right for Bargash to levy a 5 percent duty on goods shipped from coastal ports now controlled by the Germans including Witu, Kilwa, and Dar es Salaam, although he would no longer be able to collect taxes from those places.[22]

Bargash's Troubles Multiply

Portugal, aware of Bismarck's tactics and Bargash's weakness, shifted its Mozambique border north to include Tungi Bay, which had belonged to the sultanate, further reducing Bargash's kingdom (see Map 8 on page 138). On December 14 of the same eventful year, the British, French, and German governments formed a joint commission to permanently fix the frontiers of the German protectorate and the Zanzibari sultanate.[23]

Meanwhile, the African kingdoms around Lake Victoria became more volatile. Most dramatically, the local King Mwanga of Buganda, now part of Uganda, had become rabidly anti-European, believing that all Europeans wanted to gobble up his country.

When the explorer Joseph Thomson heard that James Hannington, a British Church Missionary Society bishop, was planning on traveling from Mombassa to Uganda, he warned him that he would be taking his life in his hands. Hannington ignored the warning, and he and forty-six of his porters were killed by Mwanga's men in that same year.[24]

The Germans had thought their annexation of the sultan's territory would be bloodless, but, not surprisingly, it wasn't. As L.H. Gann has noted, the area was culturally diverse when the Germans occupied it.[25] The Chaggas around Mount Kilimanjaro were farmers. The Nyamwezi specialized in providing porters for the transport of goods. The warlike Ajwas had been in the business of procuring slaves. Zulus, including the Ngoni, raided southwest Tanganyika, while Arab and Swahili slave and ivory traders, who still had a profitable business in spite of the raids, continued to run caravans into the interior. The Banyans tended to dominate business and financial markets as money lenders in coastal towns.

None of these groups warmed to German rule, and the Germans were forced to put down more bloody revolts during their thirty-year occupation of Tanganyika than in most of their other colonies. While German colonialism in Tanganyika rested on white settlement and rigid subordination requiring an extensive military presence, this was not true in their West African colony of Togo. There, German merchants formed partnerships with native farmers, and military force was hardly ever resorted to.

Kirk's Troubles

Even apart from the German issue, Kirk rarely had a moment of peace during this period. For example, at one point he received a tersely worded telegram from the Foreign Office saying that the lives of members of the Church Missionary Society in Buganda had been endangered because Kirk had disavowed them. The implication was that Kirk had sabotaged the missionaries by writing to King Mwanga that they were not bona fide representatives of the British government. It subsequently emerged that the letter had been deliberately mistranslated by unfriendly Arabs in order to weaken the British presence on the mainland, but by then the damage had been done, and King Mwanga preferred to believe the forgery. It would take military action at the end of the nineteenth century for the British to bring Uganda under their control.[26]

In another case, a missionary passing through Mirambo's territory with his own supply of ivory was accused by Mirambo of stealing his goods and thus robbed. Elsewhere, two Arabs whom the sultan had appointed as administrators in the Tabora region were fomenting anti-British feeling and threatening war with other Arabs. Kirk eventually managed to convince the sultan to recall these miscreants and to get Mirambo to return the ivory to the London Missionary Society.

Another thorny issue arose when Kirk had to decide what to do with a freed slave who had become a thief, changed his name, and sold himself back into slavery. The man who was shipped to Pemba by his new Arab slave owner managed to escape and then petitioned to have his freedom back. In this case, Kirk decided not to take action because he did not believe the man's story about reenslaving himself.[27]

The Germans Expand

In 1886, Prime Minister Salisbury attempted to curry favor with Bismarck by showing him a copy of Holmwood's secret document for the development of what would become Kenya. He confidently assured Bismarck that the British government would do nothing to interfere in any way with the new German protectorate. Bismarck decided to meet with Salisbury to establish Tanganyika's boundaries; he agreed to leave the sultan the clove island of Pemba and a narrow strip of land on the coast opposite Zanzibar.[28] At the same time, he denounced Kirk and Holmwood as troublemakers and meddlers. Salisbury, after agreeing to the new boundaries and without letting on about Bismarck's accusation, then telegraphed Kirk to find out how Bargash would view Bismarck's latest proposal. Kirk replied tersely, "The Sultan is no longer physically the same man he was. He has been disturbed by his political troubles."[29]

Looming larger than Kirk's day-to-day battles was the question of whether the sultan and the sultanate would survive. The German flag had been hoisted without warning at Gazi, twenty-five miles south of Mombassa, though the German government had agreed that the town belonged to the sultanate. In a classic political example of skullduggery, Dr. Conrad Arendt, the German consul general for Zanzibar, claimed his government had not sanctioned the takeover and had known nothing about it. But the flag nevertheless remained. General Horatio Kitchener,[30] the British member of the Boundary Commission who had traveled to Zanzibar with Arendt and knew about plans for the takeover, later confided in Kirk that Arendt had told him confidentially "of the great help Bismarck would give to England in Egypt if I acted on the Commission in the German interest."[31]

When in early 1886, the commission decided to give the sultan authority only over a 10-mile-wide by 450-mile-long coastal strip north of Kilwa and several small islands, including Pemba, Bargash became deeply depressed.[32] "I no longer have any hope of keeping the interior," he reportedly told Tippu Tib, the wealthy and influential ex-slave dealer who had retired on Zanzibar. "The Europeans here in Zanzibar are after my possessions. Will it be the hinterland they want? Happy are those who died before now and know nothing of this."[33]

Now that Germany had Dar es Salaam, Kitchener suggested that the British annex Mombassa to maintain the balance of power. For one of the last times, the Foreign Office solicited Kirk's opinion. Kirk responded with his usual candor:

> In discussing such a question as this one, I cannot assume that the relations of Germany and Zanzibar will long remain what they are or that our position will continue to be what it is. If Germany is to retain her protectorates inland, and of this there cannot any longer be a doubt, she will be compelled by the inevitable course of events to obtain possession of the coast opposite.
>
> Treaties, agreements or commissions will all be powerless to stop her from obtaining by purchase, cession or alliance. . . . The time is, in my opinion, not far distant, when the Sultan's

> authority, unable to bear the constant strain to which it is now being exposed by a system of active intrigue, intimidation and bribery, will give way. . . . In such a contingency, with German influence strong, Dar es Salaam being in her hands, Germany would be able at any moment, in case of war, to seize our coal and other stores.
>
> The question to be decided practically is this: Whether we are prepared to see Germany paramount over the Zanzibar coast, using the trading capacities of our Indian subjects to advance and develop her commerce, or whether some compromise cannot be come to whereby our influence is upheld and admitted as legitimately paramount over a certain district, without necessarily affecting the independence of the Sultan so long as that State hangs together.[34]

Kirk had foreseen the importance of saving as much of East Africa as possible from the Germans, and though his loyalty to the sultan had remained unquestioned, he decried the British prime minister and foreign secretary's actions, for he felt they were not in the best interests of the British Empire. Yet he had to obey or to forfeit his position.

On the verge of the German takeover, Bargash, in a desperate mood, offered to put his realm under British sovereignty, but the Foreign Office turned down his request, just as it had previously turned down Holmwood, Gordon, and others who thought British control of the interior was needed to sustain influence in the region, enforce the slave-trade ban, and enable British commercial development in the area. But it was too late; the Germans kept tightening the vice. The sultan's governor of Lamu arrested an African servant of the Denhardt brothers and imprisoned him for three months. Bismarck felt this demanded armed intervention to show that the Germans were truly in charge and arranged another show of military force.

A representative from the German Foreign Office arrived at Zanzibar on October 14, 1886, with the draft of a new treaty with Germany, which had already been cleared with London. The agreement recognized that the sultan's authority would now cover only the islands of Zanzibar, Pemba, Mafia, and Lamu, and his coastal jurisdiction was reduced from ten miles to five, from the Mininjani River to Kipini and the towns of Kismayu, Barawa, Merka, and Mogadishu. The remainder of his once vast mainland sultanate would soon be divided between the Germans and the British into their respective colonies.

Time Runs Out

For Bargash and Kirk, time was running out, and they knew it. The sultan, according to Holmwood, complained of physical weakness and paid less and less attention to his affairs of state. He was only interested in "the acquirement of ready money."[35]

But Bargash still had enough wits about him to request a six-month extension from Bismarck and Lord Iddelsleigh of the Foreign Office before agreeing to the final treaty boundaries. On December 6, 1886, Iddelsleigh telegraphed Bargash: "No extension can be given. We have done our best on your Highness' behalf. Our friendly advice is that you should accept at once. Your interests would be endangered by delay." The following day, a broken-hearted Bargash signed the new treaty.[36]

Dr. Conrad Arendt, the German consul general for Zanzibar, along with Dr. Schmidt, the German consul general for Cairo who had been the third boundary commissioner, sent word to Bismarck that Kirk had continued to obstruct German plans. He had given the sultan such bad advice, they charged, that Bargash had "degraded the work of the Commission to a farce."[37]

Bismarck, in turn, wrote to Count Hatzfeldt, the German ambassador to England, that Kirk's activities were a continued source of trouble. Although Kirk was informed of the complaint, he had no idea the ax would fall so soon. For twenty years he had been a loyal servant of the British Empire in Zanzibar, and he had thought it only right to point out the reality and consequences of the German acquisition of the sultan's domains. But he had dared to question the Foreign Office and the prime minister's appeasement of the Germans at the expense of the Zanzibari sultanate.

Kirk suspected his useful life as chief consul was drawing to a close. He wrote in March 1887 to a friend at the Foreign Office, "I have kept our influence supreme through all, and can fairly ask for leave when the new treaty is signed." He was referring to a proposed new commercial treaty between Germany, Zanzibar, and Great Britain.[38]

Only three months later, he received a note from the Foreign Office saying he was needed in London to give advice on how to handle the Germans. He realized that this was a pretext for his dismissal and that his career as a colonial administrator was finished.

When he left Zanzibar that July, he was only fifty-five years old. Although a bit heavier, he was still physically very fit, and he retained that energy and perceptiveness that had marked his distinguished career.

But he had bucked British bureaucracy too long, and his anti-Bismarck feelings were too well-known. After he and his family returned to England, he was thus not surprised to find himself without another government job. He officially retired from the consular service a year later, reportedly for health reasons, though, in truth, his health remained surprisingly good for another thirty years.

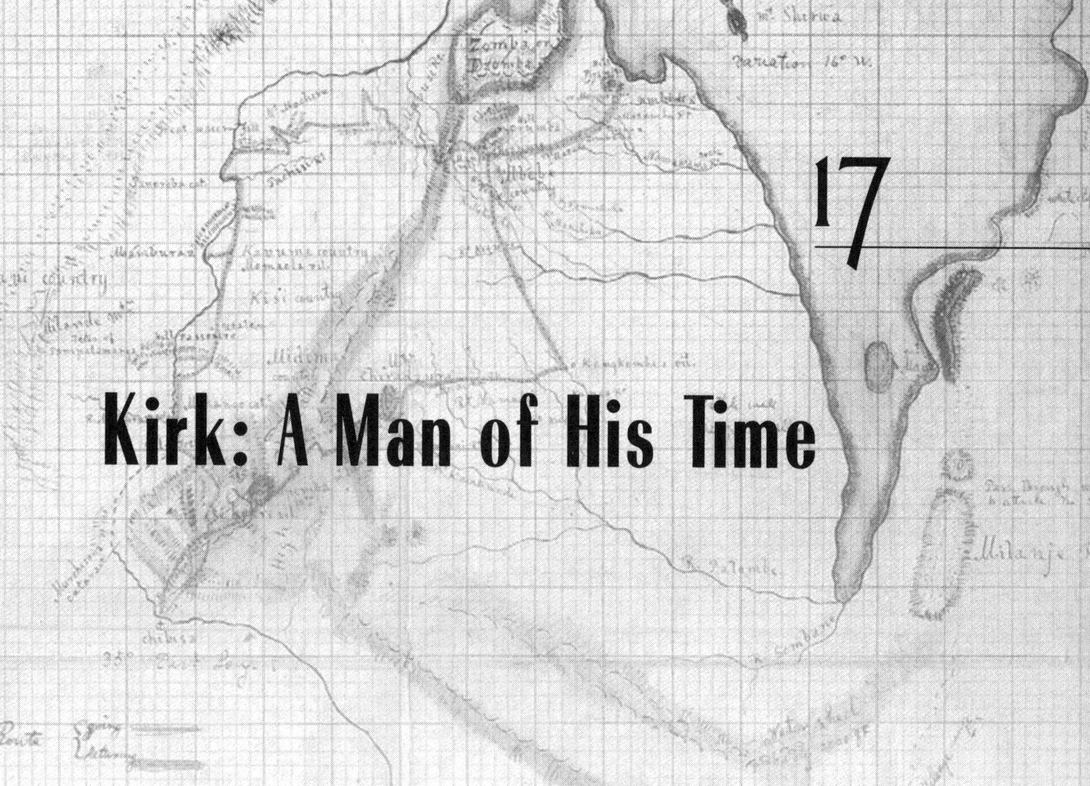

17

Kirk: A Man of His Time

When Kirk, Helen, and their family returned to England, they moved into their home at Seven Oaks. Kirk would never see Bargash again, but he would revisit Zanzibar and have more than a small hand in the way East Africa was ultimately shaped.

Details about Kirk's family life during these years in England are scant, though they reveal that he was an active member of the Seven Oaks community and sang in the church choir. His granddaughter, Daphne Foskett, recalled him as a warm and affectionate man; she also remembered the house at Seven Oaks as filled with African memorabilia.[1]

Always a prodigious letter writer, Kirk continued to correspond regularly with the people he'd met in Africa and to watch with interest as events unfolded there. As a senior diplomat and authority on East Africa and the slave trade, he continued to be solicited for advice on African affairs and was involved in a number of government and quasi-government projects, even undertaking occasional missions for the Foreign Office.

In 1895, for example, he was asked to journey to the Niger River in West Africa to investigate disturbances in Brass. A small kingdom on the Niger River delta, Brass had recently been occupied by the Royal Niger Company, whose director was Sir George Goldie Taubman. Taubman was descended from a family of smugglers who had become landowners and aristocrats on the Isle of Man. At forty-three, he was cunning and aggressive, and, with a private army and a charter from the British government, he dominated the Niger River trade, long coveted by the French.

The little kingdom of Brass had previously controlled the palm oil and palm wine trade, and Koko, the king of Brass, was not happy with the arrangement made with the Royal Niger Company. Under his leadership, the Brassmen, many of whom were cannibals, sacked and burned the Royal Niger Company's shipyard. Seventy-five African employees of the company were killed, cooked, and eaten, though some of the Christian converts among the attackers refused to take part.

The motive for the uprising, Taubman claimed, was theft of the company's possessions, but the British governor and consul general of the Niger Protectorate, Major Claude MacDonald, felt the revolt had been engendered by the company's having usurped the Brassmen's traditional role of middleman in the lucrative palm oil and wine industry. When Kirk returned to England, he reported to the Foreign Office that Taubman's Royal Niger Company had indeed supplanted the Brassmen's oil and wine trade and that the people of Brass were starving. At the same time, a smallpox epidemic was sweeping through the country. The solution: stop Taubman from monopolizing the Niger trade so the Brassmen could recover their economic standing.

Unfortunately, in June 1895, Lord Salisbury was elected prime minister for a third term and ran the Foreign Office himself once again for the next five years. In league with Taubman, he refused to approve Kirk's report or its recommendations. Consequently, many people in Brass died of starvation and disease. Kirk may have shrugged his shoulders in disgust, as it was not the first time his efforts had been sabotaged by Salisbury.[2]

Even when back in England, Africa was never far away for Kirk. For one thing, his house was filled with African artifacts. "The house is almost like a museum, so full it is of curios . . . ," the London *Morning Post* reported in an interview with Kirk. "A little group of spears, cunningly arranged in a geometrical pattern, have little spurs on them that are poisoned."[3] The spears had been hurled at Kirk and Livingstone during an ambush, and Kirk had picked them up and kept them. The poison was from the Kombé plant.

One of Kirk's most important contributions was his discovery of a native rubber tree, Landolphia. Under Kirk's guidance, the establishment of the East African rubber trade in 1878 more than made up for the loss of income by the Arabs from the slave trade.

He also studied the tree resin, copal, and his notes were published by the Linnaean Society in England in 1871.

Among his botanical and zoological contributions, he sent several large collections of plants and animals to England and identified a red colobus monkey on Zanzibar now called Kirk's Red Colobus or Colobus Kirkii, as well as a gazelle to which his name was also appended. In 1874, his study of the Rufiji River delta was published by the Royal Geographic Society.

Lust for Territory

After Kirk left Africa, the European lust for territory did not abate. He learned that the governor of Mozambique had given Bargash an ultimatum in 1887 to accept the Rovuma River as the northern boundary of the Portuguese colony. The sultan refused, and a Portuguese squadron captured one of the sultan's ships and bombarded Tungi and Minjani for five days. Neither the British nor the Germans were interested in interfering on the sultan's behalf, and Bargash capitulated.[4]

A chief called Bushiri, who was Tippu Tib's relative, led a revolt against the Germans in Witu, a town on the coast 300 miles north of Zanzibar, which had been ceded to them by Bargash. The Germans called for help and the Italians, French, Portuguese, and British obliged with a blockade of the town. But the revolt spread north and was not quelled until Bushiri was caught and hanged by the Germans. Bismarck then picked Hermann Wissmann, the explorer who had crossed Africa twice in 1880–83 and 1886–87, to head the new German protectorate of Tanganyika.

A little less than two years after Kirk left Zanzibar, Bargash died at age fifty. Bargash's younger half-brother, Khalifa, who had failed in an earlier attempted palace coup against him, now succeeded him in 1888. It was under Khalifa's rule that the British, faced with the takeover of most of the sultanate by the Germans, decided to officially make Zanzibar their protectorate.

The area encompassed was just a shadow of the sultan's former lands, however. And to trim the sultanate even further, this time with Britain's approval, Germany paid Sultan Khalifa $1 million for Zanzibar's remaining narrow coastal strip, which was then incorporated into Tanganyika. Thus, only the islands of Pemba and Mafia were left to Zanzibar.

Kirk, observing from afar the European nations tearing apart Africa like carnivores, undoubtedly had mixed feelings about the outcomes. He certainly had misgivings about Belgium's King Leopold's rule in the Congo and about the newest predator, Italy, which had established its own protectorate over Somalia north of the Juba River and had an eye on Abyssinia as well.

At the same time, a new movement for the total abolition of slavery, including emancipation of currently owned slaves, was growing in Britain. The British were convinced that by enforcing manumission they were fulfilling their national mission. In referring to the need for military action against certain West African tribes, the British imperialist Joseph Chamberlain, then Secretary of State for the colonies under Lord Salisbury, put it succinctly at the Royal Colonial Institute's annual dinner in 1897, "You cannot have omelets without breaking eggs; you cannot destroy the practices of barbarism, of slavery, of superstitions, which for centuries have desolated the interior of Africa, without using force."[5]

British government policy thus came to include exerting pressure for the total abolition of African slavery, including the manumission of currently owned slaves. In 1889 the Church Missionary Society wrote the Foreign Office: "The committee recalls with pain the debasing and distressing practice of the Slave Trade which has existed so long in Africa. . . . [Now] is the time to urge upon the great powers the necessity of immediate and combined action for its entire suppression."[6]

As a consequence of British pressure, King Leopold convened another conference in November 1889 which lasted into 1890. When it was time for Britain to select delegates for the conference, Lord Vivian wrote in a memorandum, "I would suggest Sir John Kirk, from his greater experience and knowledge of the subject, is best qualified to act, with our delegates, as British Representative on the Commissions."[7] Kirk was indeed chosen as the British government's plenipotentiary.

In a dispatch from Brussels to the Foreign Office, Kirk wrote:

> The first thing to be done to remedy the state of things now existing at Zanzibar is to insist upon the abolition of the status of slavery as a condition recognized at law within the islands of Zanzibar and Pemba. . . . The Treaty which I concluded with the Sultan . . . provided that no slaves could be legally introduced by sea. It is notorious that slaves do not have families and that they are short-lived. Not one in ten of the slaves in Zanzibar and Pemba have been born in the islands, nine-tenths have certainly been smuggled, and the authorities have been over and over again warned that the time would

> come when England would see justice done and the slaves illegally imported set free.
>
> I would not propose, however, to manumit slaves and so dislocate all the present relations of master and servant. I would simply insist upon the Sultan abolishing the recognition of slavery, leaving the system to die out as it did in India and as it is doing in the Portuguese possessions. One thing I would insist upon is that no compensation be offered to the slave holder: to do so would vitiate the argument I propose to use, namely, that the present owners have no legal right to the possession of slaves introduced since 1873.[8]

During the meeting, the U.S. minister to London, Robert T. Lincoln, son of President Abraham Lincoln and one of the delegates, wrote to Salisbury to lend support, including, if need be, naval forces to stop exportation of slaves from Africa once and for all.[9]

Kirk put his knowledge and enthusiasm to work, as always, and helped guide the conference, attended by seventeen nations, to a satisfactory conclusion. A draft of the maritime treaty based on Kirk's proposals was sent from the Foreign Office to the delegates and adopted in toto January 28, 1890. (See Appendix D for the full text of the treaty.)

It must be pointed out that this treaty, like the 1873 treaty, was concerned with the elimination of the slave trade, not freedom for those already enslaved. Kirk felt, based on his long association with the Arabs on Zanzibar and his vast experience with the slave trade, that manumission would inevitably have to be brought about slowly to avoid local rebellions, which he foresaw having to be suppressed by British troops. This, he was afraid, would not be countenanced by the Foreign Office or the prime minister, for, in Kirk's opinion, they could not be expected to do anything substantial, or risk anything of substance, but merely give voice to antislavery rhetoric.

Among the signatories to the treaty were the principal players in the scramble to grab African territory. These included Britain, France, Germany, Portugal, and Italy. After the treaty was ratified, the delegates passed a resolution showing their appreciation for the way Kirk had guided the drafting of the new treaty.

In 1890, Seyyid Ali-bin Said succeeded to the throne of Zanzibar after only two years of Khalifa's reign. In a separate treaty with Britain that same year, he declared, "Slaves shall be inherited at the death of their owner only by the lawful children of the deceased. If the owner has no children, his slaves shall, *ipso facto,* become free on the death of the owner" and "Every slave shall be entitled as a right at any time henceforth to purchase his freedom at a just and reasonable tariff."

Because the sultan was also afraid slaves would run away to earn money to purchase their freedom, he issued two new proclamations: "Be it known to all that slaves who shall run away without just cause . . . shall be punished as before," and "If any slave runs away from his master, or does anything wrong, punish him as before." Then he added as another precaution, "If any slave brings money to the Kadi [judge] to purchase his freedom, his master will not be forced to take the money."

Since this loophole allowed the owner to hold onto his slave, the treaty did not truly enfranchise those slaves. After Ali died, his successor, Mamoud bin Mahomed bin Said, decreed in 1897 that slaves could not obtain their freedom without making formal application for the issue of freedom papers and that concubines were considered equivalent to wives and would not be manumitted without due cause, namely cruelty witnessed by two disinterested parties. By 1897 the total slave population of Zanzibar and Pemba had dropped to 100,000, but by the end of 1901, there were still 47,000 slaves on those islands.[10]

Though slave trafficking by sea was mostly dead as a result of the treaty, it persisted perniciously in some regions of eastern and southern Africa. In Tanganyika, for example, the German colonial government maintained a lackadaisical attitude about domestic slavery, and slavery was not legally abolished there until 1907.

Some British who had settled in Zanzibar and along the coast felt the same way. For example, J.P. Farler, the former missionary who had accused Stanley of acquiring slaves and who himself became British Commissioner on Pemba, made this curious comment about the meaning of the word "slave":

> There is no doubt that the institution of slavery in any country does degrade not only the slave, but also the slave owners. But the slaves themselves do not feel any degradation in being called a slave. The word "slave" has a very different meaning in Swahili from what it has in English, and there is no stigma attached to it.
>
> The swahili word, Mtumwa [slave] is derived from the verb "kutuma," to send. The title of Mohammed, the Apostle of God is Mtume (i.e., the one sent). It has exactly the same meaning as our word, Apostle; while mtumwa [slave] is merely one who can be sent. So you see what an honorable connection the word

> has. The greatest Arabs, in writing to the Sultan, always sign themselves, your slave, so and so. In many parts of the country, especially the mainland coastal tribes, the word Mtume is frequently used for supreme being. The household slaves, in large families are most scornful towards slaves freed by the government, will hold no intercourse with them, and call them mateka (or the spoils of the enemy), and this is a deadly insult.[11]

Subterfuges continued to get around the antislavery proclamations, treaties, and decrees. In Abyssinia (Ethiopia), a predominantly Christian country, the British official G.R. Clerk described one such pretense in a letter to the Foreign Office in 1903:

> A soldier from Kaffa or Wallamo (the two provinces where slaves are most easily come by) gets leave to go to Addis Abbaba with two or three servants. On arrival at the capital he soon finds where he can best dispose of them. He then offers them as a gift to the would-be-owner: the latter accepts them, and in return presses a gift of so many dollars to his friend. These preliminaries are kept secret. A day or two later the soldier pays a formal visit to the purchaser, accompanied by his servants and some witnesses. He then explains that he has been suddenly recalled to his post, that his servants will delay him, and that therefore, he will be very grateful if his friend will keep them in his house until he returns to claim them, an event that never happens.[12]

All in all, however, there had been a persistent decline in slavery in that part of the world, thanks in great part to Kirk. Aside from his antislavery efforts, Kirk also served as a director of the Imperial British East Africa Company, founded in 1888 by his old friend William Mackinnon. Mackinnon, who had become one of the wealthiest men in England, was convinced, like Livingstone and Kirk, that only by developing African commerce could the misery of African peoples be ended. To counterbalance the German annexation of Tanganyika, the British government, backed by Kirk, gave the company a charter to carry out commercial development in East Africa and lay the groundwork for the soon-to-be-British colonies of Kenya and Uganda.[13]

In 1894, the British government formally declared a protectorate over Buganda (to become part of Uganda) and a year later named it The East Africa Protectorate, which included the future Kenya Colony.

Next, construction of a railway was begun to provide rail transport through and open up the territories. Some £250,000 was initially raised. Mackinnon contributed £25,000, and Kirk and Holmwood each gave £1,000. The railway would link Mombassa to the town of Kismayu on Lake Victoria. From there, a steamer would transport goods to Uganda, where they would in turn be transported by land and across Lakes Victoria, Albert, and Edward to the Nile.

The cost of construction turned out to be far more than the company had anticipated, both in money and in lives. Hundreds of construction workers imported from India died of illness or were eaten by man-eating lions in the stretch through what is now Tsavo National Park in Kenya. The project's detractors called it the "Lunatic Express." It was finally completed in 1903 at a cost of over £5 million.

In the railroad's favor was the fact that walking from Mombassa to Uganda took three months. Furthermore, after the abolition of slavery, head porterage had become very expensive. In fact, bulk freight via head porterage cost £250 a ton, leaving only ivory profitable by this means. Not only did sending goods by rail promise to make goods far cheaper, but the steel link from the Indian Ocean to the rift lakes almost immediately spurred commerce and colonization.[14]

Europeans with antislavery beliefs began to trickle into East Africa, and their presence was considered by Kirk and others to have given a final blow to the slave trade in that region. In point of fact, British settlers came in driblets to Kenya in the early years of the twentieth century. Many were low-income, single men hoping to wrest their fortunes from the land. For every Lord Delamere and other relatively well-off settler, there were many poor English families who hung on by the skin of their teeth fighting crop-decimating insects and periodic drought. South African Boers, some dispossessed by the Boer War, also drove their ox-wagons north to settle in Kenya to become farmers. Indians who had worked on the railroad brought their families over from India and became businessmen and clerks in the new British-run Kenya bureaucracy. In 1935 it was estimated that there were fewer than 18,000 European settlers in Kenya, mostly British.[15]

Kirk welcomed these changes and the British colonial effort more generally. Yet he had spent the better part of his life fighting and then successfully stopping the slave trade and had been horrified by the depredations of the Belgians in the Congo and the ruthlessness of the Germans in Tanganyika.

He had devoted his life to the elimination of slavery and abhorred it in any form, and had he lived long enough, there is no doubt that he would have fully endorsed the mandate Great Britain signed for its East African colonies at the League of Nations in 1922, the year of Kirk's death: "to promote to the utmost the material and moral well-being and the social progress of its inhabitants" and to help them over time "to stand by themselves."

In 1886, in addition to his previous two knighthoods, Kirk received the G.C.M.G (Grand Companion of the Most Distinguished Order of the Grand Cross), the highest degree of knighthood in the order of St. Michael and St. George, in recognition of his service to the Empire. Other honors included the Patron's Gold Medal of the Royal Geographic Society in 1882 for "his long continued and unremitting services to geography in Africa." The prestigious Royal Society elected him a fellow in 1887, and the University of Edinburgh honored him with an L.L.D. in 1890.

In spite of Livingstone's friction with the Portuguese in Mozambique during the Second Zambezi Expedition, Kirk's services to Portugal, while serving as their consul in Zanzibar, were recognized when Portugal awarded him the Grand Cross of the Royal Military Order of Jesus Christ. In 1887, after Kirk returned to England, he was asked to join the Royal Geographic Society Council. He served as vice-president from 1891–94 and foreign secretary from 1894–1911. In 1887 he was made a fellow of the prestigious Royal Society of London, which recognized outstanding scientific contributions, and served as vice-president of that scientific organization from 1894–95. A year later he was appointed to their Tsetse Fly Committee to study all tropical diseases, including malaria. Honors continued to multiply. Recognizing Kirk's humanitarian services while he was British consul at Zanzibar, Italy appointed him Knight Commander of the Order of the Crown of Italy in 1889. The University of Edinburgh honored him with an L.L.D. in 1890. Cambridge University awarded him an honorary Doctor of Science (Sc.D.) in 1897, and Oxford a Doctor of Civil Law (D.C.L.) in 1898. In 1897 the Cambridge Philosophical Society made him an honorary member. A year later, the Marseille, France, Geographical Society did likewise. This was followed, in 1888, with his election to the Zoological Society. Kirk was held in such esteem that even many years later, when his eyesight failed and he could no longer attend meetings, he was frequently consulted by these organizations.

And what of Henry Morton Stanley? In contrast to Kirk, Stanley was propelled by a burning desire to elevate himself above the poverty and degradation he had experienced as an orphan. By employing a combination of guile, ruthlessness, and brutality and exploiting his talent for describing people and events in a sensational manner, he achieved fame and fortune. As a geographic explorer, he was in the forefront, circumnavigating Lakes Tanganyika and Victoria, and then traveling down the entire length of the Congo River. He then made a fortune by expropriating the Congo from African chiefs for the Belgian king, Leopold.[16]

Over the years, his battle with Kirk had cooled down, and Kirk, among others, voted him the most likely candidate to lead the Emin Pasha Relief Expedition. Dr. Emin Pasha, physician and governor of Egypt's most southern province, Equatoria, was about to fall into the hands of the soldiers of the Mahdi who had advanced on Equatoria after sacking Khartoum. On this expedition, Stanley fared badly, losing half of his men and almost his own life. Still, he eventually succeeded in bringing the fabled physician of Equatoria to the east coast.

When Stanley returned to England from his last foray into Africa in April 1890, he was honored at Windsor Castle by Queen Victoria. His numerous lectures and the honorary degrees he received gave him an entry into England's highest and social circles, where he met and eventually married Dorothy Tennant. He also received word that he was being considered for knighthood. This meant renouncing his American citizenship, which he did without the least hesitation, and in 1899 he was made knight of the Grand Cross of Bath. He subsequently served one term as a conservative member of Parliament, and the orphan from Wales lived the rest of his life as a well-respected member of British society until his death in 1904.

Return to East Africa

In 1903, Kirk returned to Africa for a nonofficial visit and had the satisfaction of traveling to Lake Nyassa (Malawi) on a newly completed railway extension from Mozambique (see Map 9 on page 253). One can imagine that as he sat in his compartment he stared in wonder at a landscape he had so painfully crossed almost half a century earlier. Now, it took only a couple of days to reach the lake; with Livingstone it had taken many dreary months of danger and privation.

There were new white settlements to be seen in the highlands. Tribal wars and slavery were apparently gone, and new villages were being built alongside the tracks. In the last year of the nineteenth

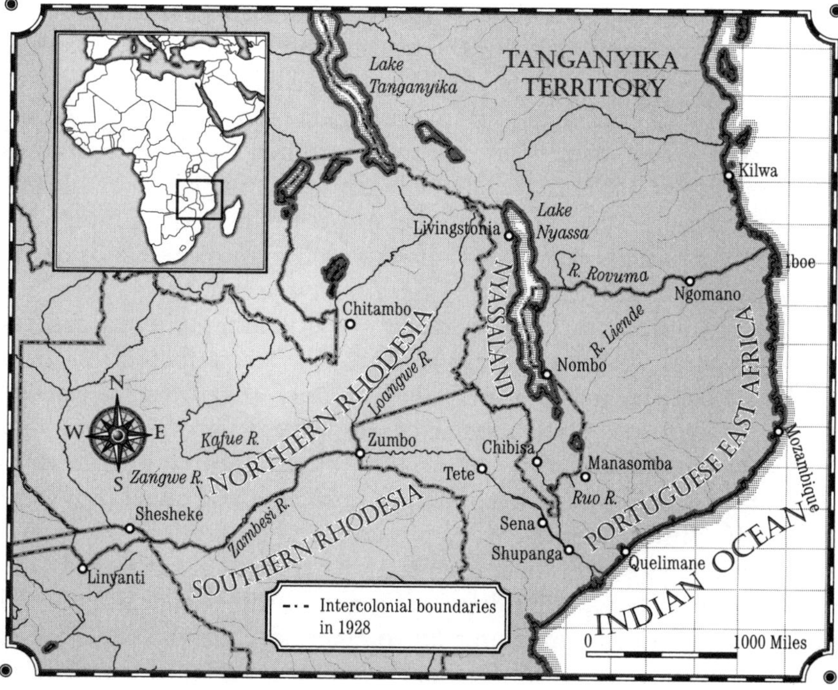

MAP 9 *Intercolonial Boundaries, 1928.*

century, the great Lake Nyassa with its surrounding territory had become a British protectorate called Nyassaland (now Malawi).[17]

Christianity competed with Islam for the souls of the different African groups in the area. The Yaos at the southern end of Lake Nyassa (Malawi), having worked for the Arabs as kidnappers of Manganjas, converted to Islam, while most of the others, including the Manganjas themselves, became Christians.

As Kirk watched through his coach window, memories may have flooded his mind of his five long years on the Zambezi, the joy of discovering new plants and trees, the tremendous number and variety of wild animals he had seen, the elephant hunts, the arduous climbs on the cliffs above the Kebrabasa Rapids, Baines's unjust sentence, his own temporary blindness and near-drowning, David Livingstone's erratic leadership, Mary Livingstone's tragic death at Shupanga, the horror of slave caravans, escapes from ambushes by the Ajwas and Makonde, and his anguish at having killed men. These were only memories now, memories of a life rich and exciting.

In 1903, Kirk also revisited the island of Zanzibar for the first time since his consul days. In some respects he found it surprisingly the same as when he had left it 17 years earlier, with the same narrow streets and buildings with overhanging second-story balconies. But slavery had been completely abolished, and Arab dhows anchored in the harbor now shipped only copal, india rubber, cloves, and other articles of legal commerce. Above all hung the Union Jack, and Kirk was relieved the island had not fallen into the hands of the Germans but had finally become a British protectorate.

It is difficult from the perspective of this biographer to categorize Kirk as an imperialist. He appears to have reflected the view held by most servants of the Crown, namely, that Africans needed "civilizing," in the British sense of the word, to bring out the dignity inherent in all human beings.[18] In the tradition of Livingstone, this meant that Christianity, commerce, and education were needed to eliminate tribal wars, poverty, and ignorance.

But there was more to it than that. There was also the question of race. D.C.R.A. Goonetelleke, referring to the European colonial period, wrote in his introduction to *Heart of Darkness* by Joseph Conrad, "It was a period of high flown ideals as to the supposed *civilizing* influence of European civilization—and a period in which it would not have occurred to many Europeans to think of non-whites in terms of words other than *savage* and *nigger.* Even those who were among the most enlightened on such issues held some views that are likely to strike modern readers as condescending; indeed, they may sometimes seem to resemble the outright racists of their day in finding the native peoples of Africa or of Asia *backwards* or *childlike.* . . . The more enlightened, by contrast, felt that the perceived backwardness was merely a product of circumstance—that, in other circumstances, with education and so on, native peoples of the world could become just as *enlightened* as themselves. The essentialist view was the foundation for racial brutality, whereas the anti-essentialist view (ethnocentric though it unquestionably was) laid the path for progress away from imperialist oppression and indeed from racism of any sort."[19]

Kirk was very well aware that imperialism was a mixed bag. The negative impact, aside from the wars of conquest and subjugation, was that the internal structure of African society was weakened, if not destroyed, when supplanted by colonial regimes with their beliefs in their own inherent superiority and their tendency to exploit native labor. There were also adverse effects on family life through migration of labor, mainly single men, to mines, lumber camps, or for large-scale agricultural or industrial projects.

The positive result, on the other hand, at least for a few, was that the French and British offered an education to those Africans who were deemed by their colonial masters to be the most gifted. These "educated and trained" Africans, it was hoped, would then help "uplift" their own people.

Although the negative side of colonialism is easy to see, and often justly remarked on, there is evidence to suggest that the British colonial system in some cases did more good than harm, though the legacy has often been a checkered one. For example, warring groups were forced to coexist relatively peacefully in the colonies. In Nigeria alone, over 600 different groups of Africans were unified into a state, though tribal divisions continued to plague the country for a long time and even resulted in a civil war. On the other hand, the basis of African nationalism was born out of the colonial system.

During the colonial era, King Leopold's legacy of rank exploitation of the Congo was followed by the Belgian government's general indifference to the fate of its African subjects. The Belgians left this huge, mineral-rich, and well-watered country—known later as Zaire—and now as the Democratic Republic of the Congo, in a hurry in 1960 without providing sufficient training for Africans to develop their country's infrastructure. Power became concentrated in the hands of a few and brought on a vicious civil war and corruption at the highest levels of government. In the former Belgian colonies of Rwanda and Burundi, extreme overpopulation coupled with poverty and limited education may have been factors in the continued tribal warfare between Tutsis and Hutus.

Peter Duignan writes that European empire builders stood for modernization. Roads, railways, ports, schools, hospitals, agriculture and veterinary centers, mines, and manufacturing centers were all built by them.[20]

Although there were regional and group differences, medical care, as well as the control of epidemic diseases through immunization and sanitation, resulted in decreased mortality and morbidity, especially among infants and children.

Where there had been few or no roads and goods had been transported by human porterage, where cattle had been moved on foot for sale to nearby markets, the introduction of bicycles, motorcycles, cars, buses, trucks, and trains made long-distance movement of populations, livestock, and goods feasible for the first time. Not only that, but public security enforced by colonial troops and consequent reduction of tribal warfare permitted a vast increase in intra- and international trade.

Forced labor, which had occurred in precolonial Africa where local wars, slave raiding, and slavery had been commonplace, ceased, but the colonial powers instituted their own forms of forced labor or economic slavery. For example, before there was enough capital and money in native African hands for monetary taxation to take place, it was common for the Europeans to coerce native Africans to work as laborers or porters. This practice actually continued well into the middle 1920s.

Finally, on the political scene after the Second World War, American and European hopes of establishing democracies, à la the United States, among the newly independent African states was slow to materialize, for one-man rule, which had prevailed historically with both tribal chiefdoms and colonial powers, continued to do so with many new African heads of state.

Kirk's Legacy

Although John Kirk's name is not well known outside Britain and East Africa, it was he, far more than Livingstone, who played a crucial role in stopping the slave trade. With his loyal defense of British interests, Kirk paved the way for the relatively enlightened British colonial rule that followed his tenure in East Africa.

His relationship to Livingstone, though at times stormy, ended, as it had begun, with respect and friendship for the man who had so profoundly influenced his life. In 1913, at age 81, Kirk was invited to a dinner at the Royal Geographic Society honoring the memory of Livingstone. Influenza and a lung infection kept him from actually attending. Instead, he sent a telegram: "Deeply regret illness prevents attendance at meeting to mark Livingstone's great work and the support given by the Royal Geographic Society ever since its foundation to African Exploration."[21]

Kirk's wife, Helen, died in 1914, and his old age was marred by the loss of sight in one eye in 1907 and partial blindness in the other, but that didn't stop him from spending much of his time in his darkroom making professional-quality photographs. He held the position of foreign secretary of the Royal Geographic Society until his eyesight almost completely failed.

There is a photograph of Kirk in his late 80s, sitting in front of Wavetree, his home at Seven Oaks. He is dressed in his consular uniform. His hair and beard have turned white. His blue eyes are by now blind, but seem to lock on the photographer, and there is a gentle, sweet smile on his face as if he is satisfied that during his life he accomplished what he set out to do.

His last public act was to attend King George V's coronation in 1910. Kirk died at Seven Oaks on January 15, 1922, at age 90.

Sir Henry H. Johnston, the same young explorer who had wanted to buy land for British colonists around Mount Kilimanjaro, became an administrator, novelist, and friend of Kirk's and who wrote a fitting eulogy:

> I have always thought Sir John, one of the greatest men produced by Great Britain during the nineteenth century, was never properly appreciated until long after his official career was closed. . . . It was to him that all those interested in central African questions—especially regarding the slave trade—turned for advice. . . . But he still found time to know personally and to assist with his advice and kind sympathy almost everyone who twenty or thirty years ago went to Africa. From my earliest African days in 1888 he has been my counselor and friend, for whom admiration vies with affection and whose example it has been my greatest ambition to follow—the ablest, the most sympathetic, and the most modest of all men. [22]

Lord Frederick D. Lugard, former administrator of Uganda and governor general of Nigeria, where he had stopped the slave trade, was present at Kirk's funeral at St. George's Church in Seven Oaks. He wrote in the London *Times* a fitting tribute to his old friend after his death:

> I had for him a deep affection which I know was reciprocated. He was to me the ideal of a wise and sympathetic administrator on whom I endeavored to model my own action and to whose inexhaustible fund of knowledge I constantly appealed. Never was there a man . . . more careless of recognition for himself, or more ready to persuade even himself that the credit belonged to another.
>
> I entered on the track where he had blazed the way, and essayed, with his advice and help, to carry on the campaign against slavery where he had left it.
>
> His was an extraordinarily original brain. Even the topics of the day, on which every conceivable opinion seemed to have been expressed, he would illumine by some wholly original point of view and some striking suggestion. . . .
>
> Almost blind, struggling for breath with the aid of oxygen through long, sleepless nights of incessant pain, never a word

of complaint escaped him. He faced death as he had faced life, with calm courage, self-possessed . . . thinking of his friends and not of himself.

I believe it is fair to say that Sir John Kirk was one of the greatest men produced by Great Britain during the nineteenth century. The services he rendered to Africa by helping to abolish the slave trade may have been forgotten, but the very fact that descendants of those former slaves rule their own countries is testimony to his unique contribution to human freedom. It was to him that all those interested in Central and East African questions—especially regarding the slave trade—turned for advice, and he never failed to suggest a practical solution.[23]

Appendix A

From David Livingstone to John Kirk

Screw Ship Pearl
at Sea off Madeira
18 Mar. 1858

Dr. John Kirk.
Sir,

1. The main object of the Expedition to which you are appointed Economic Botanist and Medical Officer is to extend the knowledge already attained of the geography and mineral and agricultural resources of Eastern and Central Africa, to improve our acquaintance with the inhabitants and to engage them to apply their energies to industrial pursuits and to the cultivation of their lands with a view to the production of a raw material to be exported to England in return for British manufactures and it may be hoped that by encouraging the natives to occupy themselves in the development of the resources of their own country, a considerable advance may be made towards the extinction of the slave trade, as the natives will not be long in discovering that the former will eventually become a more certain source of profit than the latter.

2. It is intended that the Expedition should pass through the malarious district at the lower portion of the Zambesi river as quickly as possible, and it will be necessary for you to put into practice those precautionary measures against fever by the use of Quinine which the experience of the Niger Expedition and your own judgement may suggest as likely to secure the health of your companions.

3. The efforts of every member of the Expedition will probably be required to facilitate the transport of the luggage to and beyond Tette, the most advanced post of civilisation, but the chief power in the country adjacent being in the hands of two or three influential chiefs it will be our duty to visit them and invite

them to turn the attention of their people to the cultivation of cotton, by giving them a supply of better seed than that which they already possess, and also to explain the benefit that they would derive from an exchange of the natural productions of Africa, as ivory, cotton, oil, beeswax, buaze, etc. for the manufactures of Europe, and generally to hold out every encouragement, in order to induce them to give up their warlike and predatory habits and substitute the more peaceable pursuits of agriculture and commerce; the time occupied in attending to these matters will enable you, if you find it to be consistent with your personal safety, to glean a general idea of the resources of the country to the North of Tette and to ascertain, in as full detail as the time will allow, the nature of the plant called Buaze, paying particular attention to the probable amount to which it and any other fibrous substances might be obtained. You will be good enough to furnish me with a Report thereon for transmission home to the Foreign Office.

4. Your attention is particularly requested to the discovery of dye stuffs, gums and medicinal substances, in the hope that should either these or fibrous tissues exist in quantities sufficient to warrant commercial enterprise, you may aid in the great work of supplanting by lawful commerce, the odious traffic in slaves.

It is gratifying to me to feel assured that this object commend itself to your mind as a most important and noble one, and I have the pleasure of handing you a copy of a sketch of the principal duties expected of you in the botanical department, drawn up by that eminent traveller and Botanist, Dr. J.D. Hooker whose success in reflecting honour on our country, I heartily wish you may equal and for requesting, for this part of our travels at least, your earnest and exclusive attention to the same; other objects of interest will no doubt press on your notice, but considering that the botany of this region is nearly unexplored, there is a danger of your over-working yourself—your energies will be greater in the second than in the first year—and that the primary object of the expedition is to gain accurate information respecting the vegetable and mineral resources of the country, I trust you will see the propriety of limiting, for a time, the range of your pursuits.

5. Our stay in the vicinity of Tette must necessarily be short because it is essential to proceed at an early period to the rapid, Kebrabasa or Chicova, to ascertain the possibility of

passing it while the river is still comparatively high and thus avoid the necessity of taking the launch to pieces for portage. The people near the Portuguese settlements who have been in contact with slave traders, not being so trustworthy as those farther inland who have not been subjected to the prejudicial influence of such communication, it will be unadvisable to make any distant excursions. Our energies must be bent to the establishment of a depot at some eligible spot beyond the confluence of the Kafue and Zambezi. Having reached a tolerable elevation and examined the country adjacent it will be advisable after obtaining the consent of any natives who may lay claim to the soil, to set up the iron house to serve as a central station As the spot selected will probably be on the side of one of the hills which flank the river and high to secure salubrity, a small plot of ground may at that altitude be planted with wheat and European vegetables as an experiment, and also in order to promote the comfort and health of the Expedition; while another small plot at the lower level may be planted with cotton and sugar cane, and given in charge to the headman of any village adjacent, in order to induce the natives to take an interest in the result.

6. The central depot, once established and intercourse with the natives set on foot, a more extended range of scientific observation will then be advisable. You may then follow out as opportunity offers, the instructions on Zoology from Professor Owen, contained in Appendix No. 2, and without discarding your botanical labours, collect any new or rare animals, birds, fishes or insects that may be met with on excursions which in company with the Makololo may safely be made, and the results be deposited at the central station.

7. Although these explorations and collections are very desirable you will understand that Her Majesty's Government attach more importance to the moral influence which may be exerted on the mind of the natives by a well regulated and orderly household of Europeans setting an example to all who may congregate around the settlement—treating the people with kindness and relieving their wants, teaching them to make experiments in agriculture—explaining to them the more simple arts—imparting to them religious instruction as far as they are capable of receiving it and inculcation of peace and good will to each other.

8. One especial means of gaining their favour will be by giving them the benefit of your medical skill and remedial aid. They possess medical men among themselves who are generally the most observant people to be met with; it is desirable to be at all times on good terms with them. In order to accomplish this, slight complaints, except among the very poor, ought to be referred to their care, and severe cases, before being undertaken, should be enquired with the doctor himself and no disparaging remark ever made on the previous treatment in the presence of the patient. This line of conduct will lead to the more urgent cases only being referred to you; time and medicine will both be saved, while your influence will be extended. Never neglect the opportunity which the bed of sickness presents of saying a few kinds words in a natural respectful manner and imitate in as far as you can, the conduct of the Great Physician, whose followers we profess to be.

9. The Expedition is well supplied with arms and ammunition and it will be necessary at all times to use these in order to obtain supplies of food, as well as specimens of animals for the purposes of Natural history. In many parts of the country which we hope to traverse, the larger animals exist in great numbers and being comparatively tame may be easily secured. I would earnestly press on you the duty of a sacred regard of life and never to destroy it, unless some justifiable end is to be answered by its extinction. The most vital part ought to be aimed at and no shot fired unless the animal be within a range that renders it probable that the mortal part will be struck. The wanton waste of animal life which I have witnessed from night hunting and from the precocious but child-like use of instruments of destruction as well as the wish that the habits of certain races of animated creation which are evidently destined at no very distant date to extinction should be calmly and philosophically observed while there remains the opportunity, make me anxious that none of my companions should be guilty of similar abominations.

10. It is hoped we may never have occasion to use our arms for protection from the natives but the best security from attack consists in upright conduct and the natives seeing that we are prepared to meet it. At the same time you are strictly enjoined to exercise the utmost forbearance towards the people and while retaining proper firmness in the event of any misunderstanding, to conciliate, as far as possible can be admitted with safety to our own party.

11. It is unnecessary for me to enjoin the strictest justice in dealing with the people. This your own principles will lead you invariably to follow, but it is decidedly necessary to be careful not to appear to over reach or insult anyone. Care must be taken in every case in which a native is to be employed that the terms be well understood and a little patience in settling the amount of renumeration in the presence of witnesses and the exact number of persons engaged will prevent that heart burning and discontent which otherwise may ensue. Let the payment be invariably made into the hands of the man who has performed the work. Unless this is done, the idea of property in the labour of the lower classes of the population is apt to be engendered in the minds of the under chiefs but by direct payment, a most important doctrine is widely inculcated and in process of time each man comes to feel that he owes subjection to the head chief alone and is otherwise a free subject.

12. The chiefs of tribes and leading men of villages ought always to be treated with great respect and nothing should be done to weaken their authority. Any present of food should be accepted frankly. It is impolitic to allow the ancient custom of feeding strangers to go into disuse. We come among them as members of a superior race and servants of a Government that desires to elevate the more degraded portions of the human family. We are also adherents of a holy benign religion, patient effort be the harbingers of peace to a hitherto distracted and trodden down race. No great result is ever obtained without patient and long continued efforts. In this enterprise in which we have the honour to be engaged, sympathy, consideration and kindness which when viewed in detail, may seem thrown away, if steadily persisted in, are sure ultimately to exercise a commanding influence. Depend upon it, a kind word or deed is never lost.

13. You will have access to Koelbes Polyglotta Africana, Bleeks vocabulary of the languages of Mosambique and an analysis of the Sechuana tongue, and you are to endeavour to master the latter language, as it is generally spoken in the Makololo country and its acquisition will materially aid you in all your pursuits. Should opportunity offer, you are expected to collect vocabularies of other dialects, using the system already employed in the Sechuana, taking the English consonants and giving the vowels the sound they have in Italian, Spanish and in most European languages.

14. You are distinctly to understand that your services are engaged for two years, unless any unforeseen accident should happen to the expedition, when you will be set free as soon as an opportunity is afforded for returning to England.
15. In the event of my being prostrated by illness or by accident, rendered incapable of conducting the Expedition, the charge of it will devolve on Commander Bedingfeld. If he too should fail, it will devolve on you and then on Mr. Charles Livingstone, but immediate information of such an event is, if possible, to be transmitted to England for further instructions.
16. You are at liberty to consult a copy of the original instructions I hold from Her Majesty's Government and it is hoped that you will enter cordially into the spirit of them and so far as circumstances will allow, endeavour to carry them into effect.
17. Finally, you are strictly enjoined to take the greatest care of your own health and that of the Expedition. My own experience teaches the necessity of more than ordinary attention to the state of the alimentary canal, constipation is almost sure to bring on fever, and it would be well if you kindly explain to the different members, the necessity of timely remedial aid to overcome any tendency to it, especially if accompanied by dreaming, drowsiness, want of appetite or unpleasant taste in the mouth in the mornings. If quinine combined with a mild aperient be administered this precautionary measure will often ward off an attack of this formidable disease. Feeling the fullest confidence in your zeal in the great cause of African civilisation and rejoicing in being associated with you in this noble work I heartily commit you and the cause in which you will, I hope be an influential pioneer, to the safe keeping of the Almighty Disposer of events.

I am your
most obedient servant
David Livingstone.

Appendix B

Medical Stores from Apothecaries' Hall, 17th Feb. 1858, for the Use of Dr. Livingstone's Expedition

On pages 38–40 of Vol. I of the journal, a list of medical stores is inserted, after the narrative for May 3rd, 1858.

		Avoirdupois.
Quinae Disulph:	lb. 5	
Bi: Sulph.	"	2 oz.
Magnsiae	"	8
Pulv: Rhei	"	3
Sodae nicarb.	5	
Zinc Sulphat:		5
Calomel	1	
Morphiae Muriat:		2
Opii		8
Antimon tartarizat		3
Arsenici Albi: pulv:		1
Albumen	1	
Argent Nitrat:		5
Tannin		4
Potass iodidi	1	
Ferri Sulp: exsiccat		4
Plumb acetat:	2	
Mass pil Plumb opiat		6
" " Hydrarg		4
" " Colosynth & Hyoscyami		6
" " Rhei Co. (Edin)		4
Extract Hematoxyli		6
Pulv: Ipacae		4
" " Comp:		4
Resinae Jalap:		10

Unguent Hydrarg Nitrat: Fort:		4
" Simplicis	1	
Acid Tartarici pulv:	3	12
Potass: bitartarat pulv:	12	
Magnesiae Sulphat	50	
Corrosive Sublimate	2	
Camphor	2	
Arsenical Soap	6	
Tinct: Myrrhae		8
Liq: Ammon: fort		8
Acid Hydrocyanic dilut		2
" Nitrici		8
" Sulphurici		8
" Acet: glacial		8
Blistering fluid		10
Liquid Arsenical:		8
Conserv: Rosae	1	2
Creosotum		1
Chloroform		10
Tinct: Cardamon Comp:	2	8
Balance and weights	2 sets	
Fluid measure	6 oz. 2 sets 2	
" "	1 oz. "	2
" "	minim "	2
Bandages Calico	Dozen	6
Lint	12 lbs.	
Emplast: Lithargyn- on Linen	10 yds.	
Thin Gutta Percha	6 yds	
Mortar & Pestle small	1	
Spatulas (5 & 6 inch)	2	
Glass test tubes	Doz. 1	
Chloride of Tin solution	2 oz.	

Carbonae of Amonia	12 oz.
Sulphate of Aluminia	12 oz.
Causic Potash	12 oz.
Caustic Lime	12 oz.
Bleaching powder	3 lbs.
Test papers blue & red Litmus	6 books each
Tin foil	8 lbs.
Thompson's Conspectus of the Pharmacopoeia	No. 1
4 oz. Glass Stopper bottles	4 dozen
12 oz. " " "	2 dozen
Hydrometer for Sp. G. higher than w.	No. 1
Methylated Spirit	6 galls.
Filter paper	1 quire
Glass Funnels 1/4 pint	2
Ol: Cajuputi	8 oz.
Porcelain capsules	No. 12
Packing Tow	33 lbs.

Packed in 8 cases thus

No. 1. Med: Chest
- 2. do do /Solids
- 3. do do /Liquids
- 4. Sulp: Mag: & Lint.
- 5. Glass Stoppered Bottle
- 6. Large Specimen Jars
- 7./8. Methylated Spirits

Besides the above we have Warburg's drops.

One case of Amputatry and cupping instruments.

One case of dissecting instruments.

The stores in the preceding list includes chemicals for examination of dyes and preservative substances for specimens.

Appendix C

Text of the Treaty of 1847

I. His Highness the Sultan of Muscat (Capitol of Oman) hereby engages to prohibit, under the severest penalties, the export of slaves from his African dominions, and to issue orders to his officers to prevent and suppress such trade.

II. His Highness the Sultan of Muscat further engages to prohibit, under the severest penalties, the importation of slaves from any part of Africa into his possessions in Asia and to use his utmost influence with the chiefs of Arabia, the Red Sea, and the Persian Gulf, in like manner to prevent the introduction of slaves from Africa into their respective territories.

III. His Highness the Sultan of Muscat grants to the ships of her Majesty's navy, as well as those of the East India Company, permission to seize and confiscate any vessels the property of His Highness or of his subjects carrying on Slave Trade, except such as only are engaged in the transport of slaves from one part to another of his own dominions in Africa, between the port of Lamu to the north, and its dependent cites, the northern limit of which is Kismayu Island in 1°57′ south latitude, and the port of Kilwa to the south, and its dependencies, the southern limit of which is the Songo Mnara or Pagodas Point in 9°2′ south latitude, including the islands of Zanzibar, Pemba and Mafia.

IV. This agreement to commence and have effect from the 1st. Day of January, 1847, of the year of Christ, and the 15th day of the month of Moharram, 1263 of the Hegira.

Appendix D

Text of the 1890 Treaty

Article I
The Signatory Powers agree to define a zone comprising the area affected by the export trade in African slaves. This zone, commencing from the Isthmus of Suez, shall extend southward on the African coast to 25 degrees south latitude. It shall include the Island of Madagascar and all other islands in those seas. It shall also include both coasts of the Red Sea, the coasts of Arabia, and those of the Persian Gulf, with the islands situated in those waters.

Article II
Those of the Signatory Powers between whom Treaties exist for the suppression of the Slave Trade agree to restrict the provisions of those Treaties, so far as regards, visit, search, and detention of those vessels afloat to the zone above defined, and to vessels under 500 tons measurement. In all other respects the existing Treaties shall remain in force.

Article III
All African slaves found on board vessels, detained against their will, shall be at once liberated.

Article IV
All African slaves taking refuge on board a man-of-war of a Signatory Power shall be at once liberated. Their freedom shall be recognized by all local authorities.

Article V
The Signatory Powers engage to facilitate the prompt interchange of information which may lead to the discovery of persons connected, directly or indirectly, with the trade in slaves. For this purpose International Bureaux[s] shall be established, to be watched over by the Signatory Powers engaged to communicate the names and particulars of all native vessels to which the right of flying their respective flags in the said zone shall be accorded, as well as information of every description calculated to assist the suppression of the Slave Trade. The archives of these Bureaux will always be open to the naval officers of the Signatory Powers authorized to act within the limits of the zone defined in Article I.

Article VI

The Signatory Powers engage to adopt efficacious measures to prevent the abuse of their flags in connection with the Slave Trade, and, further, to prevent the transport of slaves on the vessels authorized to fly their colors. The details of these measures will be comprised in an International Regulation annexed to the present Convention, and having, in the same manner as the Convention itself, the force of law as regards the Signatory Powers.

R.W. Beachey, *The Slave Trade of Eastern Africa* (London: Rex Collings, 1976), 225–227; Foreign Office C.P. 7946, Pt. LXVIII, Inclosure 2 in No. 15821, February, 1902.

Appendix E

John Kirk's Scientific Publications

With David Christison. "Notice of the Plants of Mount Olympus by Dr. John Kirk, With an Account of the Ascent of the Mountain, and Observations on the Country Near Broussa by Dr. David Christison." *Transactions of the Botanical Society* [Edinburgh] 5 (1858): 162–165.

"Notice of Egyptian Plants." *Transactions of the Botanical Society* [Edinburgh] 6 (1860): 22–23.

"On the Occurrence of a New Muscari on Mount Ida." *Transactions of the Botanical Society* [Edinburgh] 6 (1860): 28–29.

Letter from Dr. Kirk to Dr. Livingstone, part of a larger article.

Livingstone, David. "Extracts from the Despatches of Dr. David Livingstone, M.D." *Journal of the Royal Geographical Society* [London] 31 (1861): 256–296. [Kirk extract is pp. 284–286.]

"On a Few Fossil Bones from the Alluvial Strata of the Zambesi Delta." *Journal of the Royal Geographical Society* [London] 34 (1864): 199–201.

Extracts from a letter from John Kirk are included in a larger article: Back, George, Rear Admiral Collinson, and Frances Galton. "Hints to Travellers (Revised and Augmented Edition)." *Journal of the Royal Geographical Society* [London] 34 (1864): 272–316. [The Kirk extracts occur on pages 290–292.]

"List of Mammalia met with in Zambesia, East Tropical Africa." *Proceedings of the Scientific Meetings of the Zoological Society of London* (1864): 649. [Stanford does not own this volume. Information is from the journal's index and does not include a terminal page number.]

"On a new genus of *Liliaceae* from East Tropical Africa." *Transactions of the Linnean Society of London* 24 (1864): 497–499.

"On the Birds of the Zambesi Region of Eastern Tropical Africa." *Ibis* 6 (1864): 307–339.

"Dimorphism in the Flowers of Monochoria vaginalis." *Botanical Journal of the Linnean Society* [London] 8 (1865): 147–148.

"Letter containing a reply to the Observations of Dr. W. Peters, F.M.Z.S., relation to Gerrhosaurus robustus." *Proceedings of the Scientific Meetings of the Zoological Society of London* (1865): 227–228.

Dohrn, H. "List of the Land and Freshwater Shells of the Zambesi and Lake Nyassa, Eastern Tropical Africa collected by John Kirk, M.D., F.L.S., &c." *Proceedings of the Scientific Meetings of the Zoological Society of London* (1865): 231–234. There is an introductory note by J.K. and a correction for "List of Mammalia met with in Zambesia."

"Notes on two Expeditions up the River Rovuma, East Africa." *Journal of the Royal Geographical Society* [London] 35 (1865): 154–167.

"Notes on the Gradient of the Zambesi, on the Level of Lake Nyassa, on the Murchison Rapids, and on Lake Shirwa." *Journal of the Royal Geographical Society* [London] 35 (1865): 167–169.

"On the Tsetse Fly of Tropical Africa (Glossina morsitans, Westwood). *Zoological Journal of the Linnean Society* [London] 8 (1865): 149–156.

"On a new Antelope from Zambesia." *Annals and Magazine of Natural History,* 3.15 (1865): 360.

"Note on Bauhinia." *Transactions of the Botanical Society* [Edinburgh] 8 (1866): 110–111.

"Account of the Zambesi District, in South Africa, with a Notice of its Vegetable and other Products." *Transactions of the Botanical Society* [Edinburgh] 8 (1866): 197–202.

Baikie, W. B. "Notes of a Journey from Bida in Nupe, to Kano in Haussa, performed in 1862." *Journal of the Royal Geographical Society* [London] 37 (1867): 92–107. After the title, a note states, "Extracted from portions of Dr. Baikie's Journals in the possession of the Foreign Office, by J. Kirk, Esq., M.D."

"On *Musa Livingstoniana,* a new Banana from Tropical Africa." *Botanical Journal of the Linnean Society* [London] 9 (1867): 128.

"On a new Dye-wood, of the genus *Cudranea,* from East Tropical Africa." *Botanical Journal of the Linnean Society* [London] 9 (1867): 229–230.

"On the Palms of East Tropical Africa." *Botanical Journal of the Linnean Society* [London] 9 (1867): 230–235.

"Letter relating to the Animals of Zanzibar." *Proceedings of the Scientific Meetings of the Zoological Society of London* (1867): 952–953.

"On the Copal of Zanzibar." *Botanical Journal of the Linnean Society* [London] 11 (1871): 1–4.

"On Copal (Extract from a Letter to Dr. Hooker dated Zanzibar, November 13, 1869)." *Botanical Journal of the Linnean Society* [London] 11 (1871): 479–481.

"Letter from Dr. John Kirk concerning a Koodoo (Tragelaphus strepsiceros?) and other animals destined for the Society." *Proceedings of the Scientific Meetings of the Zoological Society of London* (1873): 195–196.

"Identification of the Modern Copal Tree (Trachylobium Hornemmanianum) with that which yielded the Copal or Animi, now found in the earth on the East Coast of Africa, often where no copal-yielding trees now exist." *Botanical Journal of the Linnean Society* [London] 15 (1877): 234–235.

"Note on specimens of Hibiscus allied to H. Rosa-sinensis., L., collected in E. Tropical Africa." *Botanical Journal of the Linnean Society* [London] 15 (1877): 478–479.

"Cattle Plague in Africa." *Nature* 54.1391 (June 25, 1896): 171.

"African Rinderpest." *Nature* 55.1412 (November 19, 1896): 53–54.

Appendix F

Sultans of Zanzibar

1828–1856	Said bin Sultan, b. 1791
1856–1870	Majid bin Said
1870–1888	Barghash bin Said
1888–1890	Khalifa bin Said
1890–1893	Ali bin Said (British Protectorate declared during his reign)
1893–1896	Hamed bin Thwain
1896–1902	Hamoud bin Muhammad
1902–1911	Ali bin Hamoud (abdicated due to ill health)
1911–1960	Khalifa II bin Harub (born in Oman August 26, 1879)
1960–1963	Abdulla bin Khalifa
1960–1964	Jamshid bin Abdullah (banished after the Zanzibar Revolution)

Notes

Prologue

1. Hugh Thomas, *The Slave Trade* (Simon & Shuster, New York, 1987, 804–805; L. H. Gann and Peter Duignan, eds., *Colonialism in Africa, 1870–1960,* Vol. 4 (Stanford: Hoover Institution, 1975), Publication 127, 44–45.
2. Ibid.
3. Joseph Thomson, *To the Central African Lakes and Back: The Narrative of the Royal Geographical Society's East Central African Expedition, 1878–1880* (London: Sampson Low, Marston, Searle and Rivington, 1881), 74–75.
4. Ibid., 73.
5. Sir Reginald Coupland, *Kirk on the Zambesi: A Chapter of African History* (Oxford: Clarendon Press, 1928); Reginald Foskett, *The Zambesi Doctors: David Livingstone's Letters to John Kirk, 1858–1872* (Edinburgh: University of Edinburgh Press, 1964).

Chapter 1

1. John Beddoe, *Memories of Eighty Years* (Bristol: J.W. Arrowsmith, 1910), 54–55.
2. Ibid.
3. The term "tribe" has been supplanted in the vocabulary of some historians by the term "ethnic group." However, tribe was the term customarily used by the Victorians.
4. At that time "South Africa" included areas unexplored or poorly explored which were subsequently divided into the independent countries of Zambia, Zimbabwe, Botswana, and Namibia.
5. Oliver Ransford, *David Livingstone: The Dark Interior* (London: John Murray, 1978), 4.
6. Sir Reginald Coupland, *Kirk on the Zambesi: A Chapter of African History* (Oxford: Clarendon Press, 1928), 45.
7. Ransford, *David Livingstone: The Dark Interior*, 80–81; David Livingstone and Charles Livingstone, *Narrative of an Expedition to the Zambesi and Its Tributaries and of the Discovery of the Lakes Shirwa and Nyassa* (New York: Harper, 1866), 277–278.

8. Ransford, *David Livingstone: The Dark Interior*, 101–103.
9. David Livingstone, *Missionary Travels and Researches in South Africa* (New York: Harper, 1858), 558.

Chapter 2

1. A. Eames, ed., *The Nile* (Boston: Houghton Mifflin, 1996), 189–190.
2. *The Koran*, translated by George Sales, 1734, republished by Frederick Warne, New York, p. 75.
3. R. W. Beachey, *The Slave Trade of Eastern Africa* (New York: Harper & Row, 1976).
4. M. Cary and E. H. Warmington, *The Ancient Explorers* (London: Methuen, 1963), 11, 123–124 (4, 19, 28).
5. Beachey, *The Slave Trade of Eastern Africa.*
6. John Peter Richard Wallis, ed., *The Zambesi Expedition of David Livingstone, 1858–1863* (London: Chatto and Windus, 1956).
7. David Livingstone and Charles Livingstone, *Narrative of an Expedition to the Zambesi and Its Tributaries and of the Discovery of the Lakes Shirwa and Nyassa* (London: John Murray, 1865), 63, 155–204.
8. Ibid.
9. Ibid.
10. Ibid.
11. William Garden Blaikie, *The Personal Life of David Livingstone,* 6th ed. (London, 1925; reprint, New York: Negro Universities Press, Greenwood Publishing Corporation, 1969).
12. Beachey, *The Slave Trade of Eastern Africa.*
13. Ibid.; E. A. Alpers, *Ivory and Slaves in East Central Africa* (London: Heinemann, 1975), 93.
14. An honorific title.
15. Beachey, *The Slave Trade of Eastern Africa.*
16. Ibid.
17. Owen, Vol. 1, in Beachey, *The Slave Trade of Eastern Africa*, 292–293.
18. *Anti-Slavery Reporter*, Vol. 5, New Series, 1850.
19. United Kingdom. Parliament. *Sessional Papers* (S.P.), XXXIX, 1852/1853, Select Committee Q. 1627, p. 18.

20. Beachey, *The Slave Trade of Eastern Africa.*

21. Ibid.

22. Ibid.

23. Ibid.

24. Because the "Freedom of the Seas" treaty provision dated from the War of 1812, the British were prohibited from boarding American ships. Thus, slave ships attempting to sneak past British patrols frequently got away with it by flying the Stars and Stripes.

25. Norman R. Bennett and George E. Brooks, Jr., *New England Merchants in Africa: A History Through Documents, 1802 to 1865* (Boston: Boston University Press, 1965), 258.

26. Beachey, *The Slave Trade of Eastern Africa.*

27. Howard Temperley, *British Antislavery, 1833–1870* (London: Longman, 1972).

28. Ibid.

29. Ibid.

30. Today, in addition to clitoridectomy, infundulectomy, or the snipping off of the labia majora of the vagina and variants thereof, is practiced among some sub-Saharan Africans and Muslims.

31. Beachey, *The Slave Trade of Eastern Africa.*

32. Temperly, *British Antislavery.*

33. Ibid.

34. Beachey, *The Slave Trade of Eastern Africa.*

35. George T. K. Keppel, Earl of Albermarle, *Personal Narrative of a Journey from India to England,* Vol. I (London, 1834, reprint, London: H. Colburn, 1927), pp. 21–22.

36. Beachey, *The Slave Trade of Eastern Africa.*

Chapter 3

1. Sir Reginald Coupland, *Kirk on the Zambesi: A Chapter of African History* (Oxford: Clarendon Press, 1928), 27.

2. Ibid.

3. Oliver Ransford, *David Livingstone: The Dark Interior* (London: John Murray, 1978), 3–4.

4. Coupland, *Kirk on the Zambesi,* 80–81.

5. Ransford, *David Livingstone: The Dark Interior,* 227.
6. Coupland, *Kirk on the Zambesi,* 92.
7. Ibid., 92–93.
8. Malaria is considered the number one killer in the emerging world. Between 300 and 500 million persons get malaria each year and someone dies of it every fifteen minutes, according to Nicolas D. Kristof, "Everyday Killers," *The New York Times,* January 8, 1997, Section A1. The parasite is also becoming more resistant to antimalarials, while the mosquito which carries it has developed increasing resistance to insecticides.
9. M. Gelfand, *Rivers of Death in Africa* (London: Oxford University Press, 1964); R.S. Dersowitz, *The Malaria Capers* (New York: W.W. Norton, 1991).
10. Coupland, *Kirk on the Zambesi,* 105–106.
11. David Livingstone and Charles Livingstone, *Narrative of an Expedition to the Zambesi and Its Tributaries and of the Discovery of the Lakes Shirwa and Nyassa* (New York: Harper, 1866), 57.
12. Coupland, *Kirk on the Zambesi,* 106.
13. Ibid., 107.
14. Ibid., 108.

Chapter 4

1. Kirk's Diary, 27.vi–19.viii.58.
2. George Martelli, *Livingstone's River: A History of the Zambezi Expedition, 1858–1864* (New York: Simon & Schuster, 1969), 77.
3. Kirk's Diary, 11–24.viii.58.
4. Joseph Conrad, *The Heart of Darkness* (Peterborough, Ontario: Broadview Press, 1995), 99, 100. This complex story has elements that have been interpreted as both imperialistic and racist. The excerpt is used here to illustrate the impact of the "jungle" on the Victorian explorer. Ibid., 14, 15.
5. David Livingstone and Charles Livingstone, *Narrative of an Expedition to the Zambesi and to Its Tributaries and of the Discovery of the Lakes Shirwa and Nyassa* (London: John Murray, 1865), 21.
6. Reginald Foskett, ed., *The Zambesi Journal and Letters of Dr. John Kirk* (London: Oliver and Boyd, 1965), 52.
7. Coupland, *Kirk on the Zambesi: A Chapter of African History* (Oxford: Clarendon Press, 1928), 115.

8. Foskett, *The Zambesi Journal and Letters of Dr. John Kirk*, 62.
9. Ibid., 62–63.
10. Coupland, *Kirk on the Zambezi*, 88, 122; Foskett, *The Zambezi Journal and Letters of Dr. John Kirk*, 198.
11. John Beddoe, *Memories of Eighty Years* (Bristol: J.W. Arrowsmith, 1910), 54–55.
12. Foskett, *The Zambesi Journal and Letters of Dr. John Kirk*, 77.
13. David Livingstone and Charles Livingstone, *Narrative of an Expedition to the Zambesi and Its Tributaries and of the Discovery of the Lakes Shirwa and Nyassa* (New York: Harper, 1866), 55.
14. Kirk's Diary 26.xii.58; F.O. 63/843.
15. Coupland, *Kirk on the Zambesi*, 133.
16. Ibid., 131.
17. Foskett, *The Zambesi Journal and Letters of Dr. John Kirk*, 124.
18. Ibid., 134.
19. Coupland, *Kirk on the Zambesi*, 135.

Chapter 5

1. The Manganjas are now called Nyanjas or Cherwa.
2. Reginald Foskett, ed., *The Zambesi Journal and Letters of Dr. John Kirk* (London: Oliver and Boyd, 1965), 144.
3. David Livingstone and Charles Livingstone, *Narrative of an Expedition to the Zambezi and Is Tributaries and of the Discovery of the Lakes Shirwa and Nyassa* (New York: Harper, 1866), 110.
4. John Peter Richard Wallis, ed., *The Zambesi Expedition of David Livingstone, 1858–1863* (London: Chatto and Windus, 1956), 343.
5. Livingstone and Livingstone, *Narrative of an Expedition*, 126–128.
6. Ibid.
7. Today a railroad runs along the Shire. When the British annexed the lake country, they called it Nyassaland and built the colony's capital on the cool slopes of Mount Zomba. The capital has since been moved to Blantyre, named after Livingstone's birthplace.
8. One can still see a faint red coloring on the boulder. John Marshall, an amateur archeologist who has a resort on the Shire, believes Livingstone put the letters there to indicate the highest water level when the river ran full.

9. Sir Reginald Coupland, *Kirk on the Zambesi: A Chapter of African History* (Oxford: Clarendon Press, 1928), 143.
10. M. Main, *Zambezi, Journey of a River* (Capetown, S.A.: Southern Book Publishing Company, 1990), 240–241.
11. David Livingstone and Charles Livingstone, *Narrative of an Expedition to the Zambesi and Its Tributaries and of the Discovery of the Lakes Shirwa and Nyassa* (London: John Murray, 1865), 81–82.
12. Foskett, *The Zambesi Journal and Letters of Dr. John Kirk*, 210.
13. Coupland, *Kirk on the Zambesi*, 146; Kirk's Diary, 18–27.vii.59.
14. When Rae's contract expired in January 1860, he decided to return home and was entrusted with Kirk's botanical specimens. He left from Quelimane on a British ship, but the specimens never reached Professor Hooker. Hooker and Kirk presumed Rae had lost them. Over twenty years later they were found in a Portsmouth warehouse, and subsequently catologued at the Royal Kew Botanical Gardens, but the mystery of why they had been deposited there was never solved.
15. Coupland, *Kirk on the Zambesi*, 153.
16. Foskett, *The Zambesi Journal and Letters of Dr. John Kirk*, 241.
17. Ibid., 253.
18. Coupland, *Kirk on the Zambesi*, 155.
19. Roscher reached the northern portion of the lake, but was murdered on his way back to Zanzibar. His diary was found verifying his discovery.
20. Livingstone and Livingstone, *Narrative of an Expedition*, 135.
21. Ibid., 137–138.
22. Coupland, *Kirk on the Zambesi*, 158.
23. Ibid., 160.
24. Ibid., 163.
25. Ibid., 159–162.

Chapter 6

1. Sir Reginald Coupland, *Kirk on the Zambesi: A Chapter of African History* (Oxford: Clarendon Press, 1928), 167.
2. David Livingstone and Charles Livingstone, *Narrative of an Expedition to the Zambezi and Its Tributaries and of the Discovery of the Lakes Shirwa and Nyassa* (New York: Harper, 1866), 97.
3. Reginald Foskett, ed., *The Zambesi Journal and Letters of Dr. John Kirk* (London: Oliver and Boyd, 1965), 233.

4. Livingstone and Livingstone, *Narrative of an Expedition*, 168.
5. Coupland, *Kirk on the Zambesi*, 162; Oliver Ransford, *David Livingstone: The Dark Interior* (London: John Murray, 1978), 168.
6. Livingstone and Livingstone, *Narrative of an Expedition*, 222.
7. Coupland, *Kirk on the Zambesi*, 168; Kirk's Diary, 26.ii.60.
8. Foskett, *The Zambesi Journal and Letters of Dr. John Kirk*, 190.
9. Livingstone and Livingstone, *Narrative of an Expedition*, 291, 293.
10. Ransford, *David Livingstone: The Dark Interior*, 169.
11. Sekeletu's father, Sebutane, had built up the Makololo kingdom, but it had been smashed by the Matabele, and Sekeletu and the remnants of his tribe had been forced back to the disease-infested shores of the Zambezi. Still, according to Livingstone, the Makololo had been able to conquer the Makalaka and Mashona (Shona) tribes and were employing them as slaves and servants. Today, Zimbabwe's Shona artists are some of the world's finest stone carvers.
12. Livingstone and Livingstone, *Narrative of an Expedition*, 304.
13. Coupland, *Kirk on the Zambesi*, 176; Russell to Livingstone 17.iv.60, F.O. 63/871.
14. During our 1995 expedition retracing the footsteps of Kirk and Livingstone, my wife and I found that Sesheke, as shown on present-day maps, is a new town, located forty miles away from old Sesheke (now called Mwandi). We couldn't find anyone who admitted to Makololo ancestry until one young man told me he was Lhosi, but that his ancestors were both Lhosi and Makololo. This seemed to reinforce the story.
15. Coupland, *Kirk on the Zambesi*, 177–179; Kirk's Diary 12. xi.60; Livingstone and Livingstone, *Narrative of an Expedition*, 352–353; *Morning Post* (London), December 19, 1913.
16. Ibid.
17. Ibid.
18. Coupland, *Kirk on the Zambesi*, 180–181.
19. Livingstone and Livingstone, *Narrative of an Expedition*, 196–199.
20. Ibid., 207–209.
21. Kirk's Diary, 9 and 15.vii.61.
22. Kirk's Diary, 6–23.xii.60 and 16.vii.61.
23. Coupland, *Kirk on the Zambesi*, 200; Kirk's Diary 1.viii.61.
24. Kirk's Diary, 9 and 15.vii.61.
25. Coupland, *Kirk on the Zambesi*, 205.

26. Much later the story of an underground river got into the hands of popular Victorian adventure writer H. Rider Haggard, whose brother became British consul to Mombassa, and he used it in one of his novels.
27. Foskett, *The Zambesi Journal and Letters of Dr. John Kirk,* 376.
28. Ibid., 383.
29. Coupland, *Kirk on the Zambesi,* 208.
30. Livingstone and Livingstone, *Narrative of an Expedition*, 412.
31. Ransford, *David Livingstone: The Dark Interior,* 192.
32. Time proved Livingstone wrong. The British protectorate of Nyassaland (now Malawi) established British settlements on those same shores fifty years later.

Chapter 7

1. Reginald Foskett, ed., *The Zambesi Journal and Letters of Dr. John Kirk* (London: Oliver and Boyd, 1965), 401–402.
2. Ibid., 415.
3. John Peter Richard Wallis, ed., *The Zambesi Journal of James Stewart, 1862–1863* (London: Chatto and Windus, 1952), 228.
4. E. Healey, *Wives of Fame* (London: Sidgwick and Jackson, 1986).
5. The use of laudanum in Victorian England was quite common. This derivative of opium was employed for relief of a variety of "female troubles," including migraines, depression, and insomnia.
6. Oliver Ransford, *David Livingstone: The Dark Interior* (London: John Murray, 1978), 195–196.
7. Foskett, *The Zambesi Journal and Letters of Dr. John Kirk,* 415, 438.
8. Ibid., 416.
9. C. W. Devereux, *A Cruise in the "Gorgon"* (1869; reprint London: Dawsons of Pall Mall, 1968); George Martelli, *Livingstone's River: A History of the Zambezi Expedition, 1858–1864* (New York: Simon & Schuster, 1969), 214.
10. Foskett, *The Zambesi Journal and Letters of Dr. John Kirk,* 416.
11. Ransford, *David Livingstone: The Dark Interior*, 196.
12. Sir Reginald Coupland, *Kirk on the Zambesi: A Chapter of African* History (Oxford: Clarendon Press, 1928), 225–228.
13. Ibid., 229.
14. Ransford, *David Livingstone: The Dark Interior*, 202.

15. Foskett, *The Zambesi Journal and Letters of Dr. John Kirk,* 439–440.

16. Wallis, *The Zambesi Journal of James Stewart, 1862–1863,* 57; Ransford, *David Livingstone: The Dark Interior,* 204.

17. Ransford, *David Livingstone: The Dark Interior,* 204.

18. Wallis, *The Zambesi Journal of James Stewart, 1862–1863,* 34.

19. Ibid., 170–171.

20. Ibid., 165.

21. When steam ships began to replace sailing vessels in the 1830s and 1840s, the British navy became dependent on coal to fuel the steam boilers. Supplies of coal had to be brought in British ships to be stored at naval bases in various parts of the world. One such base was the island of Johanna in the Comoro Islands off the coast of Mozambique between Madagascar and Cape Delgado on Mozambique's northern frontier.

22. Foskett, *The Zambesi Journal and Letters of Dr. John Kirk,* 471.

23. Ibid., 475; Ransford, *David Livingstone: The Dark Interior.*

24. Although the British were unprepared for the Makonde ambush and the hostility of the Ajwas, these should not really have come as surprises. For those Africans who did not know Livingstone, or who mistook the expedition members for Arab slavers, such actions were predictable. In these and in other instances, there could also be a psychological factor involved. For many Africans, the color white was traditionally associated with the ghosts of ancestors, personifying evil and death. The strange appearance of these whites—plus their unpleasant smell, their strange clothes, their guns, the plethora of strange objects they carried with them, and their behavior toward each other and the African peoples they met—all could strengthen a belief that these were demons from an alien and hostile culture intent on destroying the African way of life. In spite of the guns, whiskey, cloth, beads, mirrors, and other prized trade items, even in areas not yet depopulated by slave raids, the fear of whites remained among many Africans. Furthermore, the missionaries' preachments against slavery, polygamy, and ritual circumcision did nothing to endear the British or other Europeans to Africans who followed these practices.

25. Foskett, *The Zambesi Journal and Letters of Dr. John Kirk,* 476; Coupland, *Kirk on the Zambesi,* 243.

26. Foskett, *The Zambesi Journal and Letters of Dr. John Kirk,* 479.

27. Ibid., 482.

28. Ibid., 483–484.

Chapter 8

1. Sir Reginald Coupland, *Kirk on the Zambesi: A Chapter of African History* (Oxford: Clarendon Press, 1928), 246.
2. Bishop W. G. Tozer, a thirty-three-year-old missionary with no experience in Africa, was appointed by the Universities Mission to Central Africa to investigate and recommend measures to put an end to the high mortality rate among the missionaries. After visiting the Mikorongo mission he recommended that it be withdrawn to Zanzibar as there was no hope of effective military and medical protection. Establishing the mission on the island off the coast of present-day Tanzania would pose no problem because Sultan Majid, as long ago as 1846, had allowed the London Missionary Society to establish a mission at Mombassa, one of the coastal cites of the sultan's mainland domain. The sultan, a devout Muslim, was being practical. He expected the missionaries to be backed by the might of the British Navy, which he needed to help protect him against any designs on the sultanate by his brother in Oman or by other foreign powers.

   Although Livingstone's fond hope of founding a string of missions on the African mainland had come to naught, twelve years later, in 1875, a steamboat was launched on the lake and two Scottish missions were founded. One was built on the lakeshore and the other in the Shire highlands at the site where Blantyre, named after Livingstone's birthplace in Scotland, was founded. The country was eventually annexed by the British and called the Nyassaland Protectorate until it was renamed Malawi in 1964 when it became independent.
3. Coupland, *Kirk on the Zambesi: A Chapter of African History,* 243.
4. Oliver Ransford, *David Livingstone: The Dark Interior* (London: John Murray, 1978), 100.
5. Ibid., 210.
6. Ibid., 209.
7. Ibid., 208.
8. Reginald Fosket, ed., *The Zambesi Journal and Letters of Dr. John Kirk* (London: Oliver and Boyd, 1965), 498.
9. Ibid., 502, 504.
10. Ransford, *David Livingstone: The Dark Interior,* 211.
11. Fosket, *The Zambesi Journal and Letters of Dr. John Kirk,* 515.
12. Ransford, *David Livingstone: The Dark Interior,* 218.
13. Ibid., 213.
14. Ibid., 212.

15. John Peter Richard Wallis, *The Zambezi Journal of James Stewart, 1862–1863* (London: Chatto and Windus, 1952), 189.
16. Coupland, *Kirk on the Zambesi: A Chapter of African History,* 256.
17. Letter to his daughter Agnes, 24 Feb. 1864, in William Gordon, *The Personal Life of David Livingstone* (New York: Negro Universities Press, 1969; originally published in 1880 by Fleming H. Revell Co.), 345.
18. The French subterfuge of using Africans as economic slaves under the aegis of the "Free Labor Emigration System" was outlawed by Napoleon III in 1864, possibly as a result of the strong antislavery publicity associated with Livingstone's lectures and writings after his return to England.
19. Two rivers joined to form the Nile, at Khartoum in Sudan. The *Blue* comes from Lake Tana in Ethiopia, and the *White* from Lake Victoria in Uganda.
20. David Livingstone and Charles Livingstone, *Narrative of an Expedition to the Zambesi and to Its Tributaries and of the Discovery of the Lakes Shirwa and Nyassa* (London: John Murray, 1865), 10–11.
21. Reginald Foskett, ed., *The Zambesi Doctors; David Livingstone's Letters to John Kirk 1858–1872* (Edinburgh: Edinburgh University Press, 1964), 84.

Chapter 9

1. Sir Reginald Coupland, *The Exploitation of East Africa, 1856–1890* (Evanston: Northwestern University Press, 1967), 39–40.
2. The sultantate of Zanzibar was under the jurisdiction of Bombay, India, until 1883, when the Foreign Office had Kirk report directly to London.
3. William Garden Blaikie, *The Personal Life of David Livingstone,* 6th ed. (London, 1925; reprint, New York: Negro Universities Press, Greenwood Publishing Corporation, 1969), 308–309.
4. The political officer was under the consul and worked directly with the country's officials, in this case, the sultan and his advisors.
5. I.O. to F.O. 15.viii.67; F.O. 84, 1284.
6. Zanzibar Archives, Hammerton to Bombay Government, 13 July, 16. S.P. LXI, No. 102, Rigby to Russell, 5 Oct., 1861 (35).
7. Coupland, *The Exploitation of East Africa,* 172–173.
8. Ibid., 164–165; Captain Colomb, *Slave Catching in the Indian Ocean* (London: Dawsons, 1968), 197, 233; Norman R. Bennett and George E. Brooks, *New England Merchants in Africa: A History through Documents, 1802–1865* (Boston: Boston University Press, 1965), 515; R. L.

Playfair, Report on the Various Countries around Zanzibar Transactions of the Bombay Geographical Society, Volume VIII, 1865; R. W. Beachey, *The Slave Trade of Eastern Africa* (London: Rex Collings, 1976), 61.

9. Beachey, *The Slave Trade of Eastern Africa,* 192.
10. The dollar fluctuated wildly between 1860 and 1870 as a result of the American Civil War. Best estimates are that in 1997 it was worth over 30 times the 1870 dollar. See *Value of a Dollar* (Detroit: Gale Research, 1994); Antony Thomas, *Rhodes* (New York: St. Martin's Press, 1996), 73.
11. Coupland, *The Exploitation of East Africa,* 164.
12. James Juma, *The Freeing of the Slaves in East Africa* (London: Evans Brothers Limited, Montague House, Russell Square, 1956), 9, 39.
13. The cities that Said added were members of the Hanseatic League of north German trading cities, which was formed back in the thirteenth century. In Kirk's day Hamburg and Lubeck were the most prominent of the group.
14. In 1880 the exchange rate was approximately six dollars to one pound sterling, according to *British Historical Studies* (Cambridge, England: Cambridge University Press, 1988).
15. Coupland, *The Exploitation of East Africa,* 23–25; Sir Reginald Coupland, *East Africa and Its Invaders from the Earliest Times to the Death of Seyyid Said in 1856* (Oxford: Oxford University Press, 1938), 553–554.
16. Coupland, *The Exploitation of East Africa,* 46–48.
17. Ibid.
18. *The Graphic,* 9.v.85; Roland Oliver, *Sir Harry Johnston and the Scramble for Africa* (London: Chatto and Windus, 1957), 56–57.
19. Foreign Office Confidential Print Series 1858–1892, Volumes 1–6, Public Records Office, London, 541/19 Inclosure 1 in 201.

Chapter 10

1. The term "Agency" referred not only to the British consulate but to the office of the British political agent; in this case they were in the same office in the British consulate building in Zanzibar. As in Kirk's situation, the two jobs were frequently entrusted to one person representing the interests of both Great Britain and the sultan.
2. Sir Reginald Coupland, *The Exploitation of East Africa, 1856–1890* (Evanston, Illinois: Northwestern University Press, 1967), 75–79.

3. The Mlawas adhered to the Abathi version of Muslim law, the strictest of interpretations, and were fanatically anti-European. They would become a thorn in Kirk's side, doing everything they could to drive wedges between him, the British government, and the sultanate.
4. Foreign Office Confidential Print Series 1858–1892, Volumes 1–6, Public Records Office, London, 84/1326 and 541/19, Inclosure 5; Coupland, *The Exploitation of East Africa*, 56–59, 93–95, 157–158.
5. Joseph Thomson, *To the Central African Lakes and Back: The Narrative of the Royal Geographical Society's East Central African Expedition, 1878–80* (London: Sampson Low, Marston, Searle and Rivington, 1881), Vol. I, 23.
6. Kirk to Government of Bombay, 24.xii.70 and 30.i.71; Kirk to Granville, 8.i.71; Kirk to Sultan 27.i.71; F.O. 84, 1344.
7. Ibid.
8. Ibid.
9. Kirk to Sultan 27.i.71; Kirk to Government of Bombay 30.i.71; F.O. 84, 1344.
10. Foreign Office Confidential Print Series 1858–1892, Volumes 1–6, Public Records Office, London, 541/19, Inclosure 3 and 7 in No. 17, 187.

Chapter 11

1. Hookworm is caused by the worms prevalent in warm, tropical, moist soil, which penetrate through the soles of the feet to eventually lodge in the upper small intestine. They live on blood oozing from minute ulcers they cause. Hookworm can cause anemia, the hemoglobin dropping as low as 3 grams per deciliter (normal range for a male is 13.75–17.5 grams), according to Lawrence M. Tierney, Jr., Steven J. McPhee, and Maxine A. Papadakis, *Current Medical Diagnosis and Treatment* (Stamford, Connecticut: Appleton, Lang, 1998), 1534.
2. M. Gelfand, *Livingstone the Doctor, His Life and Travels: A Study in Medical History* (Oxford: Basil Blackwell, 1957).
3. Oliver Ransford, *David Livingstone: The Dark Interior* (London: John Murray, 1978), 262.
4. J. Becker, *La Vie en Afrique* II (Paris: Bibliotheque Nationale, 1886), 45–46 (loose translation of conversation between Becker and Tippu Tib at Tabora in 1886).
5. Horace Waller, *The Last Journals of David Livingstone in Central Africa* (New York: Harper, 1875), 383.
6. *The Times* (London), 20th Jan., 19; 20 Apr.; 16 July; Sept. 6, 7, 15; Oct. 1, 1869.

7. Henry Morton Stanley, *How I Found Livingstone: Travels, Adventures, and Discoveries in Central Africa, Including Four Months' Residence with Dr. Livingstone* (London: Sampson, Low, Marston, Low and Searle, 1872), 12–15.
8. R. Hall, *Stanley, An Adventurer Explored* (Boston: Houghton Mifflin, 1975), 188.
9. Stanley, *How I Found Livingstone,* 412.
10. William Garden Blaikie, *The Personal Life of David Livingstone,* 6th ed. (London, 1925; reprint, New York: Negro Universities Press, Greenwood Publishing Corporation, 1969), 442, 445.
11. Sir Reginald Coupland, *Livingstone's Last Journey* (London: Readers Union/Collins, 1947), 184–185.
12. Stanley, *How I Found Livingstone,* 704–707.
13. Coupland, *Livingstone's Last Journey,* 185.
14. Foreign Office Confidential Print Series 1858–1892, Volumes 1–6, Public Records Office, London, 541/19 Inclosure 3, and 7 in No. 17. 1872.
15. Stanley, *How I Found Livingstone,* 675.
16. *The Times of India* 13.viii.73; *The Times* (London), 29.viii.73.
17. Stanley, *How I Found Livingstone,* 713.
18. Ibid.
19. Foreign Office Confidential Print Series 1858–1892, Volumes 1–6, Inclosures 1, 4, 11, 23.
20. Kirk's Memorandum, *Correspondence on Frere Mission,* 67–69; Public Records Office, London, 541/19, Inclosure 1 in 29; Kirk's Papers, 8.ii.73; Frere to Granville, F.O. 14.i.73; 10.ii.73; India Office Records, Correspondence Respecting Sir Bartle Frere's Mission, 1873 (C-820); Coupland, *Livingstone's Last Journey,* 213–215.
21. Coupland, *Livingstone's Last Journey,* 187; Livingstone to Kirk, vi.72, Kirk's Papers.
22. Blaikie, *The Personal Life of David Livingstone,* 448.
23. Verney L. Cameron, *Across Africa* (London: Daldy, Isbister & Co., 1877).
24. Gelfand, *Livingstone the Doctor, His Life and Travels: A Study in Medical History.*
25. Coupland, *Livingstone's Last Journey,* 250–251.
26. *Journal of the Society of Arts,* March 12, 1875, 364.

Chapter 12

1. Kirk to Granville, 25.i.72; F.O. 84, 1357.
2. Ibid.
3. A Maria Theresa dollar was worth a little less than a quarter of a British pound sterling at the time.
4. A. Sheriff, *Slaves, Spices & Ivory in Zanzibar* (London: James Currey, 1987), 50–54; Sir Reginald Coupland, *The Exploitation of East Africa, 1856–1890* (Evanston, Illinois: Northwestern University Press, 1967), 147.
5. Coupland, *The Exploitation of East Africa, 1856–1890*, 12, 153–159.
6. Kirk to Granville, 25.i.72, F.O. 84, 1357. Frere to Granville, F.O. 14. i. 73; 10. ii. 73; Kirk's Papers, III a. 44, 46, 51, 52-6, 150; Kirk's Papers 8. ii. 73; Kirk's Memorandum, Correspondence on Frere Mission, 67–9; Kirk to Euan Smith 8.ii.73, Correspondence on Frere Mission, Parliamentary Papers, 1873, 67-9; Coupland, *The Exploitation of East Africa, 1856–1890*, 186–189.
7. Ibid.
8. Coupland, *The Exploitation of East Africa, 1856–1890*, 193–194.
9. Ibid., 194; Thornton to Granville, 28.x.72, 3.iii, 15; 29.iv.73, and 3.v.73; Kirk's Papers IIIb. U.S.A., 1–9.
10. Frere to Granville 10.ii.73; F.O. 84, 1389; Frere to Viceroy of India, 20.iii.73.
11. R. T. Nightingale, *The Personnel of the British Foreign Office and Diplomatic Service 1851–1929* (London: Fabian Society, 1930).
12. Coupland, *The Exploitation of East Africa, 1856–1890*, 204; Kirk to Granville 5.vi.73; F.O. 84, 1374.
13. Coupland, *The Exploitation of East Africa, 1856–1890*, 207–209.
14. Ibid.
15. Ibid.
16. Ibid., 210-211.
17. Kirk to Granville, 5.vi.73; F.O. 84, 1374, 1375; Kirk to Granville, 2.vii.73.
18. Kirk felt it was more diplomatic to sign as political agent rather than consul, since he would be acting on behalf of the sultan for the British rather than for the British government per se, a fine distinction.
19. Coupland, *The Exploitation of East Africa, 1856–1890*, 212–213; Special Papers I.xi (1872–1873), 173–174; Kirk to Granville, 5.vi.73 and 2.vii.73; 10.vi.73; F.O. 84, 1374.

20. Coupland, *The Exploitation of East Africa, 1856–1890*, 214, 220; Kirk to Granville 2.vii.73; F.O. 84, 1375.
21. Prideaux to Derby, 24.xi. 4; F.O. 84, 1400, 1453; Coupland, *The Exploitation of East Africa, 1856–1890*, 219, 221–222.
22. Ibid.
23. Ibid.
24. Ibid.
25. Ibid., 225–226; Euan Smith to Derby, 4.iii.74; F.O. 84, 1407; Kirk to Derby, 24.iv.76; F.O. 84, 1453; Special Papers I.xvii (1875–1876), 455–456.
26. Coupland, *The Exploitation of East Africa, 1856–1890*, 227–229; R.N. Lyne, *Zanzibar in Contemporary Times: A Short History of the Southern East Africa in the 19th Century* (London: Hurst and Blockett, 1905), 92–95; Kirk to Derby, 24.viii.77; F.O. 84, 1486.
27. Lloyd William Mathews served as a sub-lieutenant on the British warship *Active* during the Ashanti campaign in West Africa in 1873–74, and as lieutenant on the *London* in 1875 chasing slave runners off the East African coast. After volunteering to lead and train Sultan Bargash's army, Mathews defeated the rebellious Mazrui clan of Pemba and Mombassa. When Captain Brownrigg was killed, Mathews captured the culprit, Hindi Bin Hattam. Mathews eventually became a brigadier general and was knighted for his services by Bargash's successor, Khalifa. Khalifa died in 1890 and was suceeded by another brother, Ali. Zanzibar became a British protectorate following the Berlin Conference of 1890, and a year later, Mathews was appointed First Minister of Zanzibar. He held this position for ten years and served under two more sultans after Ali died in 1893. Because of a persistent fever, considered by some to be malaria, he returned to England in 1900 and died in 1901 at age fifty-one. See R.N. Lyne, *An Apostle of Empire: Being the Life of Sir Lloyd William Mathews, K.C.M.G.* (London: G. Allen & Unwin, 1936), 41.

Chapter 13

1. While near Shupanga in 1859, Kirk discovered an indigenous, latex-yielding rubber tree, Landolphia. After seeing a boy playing with an elastic ball made of the native substance, Kirk's investigations revealed that it grew plentifully on the mainland. In 1878, backed by the sultan and other prominent Zanzibaris, he organized the East African rubber trade, which more than made up for the loss incurred by the elimination of the slave trade.

Kirk also introduced to the West the flower *Impatients sultani,* which was so named because the seed pods open rapidly if they are touched or brushed by anything.

2. Katherine G. Endicott, *San Francisco Chronicle,* House section p. 5, April 29, 1998.
3. Sir Reginald Coupland, *The Exploitation of East Africa, 1856–1890* (Evanston, Illinois: Northwestern University Press, 1967), 320.
4. Ibid., 248–249, 253–255.
5. Gordon commanded British troops and irregulars in China during the T'ai P'ing rebellion, 1863–65, before accepting the governorship of he Egyptian province of Equatoria in 1874.
6. Coupland, *The Exploitation of East Africa, 1856–1890,* 276; Gordon to Burton 17.vii.75.
7. Ibid., 283.
8. Ibid., 284; *The Times* (London), i.xii.75; C. Chaillé Long, *My Life in Four Continents* (London:Hutchinson, 1912), I, 182–183.
9. Coupland, *The Exploitation of East Africa, 1856–1890,* 285; Kirk to Derby, 14.xii.75; Kirk's Papers Vb, 325.
10. Coupland, *The Exploitation of East Africa, 1856–1890,* 287 footnote; McKillop to Stanton ii.iv.76; *Journal of the Royal African Society* 1935 (xxxiv), 282.
11. Coupland, *The Exploitation of East Africa, 1856–1890,* 297–299; Gordon to Kirk, 7.v.80.
12. Kirk to Gordon, 22.ix.80; Kirk's Papers, VII, 519.
13. Kirk to Granville 22.ix.80.
14. Foreign Office Inclosure 1/188 and Inclosure 3/188, November 30 and December 10, 1875.
15. Foreign Office Confidential Print Series, 1858–1892, Volumes 1–6, Public Records Office, London, 541/20, 123.
16. Foreign Office Confidential Print Series 1858–1892, Volumes 1–6, Public Records Office, London, 541/21, Inclosure 4 in No. 528 and Inclosure 1 in No. 633.
17. Miles to Granville, 8,14,31.xii.81; Kirk's Papers, IX.125–150.
18. Foreign Office Confidential Print Series 1858–1892, Volumes 1–6, Public Records Office, London, 541/47, Inclosure in No. 574/57.
19. Ibid.
20. This was not the end of it. Despite her new status as an ex-slave, her former owner tried to retrieve her, and the ex-slave sought Kirk's protection. The Kirks ended up hiring her as a domestic servant and paying her a regular wage.
21. Miles to Granville, 1.iii.83; Kirk to Granville, 14.iv.83; F.O. 84, 1644.

Chapter 14

1. A protectorate is almost a colony, though not legally. Nevertheless, it is ruled by a colonial power in judicial, economic, and military respects.
2. William Mackinnon was one of a number of British entrepreneurs with investments in various parts of the British Empire. He had founded the British East India Company in 1862, and subsequently the Imperial British East Africa Company in 1887. His profits came not only from freightage from his fleet of merchant ships but also from mail contracts with the Indian colonial government and involvement in road and railroad building. Sir Bartle Frere's family was one of the investors. In order to receive backing for their enterprises, and a discreet go-ahead by the British government, men like Mackinnon enlisted the help of the powerful British ruling class, in his case the Duke of Sutherland. Mackinnon, like Kirk, had vowed to do his best to eliminate slavery in East Africa and felt this could be done more effectively by facilitating transportation. His company built bridges to replace logs thrown across streams and rivers, and his roads eventually helped open up the interior. However, unlike southern Africa and Katanga in the Congo, there were few mineral deposits in East Africa, and rich agricultural lands were limited despite Livingstone's touted plans for growing cotton for British mills. Profits failed to materialize and by 1890 Mackinnon's company was virtually bankrupt, but his investments elsewhere kept him solvent long enough to raise more money for his most grandiose scheme, the construction at the end of the nineteenth century of a railroad from Mombassa to Lake Victoria which would be dubbed *The Lunatic Express*.

   Although the British government had an official hands-off policy in East Africa, British influence was felt indirectly through royal charter companies like Mackinnon's Imperial British East Africa Company; these would prove a stumbling block to the German takeover of the region. Mackinnon and his associates had temporarily brought British administration to those territories where Britain wanted some degree of control. This suited Kirk and Bargash, for at the Treaty of Berlin in 1879–80, the European powers would decide that protectorates or colonies could not be acquired without first obtaining treaties with native chiefs, investing money, and setting up some sort of administration, usually by the charter companies of the various European states with a stake in Africa. Thus the charter companies, whether Belgian, French, German, or British, were a prelude to the the partition of Africa.
3. Sir Reginald Coupland, *The Exploitation of East Africa, 1856–1890* (Evanston, Illinois: Northwestern University Press, 1967), 308, 311; F.O. to Kirk, 26.ii.78; Kirk's Papers VIb, 312; Prideaux to Derby, 23.i.75.

4. Kirk to Salisbury, 31.v.78; Kirk's Papers VIb, 400.

5. Kirk to Wylde, 3.v.78 (private correspondence); Coupland, *The Exploitation of East Africa, 1856–1890*, 316.

6. Salisbury may also have had second thoughts in the belief that once Mackinnon had secured the concession, Britain would be obligated to protect it both militarily and financially.

7. Sir Reginald Coupland, *The Exploitation of East Africa, 1856–1890*, 317; Kirk to Horace Waller, 14.xi.78 (private correspondence).

8. Foreign Office Confidential Print Series 1858–1892, Vols 1–6, Public Records Office, London, 541/22, No. 394/21.24, Inclosure 2 in No. 397.

9. Kirk to Derby, 7.iii.77; Kirk's Papers VIb, 361.

10. Henry Morton Stanley, *The Congo and the Founding of the Free State* (London: 1885), I, 20–28; F. Masoin, *Histoire de l'Etat Independant du Congo* (Namur: 1912), I, 19–25, 228–229.

11. After Livingstone's death in 1874, the *New York Herald* and *Daily Telegraph* (London), eager to capitalize further on the fame Stanley had obtained from "finding" Livingstone and writing a book about it, commissioned Stanley to return to Africa to explore Lakes Tanganyika and Victoria in more detail. His massively equipped expedition circumnavigated the huge 200-by-125-mile Lake Victoria in 1874. Stanley became involved in a battle with the people on the lake's Bumbire Island: he wrote a hair-raising account for the *Daily Telegraph* in which he claimed that the warriors had assumed a threatening stance with upthrust spears, and the chief, not satisfied with the bolts of cloth Stanley had given him, had his warriors seize the boats' oars to keep the interlopers from leaving.

"I never saw mad rage or cruel fury painted so truly before on human features," Stanley wrote. That afternoon they heard war drums, and Stanley's men tore up some of the boat's floor boards for makeshift oars. The natives returned to attack again. Stanley continued: "I discharged my elephant rifle with its two large conical balls into their midst. . . . My double barreled shot gun, loaded with buck shot, was next discharged with terrible effect . . . seeing the sub-chief I took deliberate aim with my elephant rifle at him. That bullet, as I have since been told, killed the chief and two others who happened to be standing a few paces behind him. On getting out of the cove we saw two canoes loaded with men coming out in pursuit from another small inlet. I permitted them to approach within 100 yards of us, and this time used the elephant gun with explosive balls. Four shots killed five men and sank the canoes. This decisive affair disheartened the enemy."

In a second dispatch he wrote: "Remembering the bitter injury I had received from the savages of Bumbire and the death . . . and starvation we had so narrowly escaped, I resolved, unless the natives made amends for their cruelty and treachery, to make war on them."

Although these lake-dwellers had only spears and bows and arrows, to teach them a further lesson, Stanley soon returned to the island in canoes with 250 spearmen and 50 musketeers.

"I formed my line of battle, the American and British flags waving as our ensigns. Having anchored each canoe so as to turn its broadside to the shore, I ordered a volley to be fired at one group which numbered about fifty, and the result was several killed and many wounded. The savages . . . advanced to the water's edge slinging stones and shooting arrows. I then ordered the canoes to advance within fifty yards of the shore and to fire at close quarters. After an hour the savages saw that they could not defend themselves and retreated up the slope where they continued still exposed to our bullets. I then caused the canoes to come together and told them to advance as if to disembark. This caused the enemy to make an effort to repulse our landing, and, accordingly, hundreds came down with their spears ready on the launch. When they were close enough, the bugle sounded . . . and another volley was poured into the spearmen. . . . 42 were counted dead and over a hundred were seen to retire wounded while on our side only two men suffered contusions from stones flung at us." [See Henry Morton Stanley, *Through the Dark Continent* (London: 1887), I, 270–296; *Daily Telegraph* (London) vii.viii., 1876; R. Hall, *Stanley, An Adventurer Explored* (Boston: Houghton Mifflin, 1975), 47–49.]

Stanley was hailed as a hero in the United States, where newspapers carried word of his exploits, accompanied by lavish illustrations of the reporter standing in his canoe firing at hundreds of screaming and gesticulating "savages" in full war paint. But Stanley met with nothing but opprobrium from much of the European world, at least for a time. He was considered no better than the Ajwas or the Arab and Portuguese slave raiders; he was viewed as a mass murderer who, in attempting to aggrandize himself, had not only killed local inhabitants who were trying to defend themselves against an invader, but also endangered the life of every white man who would attempt to penetrate the area after him.

When Kirk learned about the battle, he was appalled. The British Committee on Anti-Slavery and the Aborigines Protection Society lodged protests with the Foreign Office, and Sir Richard Burton, co-discoverer of Lake Tanganyika and now British consul at Trieste, wrote to Kirk: "Of course you have seen Stanley who still shoots Negroes as if they were monkeys." (See Burton to Kirk, F.O. 12.x.76.)

Kirk was asked by the Foreign Office to officially disassociate Stanley from the British government and condemn his actions. He tersely wrote Stanley: "you have no authority to make use of the British flag as giving countenance to your proceedings in the interior of Africa." (See Kirk to Salisbury, F.O. 11.xii.76.)

Stanley did not respond to Kirk's criticism and began an epic voyage down the 3,000-mile-long Congo River. A year later he reached the Atlantic Ocean, the first white man to do so in a canoe. As in the case of Farquhar, whom he had abandoned in his haste to find Livingstone on his first African trip, Stanley was not slowed on this trip by the deaths of three of his white companions. Nor was the death of many of his African porters of any consequence to him in his determination to accomplish this feat.

In late November 1876, Stanley stopped at Zanzibar and attempted to meet Kirk, but Kirk refused to see him as Kirk felt that Stanley's unconscionable behavior had antagonized the Congolese and incalculably harmed future European development in the region. (See Kirk to Derby, i.v.78.)

Kirk had also heard rumors that Stanley had stolen ivory at gunpoint from indigenous groups and sold it at a sizable profit. After interviewing a number of the Stanley's porters, Kirk became convinced that the allegations were basically true.

Given a hero's welcome in New York, Stanley was invited to speak before a special session of both houses of the U.S. Congress. The fickle British public then had a volte-face, recognizing him for his remarkable geographic exploits. Likewise, he was feted by most European heads of state. Queen Victoria even presented him with a gold, jewel-encrusted snuff box.

12. Foreign Office Confidential Print Series 1858–1892, Vols. 1–6, Public Records Office, London, 541/22, Inclosure 440.

13. Lytton to Kirk, 6.ii.79; Kirk to Salisbury, 24.iii.79.

14. Foreign Office Confidential Print Series 1858–1892, Vols 1–6, Public Records Office, London, 541/48, No. 469/109; Coupland, *The Exploitation of East Africa, 1856–1890,* 252–265; 335; Kirk's Papers VII.8.

15. Coupland, *The Exploitation of East Africa,* 340; Kirk to Salisbury 3.ii.78 and 24.viii.78; Granville 14.iv.83; F.O. 44,16845; Gordon to Burton, 17.vii 75.

16. V. Thompson and R. Adloff, *French Economic Policy in Tropical Africa,* 127–164, in L.H. Gann and Peter Duignan, eds., *Colonialism in Africa, 1870–1960,* Vol. 4 (Stanford: Hoover Institution, 1975), Publication 127, 127–164.

17. Coupland, *The Exploitation of East Africa, 1856–1890,* 354; L. Von Hohnel, *Discovery of Lake Rudolph and Stephanie* (London: 1894), 195; Kirk to Granville, 27.vii.80, Kirk's Papers VII, 479.

18. F. Jackson, *Early Days of East Africa* (London: Dawsons of Pall Mall, 1969), 61; Kirk to Derby, 29.xi.2 and 8.xii.75.

Chapter 15

1. The designation "wa" means "people of" in Swahili.
2. Joseph Thomson, *To the Central African Lakes and Back: The Narrative of the Royal Geographical Society's East Central African Expedition, 1878–80* (London: Sampson Low, Marston, Searle and Rivington, 1881), Vol. I, 17–18.
3. Ibid., Vol. I, 66.
4. Ibid., Vol. I, 87–90; Thomson to Kirk, 27.iii.8 in Kirk to Granville, 24.vi.80, Kirk's Papers VII, 462.
5. Ibid.
6. Thomson, *To the Central African Lakes and Back*, Vol. I, 144–145.
7. Ibid., Vol. I, 87–90; Thomson to Kirk, 27.iii.8 in Kirk to Granville, 24.vi.80, Kirk's Papers VII, 462.
8. Thomson to Kirk, 27.iii. 8 in Kirk to Granville, 24.vi.80, Kirk's Papers VII, 462.
9. Ibid.
10. Thomson, *To the Central African Lakes and Back*, Vol. II, 181–189.
11. Joseph Thomson, *Through Masai Land* (London: Sampson Low, Marston, Searle, and Rivington, 1887), Vol. II, 194, 205–206.
12. Schistosomiasis, mentioned earlier in Chapter 3, is a blood fluke or trematode. The free-swimming larvae or cercariae can penetrate the skin or mucosa of a human in less than a minute. Swimming through the lymphatics and the bloodstream, they pass through the lungs and lodge in the liver's portal system. After about thirty days, a pair of worms produce about a thousand eggs a day. In another ten days, the human host begins to excrete eggs in the stool. The eggs produce free-swimming larvae called miracidium, which find an intermediate host, a fresh water snail.

    Excreted by the snail, this ubiquitous parasite (over 150 million people are infected with one of the three species of schistosomiasis worldwide) completes its life cycle of disease and death by penetrating the flesh of humans who swim or walk in contaminated water. When these microscopic worms die in the liver they cause inflammation, fibrosis, or scarring, and eventual obstruction of blood flow. Both the liver and spleen become massively enlarged. Frequently fatal, exsanguinating hemorrhage comes from ruptured esophageal veins, which have taken up the back pressure caused by obstructed portal liver veins.
13. J. B. Thomson, *Joseph Thomson, African Explorer* (London: Sampson Low, Marston, Searle, and Rivington, 1896), Chaps. 1–4; Kirk to Granville ii.vi.84.

14. Granville to Miles, 19.vi.82; Kirk's Papers, IX, 205.

15. Foreign Office to Kirk, 1881, 23.xi.24.

16. Kirk received three degrees of knighthood, all of the Order of St. Michael and St. George. This order was founded by King George III in 1818 to be awarded to British subjects who had performed extraordinary government service overseas. There were three classes. The first was the C.M.G., or Commander of the Most Distinguished Order of the Grand Cross. The second was the K.C.M.G., or Knight Commander of the Most Distinguished Order of the Grand Cross. The third and greatest honor was the G.C.M.G., or Grand Companion of the Most Distinguished Order of the Grand Cross.

17. On that same trip, Kirk was involved in a tragic hunting accident. His guide left the party without notice one night, following the group on a parallel path. Unfortunately, Kirk's party came across an antelope herd at the same time that the guide, too, was stalking it. The guide, concealed in the bush, imitated the motions of an antelope in order to get nearer to the herd. "So completely did he mimic the animals, that knowing the game was there, and being myself deceived, I fired my ball taking him behind where the antelope's heart would have been," Kirk wrote.

    Kirk's party quickly took the wounded man back to Malindi, but he died after making a formal statement exonerating Kirk. Kirk had shown himself again to be an expert marksman. It was the third time Kirk's deadly aim had brought down an African.

    See Thomson to the Central African Lakes Back, Vol. I, 87–89, 90; Thomson to K, 27.iii.8 in Kirk to Granville, 24.vi.80; Kirk's Papers VII, 462.

18. Foreign Office Confidential Print Series 1858–1892, Volumes 1–6, Public Records Office, London, 541/25, Inclosure 264, and 541/48, No. 92.

19. Foreign Office Confidential Print Series 1858–1892, Volumes 1–6, Public Records Office, London, 541/27.

20. Foreign Office Confidential Print Series 1858–1892, Volumes 1–6, Public Records Office, London, 541/47 and 541/49, Inclosures 288–291, 299, 313, 321.

21. Ibid.

22. Ibid.

23. Foreign Office Confidential Print Series 1858–1892, Volumes 1–6, Public Records Office, London, 541/29, Inclosure 3/9, 56.

24. In 1904 a new international treaty abolished slavery, but it never completely died out. According to T.E. Lawrence in his *The Seven Pillars of Wisdom* [(London: 1926), 89], there were still slaves in Arabia in 1926.

In fact, slavery continues to this day in the Sudan and elsewhere in the guise of bonded laborers who remain forever in debt to their overlords. Because of this chronic indebtedness, subsequent generations, including their children, are "owned" by their employer and may be sold. The British-based Anti-Slavery International has documented the practice, and nongovernmental organizations claim they have solid evidence that there are fifteen million bonded workers in India, half a million in Nepal, and millions in Pakistan. Brazil, Peru, Thailand, the Philippines, and Indonesia have also been accused of harboring bonded laborers in this pernicious twist of the slave trade. Human Rights Watch, an organization based in New York, believes many are children and has estimated there are ten to fifteen million bonded child workers in India alone. See Syamn Bhatia, London Observer, "Children Snatched Sold by Some Traders in Arab Nations," *San Francisco Chronicle*, April 16, 1995; Sudarsan Raghavan, Chronicle Foreign Service, "Slavery Still Pervasive in Pakistan," *San Francisco Chronicle*, November 11, 1996. Sporadic slave-dealing also still occurs in remote parts of the People's Republic of China. An article in the *South China Morning Post* (September 9, 1998) reports of seven men executed for slave trading; 43 others were found guilty of kidnapping 110 women and 2 children and selling them to farmers as wives and field hands.

25. Foreign Office Confidential Print Series 1858–1892, Volumes 1–6, Public Records Office, London, 541/29, Inclosure 3/9, 56.
26. Foreign Office Confidential Print Series 1858–1892, Volumes 1–6, Public Records Office London, 541/48, Inclosure 1 in No. 386.
27. Later he changed his first name from Henry to Harry.
28. Sir Henry H. Johnston, *The Story of My Life* (London: Chatto and Windus, 1923) 144; Kirk's Papers XII, pt. iii, 12.
29. Ibid.
30. Sir Reginald Coupland, *The Exploitation of East Africa, 1856–1890* (Evanston: Northwestern University Press, 1967), 384.
31. Granville to Kirk, Foreign Office Correspondence, 23, 26, 29.ix.84; Kirk to Granville, 24, 27.ix.84; Ibid., 235; Granville to Kirk, 9.x.84; Ibid., 225; Kirk to Granville, 21.xii.84; Granville to Kirk, 31.xii.84; Foreign Office, 84. 1679; Kirk's Papers, XII. pt. i and ii; Ibid., pt. i.6.
32. The new viceroy's father, Ismail, was forced to abdicate as he had led his country to the verge of bankruptcy by overspending.
33. Kirk's Papers, Xb.
34. Granville to Kirk, Foreign Office Correspondence, 23, 26, 29.ix.84; Kirk to Granville, 24, 27.ix.84; Ibid., 235; Granville to Kirk, 9.x.84; Ibid., 225; Kirk to Granville, 21.xii.84; Granville to Kirk, 31.xii.84; Foreign Office, 84. 1679; Kirk's Papers, XII. pt. i and ii; Ibid., pt. i.6.
35. A. J. P. Taylor, *Germany's First Bid for Colonies* (London: Macmillan, 1938).

Chapter 16

1. L. H. Gann and Peter Duignan, *The Rulers of German Africa 1884–1914* (Stanford: Stanford University Press, 1977).
2. Sir Reginald Coupland, *The Exploitation of East Africa, 1856–1890* (Evanston, Illinois: Northwestern University Press, 1967), 401; Holmwood to Granville 23.iii.85.
3. Holmwood to Granville 23.iii.85.
4. Haggard to Kirk, 25.vii.84; Kirk's Papers Xb, 229–232.
5. Cecil Rhodes made a fortune in the South African diamond and gold mines. He entered South African politics and was instrumental, in 1891, in establishing a British Protectorate over Nyassaland (Malawi), and Northern and Southern Rhodesia, now Zambia and Zimbabwe.
6. Kirk to Granville, 28.iv.85.
7. Kirk to Granville, 7.vii.85.
8. Malet to Granville, 28.iv.85; Kirk to Granville 1.v.85.
9. Kirk to Granville, 9.v.85; Kirk's Papers XII, pt. i, 69.
10. Kirk to Granville, 9.v.85; Coupland, *The Exploitation of East Africa,* 412.
11. Kirk to Granville, 4.iv.85.
12. Kirk to Salisbury, 27.vi.85; Salisbury to Kirk 28.iv.85; Kirk's Papers XII. pt. ii, 4, 6.
13. Von Plessen to F.O. 28.viii.85.
14. Ibid.
15. Hansard Parliamentary Debates, 3d. ser., ccxcv. 964, 979; Coupland, *The Exploitation of East Africa, 1856–1890,* 423.
16. Joseph Thomson, *To the Central African Lakes and Back: The Narrative of the Royal Geographical Society's East Central African Expedition, 1878–80* (London: Sampson Low, Marston, Searle and Rivington, 1881), 248; Holmwood to Hutton (F.O.), 10.iv.85; Kirk's Papers XII, pt. i, 33–43; Aberdare to Granville, 22.iv.85; Kirk's Papers, XII, pt. i, 32; Granville to Malet (F.O.), 25.v.85 and 48.
17. Kirk to Salisbury, 21.vii.85; Ibid. 90; Kirk's Papers XII, pt. ii, 89.
18. Ibid.
19. Madame Reute to Bargash (undated), Kirk's Papers misc. in Coupland, *The Exploitation of East Africa, 1856–1890,* 438.
20. Kirk to Salisbury, 29.ix.85; Kirk's Papers XCII, pt. ii, 2; Kirk to Salisbury, 15.I.86.
21. Salisbury was not only pro-German, but he wrote to Lord Iddlesleigh on August 24, 1885: "I have been using the credit I have got with Bismarck

in the Caroline Islands and Zanzibar to get help in Russia and Turkey and Egypt. He is rather a Jew, but on the whole I have as yet got my money's worth." Although Disraeli, a converted Jew, had served as prime minister and the Earl of Roseberry had married the wealthy Jewish heiress Hannah Rothschild, anti-Semitism at that time generally continued to permeate government circles. [See Coupland, *The Exploitation of East Africa, 1856–1890,* 440; Salisbury to Iddesleigh., 24.viii.85.]

22. Kirk's Papers XIII, pt. ix, 68–92.

23. The British and French had recently come to an understanding on boundaries for their respective colonies in West Africa, so the British thought it politically beneficial to include the French in determining the boundaries of the new German colony of Tanganyika.

24. E. C. Dawson, *James Hannington, First Bishop of Eastern Equatorial Africa, a History of His Life and Work* (London: 1887).

25. L. H. Gann and Peter Duignan, eds., *Colonialism in Africa, 1870–1960,* Vol. 4 (Stanford: Hoover Institution, 1975), Publication 127.

26. Foreign Office Confidential Print Series 1858–1892, Volumes 1–6, Public Records Office, London, 541/47, Inclosure 1 in No. 635, 636; Inclosure 2 in No. 636, 637.

27. Foreign Office Confidential Print Series 1858–1892, Volumes 1–6, Public Records Office, London, 541/47, Inclosure in No. 646.

28. R. Oliver and G. Mathew, *History of East Africa* (Oxford: Clarendon Press, 1963), Vol. I.

29. Kirk's Papers XII, pt. ii, 6-1.

30. Kitchener had been too late to save Gordon at Khartoum but defeated the Mahdists in 1898 at the battle of Omdurman. He distinguished himself in the Boer War, obtaining the rank of field marshall at the onset of World War I.

31. Kirk's Papers, XII, pt. iv, 117; Kirk to Salisbury, 14.ii.86.

32. F.O. 84, 1389; Coupland, *The Exploitation of East Africa, 1856–1890,* 485.

33. Frere to Viceroy (of India), 20.iii.73.

34. Kitchener to Roseberry, 4.vi.86.; Kirk's Papers XIII, pt. vi, 8.

35. Coupland, *The Exploitation of East Africa, 1856–1890,* 479–480.

36. Ibid.

37. Ibid.

38. Kirk to Wylde, 24.iii.86.

Chapter 17

1. The Kirk residence, Wavertree, was sold at auction in 1923, the year after his death. It was subsequently torn down and a new house was built on its site. Nearby, a cul-de-sac of relatively new houses is named Kirk's Court.

   Sir John Kirk's son, John Carnegie Kirk, graduated from Cambridge University and served in the British army in the Boer War. He subsequently was stationed in Somalia, and he published a Somali dictionary which is still in use. Of the Kirks' five daughters, two died while quite young, one at eighteen of unknown cause, and the other at twenty-three of "an intestinal condition acquired in Africa," possibly a chronic amebic infection. Three daughters survived and at the time of Sir John's death were married and had children of their own. Much of the personal information about Sir John's family comes from my 1997 interview with his only surviving granddaughter, Daphne Foskett, and her two daughters, Patricia Middleton and Helen Godfrey. Daphne Foskett had married the clergyman Reverend Dr. Reginald Foskett, who compiled Kirk's journals and letters, a number of which are referenced in this book.

2. Thomas Pakenham, *The Scramble for Africa: The White Man's Conquest of the Dark Continent from 1876 to 1912* (New York: Random House, 1991), 463–464.

3. *Morning Post* (London), December 19, 1913; M. Balick and P.A. Cox, *Plants, People and Culture: The Science of Ethnobotany* (New York: Scientific American Library, W.H. Freeman, 1996), 118–119.

4. Sir Reginald Coupland, *The Exploitation of East Africa, 1856–1890* (Evanston, Illinois: Northwestern University Press, 1967), 481; Kirk to Dyer, 1.iv.87—Kew, English Letters, 1866–1900.

5. Charles W. Boyd, ed., *Mr. Chamberlain's Speeches* (London: 1914), Vol. II, 1–6, Foreign Office Confidential Print Series 1858–1892, Volumes 1–6, Public Records Office, London, 541/30 Inclosure 1 in No. 196.

6. Foreign Office Confidential Print Series 1858–1892, Volumes 1–6, Public Records Office, London, 541/21, Inclosure 560 in No. 57.

7. Foreign Office Confidential Print Series 1858–1892, Volumes 1–6, Public Records Office, London, 541/37, Inclosure in No. 54.

8. Foreign Office Confidential Print Series 1858–1892, Volumes 1–6, Public Records Office, London, 541/33.

9. Foreign Office Confidential Print Series 1858–1892, Volumes 1–6, Public Records Office, London, 541/30, Inclosure 1 in No. 217 and 541/39, Inclosure 2 in No. 56.

10. R.W. Beachey, *The Slave Trade of Eastern Africa* (London: Rex Collings, 1976), 125–127, 225–226; Foreign Office C.P. 7946, Pt. LXVIII, Inclosure 2 in No. 15821, February, 1902.

11. Ibid.

12. Beachey, *The Slave Trade of Eastern Africa*, 131–132.

13. Tanganyika was ceded to the British after the First World War. Zanzibar became part of Tanganyika when that country achieved independence in 1964 and became Tanzania.

14. R. Oliver and G. Mathew, *History of East Africa* (Oxford: Clarendon Press, 1963), Vol. I.

15. F. and L.O. Dotson, "The Economic Role of Non-Indigenous Ethnic Minorities in Colonialism in Africa," in L.H. Gann and Peter Duignan, eds., *Colonialism in Africa, 1870–1960,* Vol. 4 (Stanford: Hoover Institution, 1975), Publication 127, 612.

16. As Leopold's emissary, Stanley had found himself in direct competition with the explorer Pierre Savorgnan de Brazza, who was in service for the French. De Brazza's style was quite different from Stanley's. Like Livingstone and Kirk, he had some empathy for Africans and avoided conflict when he could, whereas Stanley would not hesitate to use firepower to teach Africans a lesson.

    When the two explorers first met on the Congo in 1880, De Brazza had already secretly signed treaties with chiefs on the northern side of the great river. This vast territory was to become the French colony of Equatorial Africa and, after the Second World War and independence, the Republic of the Congo.

    It took Stanley three years to obtain all the treaties with local chiefs ceding the vast territory to the Belgian king. During this period he also met the notorious Swahili slave trader, Tippu Tib, who had built a fort and slave-holding pens at what became known as Stanley's Pool, a widened portion of the Congo River. Twenty years later, Stanley's Pool became Leopoldville, the capital of the Belgian "Congo Free State." After independence in 1960, it was renamed Kinshasa. Stanley, too, was remembered when the next-largest town on the river, 750 miles east of Kinshasa, became Stanleyville, now Kisangani.

    Although Stanley was received with honors, there were critics as well. Horace Waller, H.M Hyndman, and Henry Yule, all members of the Royal Geographic Society, wrote in the February 11, 1878, issue of the *Pall Mall Gazette*, "Exploration under these conditions is, in fact, exploration plus buccaneering, and though the map may be improved and enlarged by the process, the cause of civilization is not a gainer thereby, but a loser. . . . You may say that by our commercial relations with African tribes we must surely have let in light. I reply, if it is to be so, it is the blaze of a burning village, or the flash of the Winchester rifle—at best it is the smoke-stack of the Congo steamer bearing away tons upon tons of ivory."

In 1884–85 Stanley attended the Berlin Conference, which "legalized" the Congo Free State as Leopold's personal possession and prohibited the slave trade. As usual, prescient Kirk saw this as a pretext for looting the country. In fact, King Leopold's agents attempted to extract the last bit of ivory and palm oil from his new posession. Although slavery, in the political sense, had been abolished, the Africans' pitiful salaries and the working conditions imposed upon them by the Belgians amounted to economic slavery in the lower Congo controlled by the Belgian king. In the upper Congo, which the Belgians had not yet reached, Tippu Tib had been appointed governor, at Stanley's insistence, for he naively hoped this would civilize the Swahili slaver and put a stop to the slave trade. Instead, Tippu Tib's henchmen continued the wholesale destruction of villages and enslavement of their inhabitants.

Joseph Conrad's eloquent and disturbing novel, *Heart of Darkness*, published in 1902, describes the fear the Belgian traders had of the dark and forbidding jungle and features as its anti-hero Kurtz, a callous and avaricious ivory trader who thought nothing of killing Africans. This tale had such a troublesome impact on European readers that some historians believe it was instrumental in pressuring the Belgian government to take the Congo Free State away from Leopold in 1908, when it became an official colony of the Belgian government.

17. The last two states which had been under charter from 1899 until 1924 to Cecil Rhodes's British South Africa Company were finally divided into Northern and Southern Rhodesia (now Zambia and Zimbabwe, respectively).

18. For a look at the the excesses of imperialism, its degradation of the natives, and the practice of local genocide, see Sven Lindqvist, *Exterminate the Brutes* (New York: New Press, 1992). Charles Darwin's epochal contributions, *On the Origin of Species* (1859) and *The Descent of Man* (1871), contributed a new awareness to human origins, but his conclusions were distorted by a new breed of racists who considered the African a member of an inferior race which at best was only fit for labor, and at worst for extermination. Justified by the term "Social Darwinism," this malignant concept placed the white race at the top of the evolutionary tree, and, in the case of rabid imperialists like Rhodes, the Englishman at its pinnacle. [See Antony Thomas, *Rhodes* (New York: St. Martin's Press, 1997), 108–109.]

19. D. C. R. A. Goonetilleke, Joseph Conrad, *The Heart of Darkness* (Peterborough, Ontario: Broadview Press, 1995), 13, 14.

20. L.H. Gann and Peter Duignan, eds., *Colonialism in Africa, 1870–1960*, (Stanford: Hoover Institution, 1975), Publication 127; 1–17.

21. Proceedings of the Royal Geographic Society, 1913.
22. Reginald Fosket, *The Zambezi Doctors: David Livingstone's Letters to John Kirk 1858–1872* (Edinburgh: Edinburgh University Press, 1964), 25–26; H. H. Johnston, *The Geographical Journal,* 59, No. 3 (March, 1922): 228.
23. *The Chronicle and Courier* (Seven Oaks), January 20, 1922; *The Times* (London), January 20, 1922.

Index

TONI MORRISON

TONI MORRISON

Great American Writer

by Lisa R. Rhodes

A Book Report Biography
FRANKLIN WATTS
A Division of Grolier Publishing
New York / London / Hong Kong / Sydney
Danbury, Connecticut

Excerpt from Toni Morrison's 1993 Nobel Prize Lecture reprinted with permission of The Nobel Foundation in Stockholm, Sweden.

Cover illustration by Dave Klaboe, interpreted from a photograph © Retna Ltd./Falour/Stills

Photographs ©: AP/Wide World Photos: 72; Archive Photos: 19 (American Stock), 13 (Reuters/Pressen Bild); Black River Historical Society, Lorain, OH: 21, 25, 28; Corbis Sygma: 77 (Danny Hoffman); Corbis-Bettmann: 107 (Michel Bourquard), 105 (Mitch Gerber), 40, 51 (UPI), 71, 75; Courtesy of Howard University Archives: 33, 36; Everett Collection, Inc.: 56 (CSU Archives), 15, 88, 90; Liaison Agency, Inc.: 2 (Ulf Anderson); Photofest: 31, 48; Retna Ltd./Camera Press Ltd.: 93 (Jim Cooper), 101 (Walter McBride), 110 (Susan Stava); Texas Southern University, Heartman Collection: 38; The Daily Princetonian: 11, 84; The Morning Journal, Lorain, OH: 98.

Visit Franklin Watts on the Internet at:
http://publishing.grolier.com

Library of Congress Cataloging-in-Publication Data

Rhodes, Lisa Renee.
Toni Morrison : great American writer / by Lisa R. Rhodes.
p. cm.—(A book report biography)
Includes bibliographical references and index.
ISBN 0-531-11677-8 (lib. bdg.) 0-531-15555-2 (pbk.)
1. Morrison, Toni—Juvenile literature. 2. Novelists, American—20th century—Biography—Juvenile literature. 3. Afro-American women novelists—Biography—Juvenile literature. [1. Morrison, Toni. 2. Authors, American. 3. Women—Biography. 4. Afro-Americans—Biography.] I. Title. II. Series.

PS3563.O8749 Z829 2001
813'.54—dc21
[B] 00-032077

Printed in the United States of America.
1 2 3 4 5 6 7 8 9 10 R 10 09 08 07 06 05 04 03 02 01

CONTENTS

CHAPTER ONE

AFRICAN-AMERICAN, FEMALE, AND FIRST

Toni Morrison walked down the stairs at the Concert Hall in Stockholm, Sweden, carefully like a queen. Her gray dreadlocks swept the nape of her neck in long tendrils. Her long flowing black gown, made by designer Bill Blass, almost touched the floor, and her black and bright-pink shoulder wrap cradled her golden-brown shoulders. Her escort, King Carl XVI Gustaf of Sweden, gently held her arm as they descended the stairs. Morrison was now a member of the world's literary royalty. She had come to Stockholm in December 1993 to receive the Nobel Prize in Literature. She was the first African-American woman to receive the award.

"This is a palpable tremor of delight for me. It was wholly unexpected and so satisfying," Morrison told a *New York Times* reporter in October 1993 when the announcement of her win was

made. "Regardless of what we say and truly believe about the irrelevance of prizes and their relationship to the real work, nevertheless, this is a signal honor for me."[1]

Morrison, then 62, received the Nobel Prize for an exceptional career as a writer. She had written six novels, all telling the triumphs and tragedies of African-Americans in the 1800s and 1900s. Her books—*The Bluest Eye* (1970), *Sula* (1973), *Song of Solomon* (1977), *Tar Baby* (1981), *Beloved* (1987), and *Jazz* (1992)—had captured the attention of critics and readers throughout the United States and the world. Her works have been translated into more than twenty different languages. The Nobel Committee of the Swedish Academy, which awards the prize, praised Morrison for her literary efforts in its announcement. The academy called Morrison "a literary artist of finest work," who "gives life to an essential aspect of American reality." Said the Academy, "She delves into the language itself, a language she wants to liberate from the fetters of race. And she addresses us with the luster of poetry."[2]

For almost twenty years, Morrison has created memorable African-American characters who struggle to live their lives as full individuals and members of the African-American community. Her characters must often overcome the brutality of slavery, racial and economic oppression, and

sexism, but they rely on their own ·inner strengths, the bonds of the African-American community, spirituality, and their love of African-American culture, to shape their lives. "It's true [my characters] go through difficult circumstances," Morrison once told an interviewer. But by the end of her novels, "people always know something profound and wonderful."[3]

Her works had helped to change the face of American literature—a literature that once told only the conquests of white men with white women as minor characters. Morrison's work introduced lyrical prose, storytelling, African-American folklore, and African-American history to the American literary establishment. African-American literature, also dominated by male characters, was similarly changed when Morrison introduced the female point of view and female sensitivities—and made them credible. "She has taken the specific and often terrible history of African-American people in America and lofted it into the tireless realm of myth," wrote critic Michiko Kakutani in *The New York Times*.[4]

Morrison, who won the Pulitzer Prize for Fiction a few years earlier, had not expected to win the Nobel. Morrison woke up to write at about 4:30 A.M. one crisp October morning in 1993. The phone rang a few hours later. "I knew it was terrible news," Morrison told *The New York Times*.

Instead, the news was joyous—a friend had called to tell Morrison that she had won the Nobel. "It took a long time for me to accept it," Morrison admitted. Several hours later, the secretary of the Swedish Academy called Morrison to deliver the good news and to let her know that a confirmation letter was on its way to her home. "I said 'Why don't you send me a fax,'" Morrison said jokingly. "Somehow, I felt that if I saw a fax, I'd know it wasn't a dream or somebody's hallucination," she told *The New York Times*. "I'll tell you one thing, we're going to have a big party here tonight!"[5]

The Nobel Prizes, founded by Alfred Bernhard Nobel, a Swedish scientist, have been given each year since 1901. The prizes are given in six different fields of study to a person who has made a valuable contribution to the "good of humanity." The prizes are awarded in physics, chemistry, medicine, international peace, economics, and literature.

The Nobel Prize in Literature is given to the person who has created the "most distinguished work of an idealistic nature." The award is usually given for a lifetime of literary efforts, rather than a single book. Prizewinners receive the award on December 10, the anniversary of Alfred Nobel's death.

Morrison answered many phone calls on the morning she heard the news. By 10:00 A.M., she

had turned off the telephone to take a hot bath. She also refused her publisher's invitation to hold a press conference about the announcement. Morrison decided to go to work instead. A professor of creative writing and humanities at Princeton University in New Jersey, Morrison met a crowd of news reporters at the university who wanted to know her response to the honor. Morrison continued to teach her classes for the day, undistracted by the media attention.

Morrison talks with reporters on the day she learned about her Nobel Prize.

Morrison had to prepare for a full week of celebratory activities. The Nobel Prize Committee had set up a dinner, a concert, and press conferences for Morrison. Many literary dignitaries would come to see her receive the award at the Swedish Academy and hear her Nobel Prize lecture. But soon after the Nobel announcement, Morrison found she hardly had any time to write her lecture—instead she had to decide what to wear for the award ceremony. "I called someone at the Nobel Committee," Morrison told *Time* magazine five years after receiving the award, "and I said 'Look, if you're going to keep giving prizes to women—and I hope you do—you're going to have to give us more warning. Men can rent tuxedos. I have to get shoes. And I have to get a dress.'"[6]

Despite her earlier concerns, when Morrison arrived in Stockholm in early December, she arrived in style. An audience of four hundred well-wishers at the Swedish Academy heard her Nobel Prize lecture about the importance of literature in shaping a humane society. Part of Morrison's lecture read:

> "Oppressive language does more than represent violence; it is violence; it does more than represent limits of knowledge; it limits knowledge. Whether it is obscuring state language or the faux-language of the mindless media; whether it is the proud but

calcified language of the academy, or the commodity-driven language of science; whether it is the malign language of law—without ethics, or language designed for the estrangement of minorities, hiding its racist plunder in its literary cheek—it must be rejected, altered, and exposed."[7]

Morrison received a standing ovation for her lecture. No one doubted that she deserved the Nobel Prize and she was presented with the

Toni Morrison receives the Nobel Prize from King Carl Gustav of Sweden.

award at a lavish ceremony. In 1993, the winner of the Nobel Prize in Literature received a monetary award of $825,000.

When Morrison returned to the United States, however, some of her fellow writers questioned whether she deserved the award. Charles Johnson, author of the novel *Middle Passage*, was critical, insisting that Morrison won the award because she "has been the beneficiary of goodwill." Johnson, in a *Washington Post* article, said Morrison, who began writing in the early 1970s (the years after the Civil Rights Movement and the beginning of the Women's Movement), had managed to combine the calls for African-American pride and equity among African-American women. "But when that particular brand of politics is filtered through her [poetic] writing, the result is often offensive, harsh," Johnson noted. "Whites are portrayed badly. Men are. African-American men are." In his final comments, Johnson said Morrison's award was "a triumph of political correctness."[8]

Other writers came to Morrison's defense. "No one writes more beautifully than Toni Morrison," said Alice Walker, author of *The Color Purple*. "She has consistently explored issues of true complexity and terror and love in the lives of blacks. Harsh criticism has not dissuaded her. Prizes have not trapped her. She is a writer who deserves this honor."[9]

Morrison had not been a stranger to controversy in her career. In the late 1980s, she had been in the midst of another dispute. During this time, other writers wondered why Morrison had not received another important award, and they wrote to *The New York Times Book Review* to complain. Some literary critics have complained

Author Alice Walker

her writing style is overdone. Some readers have complained her novels are hard to understand. Political conservatives have also criticized her scholarly exploration of the role of race in American literature. Through it all, Morrison has persevered and never lost sight of her first love—writing.

According to literature scholar Trudier Harris, Morrison is a literary giant who is as important to American culture as one of our finest athletes. "By any standard of literary evaluation, Toni Morrison is a phenomenon in the classic sense of a once-in-a-lifetime rarity, the literary equivalent of Paul Robeson, Michael Jordan . . .," Harris wrote in *World Literature Today*. Morrison has "a place in the canons of world literature."[10]

Morrison would withstand controversy to become a master writer, editor, teacher, and mentor to upcoming African-American writers who also aspire to share their vision of the world. "There were plenty of roadblocks along the way," Morrison told *Time* magazine when recalling her writing career. "The world back then didn't expect much from a little black girl, but my father and mother certainly did. She [Morrison's mother] was still alive when I won the Nobel,

"There were plenty of roadblocks along the way,"

although she died three months later. She was delighted, but not surprised."[11]

Toni Morrison's life has been one of great expectations. It all began in a small Midwestern steel-mill town in a family headed by proud and strong parents who shaped Morrison's view of life—and her writing.

CHAPTER TWO

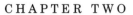

AT HOME WITH FATHER

Ardelia and John Solomon Willis woke every morning before sunrise to work the crop fields on 88 acres (36 hectares) of farmland Willis owned in Greenville, Alabama in the early 1900s. They worked the land together and raised their children there. Southern land was a link to the Willis family's past.

Willis and his parents were once slaves—among the millions of blacks whose ancestors were taken from Africa on slave ships and held in bondage for life by white Americans in the northern and southern United States. The North eventually outlawed slavery, but the South continued the practice. The slaves were made to plant and harvest cotton and other crops that their owners would later sell. The slaves never shared in the money, land, or other resources that came from their life's work. Instead, the ancestors of the

Many slaves worked the land, including Morrison's ancestors in her grandfather's family.

Willis family and other blacks endured whippings, physical torture, degradation, and the pain of being sold away from each other—separating husband from wife and mother from child.

In 1863, President Abraham Lincoln signed the Emancipation Proclamation, granting legal freedom to African-Americans in slavery, including John Solomon Willis, who was born a slave.

His granddaughter, Chloe Anthony Wofford, known later as Toni Morrison, would become one of America's most highly respected writers. She would earn that honor, in part for retelling the stories of African-American slaves and their families. "Fathers and sons, mothers and daughters—these bonds are essential to Ms. Morrison, who plays out the drama of slavery and racism in the most intimate human relationships," wrote a journalist in the *Wall Street Journal* in 1993, some sixty years after Chloe's birth.[1]

Chloe Anthony Wofford was born on February 18, 1931, in Lorain, Ohio. Her mother, Ramah Willis, had moved to Ohio with her parents from Alabama in 1912, after the family lost their land to a group of white southerners in a shady business agreement. Ramah later married George Wofford, a proud African-American laborer from Georgia. The Wofford family settled in Lorain and Chloe was born two years after the birth of their first daughter. The Woffords later had two sons.

Hard work was not a stranger to either the Wofford or Willis families. George Wofford held three jobs at the same time to provide shelter and food for his family, although work was extremely difficult to find in the early 1930s. Chloe was born during the Great Depression—a time when the U.S. economy almost collapsed. Many banks

The house where Chloe was born

failed, many people lost their homes, and countless numbers of people stood in line at soup kitchens to get food. Wofford worked in a car wash, at a road-construction site, in steel mills, and at a shipyard to earn money. Wofford was never ashamed of the type of work he did—instead he was motivated to do his best. He worked diligently in the shipyard to weld perfect

seams on the sides of steel ships. He often wrote his name after each seam as proof of his success. Grandfather John Solomon Willis worked as a carpenter and a coal miner soon after his family moved to the North.

Ramah Wofford also held her head high. At one time, the Woffords, like many Depression-era families, relied on the federal government for assistance to make ends meet. The Woffords signed up for the government's food-relief program and once found bugs in the flour and other food items they received from the government. Ramah was insulted, but she did not bow her head. She quickly wrote a letter of protest to President Franklin Delano Roosevelt to air her concerns about the quality of the food in the relief program.

Ramah also showed her inner strength when her husband was unemployed. The Woffords could not pay the $4 rent, and one day found an "Evicted" sign pasted on their front door by the landlord. Ramah quickly removed the sign and ripped it up. The landlord did not give up, though. Sometime later, the landlord burnt the Wofford home down in retaliation for the unpaid rent.

"It was this hysterical, out-of-the-ordinary, bizarre form of evil," Chloe would recall years later in an interview with a journalist. "If you internalized it [the tragedy], you'd be truly and

thoroughly depressed because that's how much your life meant. For four dollars a month, somebody would just burn you to a crisp."[2]

Luckily, no one was hurt in the fire, although Chloe, her mother, and sister were at home when it started. Despite the many hardships the family faced, Chloe and her siblings never saw their parents break under the strain, and they passed their formidable strength and self-esteem on to their children. "Social obstacles, economic obstacles, or racism were obstacles, but we ourselves were extraordinary and superior people," Chloe said years later. "My parents also responded to life like that."[3]

Life for African-Americans was far from easy—particularly during the Great Depression. African-Americans in the South struggled with the decreasing number of agricultural jobs, while most African-Americans—like the Woffords and Willis families—had moved to the North hoping to find employment, housing, and a better life. Southern blacks had to live with legal racial segregation—laws that prevented them from eating in public restaurants with whites, using the same public bathrooms, or even attending the same public schools. African-Americans were also restricted from voting. In addition, white supremacy groups, such as the Ku Klux Klan, terrorized blacks. The Klan was known for harassing

and even lynching African-Americans who dared to try to improve their lives by trying to vote or owning a plot of land. While segregation laws were not as prevalent in the North, African-Americans still faced discrimination in housing, employment, and the use of public facilities. For example, Chloe, her siblings, and other blacks in Lorain, were not allowed to swim in Lake Erie during the summer, while whites enjoyed the lake whenever they wanted to.

However, relations between blacks and whites in Lorain were better than in some parts of America, North or South. Chloe grew up in a fully integrated community. Her neighbors were Irish, Italian, Greek, and German. The one common factor between blacks and whites in town was their economic class. Most of the families were blue-collar, working-class people, and this circumstance seemed to bond everyone together. "We were all in one economic class and therefore mutually dependent upon one another," Chloe explained years later. "There was a great deal of sharing of food and services, and caring. If someone was ill, people might come and take care of him or her, regardless of race."[4]

Chloe and her siblings also went to school with white children. "They were my friends . . . There was no awe, or fear," Chloe told a journalist years later, noting that only when she became a

teenager did she notice "how clear the lines really were." Said Chloe, "But when I was in first grade, nobody thought I was inferior. I was the only black in class and the only child who could read!"[5]

"I was the only black in class and the only child who could read!"

George Wofford felt quite differently about relations between blacks and whites. George was convinced that some whites could not be trusted and that the black man had to be careful not to be taken for granted.

Chloe (second from left, first row) participated in many school activities, including the Library Aids.

George's life in Georgia shaped his perspective of white Americans. The constant threat of physical violence and the legal barriers to social progress were proof to him that the scales of justice were tipped generously toward whites—not blacks. The only advantage given to African-Americans was their humanity. "My father [in that sense] really felt that black people were better than all white people because their position was [inherently] a moral one," Chloe said.[6]

As a matter of fact, George felt so strongly about white Americans that he would not allow whites into the Wofford home. Chloe recalled years later in a 1998 interview with "60 Minutes," the television news program, that white insurance salesmen could enter the home only when her father was not there.[7]

Ramah was more likely to believe that with education, people could overcome their racial prejudices. While her husband taught the children about the separation of blacks and whites, Ramah's devotion to the Christian church shaped a more spiritual perspective—one that favored conscientious protest. Ramah dared to sit in the white-only section of the local movie theater to see Saturday matinees, rather than sit in the section reserved for blacks. For Ramah, integrating a movie theater or writing a letter to the president were simply forms of protest.

George and Ramah worked together to instill a sense of racial pride in their children. Racism and racial discrimination were unfortunate realities of life for African-Americans, and the Woffords knew their children needed a solid cultural foundation to succeed in life. Chloe's parents and grandparents often shared stories taken in part from Africa about ghosts, supernatural events, folktales, and myths. These stories were handed down in both families after slavery, a custom in many African-American families. Children like Chloe and her siblings learn at an early age that the spirit world is a natural part of life—not something to fear or criticize. The Wofford children also gathered around the family's kitchen table to hear stories and listen to music. Ramah sang in church and often sang the gospel and work songs that the slaves sang among themselves as they worked in the fields. Grandfather Willis played the violin at family gatherings and often managed to earn a few dollars using his skills as a musician.

Chloe loved the family's music and stories. Years later, as an adult, she would recall how her adult relatives always asked the Wofford children about their dreams. These family influences helped to make Chloe an advanced student. By the time she graduated from Lorain High School—with honors—Chloe had studied Latin and had read most of Europe's classical literature,

Chloe as a high school senior

ranging from Russian authors such as Dostoyevsky and Tolstoy—authors of *Crime and Punishment* and *War and Peace*, respectively—and even Gustave Flaubert, the French author of *Madame Bovary*. She also enjoyed the writings of England's Jane Austen, the author of *Pride and Prejudice*. The Wofford family's link to Africa helped Chloe to appreciate her own heritage and the fine cultural works of other ethnic groups. But for many years she yearned to read books about the deep psychological and spiritual complexities of African-American life—books by African-Americans.

Chloe hoped to read such works someday, but she had no ambitions to become a writer herself, although she did manage to scribble a few notes about her experiences. For the most part, she spent her teenage years studying hard and helping to earn money for the family. At thirteen, Chloe worked part-time after school cleaning a white family's house. It was one experience, in addition to being barred from Lake Erie, that taught Chloe the harsh inequities between African-Americans and whites. The white family she worked for was far from friendly, and Chloe hated the long hours of hard work. But George Wofford would not let his daughter walk away from an important lesson in self-respect. "Girl,

you don't live there. You live here. So go do your work, get your money, and come on home."[8] Chloe followed her father's advice and never again doubted her ability to face racial adversity.

She also learned an unspoken rule about some white Americans and their view of African-Americans. Years later in an interview with "60 Minutes," Chloe explained that although she is not prejudiced against all white Americans, her life experiences have taught her that some whites could not be trusted—they would "betray" her. Chloe called her attitude toward some whites a "constant vigilance and awareness" to ensure her physical, emotional, and spiritual well-being.[9]

College was the natural choice for Chloe after her success in high school. She decided to apply to Howard University in Washington, D.C., one of the largest mainly African-American universities in America. When Chloe graduated from high school in 1949, she thought she would become a ballerina, following in the footsteps of the famous Maria Tallchief. Tallchief, the daughter of an Osage American Indian father and a Scots-Irish mother, began her career at the New York City Ballet in 1947. Tallchief was known for her personal discipline and grace, qualities Chloe hoped to emulate. It seemed the educational opportunities at a predominantly African-American university would help Chloe achieve her dreams. After

eighteen years at home with her defiant father, Chloe left Ohio for the northeastern United States to begin her life as a young woman. Her experience at Howard University would teach her more about African-Americans than she ever imagined.

In high school, Chloe dreamed of being a ballerina like Maria Tallchief.

CHAPTER THREE

"TONI" MORRISON

Not long after Chloe arrived on the campus of Howard University in the fall of 1949, she made two decisions that would greatly influence her adult life. She changed her name from Chloe to "Toni" (a shortened version of her middle name Anthony), because some classmates could not pronounce her name properly, and she joined the Howard University Players, a campus theater group made up of students and faculty members.

The Howard University Players performed works by William Shakespeare and other revered European playwrights during the school year. The performances complemented Toni's English literature major and her minor in the classics. In the summer, the group performed for African-American audiences throughout the South. Toni's travels in the southern states made her more familiar with the life and struggles of her parents and

Toni in the Howard University Players' production of Shakespeare's Richard III

grandparents who fled legal segregation and discrimination with hopes of better opportunities in the North. Toni was able to see first-hand the poor living conditions of many rural African-Americans who had not been able to progress past generations of working as sharecroppers. They worked for menial wages and endured segregated public bathrooms and movie theaters. Although Toni—the actress—had no interest in writing about the injustices she saw in the South, she was touched by the images she saw and the African-American people who came to her theatrical performances. These memories of African-Americans made a lasting impression on the literature she wrote years later.

Unfortunately, Toni discovered that many of her African-American classmates at Howard were not particularly interested in the common life of southern African-Americans—or in the history and contributions of African-Americans. Many of the faculty and students at Howard at that time had little interest in authentic African-American culture, although the university was founded in 1867 to train African-American preachers to serve free African-Americans after the Civil War. Toni found that the history, culture, and literature of Europeans and white Americans were taught in the classroom, rather than the works of blacks. This was common practice at many colleges, both

black and white, in the 1940s. African-American studies did not become a widely taught subject in most schools and colleges until the Civil Rights Movement twenty years later.

On campus, students were preoccupied with the social status and skin color of their peers. Students from middle-class and upper middle-class backgrounds with light or fair complexions were preferred to students who came from humbler family origins and had darker skin tones. For example, Toni knew a female student who was not popular with the men on campus because of her dark brown skin. Their attitudes changed when they learned that her parents were rich. The men suddenly took an interest in the young woman and many asked her out on dates. Toni disapproved of young men's actions since they were only interested in her friend because she had money.

Toni participated in some of the social activities on campus—she joined Alpha Kappa Alpha, one of the many African-American sororities on campus, but tried her best to avoid engaging in some of the elitist, snobby attitudes and behaviors of her fellow students. Toni wanted to hold on to her family's working-class and southern roots and learn more about her African-American heritage without alienating the new middle-class social order she surprisingly found at Howard. It was a strange journey, but Toni was not afraid to test

Toni in her college yearbook

her newfound independence. Instead, she focused on her schoolwork. She graduated in 1953 and applied for a master's degree program at Cornell University.

Toni enrolled at Cornell to pursue a degree in English. She continued to love classic literature and decided to write her thesis paper on the works of William Faulkner and Virginia Woolf and the two authors' preoccupation with the theme of suicide. Toni graduated in 1955.

After her graduate studies, Toni decided to teach English. She applied for a teaching position at Texas Southern University (TSU) in Houston, Texas, and she was hired to teach introductory English to college freshmen. Toni did not mind returning to the South to teach. TSU became a place where she would celebrate African-American culture and learn more about the contributions of African-Americans—for the first time in her academic experience. "[I] began to think about black culture as a subject, as an idea, as a discipline," Toni recalled years later. "Before it had only been on a very personal level—my family."[1] Toni taught at the university for 1½ years.

Toni was not the only African-American to make a conscious connection to her racial and cultural roots and feel a sense of pride. In 1954, lawyers for the National Association for the Advancement of Colored People (NAACP), the

Toni worked as an English Instructor at Texas Southern University.

country's oldest civil rights organization, won an important legal battle on behalf of African-Americans. Thurgood Marshall, an African-American lawyer and graduate of Howard University Law School, argued before the U.S. Supreme Court that the legal separation of blacks and whites in public schools was unconstitutional—and the Court agreed. In the *Brown vs. Board of Education of Topeka* case, the Supreme Court declared that segregated schools prevent blacks (and other children of color) from receiving an equal education. In addition, Chief Justice Earl Warren also stated for the Court that the legal separation of the races—racial segregation—went against the principles of the fourteenth amendment to the Constitution. This amendment guarantees all U.S. citizens the right to equal protection under the law, regardless of their race.

On the heels of the 1954 *Brown* decision, African-Americans in Montgomery, Alabama, were taking part in a grassroots movement for African-American civil rights that was beginning to take shape. In 1955, Rosa Parks, a black seamstress, refused to give up her seat on a bus to a white passenger, and started a yearlong bus boycott. African-Americans throughout the city pledged not to use the city buses until the city agreed to abolish the custom of seating passengers according to their race. The boycott was a

major nonviolent protest against the city's public officials in the effort to strike down unfair segregation laws.

Rosa Parks's courage—she was arrested and fined for her refusal to give up her seat—led the Montgomery Improvement Association (MIA), a

Rosa Parks

local civil rights group, to take the city to court on Mrs. Parks's behalf. The lawsuit eventually led to a Supreme Court ruling declaring that state and city laws permitting racial segregation on city buses were unconstitutional. Dr. Martin Luther King Jr., a young African-American Baptist minister, led the MIA, and would someday become the most prominent leader of the Civil Rights Movement. In the meantime, the *Brown* decision and the successful Montgomery bus boycott were legal victories that gave many African-Americans hope that their children would grow up in a society that guaranteed equal rights to all.

Dr. King and other civil rights leaders favored racial integration, but Toni's childhood experiences and family influences led her to favor all-African-American institutions, particularly public schools. "I was not in favor of integration, but I couldn't officially say that, because I knew the terror and abuses of segregation," she said years later. "But integration also meant that we [blacks] would not have a fine black college or a fine black education. I didn't know why the assumption was that black children were going to learn better if they were in the company of white children."[2] Toni worried that the Supreme Court ruling to desegregate public schools would mean the end of black educational institutions. She supported increased

funding to African-American schools to provide better textbooks and notebooks and more well-trained teachers.

Toni's commitment to African-American education brought her back to Howard University in 1957 to teach English. Now in her mid-twenties, she enjoyed her life as a single woman, but a year later she fell in love and married a young architect named Harold Morrison. Toni Morrison and her new husband, who was born in Jamaica, settled into their new home in Washington, D.C., and became parents three years later. Their first son, Harold Ford Morrison, was born in 1961.

Morrison was busy with her newborn son, her teaching, and her new marriage when she heard about a writers' group on Howard's campus. Morrison still was not serious about a writing career, but she wanted to broaden her circle of friends and thought being in the company of writers and poets would be a refreshing change from her daily routine. The group met once a month and the members shared their own works, reading and discussing their writing with their peers. At first, Morrison decided to share some of the scribblings she wrote in high school. But soon she ran out of material and found that she had to share more recent work. Morrison wasn't quite sure what to do, but one night she started to write a story about a young African-American girl she had met

as a child. The girl had revealed one of her deepest secrets—she told Morrison that she had prayed to God for blue eyes for two years. Morrison knew that the girl's secret revealed a hidden desire—to have blue eyes like "pretty" white girls. But the girl's prayers were never answered. Devastated, the girl gave up her faith in God because she felt she was doomed to live her life as a black person.

One evening, Morrison shared her short story about the girl with the writers' group. Her peers were impressed with her work and wanted to hear more. Despite the group's enthusiasm, though, Morrison set the story aside. She thought nothing more of her story, except that it had done well in the writers' group.

Two years later, Morrison, pregnant with her second child, made another important decision. She resigned from her teaching position at Howard and spent the summer in Europe with her husband and young son. When Morrison returned to the United States, her marriage was over, and she had no job. Harold Morrison went back to Jamaica, and Toni returned to her family in Lorain, Ohio, to give birth to her son, Slade Kevin Morrison, in 1964.

It was one of the most difficult times in Morrison's life, and she later described it as "bleak." Despite her unhappiness, Morrison was

determined to move forward. She knew her family would help her in any way they could, but she desperately wanted to avoid becoming a burden to her parents and siblings. At age thirty-four, Morrison had two sons and she wanted to get on with her life, find a job, and build a future. Said Morrison, "I wanted to find out who I was and whether I was tough enough."[3]

"I wanted to find out who I was and whether I was tough enough."

Years later, Morrison would only briefly recall the unhappy years of her marriage. In 1979, Morrison spoke about the troubled six-year marriage in an interview with *The New York Times Magazine*. "Women in Jamaica are very subservient in their marriages," Morrison explained. "They never challenge their husbands. I was a constant nuisance to mine. He didn't need me making judgments about him, which I did. A lot."[4]

A year later, in 1965, Morrison and her sons moved to Syracuse, New York. Ramah Wofford worried that her daughter's decision to move meant the possibility that she would have few friends. But Morrison was not afraid. "You take the village with you," she told her mother. "There is no need for the community if you have a sense of it inside."[5]

Morrison's work in the classroom prepared her for an editorial position in a textbook division at the Syracuse office of Random House, a publishing company based in New York City. Morrison became an associate editor and went to work editing textbooks about African-American history and culture for elementary and high schools.

Toni Morrison was now on her own. In the next few years, literary critics would find her to be one of the country's most promising African-American writers of fiction. But that praise did not come without loneliness and hard work.

CHAPTER FOUR

A WRITER'S PEN

Pecola Breedlove hates herself. When she looks into the mirror, she finds no beauty in her brown skin, dark eyes, and tightly curled hair. She prayed to God for two years to make her beautiful and give her blue eyes, like the 1930s child film star Shirley Temple. Pecola believes she must be ugly. Perhaps that was why she was raped by her drunken father, Cholly, and later became pregnant. Perhaps that was why the baby was born but did not survive. Pecola needs a miracle. Blue eyes will certainly change her world—make it tender, caring, and loving—a world away from the poverty she lives in and the rejection she faces from her mother Pauline. Pecola prayed hard and asked Soaphead Church, a so-called minister, to help her. But will her prayers be answered?

Toni Morrison created the character Pecola for her first novel, *The Bluest Eye*, during late-night writing sessions at her new home in Syracuse.

During the day, she worked at her publishing job, editing textbooks. But in the late evening, after her two sons were fed and safe in bed, Morrison began to finish the short story she wrote years ago when she lived in Washington, D.C. The short story she presented to the writers' group had become the plot for *The Bluest Eye.*

Morrison named the book's African-American narrator Claudia. Along with her sister Frieda, she is friends with Pecola. Like Pecola, Claudia and Frieda are poor, but their family life is more stable. Claudia's and Frieda's mother is strict, but nurturing. She demands that her daughters be well behaved, but Mrs. MacTeer takes good care of her children. When Claudia becomes sick with a bad cold, her mother insists that she stay in bed and rubs her neck and chest with a medicinal salve to help her get better.

On the other hand, Pauline, Pecola's mother, does not recognize that her daughter needs her love and support. After Pecola was raped, Pauline does not realize that Pecola is suffering. She beats Pecola at a time when Pecola desperately needs to be comforted. To escape her pain, Pecola hopes to become someone she is not—and she loses her mind when she comes to believe that her eyes have indeed changed, when in reality they have not.

To write *The Bluest Eye*, Morrison relied on her childhood memories of life in Lorain, Ohio. The young characters grow up in a neighborhood

of people and places a lot like those Morrison knew as a child. But the similarity ends there. Morrison grew up with a strong sense of pride and love for her African-American heritage, while Pecola is rejected by her family and the other adults and children in her neighborhood. She has no positive role models for beauty and blackness.

For Pecola's mother Pauline, women like the film star Jean Harlow were very beautiful.

The story takes place in the early 1940s, and even Pecola's mother Pauline is drawn to white film stars, such as Jean Harlow, for her own standard of beauty.[1] Morrison's narrator Claudia tells Pecola's sad story years later as an adult when she comes to understand her friend's low self-esteem and her struggle against heartache and pain.

Morrison began writing *The Bluest Eye* in 1967, and continued to write during the eighteen months she worked in Syracuse. Morrison sent her almost completed manuscript to many publishers, but it was not quickly accepted by the industry. Morrison decided not to give the manuscript to Random House, since she felt it would be an awkward conflict of interest. However, an editor at another publishing company liked her work, offered her a contract, and encouraged her to finish the novel.

In late 1969, she received a job promotion at Random House and moved her family to New York City. Morrison was transferred from the textbook division to the trade division where she worked on books for the general readers' market. Morrison found a house in Queens and enrolled her two sons in a new school. The new senior editor position meant more exposure to the publishing field and more work, but Morrison tried her best to adjust. She continued to write at night to counter the loneliness and tremendous responsibility she

felt as a single parent. Morrison discovered that writing gave her a sense of joy she had never known before. "Whether or not it [*The Bluest Eye*] was successful—or even whether or not it was published—I was committed already," Morrison said years later.[2] In an interview with *The Chicago Tribune*, Morrison told a reporter that the experience of writing her first novel was refreshing and brought a renewed sense of living.[3] The world outside her writing seemed far less interesting.

The Bluest Eye was published in 1970. Critical reviews of the novel were positive, though the sales were modest by publishing standards. Several reputable newspapers and book-review journals, such as *The New York Times Book Review*, *The Chicago Tribune, The New Yorker*, and *Newsweek*, reviewed *The Bluest Eye* and complimented Morrison for her writing style. Other reviews praised Morrison for daring to take an honest look at American racism and its damaging effects on the mental health and spiritual development of African-American children, particularly girls. Morrison was one of the first writers, black or white, to ask what happens to the mind, heart, and soul of a young African-American girl who is raised in a society that values beauty standards that are not her own.

"I've just finished reading Toni Morrison's

book, *The Bluest Eye*, and my heart hurts," wrote Ruby Dee, an African-American actress, in a review of the novel for a publication called *Freedomways*.[4] Dee wrote that she wanted to "lie down and cry" in response to the pain that young Pecola endures. Dee asked the reading public if, after reading *The Bluest Eye*, society can find a solution to one of the brutalities of racism—the reality of self-hatred. Dee encouraged both blacks and

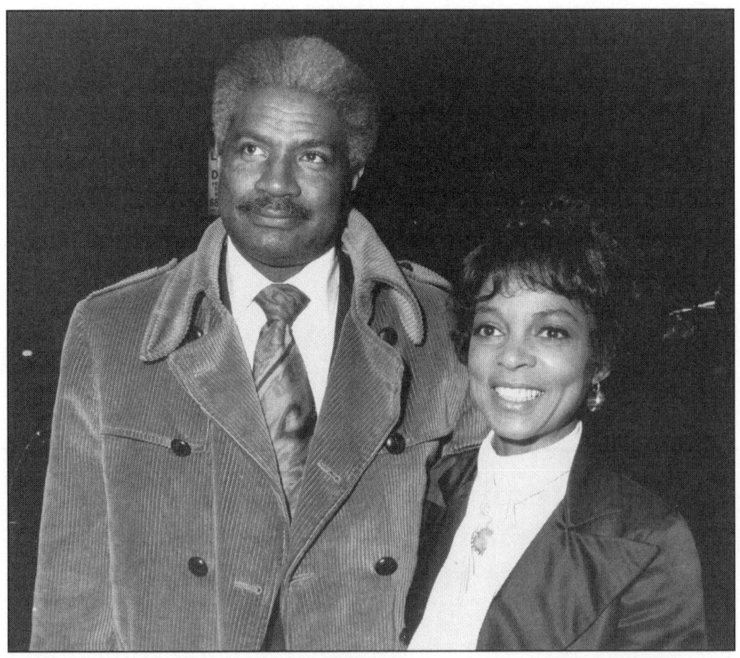

Ruby Dee (shown here with her husband Ossie Davis) wrote a very positive review of The Bluest Eye.

whites to "think faster and work harder" to create a more humane society.[5]

The Bluest Eye did not bring immediate fame to Morrison, but she became a well-respected critic and spokesperson for African-American culture, life, and literature. Several scholarly journals and literary publications approached Morrison to write book reviews and essays on the need for social, political, and legal equality for women. A new crusade called the Women's Movement was beginning to capture the nation's attention in the early 1970s. While the Women's Movement worked to solve the problems of mostly white middle-class women who were raised to take care of their husband and family rather than pursue a profession, Morrison could speak to the problems of working-class black women, like her mother Ramah, and other members of her family. These women struggled against racism and low wages in an effort to support their families. As a result of her background, Morrison was eager to respond. As an African-American woman, she brought a unique perspective to many of the social, political, and literary debates of the time. Eventually, Morrison wrote more than twenty reviews, mostly for *The New York Times*.

The Civil Rights Movement made some legal strides with the passage of two major civil rights laws such as the Civil Rights Act of 1964, which

forbids discrimination based on color, race, sex, religion, or national origin, and the Voting Rights Act of 1965, which forbids discrimination in voting. Despite these legal successes, blacks still did not enjoy many of the social, political, and economic rights that were given to whites. The door to racial equality was still not open, and the 1968 assassination of Dr. Martin Luther King Jr. left many African-Americans angry and disillusioned.

The point of view of black women in the literary and political circles of mainstream white society was invisible by the early 1970s. Two other African-American women, notably the poet Gwendolyn Brooks, winner of a Pulitzer Prize, and Lorraine Hansberry, the playwright, had been published in the 1960s, their writings were not generally used as material for literature courses in schools and colleges across the country. Nellie McKay, an editor and scholar of American and Afro-American literature, notes that at least fifty-nine books by African-American women were in print between 1859 (the publication year of *Our Nig* by Harriet Wilson, the first novel by a African-American woman) and 1964. And in the 1920s and 1930s, only one woman—Jesse Fauset—had published three novels.[6] While other African-American women writers had come before Morrison, few had received much notice for their work from mainstream literary circles. Morrison

hoped to bring attention to African-American women writers and their role in literature.

Before the publication of *The Bluest Eye*, Morrison believed something important was missing from African-American literature—the voice of the African-American female. Morrison said African-American men wrote many of the novels she read. Writers such as James Baldwin, author of the novel *Go Tell It on the Mountain*, Richard Wright, author of *Native Son*, and Ralph Ellison, author of the novel *Invisible Man*, were well-received and read by blacks and whites. But "there were no books about me, I didn't exist in all the literature I had read . . . this person, this female, this black did not exist . . .," Morrison said in an interview with the *Women's Review* in London years later.[7] Although some women writers, such as Eudora Welty, Lillian Hellman, and Nadine Gordimer, present many different perspectives of white women in society, most contemporary white female authors did not examine the complex and rich life of black women. "Where is the white woman who has written what it feels like to hate the black women who reared her?" Morrison asked in the *Women's Review*. "I'd like to hear that."[8]

"There were no books about me, I didn't exist in all the literature I had read."

Morrison hoped that someday the number and impact of African-American women writers in American literature would change, but even after the publication of *The Bluest Eye* she did not think of herself as a real writer. She still thought of herself as a book editor and teacher. In 1971, she accepted another teaching position, this time at the State University of New York at Purchase. Morrison agreed to work as a visiting professor of English with a flexible schedule, teaching for only a year. Meanwhile, she continued her editorship at Random House.

Morrison did not publish her second novel until 1973. She spent nearly two and a half years writing the story of a very close friendship between two African-American women who live completely different lives and have different points of views about what makes life worth living. The idea for *Sula* did not come easily. Morrison spent quite some time imagining the plot for the story. During her morning rides on the subway from Queens to Manhattan, Morrison would think of characters and dialogue for her novel, anxious to get home at night to write her thoughts on paper. Before she began writing, Morrison knew she wanted to examine the dilemma between good and evil. "One can never really define good and evil," Morrison said years later in an interview with the *Massachusetts Review*. "It depends on what uses you put it to. Evil is as

useful as good is."[9] In *Sula*, Morrison wanted to show that sometimes what society calls "evil" can also have a good purpose.

Morrison's characters, Sula and Nel, are the focus of the novel. Sula and Nel are born and raised in an African-American community called

Morrison after the publication of Sula

The Bottom, a tract of barren land given to a slave by a dishonest white landowner centuries earlier. The story takes place from 1919 to 1965. Sula and Nel are close friends as young girls and share most of their time and activities. As they grow older, their lives separate. Nel decides to remain in The Bottom after she gets married like most of the women in the town. Sula, however, leaves The Bottom to pursue an education and gain her independence from The Bottom's small-town ways. When Sula returns to the town ten years later, she has a series of affairs with several married men and even sleeps with Nel's husband, Jude. Soon, she becomes the outcast of the community. The men and women in The Bottom view Sula as an example of evil—a person with no conscience, a person who would do or say anything to satisfy her own desires. Sula is also criticized when she decides to place Eva, her grandmother, in a nursing home.

Despite her earlier friendship with Sula, Nel follows the popular opinion about her once-close confidante. She also views Sula as an outcast—until Sula's death. Nel is forced to come to terms with the truth of Sula's life and her own life choices. Nel must ask herself whether Sula was indeed "evil" or just misunderstood. Perhaps Sula was a good person who made bad choices—and those choices caused other people to view her as evil.

Sula dared to live her life outside the safe boundaries of her community, but she lived life on her own terms. Not many African-American women in the community had Sula's nerve or guts. Nel also wonders if the life she has led was indeed a good life, or a life lived in fear—the fear of rejection from her community or the fear of loneliness.

Literary editor and scholar Claudia Tate notes that Morrison did not consider herself to be a true writer until *Sula* was published.[10] Scholar and editor Karen Carmean agrees, pointing out that Morrison's second novel "challenges readers in ways *The Bluest Eye* does not, primarily because of Morrison's presentation of evil . . ." and the way her writing reveals that evil comes in many different forms.[11]

Critics had mixed reactions to the book. Some critics applauded Morrison for examining the reality of friendship between African-American women and for showing both the love and the estrangement that happen when two human beings relate to each other. Barbara Smith, a critic for *Freedomways*, wrote that Morrison was able to capture the strong bond between African-American women because she has personal knowledge of those relationships. "She has made a book for us that is beautiful, mysterious, and needed."[12] Scholar and editor Nellie McKay also credited Morrison for refusing to portray African-American

women in a degrading way. In the past, few African-American women characters appeared in books. And the few that did exist were portrayed as menial workers or sexual objects. Instead, Morrison created a female character, Sula, who becomes a heroine while also being a social outcast.[13]

Other critics, however, chastised Morrison for writing about the darker side of human relations, rather than portraying characters in a more uplifting and positive light, or at least presenting some statement or opinion about characters, like Sula, who make unwise life choices. For example, one critic wrote that Morrison, and other writers with similar literary aims, ignore these moral dilemmas.[14]

Sula proved to be a critical literary success for Morrison, although the book's sales were not extravagant. The book was nominated for the 1975 National Book Award for fiction, *Redbook* magazine published portions of the book, and the *Nation* and the *Harvard Advocate* praised Morrison's work.

Morrison's reputation as a book editor was also highly respected. Her work at Random House made her an editor-mentor for other upcoming African-American writers whose first books she helped to publish. Authors such as Toni Cade Bambara, author of *Tales and Stories for Black*

Folks, Gayl Jones, author of *Corregidora*, and Henry Dumas, author of *Ark of Bones and Other Stories*, worked with Morrison. Morrison also edited biographies written by famous African-American figures, such as Andrew Young, the civil rights activist, Angela Davis, the political activist, and Muhammad Ali, the champion heavyweight boxer.

Morrison's next undertaking for Random House was an African-American historical scrapbook called *The Black Book*, published in 1974. Morrison worked with four collectors of African-American culture to create a scrapbook of photographs, newspaper articles, slave narratives, song lyrics, and other memorabilia dating back to the times of slavery and covering three hundred years of African-American history. The book was put together by Morrison and Middleton (Spike) Harrison; comedian Bill Cosby wrote the introduction. The research Morrison did for *The Black Book* would someday be the inspiration for one of her most famous novels.

In her personal life, Morrison continued to juggle her work schedule, her writing, and raising her two sons. She moved her family from Queens to Spring Valley, New York, and began a daily commute to and from Manhattan. To help manage her household finances, Morrison left the State University of New York at Purchase and accepted

a visiting professor position at Yale University for the 1976–77 academic year. She agreed to teach a class on African-American women fiction writers while she also worked at Random House. To say the least, this left very little—if any—time for friends, or any social life at all. Morrison was still a single woman. "I considered marrying again, on several occasions, but I decided against it for two reasons," Morrison told *Time* magazine years later. "I didn't want to give up the delight of not having to answer to another person, and I was worried about how my two boys would react to a stepfather."[15] But the single life did not seem to bother her at all. "Sometimes I'll even forget to go if I've been invited to someone's house for dinner," Morrison would tell a reporter for *The New York Times* years later in an interview. "At this point in my life, anyone who's going to be a friend of mine is simply going to have to be able to understand that."[16]

However, the lack of male companionship in Morrison's life did not mean that she did not understand the male view of life, or that men did not interest her as characters for future novels. For example, Milkman Dead, the main character of Morrison's third novel, *Song of Solomon*, was born from Morrison's personal knowledge of the male mind and spirit. Morrison's father, George Wofford, died while she was writing the book, so

Morrison relied on her late-night conversations with his spirit to lead her through the manuscript. Morrison would imagine her father in her mind and communicate accordingly. In Morrison's family, a belief in the supernatural was a reality from which to draw strength and wisdom, and had never been something to fear. She learned this lesson as a child. Now, speaking to her father, Morrison found peace and guidance.

She relied on her experiences as the single parent of two sons and her relationship with her father to create Milkman. He was a man born in a small town in Michigan who leaves the Midwest to search for his family's roots in the South and learn whether or not it is possible to "fly."

Milkman Dead searches for peace of mind during his long journey to the South. His birth is quite an event—his mother Ruth gives birth to Milkman after she sees an insurance salesman, strapped in wings, try to fly off a hospital rooftop. The strange sight starts Ruth's labor and Milkman is born—the first black child born in a previously all-white hospital. Milkman's father, Macon Dead, the richest landowner in the African-American community, advises his son to follow in his footsteps by becoming a landowner, too. "The most important thing you'll ever need to know," Macon Dead declares, "[is to] own things. And let the things you own own other things. Then you'll own

yourself and other people too."[17] Macon Dead is a man who believes that only money and property are the measure of a person's worth.

However, Milkman eventually defies his father's wishes and instead learns his family history from his aunt Pilate, a woman born with no navel, who carries a bag of bones, and wears a brass box for earrings. Milkman learns about a miner's sack of gold buried along a riverbank in the wilderness and leaves Michigan to search for it. Instead, he discovers his true family history and uncovers the legend of his great-grandfather Solomon and his "flight" from slavery to freedom in Africa.

Song of Solomon was published in 1977. It has become, perhaps, one of the best examples of why both literary critics and readers—black and white—in time have come to consider Morrison one of the finest novelists in America—and even the world. Critics note that in *Song of Solomon*, Morrison combined some of the most important elements of African-American culture, classic Greek literature, European-American literary styles, and Christianity. Critics noted that Morrison relied upon African-American and classical Greek folktales as the foundation for the plot. They said that she drew from myths of human flight—the legends of African slaves flying to freedom, and Daedalus, the ancient Greek who makes

a pair of wings to escape prison with his son, Icarus. Morrison said later that her story was inspired by African folktales, not Greek mythology. Morrison also gave her characters common names from the Bible—Solomon, Pilate, Hagar, and Ruth. Scholar Karen Carmean notes that Morrison may have named her novel after her grandfather John Solomon Willis, in tribute to him.[18]

Morrison's ability to weave these elements into a complex and lyrical novel, with an African-American male character as its hero—a rare story plot for an African-American woman writer in the late 1970s—made *Song of Solomon* Morrison's most influential book. It won the National Book Critics Circle Award for fiction for that year and was also featured on the front page of *The New York Times Book Review*. Morrison was honored when *Song of Solomon* became a major book selection for the Book-of-the-Month Club, the only book written by an African-American to earn that tribute since Richard Wright's *Native Son* in 1940.

Critics no longer viewed Morrison as an aspiring writer. She had become an important literary presence in the publishing industry—a true writer. Melvin Dixon, a reviewer for a publication called *Callaloo*, called Morrison's novel a "brilliant, compelling achievement."[19] Samuel Allen, a critic for the *Boston University Journal*, wrote

"the novel is the product of a skilled artisan," who managed to combine the two traditions of gospel and the classics.[20]

The U.S. academic and literary establishment agreed with the critics. In 1977, Morrison was appointed to the American Academy Institute of Arts and Letters, and President Jimmy Carter appointed her to the National Council on the Arts. However, even before Morrison received critical acclaim, she placed her faith in the book's eventual success and resigned from her position at Random House to devote herself to a full-time career as a writer and teacher. She left her visiting professorship at Yale University. Her belief in *Song of Solomon*'s success became a reality—the book was hailed as a triumph. Toni Morrison was now a well-recognized and respected American writer and intellectual. Her life would never be quite the same again.

CHAPTER FIVE

BELOVED

The tremendous success of *Song of Solomon* made it possible for Morrison to once again make important changes in her personal life. The book's sales enabled her to move from Spring Valley, New York, to a three-story, newly designed boathouse on the Hudson River in Grandview-on-Hudson, New York, in the early 1980s. She now worked only part-time at an editing position at Random House. She agreed to return to Random House to work on various editorial projects for the publisher, but her main concerns now were her writing and her private life.

Morrison took time out to tend a flower garden and she changed her writing hours from late at night to the early hours of the morning. She continued to write during quiet and peaceful times, but now she woke at 5:00 A.M, rather than falling asleep in the wee hours of the morning. Morrison would sit outside on her porch or on her

own private dock on the river to jot down story ideas, characters, and dialogue. Morrison was already an intensely private person, and the increased solitude gave her even more time to write and read works by other authors.

While settling into her new home, Morrison began work on her fourth book, *Tar Baby*. The novel tells the story of a passionate, yet turbulent, love affair between a young, sophisticated, college-educated, and French-speaking black model named Jadine Childs, and Son Green, an African-American fugitive who escapes from Florida to an island called Isle des Chevaliers in the West Indies. It is on this island that Son meets Jadine and her uncle and aunt, Sydney and Ondine Childs, a butler and cook. The Childses work for Valerian Street, a wealthy white man who has retired from his candy factory in Philadelphia. Street and his wife Margaret move to the island and live in a mansion called L'Abre de la Croix. In Morrison's story Jadine and the Streets find Son in the mansion. Son is a thief who accidentally killed his wife. To escape the law, Son had gotten on a ship and jumped overboard, swimming to Isle des Chevaliers. Son's appearance causes an uproar in the home, but Valerian Street allows him to stay. During this short stay, Son and Jadine fall in love.

Jadine and Son, though from different economic and social backgrounds, have an affair.

Jadine runs off with Son to New York despite the fact that a rich man in France has asked her to marry him. In New York, Son realizes that he cannot adjust to Jadine's "superficial" world and her upper-middle-class values. He convinces Jadine to come with him to his hometown, Eloe, in Florida. However, Jadine is not satisfied with the simple, small-town country life of the South. The two lovers cannot come to terms with their differences, and Jadine's family in Isle des Chevaliers struggles to find peace when an old family secret of child abuse is discovered after Son is found in their home.

The clash of social and economic values between Jadine and Son is also part of their view of what it means to be black. Morrison based the plot of the novel partly on an African-American folktale called "Tar Baby." The folktale has its roots in West African culture. In Morrison's novel, some literary critics have come to interpret the folktale as symbolizing the differences in African-American social classes. There are many versions of the tale, but when Morrison wrote "Tar Baby" she used the version she heard as a child.

In this version, a white farmer makes a "tar baby" out of a mixture of tar and turpentine. He creates the figure to get rid of an annoying rabbit that has caused damage in his garden. The farmer dresses the tar baby in a skirt and hat and sets it

in the garden to trap the rabbit. When Brer Rabbit sees the tar baby, he comes close and says "Good morning," hoping to hear a friendly reply. When the tar baby does not respond, the rabbit gets angry and hits the figure. Unfortunately, the rabbit gets stuck in the tar. When the farmer sees Brer Rabbit in the tar, the rabbit tries to fool the farmer with a rhyme. "Boil me in oil, skin me alive, but please do not throw me in that briar patch!" Not knowing the rhyme is a trick, the farmer throws the rabbit into the briar patch. The rabbit manages to escape, saying to the farmer, "This is where I was born and bred at!" The folktale was written by Joel Chandler Harris, a white American writer.

Critics view Morrison's use of the Tar Baby folktale in different ways. Critic Robert O'Meally, a reviewer for *Callaloo* magazine, wrote that Jadine represents the tar baby and Son represents Brer Rabbit. Son views Jadine as a kind of "tar baby"—a "tricky white man's creation set to waylay the black man." Son, meanwhile, is Brer Rabbit, whose home is down in the briar patch. At the end of the novel, O'Meally wrote that Son is "loosed from her grasp and runs: lickety-split, lickety-split."[1] Literature professor Karen Carmean writes that "Son and Jadine are opposites in the most essential ways, incompatible in their personal hopes and dreams. On the other

hand, they can't entirely let go of each other, as if stuck to a tar baby."[2]

Although *Tar Baby* is the first Morrison novel to include white central characters—Valerian and Margaret Street—her use of the "Tar Baby" folktale shows her commitment to analyzing complex relationships between African-Americans and their cultural roots.

Tar Baby received mixed reviews when it was published in 1981. Some critics praised Morrison (who took three and a half years to write the book) for her lyrical language, her use of folktales, and the rich images she created to describe the people and places in the novel. However, other critics felt Morrison devoted too much energy to the book's imagery and not enough to the development of her characters or plot.

The book's reviews may have been mixed, but the media gave Morrison a lot of attention when the novel was published. *Newsweek* magazine featured Morrison on its front cover on March 30, 1981, to give readers an up-close and personal view of one of the country's finest writers. Morrison was the second African-American woman writer to receive such exposure—the first was Zora Neale Hurston, author of the 1937 novel *Their Eyes Were Watching God*. Hurston appeared on the magazine's cover some forty years earlier.[3]

"Are you really going to put a middle-aged, gray-haired colored lady on the cover of this mag-

Zora Neale Hurston was the first African-American woman writer to appear on the cover of Newsweek.

azine?" Morrison jokingly asked *Newsweek*'s editorial staff when she visited the publisher's office for the cover photograph.[4] The staff said "Yes," and they called the article, "Toni Morrison's Black Magic." The article appeared along with photos of

Morrison as a child, her parents, grandparents, and her two sons.

The *Newsweek* article gave many of Morrison's colleagues the opportunity to comment on her contributions to African-American and American literature. "Toni has done more to encourage and publish other black writers than anyone I know," said Andrew Young, the civil rights activist and politician.[5] Writer Toni Cade Bambara, a Morrison protégée, credited the author for her work as a "superb" editor and novelist. "The fact

James Baldwin praised Morrison's work in the Newsweek *article.*

that she is there, with her canny, spooky voice, gives other people inspiration to fly."[6] Perhaps one of the article's greatest compliments came from James Baldwin, the highly respected African-American writer. "We still overlook the incredible stamina—Toni would say 'sheer intelligence'—of black women in their ability to be all those things which somehow hold a black man together. Toni shows this, with a sense of humor, that is the key to a sense of life."[7]

Tar Baby sold extremely well on its own and made *The New York Times* best-seller list thirty days after its publication. Not long after *Tar Baby*'s release, Morrison told an interviewer she was pleased with her growth as a writer. She said that her goal was to become a better writer—not to become a success among critics or readers, who often commented that her novels were too complex. She believed her readers could meet the challenges presented by her work.

Two years after *Tar Baby*'s publication, Morrison finally decided to give up her part-time position at Random House. After completing her professorship at Yale University in 1977, Morrison served as a lecturer at Bard College in upstate New York in 1979. In 1984, she was appointed as the Albert Schweitzer Professor of Humanities at the State University of New York in Albany. Her new responsibilities included teaching creative

writing and African-American literature, and helping students improve their skills in writing fiction. The new teaching position also made it possible for Morrison to try her hand at another artistic form—playwriting.

The New York State Writers Institute at the State University of New York at Albany, led by William Kennedy, a Pulitzer Prize-winning writer, contracted Morrison to write a play to honor Dr. Martin Luther King, Jr., and the observance of the first federal holiday celebrating the slain civil rights leader's birthday. The holiday is observed on the third Monday in January.

Once again, Morrison looked to African-American history and culture to create her play. She decided to base her work on the 1955 murder of a fourteen-year-old African-American boy named Emmett Till. The tragedy occurred one summer day when Till, a native of Chicago, visited family members in Mississippi. Till was shot twice in the head and beaten after a group of white men kidnapped him from his uncle's house. The men claimed Till had whistled at a young white woman named Carolyn Bryant a few days before at a local store, and they had come to punish him for the offense. Three days after the kidnapping, Till's body was found in the Tallahatchie River.

Till's death was a national horror. It motivated many African-Americans to work even harder for civil rights in the South. However, when the

The story of the brutal murder of Emmett Till inspired Morrison to write a play.

men who killed Till went to trial, an all-white jury found them not guilty of murder.

In Morrison's play, titled *Dreaming Emmett*, Till overcomes death and returns to tell the audience—and the world—the truth about how he was cruelly killed. In an interview with the press,

Morrison said the play was about “a boy’s imagination,” and the possibilities that exist if an African-American child’s imagination is allowed to grow undisturbed by death. Said Morrison, “What is it like if his dreams are fulfilled?”[8] The play opened two weeks before the first observance of the King holiday in 1986.

The plot of Morrison’s next novel, *Beloved*, also included details from a terrible period in African-American and American history—the time of slavery. While doing research several years earlier for *The Black Book*, Morrison found a newspaper article about a black woman named Margaret Garner who had escaped slavery in Kentucky and relocated to Ohio in an attempt to save herself and her children from the brutalities of her white slave master. The article told the story of how Garner had cut her baby daughter’s throat with a jigsaw to prevent the slave catchers from finding her alive and bringing her back to the plantation in Kentucky. The article appeared in a newspaper called *American Baptist* in 1856.

Garner’s story became the inspiration for the plot of *Beloved*, Morrison’s fifth novel. The book would be the first in a three-part series of novels Morrison planned to examine the various kinds of love. In the novel, Morrison tells the story of a runaway slave named Sethe who escapes from her plantation, called Sweet Home, after arranging

the escape of her children. Sethe hopes to meet her husband later at an agreed-upon destination. Pregnant with a daughter, Sethe manages to find her way to a small town outside Cincinnati, Ohio. She comes to the house of an African-American woman named Baby Suggs, her mother-in-law. When Sethe arrives, her baby daughter has been born, and her three other children are safe at Baby Suggs home. However, some time later, slave catchers from Sweet Home discover Sethe and her children. Rather than see her children

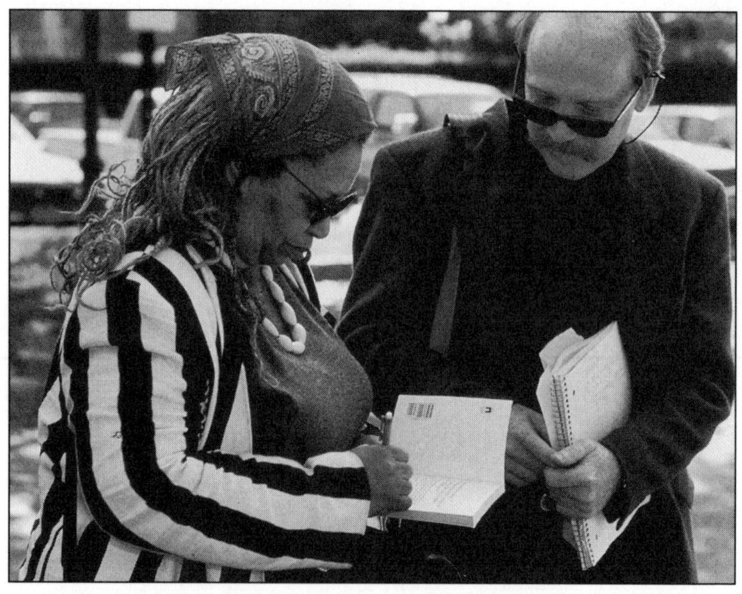

Morrison signs a copy of Beloved *for a fan.*

captured and enslaved, Sethe hits her two sons on the head with a shovel and cuts the throat of her infant daughter. A family member stops Sethe before she is able to harm her other daughter, Denver.

The novel begins in 1873, almost twenty years after the infant daughter's death. Sethe and Denver live alone together in Baby Suggs' home. Baby Suggs is dead. For several years, the home has been haunted by a ghost. The hauntings are so frightening that Sethe's two sons, who have recovered from their head injuries, run away—never to be found. Denver remains with her mother, who has become a social outcast in town because of the supernatural hauntings and the atrocity she has committed—killing her child. Paul D, a former slave who lived on the Sweet Home plantation with Sethe years ago, appears at Sethe's home and moves in with her and Denver. In time, Sethe and Paul D begin a romance, and the ghost begins to terrorize the family even more. In a fit of rage, Paul D manages to throw the ghost out of the home. But when they meet Beloved, a mysterious young woman who shows up at Sethe's home and tries to live with the family, the characters come to believe that the ghost has reappeared. In time, Sethe and Denver believe that Beloved is the ghost of the infant daughter who was killed years ago. Why has

Beloved come back? Why was she killed? Was her death necessary? Should Sethe be judged for her crime? The characters struggle with these questions throughout the novel, as well as coming to terms with the impact of slavery upon their lives.

Morrison hoped *Beloved* would tell not only Sethe's story, but the life stories of the millions of Africans who died, or survived, during slavery in the American South. To accomplish this task, Morrison buried herself in research and learned all she could about the Middle Passage—the journey of Africans who were transported from Africa to slavery in North and South America and the Caribbean. She also wanted to learn how the Africans were actually treated by their slave masters, but Morrison found few sources for her research. She did find some slave narratives—stories told by the slaves themselves—and the writings of slave owners. But even visits to museums revealed little information. She also relied on folktales and slave songs, but found little information about the horrors slaves faced. Morrison had hoped to learn about what she calls the "interior life" of slaves—their deepest and inner-most thoughts and feelings about the day-to-day struggle of their lives. However, few sources provided the story Morrison hoped to tell.

Morrison did not give up, however. She finally decided to leave the United States to do

research in Brazil. In Brazil, she visited slave museums and found exhibits that included the actual chains and other iron fixtures used to punish slaves or to keep them from running away. These artifacts helped Morrison create a novel that came very close to the reality of life for African slaves—close to their interior lives. Morrison did not want to write about slavery as a social institution, or "slavery with a capital 'S.' It was about these anonymous people called slaves," she has said, and "What they do to keep on, how they make a life. What they are willing to risk, however long it lasts, in order to relate to one another."[9]

Morrison's dedication to her research paid off when *Beloved* was published in 1987. In the first seven days after its publication, the book made *The New York Times* best-seller list and received very favorable reviews from most critics. The scene of Sethe's infant daughter's death is riveting in the novel, *New York Times* reviewer Michiko Kakutani wrote, the murder is "so brutal and disturbing that it appears to warp time before and after into a single unwavering line of fate."[10] The *Los Angeles Times* called the novel a "masterwork" that should be kept "on the highest shelf in American literature."[11] Morrison dedicated *Beloved* to the 60 million Africans who some historians believed died during the Middle Pas-

sage to North and South America and the Caribbean.

The literary establishment was impressed with Morrison's work, but several other writers and critics became gravely concerned when *Beloved* did not earn the National Book Award or the National Book Critics Circle Award for the year, both very prestigious awards in publishing. After all, Morrison's earlier novels, for example, *Sula*, was nominated for the National Book Award in 1975, and *Song of Solomon* won the National Book Critics Circle Award two years later. Forty-eight African-American writers and critics wrote a letter to *The New York Times Book Review* to lament the fact that although Morrison's literary work was exceptional, she had not received national recognition for her efforts. The letter was published on January 24, 1988.

Three months later, Morrison's *Beloved* won the Pulitzer Prize for Fiction. The Pulitzer Prize is one of the most distinguished awards in America. Each year the award is given for excellence in journalism, literature, music, and drama. Joseph Pulitzer, a prominent newspaper publisher, established the award and it has been given to exceptional writers and artists since 1917.

Some literary critics raised their eyebrows after the prize was given to Morrison, noting that the letter in *The New York Times Book Review*

may have influenced the Pulitzer Board's decision. The board, which selects the winners, made it clear that it was influenced only by the credibility of Morrison's work when it decided to give her the award. "Obviously the board was aware of the statement [letter], but, no, it didn't affect their decision," said Robert Christopher, secretary of the Pulitzer Board, when asked if the letter to *The New York Times* had an impact on the members. "I think there was some feeling that it would be unfortunate if anyone diluted the value of Toni Morrison's achievement by suggesting that her prize rested on anything but her merit."[12]

Morrison, who made it clear she was not aware of the letter before its publication, told *The New York Times Book Review* she felt the prize was given to her fairly, despite the "gossip and speculation" that surrounded the event. "In the end I feel as though I served the characters in the book well, and I hope the Pulitzer people are as proud of me as I am of them," Morrison said, calling the signed letter "a kind of blessing for me." Morrison believed her colleagues "appreciated the worth of my work for them." Said Morrison, "They redeemed me, but I am certain they played no significant role in the judgment."[13] Morrison later received the Pulitzer Prize at an award ceremony at Columbia University in New York.

Although Morrison had been given one of the

most important literary awards in the country, she did not neglect her teaching career. A month after *Beloved*'s publication, Morrison accepted an appointment to the Robert F. Goheen Professorship in the Humanities Council at Princeton University to teach creative writing. Morrison was very pleased with her position at the State University of New York at Albany, and she was not too anxious to leave the post. However, Princeton University's commitment to liberal arts and education convinced her that the new position was the right choice. "I take teaching as seriously as I do my writing," Morrison said in an interview. "Princeton's notion of what constitutes serious teaching dovetails with mine. You get a small number of students who are working on projects and stay with them for a year or even two."[14] Morrison said her aim in teaching students is to "help writers best do what they do best."

"I take teaching as seriously as I do my writing."

The professorship, which began in 1989, allowed Morrison to teach courses in African-American studies, American studies, and women's studies. To accommodate her new teaching schedule, Morrison would eventually purchase another home in Princeton, New Jersey.

Morrison took five years to complete her next

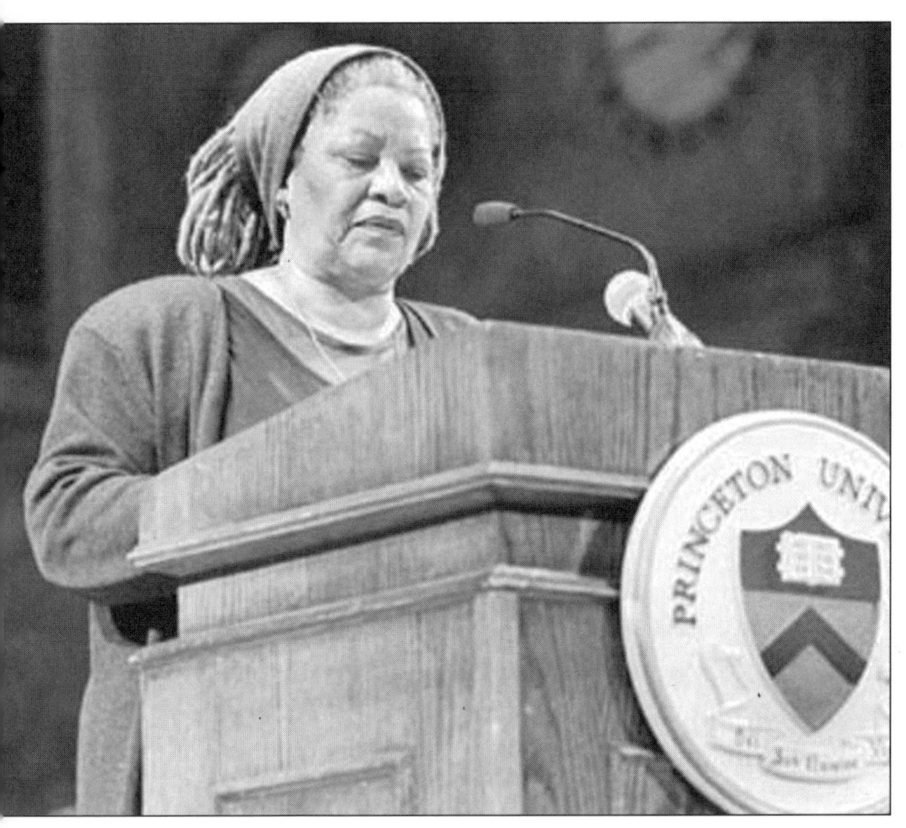

Morrison gives a reading at Princeton University.

three projects, a sixth novel called *Jazz*, a book of literary criticism called *Playing in the Dark: Whiteness and the Literary Imagination*, and a book of political essays called *Race-ing Justice, EnGendering Power: Essays on Anita Hill, Clarence Thomas, and the Constitution of Social Reality*.

Morrison published the second novel in her three-part series on love in 1992. The book, *Jazz*, tells the sad tale of the undoing of Joe and Violet Trace, a married African-American couple who leave the segregated South to live in Harlem, New York City in the mid-1920s. Like other southern African-Americans, Joe and Violet hope to find work and a better way of life in the city. However, during the early 1920s, while African-American artists, writers, and musicians in Harlem thrive, African-Americans in the cities also face racial prejudice. During the summer of 1919, blacks in cities across the country, such as Chicago and Washington, D.C., barely survive the attacks of vicious white mobs. The violence was so bad that the riots became known as the "Red Summer."

In *Jazz*, Joe and Violet's marriage crumbles when Joe, a middle-aged man, falls in love with Dorcas, an eighteen-year-old woman. In a fit of passion, Joe shoots and kills his lover Dorcas. Violet, who finds out about the affair, later tries to cut the face of the young woman's corpse at the funeral. In this novel, Morrison examined the extremes of romantic love between a man and a woman.

Similar to some of her earlier works, Morrison relies on artifacts from African-American culture to create her story. The idea for the novel is taken from a book of photographs called *The*

Harlem Book of the Dead, by James Van Der Zee, a famous African-American photographer who worked during the Harlem Renaissance. A photograph of a young girl lying in a coffin—shot by her jealous ex-boyfriend—sparked Morrison's imagination for the story.

Once again, Morrison's work drew mixed reactions from critics. Some continued to praise Morrison for her lyrical writing style and gift of storytelling, while others felt the style was too cumbersome for readers to enjoy the plot. Literature professor Karen Carmean writes that Morrison selected the title *Jazz* because the word "originally was a slang term for sexual passion" and because the word is known "for the most famous kind of black music, a special kind of music that aspires to come from and produce pure emotion."[15]

Morrison tried to organize her novel like a piece of jazz music. Carmean writes that the novel, like jazz, has a "fast opening, establishing a dominant note and theme," and then the novel "breaks into different parts—various stories [passages] and voices [instruments] . . ."[16] Carmean writes that the novel is inspired "by the whole range of human feelings,"[17] just as jazz music is a musician's vision of human emotions and life experiences.

Morrison's book of literary criticism was quite

a departure from her focus on writing fiction. In *Playing in the Dark*, Morrison examined the role of race in the works of other famous fiction writers, notably Edgar Allen Poe, Mark Twain, Ernest Hemmingway, Willa Cather, and others, to understand their treatment of African-American characters. As a result of her studies, Morrison found that many white writers shortchanged American readers by simply avoiding black characters, or portraying them as stereotypes. However, when white authors dared to create black characters, Morrison wrote that literary critics did not attempt to point out how important the African-American characters were to American literature. She also found that literary critics were reluctant to comment on the racial point of view of white American authors. "Black people and black things and Africa-type things are understood to be blank space for white imagination," Morrison said in an interview with the *Washington Post*. "It's the 'Heart of Darkness.' No Africans talk in there."[18] *Playing in the Dark* was based in part on a series of lectures Morrison gave at Harvard University while she was writing *Jazz*.[19]

Race was also an important factor in *Race-ing Justice*, Morrison's collection of political essays. A year before the book's publication, the nation had focused its attention on the controversial confirmation hearings of Clarence Thomas, a

conservative African-American judge and nominee for the U.S. Supreme Court. Anita Hill, an African-American law professor from Oklahoma, who worked with Thomas years earlier, accused Thomas of sexual harassment. The political debate between Thomas's denial of sexual harassment, and Hill's serious charges was fierce, particularly in the African-American community where no consensus could be found.

Morrison became concerned that important social and political issues were not being addressed in the furor over Thomas' confirmation, so she

Anita Hill accused Clarence Thomas of sexual harassment and sparked a national debate.

asked several scholars and intellectuals to write their opinion about whether Thomas or Hill had been given a fair hearing. Despite the allegations against him, Clarence Thomas was eventually approved for the Supreme Court by the U.S. Senate. *Race-ing Justice* was published soon after the political debate. Some critics praised the writers for their influential views on race and class, but commented that the essays seemed to be repetitive. The conservative press knocked the book for its liberal bent in favor of Hill and against Thomas.

While reviews for *Race-ing Justice* were lukewarm, *Jazz* and *Playing in the Dark* became bestsellers on *The New York Times* book list. However, the critical response to *Playing in the Dark* was not complimentary. Morrison's examination of racial stereotypes and attitudes in American literature did not win the approval of some political conservatives. Her findings were severely criticized in the conservative press, which insisted that Morrison had not contributed any worthy scholarship to the race debate.[20] However, many other scholars of African-American and American literature view *Playing in the Dark* as an important academic examination of American literature and culture.

Morrison took the criticism in stride. She was not disheartened. Instead, she devoted her time to another creative project that was also unveiled in

1992. Morrison had been contracted by Carnegie Hall a year earlier to write song lyrics to an original musical score written by composer André Previn. The project was called “Honey and Rue,” a collection of songs that was eventually performed

Kathleen Battle sang the lyrics Morrison wrote for “Honey and Rue.”

live and recorded by Kathleen Battle, the African-American opera singer.

Battle, in an interview for the project, said she thought Morrison would be a perfect match for the song collection when she thought of Morrison's novel *The Bluest Eye*. "I imagined as I read subsequent works of hers, how thrilling it would be to hear her words set to music," Battle said.[21] Morrison, in the same interview, was also excited about her creative contributions. "I was interested in the marriage of language and music," said Morrison. "The best of all possible things was to hear Kathleen sing the songs."[22]

Morrison's colleagues and critics would be surprised by the next achievement in her life. She was soon to be considered one of the finest fiction writers in the world.

CHAPTER SIX

WHAT IS PARADISE?

The Nobel Committee of the Swedish Academy in Stockholm, Sweden, made no one prouder than Toni Morrison was when it gave her the Nobel Prize in Literature in 1993. "I feel good about this, really good," Morrison said in an interview with the *Washington Post*. "Part of the pleasure is the fact that it was wholly unexpected. It's not a narrow, personal, subjective delight. I feel it on a very large scale."[1]

Morrison's family, friends, and colleagues rushed to congratulate her when they heard the news. Morrison was especially happy to hear from other African-American writers. "[The prize] feels expanded somehow, like a very large honor, because one can share it with more people than one's neighborhood, or one's family. I feel like it is shared among us [African-American writers]."[2]

The prize gave Morrison a sense of recognition she had not had before—even as the winner

of a Pulitzer Prize. The Nobel's international scope could not be ignored, but Morrison, as usual, kept the honor and its prestige in perspective. "When I heard I'd won, you heard no 'Aw, shucks,' from me," Morrison told *Time* magazine. "The prize

Morrison said that she appreciated the award, but did not let it alter her view of herself.

didn't change my inner assessment of what I'm capable of doing, but I welcomed it as a public, representational affirmation of my work . . . I felt pride that a black and a woman had been recognized in such an international forum."[3]

Morrison returned from her weeklong celebration in Sweden in mid-December 1993, and went back to work at Princeton University where her colleagues and students shared in her happiness. Unfortunately, this joyous time ended when Morrison faced a personal tragedy just a few weeks after her return. Her Grandview-on-Hudson home in upstate New York burned to the ground on Christmas Day. Morrison's son, Slade, was home when the fire started, but fortunately no one was injured.

The fire was sudden and swift. It began at 9:00 A.M. after an ember from a fireplace landed on a sofa. According to press reports, Slade tried to put out the fire himself, but the flames burned out of control and he rushed to call the fire department. Soon after the fire trucks arrived, flames could be seen coming from the house's windows. Slade called his mother at Princeton University. By the time Morrison got there, her home was already demolished. Morrison made no comments to the press, but Howard Dodson, chief of the Schomburg Center for Research in Black Culture in New York, and a friend of Morrison's, told

reporters that family members said she was "upset over the loss of the house." Immediately, both Morrison and Dodson were concerned about Morrison's original book manuscripts and whether they had been destroyed in the fire.

"The house was almost totally destroyed, but indications are that the major part of the manuscripts and other material in the basement were not severely damaged," Dodson told *The New York Times*.[4] However, since the fire, the surviving manuscripts have been kept at the Firestone Library in Princeton University. The manuscripts are being preserved and are not on view to the general public.

In a television interview three years after the tragedy, Morrison said that after the fire happened, she could not share her thoughts about it with anyone for quite some time. She became depressed and worried that she had lost belongings that could never be replaced, such as her children's report cards, or the original manuscript of her novel *Song of Solomon*. However, Morrison, later recovered, and decided to rebuild her home while she continues to live in Princeton, New Jersey, during the school year.

Morrison dedicated the next five years to writing the third novel in her three-part series on love. But in the meantime, she directed her energies to her responsibilities as a professor at

Princeton University. In 1994, Morrison created the Atelier (a French word meaning "artist's studio") Program at Princeton. The purpose of the program is to allow students to work together with professional artists and faculty members to create original projects in the visual arts, literature, music, dance, film, and theater. The students, artists, and faculty members meet in small groups at weekly workshops, in which the students work with the artists to develop a group project for the semester. The project can be an originally choreographed dance, an opera, a dramatic play, or a short film documentary, depending on what the group decides to work on. "There is a very complicated and exhilarating process that [the students] will go through when they work with people in other genres," Morrison said in an interview about the special program. "That's where the spark is."[5]

The program has received funding from the Samuel I. Newhouse Foundation, alumni, and friends of the university.[6] Students apply for admission to the program and are often recommended by faculty members. Morrison also participates in the workshops, giving her own creative guidance in addition to teaching her own creative writing classes.

Since the program began, several professional artists, including Bernice Johnson Reagon, founder of the a cappella gospel/folk group Sweet

Honey In The Rock, have participated in the Atelier. Jacques d'Amboise, a choreographer and lead dancer with the New York City Ballet, has also contributed, along with Yo-Yo Ma, a master cellist, A.S. Byatt, a master fiction writer, and Peter Sellars, a master director.

"We didn't feel like we were novices or were doing something that wasn't worthwhile," said Tom Ford, a classics major and 1997 Princeton graduate who participated in the program. Ford made his comments in an interview with *Princeton Alumni Weekly*. "The artists had the same sort of expectations of us that they would have had of people who were doing this professionally. They seemed to be operating under the same assumption that we were capable to doing something of genuine artistic worthiness and they were careful not to step on us creatively."[7]

In January 1995, Morrison and her family were honored by the Lorain Public Library in Morrison's hometown. The library opened the Toni Morrison Reading Room in Morrison's honor. Morrison was flattered and traveled back home to her family to attend a special opening ceremony. Several months later, in the spring, Morrison returned to her alma mater, Howard University in Washington, D.C., to receive a Doctor of Humane Letters degree—an honorary academic degree.

A year later, the National Endowment for the Humanities named Morrison the Jefferson

Morrison cuts the ribbon on the Toni Morrison Reading Room at the Lorain Public Library.

Lecturer in Humanities for 1996. That honor is the highest award given by the United States government for excellence and achievement in the humanities. The award is given for "distinguished intellectual achievement in the humanities." Morrison received a $10,000 cash award and delivered a speech on modern humanity and the future at the Kennedy Center in Washington, D.C. "Toni

Morrison is one of America's greatest contemporary novelists," said Sheldon Hackney, chairman of the National Endowment for the Humanities, which established the award in 1972. "Taking as her subject the cosmos of African-American experience and folklore, she brilliantly dramatizes in her novel the archetypal theme of the quest for individual and cultural identity and the sometimes confusing influence of family in that quest."[8]

In December 1996, Morrison was recognized by a new literary audience—the watchers of "The Oprah Winfrey Show." Oprah Winfrey, the popular African-American daytime talk show host, selected Morrison's novel, *Song of Solomon*, for the Oprah Winfrey Book Club. The result was a second wave of success for the novel. The book club, created by Winfrey, includes Winfrey's national audience of viewers. The viewers and Winfrey read the selected book and later a show is dedicated to the author and the book for an open discussion. Six audience members are chosen for a private dinner with Winfrey and the author to be broadcast at a later date.

Morrison had no idea of Winfrey's tremendous influence in the publishing industry and was not a regular viewer of "The Oprah Winfrey Show." "I'd never heard of such a thing," said Morrison when asked about the Oprah Winfrey Book

Club in an interview with *Time* magazine. ". . . All I could think was 'Who's going to buy a book because of Oprah?'"[9] According to Morrison, one million additional copies of *Song of Solomon* were sold, due to its selection for the book club, and sales of Morrison's other novels reportedly jumped 25 percent.

"All I could think was 'Who's going to buy a book because of Oprah?'"

Morrison's relationship with Oprah Winfrey would flourish creatively. Winfrey not only selected another Morrison novel, *The Bluest Eye,* for her book club, but she also purchased the movie rights to Morrison's novel *Beloved*. The movie became one of the most eagerly awaited films in recent years.

Morrison once again turned to writing song lyrics in 1997. This time, she collaborated with composer Richard Danielpour to write lyrics for original music called "Sweet Talk: Four Songs on Text." The project, which started in Morrison's Atelier program at Princeton University, debuted at Carnegie Hall in April 1997. Jessye Norman, the African-American opera singer, performed the songs in concert. "It's [writing lyrics] the only writing I do that is as close to thrilling as writing fiction," Morrison told a *USA Today* reporter.[10]

Morrison's third novel in her three-part series

Oprah Winfrey encouraged her viewers to read some of Morrison's books.

on love, *Paradise*, was considered long overdue by literary critics and readers. The novel, published in January 1998, was called Morrison's most ambitious book to date, and literary reviews were mixed. "I'm mad. Something I forgot to do is bothering me a lot," Morrison told *The New York Times* not long after the book's publication. "The last word in the book *Paradise* should have a small 'p,' not a capital P. The whole point is to get paradise off its pedestal as a place for anyone, to open it up

for passengers and crew. I want all the readers to put a lowercase mark on that 'p.'"[11]

Paradise readers are taken to an all-African-American town called Ruby in Oklahoma in 1976. The town's history dates back to the 1870s when a group of African-American families, former slaves, leave the misery of Mississippi and Louisiana to search for freedom and prosperity in Oklahoma. Along the way, they meet other African-Americans at a town called Fairly, but they are rejected because of their dark skin tones. The men continue their travels and eventually start their own town called Haven. Haven becomes a close-knit rural community where everyone uses the same town oven to cook. No outsiders are allowed in the town. But after World War II, the close network of families and businesses begin to dwindle as people leave for the cities. The grandsons of Haven's founders pick up their families, take apart the town's oven, and move away to start a new town called Ruby. Like Haven, Ruby is also isolated and restricted from outsiders. It is located more than 90 miles (145 kilometers) from the nearest community, except for a small house of refuge for women called the Convent.

The novel begins when one of the women in the Convent—a white girl—is shot by a group of black male leaders from Ruby. The women's con-

vent is considered to be a threat to the rigid morality in Ruby. The women, who have come to live together after surviving various life tragedies and misfortunes, practice a combination of an African and Christian religion. Some of the men in Ruby believe that the religion and the women are immoral, and so they decide to destroy the Convent and the women in it.

"The book coalesced around the idea of where paradise is, and who belongs in it," Morrison told a reporter for *The New York Times*. "All paradises are described as male enclaves, while the interloper is a woman, defenseless and threatening. When we get ourselves together and get powerful is when we are assaulted."[12] The race of characters is mentioned in other Morrison novels, however she does not reveal the race of the women at the Convent except for the first victim. "I did that on purpose," said Morrison in an interview with *Time* magazine. "I wanted the readers to wonder about the race of those girls until those readers understood that their race didn't matter. I want to dissuade people from reading literature in that way."[13]

In *Paradise*, Morrison also hoped to examine "the love of God and love for fellow human beings."[14] She wanted to explore why human beings, often influenced by religion, feel the need to create their own kind of "paradise" in society,

and why creating a paradise often means other human beings must be excluded—as the men in Ruby exclude the women at the Convent.

Critics varied in their opinion of Morrison's work. Critic Louis Menand of *The New Yorker* said Morrison was "at the novelistic best."[15] Writer Paul Gray wrote in *Time* magazine that "Morrison's prose remains the marvel that it was in her earlier novels, a melange of high literary rhetoric and plain talk."[16] However, other critics complained that the book's plot was contrived. Michiko Kakutani wrote in *The New York Times* that *Paradise* is "a heavy-handed, schematic piece of writing."[17] Deirdre Donahue wrote in *USA Today* that the book is "hard to read and at times hard to understand," but that it is "worth the struggle."[18]

As usual, Morrison took the criticism in stride. She had hoped to work on the book's manuscript a bit longer, but there was no additional time before its publication date, which was moved up to the beginning of the year rather than spring. By March, Oprah Winfrey had selected *Paradise* for her TV book club and the novel had already made *The New York Times* best-seller list.

A few months later, Morrison's next creative venture appeared on movie screens across the country. The motion picture *Beloved*, based on Morrison's novel of the same name, opened in movie theaters in October 1998. Oprah Winfrey,

who bought the movie rights to the film ten years earlier, co-produced the film and starred in the movie as Sethe, the runaway slave who kills her infant daughter and is later haunted by the infant's spirit. Many Hollywood insiders, and even

Morrison attends the premiere of Beloved *in New York City.*

Morrison herself, thought *Beloved* could not be made into a movie. The book was simply too complex and rich—the story of slavery too horrifying. But Winfrey persevered for ten years to select the right director and screenwriter for the project. Jonathan Demme, director of the Oscar-winning movie, *The Silence of the Lambs*, agreed to direct the movie. Richard LaGravenese, screenwriter for the movie *The Bridges of Madison County*, agreed to co-write the script.

Morrison, who visited the movie set while the film was being made, saw the completed movie three times before she could view it in an objective way. As the author of the book, Morrison knew it would be difficult not to see the movie through a writer's perspective. But she was finally pleased with the results. "They did something I thought they could never do: to make the film represent not the abstraction of slavery, but the individuals, the domestic qualities, and the consequences of it."[19]

Morrison also praised the cast of the film in a special appearance to promote the movie on "The Oprah Winfrey Show." Actor Danny Glover, known for his role in the "Lethal Weapon" movie series, played Paul D. Paul D not only appears at Sethe's home and becomes her love interest, but he also falls under the spell of the mysterious Beloved who has come to live with Sethe and Denver. Actress Thandie Newton, who appeared in the film *Jefferson in Paris*, portrays Beloved, and

actress Kimberly Elise, who played in the movie *Set It Off*, portrays Denver. The star four-person cast impressed Morrison, who called the movie "extraordinary."

The critical reviews for the film were general-

Danny Glover and Oprah Winfrey in a scene from the movie Beloved

ly positive, although some were mixed and the movie's reception at the box office did not meet its high expectations. Critic Janet Maslin, in a review in *The New York Times*, praised director Jonathan Demme for "taking on the most enticing and daunting job of literary adaptation since *The English Patient*," and for succeeding "uncannily well in bringing the novel's pulse to the screen." Wrote Maslin, "*Beloved* works on its own, with only occasional confusing junctures. But it is much enhanced by the familiarity with the Pulitzer Prize-winning novel. In so ambitiously bringing this story to the screen, Ms. Winfrey underscores a favorite, invaluable credo: read the book."[20]

Critic Jack Matthews wrote in *New York Newsday* that Morrison's book is far better entertainment than the movie. "It [the story] works better as a novel than the movie. You can step back from the book, and in the case of *Beloved*, you must. Morrison weaves such a tight tapestry of history, romance, adventure, and metaphysical mystery that readers have to pause now and then to absorb and reflect. You can't do that with a movie."[21]

Audiences may have also been confused by the movie's complexity. However, movie insiders said *Beloved* failed to appeal to white moviegoers, resulting in poor sales at the box office. Although it took an $80-million investment to produce and market *Beloved*, it made only $8 million during its

opening weekend in mid-October, and only pulled in $18 million by early November.[22] According to Ken Smikle of *Target Market News*, a research firm that tracks African-American media and consumers, the story of slavery is still a difficult tale to tell, unlike other historical tragedies such as the Holocaust. "You have to create empathy," Smikle told the *New York Daily News*, "and that's tricky."[23]

Despite Oprah Winfrey's immense popularity as a talk-show host, her own promotion of the film, and the quality of the acting and film direction, *Beloved*'s commercial success was marginal by film-industry standards. However, neither Winfrey nor Morrison plan to give up making movies. Winfrey has also purchased the movie rights to *Paradise* and may produce another motion picture for the big screen.

Morrison has achieved a great deal since her working-class beginnings in Lorain, Ohio, and lone writing sessions in Syracuse, New York. She is one of the finest fiction writers—of any race—in the United States and the world. She is a popular guest speaker and receives hundreds of requests to speak at colleges, universities, and bookstores around the country. She is also a successful parent—her sons, Ford and Slade, are now grown men. Ford is an architect and Slade, the father of a daughter named Kali, is a painter.

Today, Morrison helps to fight oppression

Morrison after a speaking engagement in New York

against people of color all over the world. She is a member of the Universal Academy of Cultures in Paris, France. Along with other Nobel Prize winners, artists, and scholars, she is working to write an international manual against racism. In her

role as a teacher and academic, she is helping to shape the lives of the next generation of writers and artists who also believe creativity can be used to lift the human spirit and to tell the story of those whom society often forgets. Morrison has become an important literary voice for African-Americans, women, and all others who have been excluded from America's "paradise."

Literature scholars and students who respect and admire Morrison's work come together every two years in a conference to present research papers about her novels. The conferences are sponsored by the Toni Morrison Society and began in 1998. The scholars have presented papers on topics such as the meaning of home and the portrayal of the South in Morrison's writing.

The Society's most recent conference was held September 28-October 1, 2000 at Lorain Community College in Elyria, Ohio, not far from Lorain where Morrison was born. As a matter of fact, the Society holds its conferences in or near cities that have meaning in Morrison's life. The Society's first conference, for example, was held in Atlanta, Georgia, a half-hour drive from Cartersville, where Morrison's father was born. Morrison attended the first conference and gave a special reading of her work.

The conference at Lorain Community College included a panel discussion on Morrison's work

featuring Cornel West, the African-American scholar and theologian, Bell Hooks, John Edgar Wideman, and Marita Golden, all African-American authors. A seminar on how to teach Morrison's novels in high school English classes was held, as well as a tour of Lorain.

The Toni Morrison Society was created in May 1993, by Dr. Carolyn Denard, a professor at Georgia State University in Atlanta, during a meeting of the American Literature Association. The purpose of the Society is to "initiate, sponsor, and encourage critical dialogue, scholarly publications, conferences, and projects devoted to the study of the life and works of Toni Morrison."

"My responsibilities are to do the best work I can do and to be the best human being I can be," said Morrison in an interview with *Essence* magazine in 1998. "What [the Nobel] does—which is one of my assumed responsibilities—is to make it thinkable, possible, doable, for others. Other African-Americans and other women. If one, then why not two? If two, why not twenty? If I'm able to keep learning, putting myself in a position to learn something else, and putting myself in positions where

"My responsibilities are to do the best work I can do and to be the best human being I can be,"

I can make it possible for somebody else to learn something, those are the major successes."[24]

Toni Morrison is more than a success. She is an inspiration for all writers, artists, and book readers. She is, as she likes to think of herself, a writer. A great American writer.

END NOTES

CHAPTER ONE

1. "Toni Morrison is '93 Winner of Nobel Prize in Literature," by William Grimes, *The New York Times*, October 8, 1993.
2. Ibid.
3. "Morrison's Slice of Paradise," by Deirdre Donahue, *USA Today*, January, 1998.
4. Ibid #1.
5. Ibid #1.
6. "Paradise Found," by Paul Gray, *Time* magazine, January 19, 1998.
7. "Nobel Lecture 1993," by Toni Morrison, *World Literature Today*, Winter, 1994.
8. "Author Toni Morrision Wins Nobel Prize," by David Streitfeld, *Washington Post*, October 8, 1993.
9. Ibid.
10. "Toni Morrison: Solo Flight Through Literature into History," by Trudier Harris, *World Literature Today*, Winter, 1994.
11. "Paradise Found," by Paul Gray, *Time* magazine, January 19, 1998.

CHAPTER TWO

1. "Nobel in Literature Goes to Toni Morrison," by Amy Gameron, *Wall Street Journal*, October 8, 1993.
2. "The Laureate's Life Song," by David Streitfeld, *Washington Post*, October 8, 1993.
3. *Critical Essays on Toni Morrison*, edited by Nellie Y. McKay, G.K. Hall & Co., 1988, page 49.
4. Ibid, page 52.
5. *Toni Morrison: Author*, by Douglas Century, Chelsea House Publishers, 1994, page 24.
6. "60 Minutes" transcript, March 8, 1998.
7. Ibid #5, page 23.
8. Ibid #6.
9. *Toni Morrison: Nobel Prize-Winning Author*, by Barbara Kramer, Enslow Publishers, 1996, page 18.

CHAPTER THREE

1. *Toni Morrison: Author*, by Douglas Century, Chelsea House Publishers, 1994, page 35.
2. *Toni Morrison: Nobel Prize-Winning Author*, by Barbara Kramer, Enslow Publishers, 1996, page 26-27.
3. Ibid, page 29.
4. Ibid, page 28.
5. *Critical Essays on Toni Morrison*, edited by Nellie Y. McKay, G.K. Hall & Co., 1988, page 43.

CHAPTER FOUR

1. *Toni Morrison's World of Fiction*, by Karen Carmean, The Whitson Publishing Co., 1993 page 21.
2. *Toni Morrison: Author*, by Douglas Century, Chelsea House Publishers, 1994, page 43.

3. Ibid, page 43.
4. *Critical Essays on Toni Morrison*, edited by Nellie Y. McKay, G.K. Hall & Co., 1988 page 19.
5. Ibid, page 20.
6. Ibid , page 2.
7. Ibid, page 45.
8. Ibid, page 46.
9. Ibid #1, page 44.
10. Ibid #1, page 31.
11. Ibid, page 31.
12. Ibid #4, page 24.
13. Ibid, page 4.
14. *Toni Morrison: Nobel Prize-Winning Author*, by Barbara Kramer, Enslow Publishing, 1996, pages 44–45.
15. "Paradise Found," by Paul Gray, *Time* magazine, January 19, 1998
16. Ibid #14, page 42.
17. Ibid #4, page 27.
18. Ibid #1, page 46.
19. Ibid #4, page 29.
20. Ibid, page 32.

CHAPTER FIVE

1. *Critical Essays on Toni Morrison*, edited by Nellie Y. McKay, G.K. Hall & Co., 1988, page 35.
2. *Toni Morrison's World of Fiction*, by Karen Carmean, The Whitson Publishing Company, 1993, page 64.
3. *Toni Morrison: Nobel Prize-Winning Author*, by Barbara Kramer, Enslow Publishing, 1996, page 56.
4. "Toni Morrison Magic," by Jean Strouse, *Newsweek*, March 30, 1981.
5. Ibid.
6. Ibid.
7. Ibid.
8. *Toni Morrison: Author*, by Douglas Century, Chelsea House, 1994, page 73.

9. *Toni Morrison's World of Fiction*, by Karen Carmean, The Whitson Publishing Co, 1993, page 83.
10. "Toni Morrison's Novel 'Beloved' Wins The Pultizer Prize in Fiction," by Dennis Hevesi, April 1, 1988.
11. Ibid #8, page 78.
12. Ibid #10.
13. Ibid#10.
14. "Creating The Danger I Need," by Angela Delli Santi, *Time Off*, December 2, 1987.
15. *Toni Morrison's World of Fiction*, by Karen Carmean, The Whiston Publishing Company, 1993, page 102.
16. Ibid.
17. Ibid.
18. "The Laureate's Life Song," by David Streitfeld, *Washington Post*, October 8, 1993.
19. Ibid #8, page 90.
20. Ibid #8, page 90.
21. "Honey and Rue," CD performed by Kathleen Battle, Liner Notes, page 3, Deutsche Grammophon.
22. Ibid.

CHAPTER SIX

1. "Author Toni Morrison Wins Nobel Prize," by David Streitfeld, *Washington Post*, October 8, 1993.
2. Ibid.
3. "Paradise Found," by Paul Gray, *Time* magazine, January 19, 1998.
4. "Toni Morrison's Manuscripts Spared in Christmas Fire," by Robert McFadden, *New York Times*, December 28, 1993.
5. "Morrison Organizes Program to Feature Writing, Theatre," by Howard Gertler, *The Daily Princetonian*, November 8, 1993.
6. "Toni Morrison's Atelier," by Deborah A. Kaple, *Princeton Alumni Weekly*, September 10, 1997.
7. Ibid.

8. "Morrison Wins Appointment as 1996 Jefferson Lecturer," by Mandy Terce, *The Daily Princetonian*, February 5, 1996.
9. Ibid #3.
10. "Morrison's Slice of Paradise," by Deirdre Donahue, *USA Today*, January, 1998.
11. "Toni Morrison's Mix of Tragedy, Domesticity, and Folklore," by Dinitia Smith, *The New York Times*, January 8, 1998.
12. Ibid.
13. Ibid #3.
14. Ibid #10.
15. Ibid #11.
16. Ibid #3.
17. Ibid #11.
18. "Morrison's Painful, Profound Paradise," Deirdre Donahue, *USA Today*, January 8, 1998.
19. "The Beloved Oprah," by Richard Corliss, *Time* magazine, October 5, 1998.
20. "No Peace From a Brutal Legacy," by Janet Maslin, *The New York Times*, October 16, 1998.
21. "A Restless Spirit Haunts Beloved," by Jack Matthews, *Newsday*, October 16, 1998.
22. "Cry, The Beloved Letdown," by Lewis Beale, *New York Daily News*, November 23, 1998.
23. Ibid.
24. "Paradise Found," *Essence* magazine, February, 1998.

CHRONOLOGY

1931 Born Chloe Anthony Wofford in Lorain, Ohio, on February 18.

1949 Graduates from Lorain High School.

1953 Graduates from Howard University with a bachelor's degree in English; enters Cornell University in Ithaca, New York.

1955 Receives masters degree in English from Cornell University; teaches English at Texas Southern University in Houston, Texas.

1957 Teaches English at Howard University in Washington, D.C.

1958 Marries Harold Morrison.

1961 Gives birth to son Harold Ford.

1962 Joins writers' group at Howard University.

1964 Resigns from teaching at Howard University; divorces Harold Morrison; moves to Ohio; gives birth to second son, Slade Kevin.

1965 Accepts job working as an editor for Random House in Syracuse, New York; moves to New York from Ohio.

1969 Receives promotion and becomes senior editor; moves to New York City.

1970 Publishes *The Bluest Eye.*

1971 Teaches English at the State University of New York at Purchase.
1973 Publishes *Sula*.
1974 Publishes first reference book, *The Black Book*.
1976 Teaches English at Yale University in New Haven, Connecticut.
1977 Publishes *Song of Solomon*.
1979 Serves as a lecturer at Bard College in Annadale-on-Hudson, New York.
1981 Buys a new home in Grandview-on-Hudson, New York. Publishes *Tar Baby*.
1984 Teaches creative writing at the State University of New York at Albany.
1986 Her play, *Dreaming Emmett*, is produced in New York.
1987 Publishes *Beloved*.
1988 Wins the Pulitzer Prize for fiction for *Beloved*.
1989 Accepts the Robert F. Goheen chair at Princeton University in Princeton, New Jersey; teaches creative writing and humanities courses at Princeton.
1992 Publishes *Jazz*; edits collection of essays on the Anita Hill–Clarence Thomas hearings called *Race-ing Justice, En-Gendering Power*; contributes song lyrics to "Honey and Rue," an original music score.
1993 Wins the Nobel Prize in literature for her novels; her home in Grandview-on-Hudson is destroyed by fire.
1994 Creates Atelier Program at Princeton University.
1995 The Toni Morrison Reading Room is opened at the Lorain Public Library in Lorain, Ohio.
1996 National Endowment for the Humanities names Morrison the Jefferson Lecturer in Humanities; *Song of Solomon* is selected for the Oprah Winfrey Book Club.
1997 Contributes song lyrics to "Sweet Talk: Four Songs in Text," an original music score.
1998 Publishes *Paradise*; *Beloved*, the movie based on Morrison's novel, is released.

A NOTE ON SOURCES

My first step in researching was to contact Alfred A. Knopf, the New York book publishing company that published Toni Morrison's most recent novel, *Paradise*, in 1998. I wrote the company a letter to ask if I could interview Morrison and get more information about Morrison and her life. While the company said no to an interview, they did send me a packet with copies of articles on Morrison.

Next I visited my local library to learn more about Morrison's life and the importance of her writing to American literature. I found several books that helped me, including *Toni Morrison: Author* by Douglas Century, *Toni Morrison: Nobel Prize-Winning Author* by Barbara Kramer, *Critical Essays on Toni Morrison*, edited by Nellie Y. McKay, and *Toni Morrison's World of Fiction* by Karen Carmean.

Besides books, I also found more newspaper and magazine articles and I ordered transcripts and video tapes from shows that Morrison had appeared on, including "60 Minutes" and "The Oprah Winfrey Show."

FOR MORE INFORMATION

BOOKS BY TONI MORRISON

Beloved. Alfred A. Knopf, 1998.
The Big Box. Hyperion Press, 1999.
The Bluest Eye. Alfred A. Knopf, 2000.
Jazz. Alfred A. Knopf, 1992.
Paradise. Alfred A. Knopf, 1997.
Song of Solomon. Plume, 1987.
Sula. Alfred A. Knopf, 1973.
Tar Baby. Alfred A. Knopf, 1987.

BOOKS ABOUT TONI MORRISON

Bloom, Harold, ed. *Toni Morrison*. Chelsea House Publishers, 1999.

Century, Douglas. *Toni Morrison: Author*. Chelsea House Publishers, 1994.

Kramer, Barbara. *Toni Morrison: Nobel Prize-Winning Author*. Enslow Publishers, 1996.

Patrick-Wexler, Diane. *Toni Morrison*. Raintree/Steck-Vaughn, 1997.

MAGAZINE ARTICLES ABOUT TONI MORRISON

"The Beloved Oprah," by Richard Corliss, *Time* magazine, October 5, 1998.
"Creating the Danger I Need," by Angela Delli Santi, *Time Off,* December 2, 1987.
"Paradise Found," *Essence Magazine*, February, 1998.
"Paradise Found," by Paul Gray, *Time* magazine, January 19, 1998.
"Toni Morrison's Magic," by Jean Strouse, *Newsweek*, March 30, 1981.

ORGANIZATIONS AND ONLINE SITES

The African-American Mosaic Exhibition
http://www.loc.gov/exhibits/african/intro.html
Discover some of the history that inspired Morrison's work from this online resource guide from the Library of Congress.

Africana.com
http://www.africana.com/tt_196.htm
Read a biography of Toni Morrison and explore the lives of other famous African-Americans.

Nobel Prize Internet Archive
http://nobelprizes.com/nobel/literature/1993a.html
Lists books by and about Morrison, her Nobel acceptance speech, a biography, interviews with Morrison, a bibliography, and excerpts from *Beloved*.

Time Magazine
http://www.time.com/time/magazine/1998/dom/980119/cover1.html

Read the cover story on Toni Morrison from the January 18, 1998 issue of *Time* magazine.

The Toni Morrison Society
http://www.gsu.edu/~wwwtms.index.html.
The Toni Morrison Society publishes a newsletter twice a year and maintains a website through the English Department at Georgia State University.

INDEX

ABOUT THE AUTHOR

Lisa R. Rhodes is a journalist and author of children's literature. She is the author of *Barbara Jordan: Voice of Democracy*, and a graduate of Baruch College, City University of New York, and the Columbia Graduate School of Journalism.